POLICE–COMMUNITY RELATIONS AND THE ADMINISTRATION OF JUSTICE

POLICE–COMMUNITY RELATIONS AND THE ADMINISTRATION OF JUSTICE

Fourth Edition

PAMELA D. MAYHALL

THOMAS BARKER

RONALD D. HUNTER

Prentice Hall, Englewood Cliffs, New Jersey 07632

Library of Congress Cataloging-in-Publication Data

Mayhall, Pamela D. (Pamela Douglass)
    Police–community relations and the administration of justice/
  Pamela D. Mayhall, Thomas Barker, Ronald D. Hunter.—4th ed.
      p. cm.
  Includes bibliographical references and index.
  ISBN 0-13-097791-8
    1. Public relations—United States—Police. 2. Police—United
States. 3. Criminal justice, Administration of—United States.
I. Barker, Thomas. II. Hunter, Ronald D. III. Title.
HV7936.P8M34   1995
363.2'0973—dc20   94-5158
                                         CIP

Editorial/production supervision: Janet M. McGillicuddy
Cover design: Laurel Marx
Cover art: Laurel Marx
Manufacturing buyer: Ed O'Dougherty
Acquisition editor: Robin Baliszewski
Editorial assistant: Rose Mary Florio

© 1995 by Prentice-Hall, Inc.
A Simon & Schuster Company
Englewood Cliffs, New Jersey 07632

10 9 8 7 6 5 4

ISBN 0-13-097791-8

Prentice-Hall International (UK) Limited, *London*
Prentice-Hall of Australia Pty. Limited, *Sydney*
Prentice-Hall Canada Inc., *Toronto*
Prentice-Hall Hispanoamericana, S.A., *Mexico*
Prentice-Hall of India Private Limited, *New Delhi*
Prentice-Hall of Japan, Inc., *Tokyo*
Simon & Schuster Asia Pte. Ltd., *Singapore*
Editora Prentice-Hall do Brasil, Ltda., *Rio de Janeiro*

To the memory of Pamela D. Mayhall

CONTENTS

7 POLICE DISCRETION AND COMMUNITY RELATIONS   *141*

8 THE MEDIA LINK   *166*

9 THE YOUNG, THE ELDERLY, AND THE POLICE   *196*

PREFACE

Relationships change as individuals, communities, and societies change. They change as the needs and responsibilities of each member in the relationship change. This book addresses a challenge that all criminal justice practitioners—police, courts, and corrections—must confront. It is the challenge of developing and maintaining meaningful relationships with each other and with the citizens they serve in an atmosphere of change.

The police are the edge, the most visible and, according to many citizens, the most approachable of these criminal justice practitioners. A police–citizen partnership is essential to reducing crime. Shaping the partnership in positive ways requires effective police–community relations practice. Many disciplines are involved: criminology, law, history, philosophy, psychology, political science, communication, sociology, economics, and more.

In this book we draw from all of the above in order to help the reader better understand and practice positive police–community relations. To achieve our purpose, many topics are addressed in the context of community relations. For example: What are the psychological processes that accompany the business of enforcing laws in America today? What is the relationship between crime prevention and community relations? How can systems principles be applied to police–community relations? What is the nature of the media link to the community? The reader is encouraged to explore the dynamics and problems of communication, to relate these to a variety of issues associated with discretion, and to discover ways in which the police and the community can interact more effectively.

This text is designed for use in a one- or two-semester course on Police–Community Relations or Police and Society. It represents an overview. Much more can be said about every topic included. We address these topics in the context of community relations, and encourage the reader to pursue further study in areas of special interests.

The third edition of this text had many friends. To them we would like to say that every chapter in this fourth edition has been updated to reflect current issues and research. Some chapters have only been updated, others have seen extensive revisions, a couple have been incorporated within other chapters, and a new chapter on community policing has been added. Yet, we have tried very hard to maintain the style and integrity of the previous edition.

As in the third edition, we have attempted to make the subject matter accessible to students. The pedagogical devices utilized there have been maintained to ensure student comprehension. Each chapter begins with a summary overview and learning objectives. Each chapter ends with conclusions, a student checklist, questions for discussion, and the feature "One Step Forward," designed to apply concepts, increase understanding, and offer new learning opportunities.

It is our fervent desire that this edition continue the tradition established by Pamela D. Mayhall of providing both instructors and students with an interesting and challenging overview of the many issues relative to police–community relations.

Thomas Barker
Ronald D. Hunter

ACKNOWLEDGMENTS

This book is dedicated to the late Pamela D. Mayhall for good reason. She authored the finest undergraduate text ever written on the topic of police–community relations. We are honored that Mr. Travis Mayhall and Prentice Hall, Inc. allowed us to revise such an important contribution to the study of criminal justice.

The pressures of maintaining the integrity of the previous edition, resolving our creative differences, meeting production deadlines, and responding to manuscript reviews did little to enhance the quality of life for our loved ones. We are extremely grateful for the tolerance, understanding, and support provided by our spouses and families.

We are also grateful for the encouragement provided by our colleagues and the students in the College of Criminal Justice at Jacksonville State University. We are especially thankful for the supportive efforts of Ms. Patsy Meadows, our college secretary and Ms. Candy Fortune, our student assistant.

The professional staff at Prentice Hall is also greatly appreciated. The guidance and editorial skills provided by Robin Baliszewski, Rose Mary Florio, Janet McGillicuddy, and Judy Casillo were outstanding. Their dedicated efforts made our work much easier.

No writing project can be successful without the helpful insights provided by colleagues in the field who perform the difficult task of manuscript review. We offer our thanks to the following individuals whose comments enabled us to revise and strengthen our original manuscript: Professor Donald J. Melisi, Middlesex Community College; Professor James D. Stinchcomb, Miami-Dade Community College; Professor Tom Dempsey, Thomas Nelson College; Professor Lois A. Wims, Salve Regina University; and Professor Ronald A. Pincomb, New Mexico State University.

Several law enforcement agencies provided information, photographs, or other materials which greatly aided us in our efforts. We wish to thank Dr. David Nichols, Jacksonville State University Police Department; Sgt. Phil Kiracofe, Tallahassee Police Department; Sgt. Vincent Henry, New York City Police Department; Chief Johnnie Johnson and Mr. Don R. Sharpe, Birmingham Police Department; Sgt. Richard Morris, Pennsylvania State Police; and Deputy Roy Turman, Calhoun County Sheriff's Department for their contributions.

We also wish to thank Professor Richard C. Lumb of the University of North Carolina at Charlotte, and Professors Patrick Ryan and Sean Grennan of the Long Island University–C.W. Post Campus for their contributions and support.

1

POLICE–COMMUNITY RELATIONS: AN OVERVIEW

. . . the police are the public and the public are the police. (Peel's Principles)

In the last few years, American law enforcement has accepted (begrudgingly at times) the notion that community relations is an important and even indispensable part of police work. In so doing, it has recaptured the old belief that a police force can and should be "the people's police"—an agency that is responsive to the public it serves.

Philosophically, not every officer agrees, and practically, the nature of community relations varies widely from agency to agency, community to community, but change has occurred. Awareness and acceptance of community relations—the process of developing and maintaining meaningful, two-way communication between the agency and specific populations served toward identifying, defining, and resolving problems of mutual concern—have increased.

STUDYING THIS CHAPTER WILL ENABLE YOU TO:

1. Provide an overview of police–community relations and its impact on the police system.
2. Explain how police–community relations are complex interactions among a multitude of internal and external communities.
3. Define the *people's police* and *community.*
4. Describe the evolution of police–community relations programs in the United States.
5. Identify the current status of and prospects for police–community relations.

THE POLICE–COMMUNITY ENVIRONMENT

Of all the issues that affect the police in the United States, none is more important than the manner in which the police and the public interrelate. Despite our democratic traditions (or perhaps because of them), we in the United States have been slow to accept the concept that "police are the public and the public the police" (Greene, 1989, p. 354). Yet the police and the community are not only interdependent, but are in fact inseparable from one another.

Readers, both police and civilian, may find it difficult to accept the assertion that police and community are inseparable. If one adheres to the traditional concept of police–community relations (as shown in Figure 1-1), such a statement may actually appear to be ludicrous. Typically, the police have responded to pressure from politicians and others who have reacted to complaints from groups or individual citizens regarding police procedures. Such an isolationist view has perpetuated an "us against them" mentality that has detracted from police–community interaction.

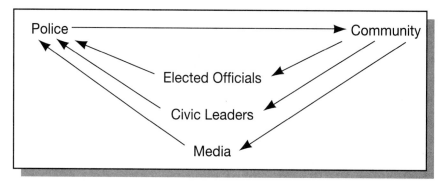

FIGURE 1-1   Traditional police–community relations.

However, if one adheres to the more contemporary view that the individuals within various police organizations are but a microcosm of the general society and that this society is composed of numerous interrelated communities, the previous assertion is valid. Today's police organizations are not isolated monoliths that are impervious to the communities they serve. The police organization is not a unified community. Nor is there a single community to which they respond. There are in actuality a myriad of sometimes cooperating, often competing communities that are constantly influencing and being influenced by one another.

Police organizations are in truth very responsive to this rapidly changing "community environment." To understand police–community interaction, it is necessary for the student of police to realize that there are constant exchanges between the various communities which exist both within and without the police organization. Figure 1-2 demonstrates how these "exchange relationships" (Cole, 1992, pp. 169–172) between communities occur.

As displayed in Figure 1-2, the police organization is comprised of a number of *internal communities* engaged in constant interaction with one another. These internal communities are engaged in numerous individual and group exchanges with a myriad of *external communities.* Within the *overlapping communities* displayed are those groups from which both the internal and external communities are comprised.

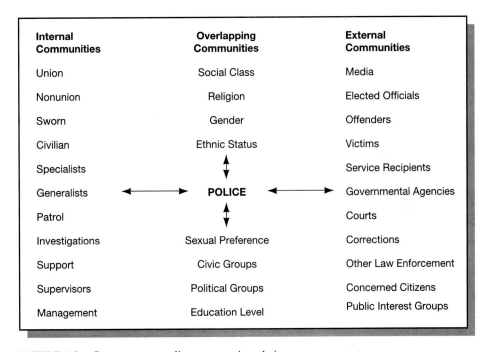

Internal Communities	Overlapping Communities	External Communities
Union	Social Class	Media
Nonunion	Religion	Elected Officials
Sworn	Gender	Offenders
Civilian	Ethnic Status	Victims
Specialists	↕	Service Recipients
Generalists ⟷	**POLICE** ⟷	Governmental Agencies
Patrol	↕	Courts
Investigations	Sexual Preference	Corrections
Support	Civic Groups	Other Law Enforcement
Supervisors	Political Groups	Concerned Citizens
Management	Education Level	Public Interest Groups

FIGURE 1-2   Contemporary police–community relations.

DEFINING POLICE–COMMUNITY RELATIONS

As argued in the preceding section, there is no one "community" that is served by the police. Instead, there are numerous communities that make up an often indefinable "public." As a result, "public opinion" is usually not a clear consensus of viewpoint within a nation, state, county, or municipality but a chorus of differing opinions from various communities.

Police–community relations are complicated and constantly changing interactions between representatives of the police organization and an assortment of governmental agencies, public groups, and private individuals representing a wide range of competing and often conflicting interests.

Throughout this book we focus our discussion of police and community interaction on both the external communities outside the police organization and the internal communities within the police organization. Our primary contention is that successful police–community relations must take into account exchange relationships among community groups located both within and without the police organization.

ACCEPTANCE OF THE CONCEPT OF POLICE–COMMUNITY RELATIONS

Secrecy and institutional separation have ceased to be defensible positions for police agencies to take in relation to the community they serve. Although secrecy and institutional separation have not totally disappeared, it is valid to state that in less than two decades the most insular of all institutions in American society is becoming committed, at least in principle, to programs of ongoing exchanges with the community and with other agencies about its mandate and practices.

The concept of police–community relations has gained a secure level of acceptance in the law enforcement establishment and in urban government. *Acceptance,* in a working sense, means that proposals to establish and maintain such programs have a fair chance of success. There are no longer any organized factions publicly opposing police efforts to open and cultivate channels of communication with the public in general and with civic groups and social movements in particular. Whether those who were aligned against such attempts are now merely silent for the time being, or whether they have changed their views, is an open question. But there is no doubt that activities included under the heading of police–community relations are achieving respectability, and that a large and growing number of police officials in positions of responsibility have come to view them as indispensable for effective law enforcement and peacekeeping.

ACCEPTANCE AS A SIGN OF PROGRESS

This acceptance alone is a sign of progress, a remarkable achievement. It is, however, only a first step toward implementation. It is much easier to agree with the reasonableness and justice of a proposal than to implement it and live with the consequences of its implementation. Above all, when the task is to decide what must and can be done, it is important to measure aspirations against resistance, inertia, and regression. Thus, for example, despite the acceptance of the principle of police–community relations, few, if any, actually functioning police–community relations programs are fully deserving of the name. Most have barely succeeded in laying the foundations for their own existence. A positive statement of present circumstances is that although newly functioning programs have been accepted in principle, the kinds of activities that total acceptance would lead one to expect have yet to be implemented.

TIGHT FINANCES AND THEIR EFFECTS

Today, in times of tight finances, new and existing programs must compete for reduced funding and human resources with other programs that meet long-established police obligations (e.g., crime, traffic, and vice control). In such circumstances it becomes necessary to demonstrate a high level of cost-effectiveness in meeting police goals. Often, community relations programs become locked into quick and relatively safe ways of demonstrating success: (1) "busy work" activities, which show that something is happening, and presumably goals are being accomplished; and (2) solving easy problems and postponing (sometimes indefinitely) the more difficult ones (e.g., maintaining contact with civic and political groups that are receptive to the police, and failing to reach out to those that are not receptive).

Such difficulties can arise with virtually any kind of program in which success is expected. The way police–community relations programs have developed seems to pose some unique difficulties, however, for these programs in particular.

A HISTORICAL PERSPECTIVE

The Nineteenth-Century Origins

The concept of police–community relations is not a new one. When Sir Robert Peel undertook reform of the London police with the Metropolitan Police Act of 1829, he and the two key commissioners that he appointed, Charles Rowan and Richard Mayne, emphasized that the police should work in cooperation with the people and that members of the office should protect the rights, serve the needs, and earn the *trust* of the population they policed (Critchley, 1967; Reith, 1952).

Writing at the turn of the century, Melville Lee discussed Peel's principles of law enforcement. The following excerpts from Lee's text retain the flavor of the period in which they were written. They also reflect many of the concepts of police–community relations that are being proposed today. According to Lee, police officers are "public servants in the fullest sense of the term."

> It should be understood at the outset that the principal object to be attained is the prevention of crime. To this great end every effort of the police is to be directed.
>
> The absence of crime will be considered the best proof of the complete efficiency of the police.
>
> . . . There is no qualification more indispensable to a police officer than a perfect command of temper, never suffering himself to be moved in the slightest degree by any language or threats that may be used; if he does his duty in a quiet and determined manner, such conduct will probably induce well-disposed bystanders to assist him should he require it.
>
> . . . What is wanted is the respect and approval of all good citizens.
>
> The wisdom of fostering cordial relations between the people and the civil defenders of their lives and properties seems so obvious, that it is a source of wonder that so little attention has been given to the study of how best to promote this desirable *entente cordiale.*
>
> The police . . . are simply a disciplined body of men, specially engaged in protecting "masses" as well as "classes," from any infringement of their rights on the part of those who are not law-abiding.
>
> . . . It is necessary also that they [the public] should be acquainted with the conditions that govern the mutual relationship.
>
> We are well served by our police because we have wisely made them personally responsible for their actions.
>
> . . . That is to say, the modern system rests, as the ancient one did, on the sure foundation of mutual reliance. (Lee, 1971)

These principles were imported into American police departments; in a way, they had to be. There was strenuous opposition to establishing organized police forces on the grounds that they would be the exclusive organ of executive government and indifferent to public influence. They would function against the people, resulting in a "police state." Opposition was in part silenced by assurances that the new institution would be "the people's police" (Astor, 1971).

In many ways the institution focused on the needs of the people. Engaging in community service activities is a part of the American police heritage (see Figure 1-3). As Zumbrun notes, "During the early part of the 20th century, the New York City Police Department engaged in such non-stereotyped activities as massive Christmas parties for poverty-stricken children and their families, engaging in job hunts for released prisoners from Sing Sing prison and other non-crime fighting endeavors" (Zumbrun, 1983).

FIGURE 1-3   Service is part of the American police heritage.

The "police state" issue did not die. World War II (and many wars and cold war struggles before and since) have been waged against so-called "police states." In many European countries and in the United States, the police worked hard to disassociate themselves from such a label in the aftermath of World War II. Still, many Americans found adequate evidence to support the view that during their first century of existence in the United States, the police were often corrupt agents of boss-dominated urban governments (Berkley, 1969).

Selling the Police to the People

The reformers of the 1950s felt that it was necessary to overcome the attitudes of contempt that middle-class citizens held toward police, and literally, to sell the police to the people. This was done by sending speakers to high schools, to business luncheons, to meetings of civil organizations, and so on. These speakers argued that the police are the "thin blue line," the last bulwark of defense against the dark forces of crime and disorder.

Three key elements were notable in these efforts:

1. At their best, they employed highly sophisticated techniques of advertising, selling, and, of course, public relations.
2. To police the "public" in a public relations sense meant, essentially, middle-class adults and youth ("solid citizens" and their offspring).
3. No attempt was made to improve the "product"; the programs were designed solely to improve the police "image"; there was little or no provision to recommend or effect needed changes in departmental policy or procedures.

Although these police–community contacts were chosen very selectively, in the 1950s they did constitute a movement away from the exclusive dominance of police departments by city-hall bosses.

The 1960s: From Public Relations to Community Relations

At the beginning of the 1960s, the police had reason to believe their public relations programs had been a success. But then minorities, disaffected young people, the poor, recent immigrants, antiwar activists, and street people in general made new claims and demands. Their quarrel was with the "system," or with society as a whole, but their confrontations were often with the police, who usually responded with force. One lesson should have been clear: Public relations programs designed to appeal to "solid citizens" were ineffective in dealing with the disadvantaged and the aggrieved—many of whom were openly hostile to the police.

Something else was needed—police–community relations—where *community* was defined realistically to include, as one reviewer of this text stated: all of the "stratified, segmentalized, unintegrated, and differential environments where police work." This focus includes precisely those segments of society ignored by the earlier public-relations approach. New police–community relations programs were built on the foundations of already existing public relations programs.

The San Francisco Community Relations Unit

In the mid-1950s, the Metropolitan Police Department of St. Louis, Missouri, established a public relations division that became known as one of the best functioning programs of its kind in the country (School of Police Administration, 1967). The division contained a speakers' bureau, published a newsletter, organized citizens' councils, and maintained school contacts, all of which were considered to be effective in accordance with their aims. There were also police and community relations committees in housing projects, which, in the department's own estimate, did not function well even as late as 1966. Nevertheless, the undertaking as a whole had an enviable reputation. In 1962, Chief Thomas Cahill of San Francisco visited St. Louis to help obtain answers to his own problems. Chief Cahill realized that it was important to use other resources, not just force, to deal with outbreaks of discontent. His department was faced with student protests against hearings being conducted by the House Un-American Activities Committee in the San Francisco City Hall. Chief Cahill took the new director of his community relations program, Lieutenant Dante Andreotti, to St. Louis to study their methods. Cahill and Andreotti went to St. Louis to learn because they had a problem on their hands; their problem, however, was quite different from the situation that had motivated the St. Louis department. The St. Louis program was formulated primarily to address the "solid citizens." No one considered the program seriously impaired by the fact that the project that was directed toward working with the disadvantaged and the aggrieved did not function.

In the ensuing years, Lieutenant Andreotti developed a program in San Francisco that was vastly different from the St. Louis program. The direction of work that was permitted to lie fallow in St. Louis became the central interest of the San Francisco community relations unit. While Andreotti commanded the unit, "community relations" meant working primarily with the disadvantaged and the aggrieved segments of the population. The unit's officers were attached to organizations such as the Youth Opportunity Center, which served ghetto youngsters, and the Office of Economic Opportunity. They also exerted themselves to meet with, talk and listen to, and help people living in the Tenderloin, the skid row, and the ghetto. The activities of the San Francisco unit are illustrated by the following example.

> A robbery and beating of a white grocery store operator in a minority group neighborhood resulted in community-wide concern, and tension. As a result of the efforts of the police and the community relations unit, together with minority group leaders, a group of youngsters (many of whom had juvenile records) were organized into a picket line which marched back and forth in front of the store carrying signs condemning violence and stating that they were ashamed of what had happened. Although the boys picketing were not involved in the robbery or the beating, they offered verbal apologies to the family of the victim for the act done by members of their race. The publicity given this parade by the various media communications resulted in an almost immediate lessening of tensions. (School of Police Administration, 1967, p. 49)

This incident should not be taken as indicating the scope of the unit's program nor even its focal concerns. The routine work of the officers assigned to the unit concentrated much more on everyday kinds of predicaments, such as protecting persons who were not resourceful on their own or helping persons with police records find employment or lodgings. The officers acted upon the realization that life in the city has many conditions, circumstances, and troubled people. They worked on the assumptions that ex-cons without jobs are likely to commit crimes again; intergroup tension may lead to violent confrontations; children without recreational facilities tend to get into mischief, and so on. When such potential is not checked, it leads to consequences that will sooner or later have to be handled by detectives, riot squads, or juvenile officers, depending on the specific situation.

Those in the San Francisco community relations unit were not the first police officers ever to help a former criminal find a job, nor were they the first to succeed in preventing a public disorder. Their innovation was in two additional aspects of their work: First, they did not simply go out to solve some problem; rather, they always dealt with problems in conjunction with other community resources. In the example cited earlier, they worked together with minority group leaders. Cooperation was not simply a convenient expedient; it involved an established and ongoing mutually cooperative arrangement between members of the police and members of the community. Second, persons in the unit felt that providing services to citizens was their *primary* job. In the past such services were rendered on rare occasions and only after the officers took care of more demanding crime control problems.

The establishment of the community relations unit in San Francisco meant that personnel resources were specifically assigned to the task of working cooperatively with the people. More important, the chief of the department referred to the existence of the unit with pride. He claimed credit for creating it, and gave weight to its importance by having its commanding officer report directly to the office of the chief, rather than through the chain of command. Nevertheless, some commanding officers and several line officers did not like the unit. Even without total acceptance within the department, the unit gained momentum. It soon was regarded locally and nationally as conspicuously successful.

Although others considered the unit to be a success, its commander, Lieutenant Andreotti, recognized the problems that still had to be faced. Speaking at a law enforcement conference in 1968, he said:

> It is my belief that there isn't a successful police–community program anywhere in the country today, in terms of commitment by all members of the law enforcement agency. There have been successful police–community relations units, but practically all of them have been frustrated in their efforts to get the rank and file involved to the point of a genuine, personal interest and commitment. (Andreotti, 1971, p. 120)

Police–Community Relations Since the 1960s

The themes of the 1970s were Vietnam, the Watergate scandal of the Nixon administration, inflation, and the energy crisis. Compared with the 1960s the 1970s were relatively subdued—except for a notable and disturbing increase in violence. It was a period of "finding" oneself, or, as one author called it, the "Me Decade."

Out of the turmoil of the 1960s, and based on the findings of several presidential commissions, funding was made available through the Law Enforcement Assistance Administration for research, education and training, and projects of criminal justice agencies designed to reduce crime. Law enforcement agencies had the opportunity to develop and implement new programs—and they did. Many were described as community relations projects and some of these were innovative and elaborate. Many, in practice, were simply public relations activities. Few were carefully evaluated. As federal funding for them ended, many projects ended. Others, not necessarily as originally conceived, are still part of agency function today.

During the 1980s, the increasing fear of crime throughout American society resulted in a transition of focus from enhancing relations with minority communities to providing reassurances to the general public that crime was not running rampant. Crime prevention units became popular with police agencies throughout the nation.

These units served not only as a means of educating the public about crime prevention strategies but became valuable tools in enhancing public perceptions of the police.

In addition to developing crime prevention units, the police also sought to enhance their relationship with the media. Specialized public information units sprang into existence across the country in agencies that previously had sought to suppress information. These units not only made information more accessible to the media and civic groups but also promoted support for police programs.

The results of the previous strategies led progressive police administrators to seek out new programs in which the public could become more actively involved with their police agencies. An array of community liaison units, school resource programs, joint police–community activities, and enhanced civilian oversight of police operations were experimented with. The culmination of these efforts is community-oriented policing, which is discussed in detail in Chapter 13.

Despite the advances in police–community relations since the 1960s, few programs receive the total support of their agencies. Andreotti's concern voiced in 1968 continues to be a community relations concern of the 1990s. In terms of commitment by all members of the law enforcement agency, the status of police–community relations has not changed dramatically since 1968.

The rise of gangs in the inner cities and their rapid spread to suburban America, the detrimental effects of a flourishing illicit drug trade, the dramatic increase in hate crimes by both right-wing extremists and frustrated minorities, as well as the fear and instability produced by a declining economy demonstrate the need for enhanced police–community relations in the 1990s. The riots in Los Angeles and other major cities during the 1960s served to motivate police agencies to begin police–community relations. The distrust and resentment of police expressed in many American cities following the Los Angeles riot of 1992, provoked by the acquittal of police officers charged with beating an African-American motorist, will hopefully serve as the catalyst for new developments in police–community relations.

The Police and Social Work

Even under the best circumstances community relations programs suffer both from neglect and from being given low priority by police departments. Many police officers have little interest in community relations programs, and even resist and condemn them. Social problems, as the thinking in police circles sometimes goes, are best left to social workers; they are not "proper" police business, (i.e., they have little to do with preventing people from committing crimes and with bringing them to justice when they do). This view persists. Academy training often continues to focus predominantly on "crime fighting" behavior, even though it is generally known that the major portion of police work (some references note as high as 80 percent), is social service related rather than "crime fighting" behavior.

To say that only social workers should deal with these problems is similar to arguing that a champion swimmer should not pull a drowning person from the water unless the swimmer has a Red Cross Life Saving Certificate. Commitment to the principles of police–community relations means acting on the assumption that the police are a service organization dedicated to keeping the peace, to the defense of the rights of the people, and to the enforcement of laws. In all these fields they are not merely an independent instrument of government; rather, they must work with individuals, community groups, and community institutions to achieve the desired objectives.

It was this latter attitude that governed the intervention of the San Francisco community relations unit in the incident mentioned earlier. This incident is a good example of commitment to the principles of police–community relations on the level of departmental organization. It is not clear in this case at which point community leaders would be told to stay out of it and let the experts take over (and the community relations unit would move on to the next case). Typically that would be most likely to occur as procedures leading to the apprehension and trial of the assailants were set into motion.

Such a move may seem appropriate. Citizens are not expected to be involved in "catching criminals." In fact, when they insist upon becoming involved, police believe that they are likely to cause more harm than good. This is also the view of many judges, public prosecutors, city council members, and citizens. Thinking in terms of isolated offenses, it is difficult to reason otherwise.

Thus, even those who are in favor of genuine police–community relations are forced to agree that the work must be assigned to special units that work independently while the rest of policing takes its ordinary course. In other words, progressive departments establish external units to deal with the community, but these units must follow the department's conditions. In still different terms, it appears that accepting the principles of police–community relations in its present exclusively outward-oriented direction (somewhat in the way nations send envoys to other nations) does not mean that two-way police–community relations are the norm (or, to continue the analogy, that the other nations send them envoys).

This situation is not unique. The police are not alone in thinking that they can communicate adequately with the people by means of external ambassadors. Indeed, they have done better with this approach than other institutions. The educational system, for example, keeps parents at arm's length while pretending to allow involvement by letting assistant principals of schools deal with the PTA. Similarly, institutions that deliver medical services often do not even pretend to communicate with the people they serve. In each of these cases, it is argued that lay people could not possibly contribute to solving the problem of a slow-learning child or a diabetic patient, just as it is said that lay people could not be helpful in solving a robbery.

All communities have educational needs, health needs, and law enforcement and peacekeeping needs. It is neither proper nor efficient for the specialists alone to define the nature of these needs or the way in which they will be met. Specialists bring competence and skills to bear on meeting these needs, but they must communicate with lay citizens to determine what those needs are.

The Success of Police–Community Relations

The establishment of police–community relations units is a first, long step in recognition of the usefulness of bringing needs and special resources together in a harmonious relationship. Nevertheless, it is just that—a first step. The establishment of *community–police relations,* in a much broader sense, is a logical next step. An example might help in making clear what this involves. It is commonly accepted that the ghettos of our cities produce a disproportionately large number of people who are arrested for criminal activities and that people living in these ghettos are exposed to a far greater risk of being criminally victimized than other citizens. Finally, it is no secret that people living in these areas distrust the police and often are reluctant to help officers in their efforts to control crime. What would be more sensible than for the police to consider these three facts, together with their present ways of dealing with suspects and victims, as systematically related? Joint consideration of the larger problem suggests that a successful attack on the problem can come only from the establishment of a program of trusting and fully cooperative relations between ghetto communities and the police.

The reversal of terms for police–community relations to community–police relations was not done simply to coin a new term. It does not matter what the arrangement is called! What matters is that the full effectiveness of the program cannot be attained merely by having a special unit to implement it. At best, such units can only succeed in doing an occasional good deed and putting out an occasional fire, while leaving the rest of the police department's work unaffected by even these accomplishments.

Success of community–police relations requires a "people's police" attitude. Rank-and-file officers need to recognize that the police are a service organization dedicated to keeping the peace, defending the rights of the people, and enforcing the laws. Community–police relations is a broad, two-way program that involves every officer.

INTERNALIZING COMMUNITY RELATIONS

Perhaps it would be easiest to explain the concept of incorporating community relations into police work by first discussing what it does not mean.

What the Concept Does Not Mean

- *Making entire departments do what police–community relations units do now.* Special programs would remain the responsibility of the units, just as other units in police agencies also have special responsibilities. Although support for programs needs to be broadly based, it would be inefficient to have all units specializing in all programs.
- *Weakening law enforcement.* Viewing crime as a social problem does not imply that crime control would be "soft." Actually, police might become more strongly dedicated to crime control than they are now, and possibly become more effective in that task.
- *Close involvement with partisan politics.* Mobilizing support for police–community relations at state, county, and community levels may involve working with "political" figures and organizations, but it is a position that is not partisan, conservative, or liberal. It is a method for doing police work that considers the distribution of political forces in any community and seeks the cooperation of all.
- *"Bending" to community pressures.* Clearly, this is a danger in the face of conflicting demands, but risks can be contained provided that responsiveness to

community needs and demands is not interpreted as bargaining away the police mandate. Because openness is reciprocal, the risk can become an opportunity for citizens to understand and respect the police mandate in society.

- *Turning police officers into social workers.* Social interaction is a critical part of police work, and police perform "social" work as part of their everyday tasks. The basic functions of social work, according to Siporin (1975), are to develop, maintain, and strengthen the social welfare system so that it can meet basic human needs; to assure adequate standards of subsistence, health, and welfare for all; to enable people to function optimally within their social institutional roles and statuses; and to support and improve the social order and institutional structure of society (Siporin, 1975, pp. 13–14). Police also are involved in such a function as part of the overall mission of a service organization, dedicated to keeping the peace, defending the rights of the people, and enforcing the laws. The common interests are apparent, but the professional specialty and the context within which each function may vary (see also Friedlander and Apte, 1980, pp. 111–122). Improving police–community relations in all aspects of police work will allow officers to be more effective public servants while exercising their full range of proper police duties and service responsibilities.

What the Concept Does Mean

- *Reviving the ideas of "the people's police."* This is the basic notion on which modern, urban police departments were founded. Needs for police service must be determined on the basis of ongoing communication between the people and the police.

- *A more reasoned basis for police work.* Police officers usually operate with a repertoire of responses determined by penal codes, municipal ordinances, and demands of the often recurrent types of situations and emergencies with which they deal. The police–community relations concept encourages police to deal with complex problems in complex ways, going beyond traditional constraints and procedures where necessary (see Bittner, 1970).

- *A deeper, more comprehensive interest in human life.* To some, this phrase may sound sentimental, and to others, unnecessary, because many effective police officers now operate with humanity and compassion. Still, many police officers do not find it improper to adopt cynical attitudes toward human life. The police–community relations approach, by contrast, stresses that police are both entitled and required to take an interest in and help to resolve human problems.

- *An acceptance of the view that "relations" is a process, not a product.* It is vital, ongoing, and constantly changing. It requires mutual respect and mutual exchange and cannot be compartmentalized if it is to be effective.

SYSTEMS AND COMMUNITIES

A system is a set of elements, or components, interacting with each other. These elements may be physiological, as in organic systems in the human body, individuals within a family, groups of individuals as in a police department, or groups of systems as in the criminal justice system. Systems, according to systems theory, are guided by major principles which include:

1. The whole is greater than the sum of its parts.
2. Elements of a system interact in repetitive patterns.
3. A change in one part of the system will reverberate throughout the system (transactional reciprocity).
4. Interactions are governed by a set of rules.
5. Systems tend to maintain a balance among the elements.
6. Open systems exchange energy, or information flow, with the surrounding environment (Norgard and Whitman, 1980).

Police agencies are a part of several systems and are also a system within a system. They are part of the criminal justice, the human services delivery, and the community social systems. Each person in the police agency is a part of a family system and of the police agency system. Police agencies and police officers are affected by systems principles in all of these contexts. They help to shape the systems in which they participate, and they are shaped by them. Each of these systems is, in effect, a community with which the police must relate. Community is defined as a group of people sharing common boundaries, such as common goals, needs, interests, and/or geographical location. The task of police–community relations appears more complex as each community is considered.

THE MANY COMMUNITIES IN COMMUNITY RELATIONS

In future chapters, each of these communities, and others, will receive individual attention. At this point, however, it is important to recognize a few of the many communities that make up the environment in which police work. Each has a distinct identity of its own; each has its own elements and each interacts in some distinct way with police and with each other. Each community must be a part of police–community relations if it is to be truly effective.

External Communities

The Justice Community

Other police agencies, jurisdictions, courts, and corrections departments existing at many levels of government, are a part of the justice community with which police must interact. The nature of the relationship between police and members of the justice community has a direct impact on police effectiveness in achieving their goals. A lack of coordination, communication, and mutual respect within this community, or system, is legendary. Community relations includes relations with this community as a whole and with its individual members.

The Human Services Community

The human services umbrella includes many public and private social service resources, mental health general medical services, media, civic, and religious groups, and educational services. These also form a community, and sometimes many communities with which police officers and agencies interact. Mutual support and availability of services may be lacking because of poor police–community relations. Keeping the peace may depend upon access to and coordination of such resources.

Citizens and the Police

Peel's principles state that "the police must secure the willing cooperation of the public in voluntary observance of the law to be able to secure and maintain public respect." Part of police–community relations is understanding the public that police serve and having the public understand police. That is no easy task. The public is many people with many varying needs and hopes, who live in a changing society and bring to that society conflicting values and cultural rules. The police agency is relatively closed, somewhat secretive, and vague as to what the police role and the citizen role should be. Citizen participation in policing, particularly in crime prevention aspects, has increased in recent years. The business community actively participates in police-designed crime prevention programs. Neighborhoods operate effective block watches. Many of these efforts are models in cost-effective crime prevention. Citizen volunteers now participate in many areas of police work. Even those that have been little more than public relations efforts could be redefined and expanded in the context of community relations.

Thus far, however, much of this redefinition and expansion is in rhetoric rather than in practice, and those communities and neighborhoods most in need of improved police–community relationships are the ones least likely to be involved in such projects. The cooperation and support of other groups are much easier to gain and maintain.

Internal Communities

The Personal Support Community

The officer's support groups, both in the sense of family system and close personal relationships, affect the officer's perspective and effectiveness. The officer has an impact on the support groups as well. This relationship may be one of the most critical in determining the officer's ability to cope with the human experience of being a cop. It may also determine to a large degree how the individual officer will relate with other communities.

The Police Community

The police officer as a member of the police agency and police structure must also be considered. It is this community that can determine whether police–community relations outside the agency will be supported or undermined both as a matter of policy and practice. The first positive relationship that must be formed if effective community relations in a larger sense is to be accomplished is within the agency itself (Fischer, 1981, pp. 54–55).

CONCLUSIONS

Police–community relations programs were built on the foundations of *already existing public relations programs* and, like those programs, involved working with the community in ways that *leave little or no room for recommending or effecting changes* in departmental policy or procedures.

Police–community work concentrated on precisely the segments of the community (e.g., blacks, lower-class youth, and poor) that were most neglected by the earlier public-relations approach, a change that called for new attitudes and procedures.

Police–community relations (following a familiar tendency of our age and bureaucracies everywhere) have become a specialized function to be carried out by special units.

Programs were begun in the 1970s because it was apparent that some response to injustice, discrimination, and poverty was needed, but the response was rarely the result of careful analysis and planning.

Police–community relations work to date has revealed the *isolation* of the police in society, particularly their isolation from what is going on in ghettos, universities, hospitals, union halls, various government agencies and, most important, other institutions of the criminal justice system.

If police wish to maintain ongoing dialogues with all members of society, community relations must be a part of every officer's job and the department's mission.

A police agency is part of several systems and is also a system within a system. Each of these systems is, in effect, a community with which the police must relate. These include the justice community, the human services community, the personal support community, the system within a system, and citizens and the police. The task of police–community relations appears increasingly complex as each community is considered. However, understanding the concept of police–community relations, the people who are involved in its processes, the systems in which they function, the problems they encounter, and the successes they achieve, provides a basis for improving police–community relationships in all communities.

STUDENT CHECKLIST

1. Describe the different views of communities utilized within "traditional" police–community relations and "contemporary" police–community relations.
2. What is police–community relations as described in this chapter?
3. Define the *people's police* and *community.*
4. Describe briefly the impact of police–community relations on the police system.
5. Describe briefly the evolution of police–community relations programs in the United States.
6. List some of the difficulties surrounding a new police–community relations program.
7. Identify several "communities" within which the police play important roles.
8. Describe the current status of and prospects for police–community programs in the United States.

TOPICS FOR DISCUSSION

1. Describe some of the difficulties that might be encountered by a new police–community relations program in your community.

2. How can police, psychiatrists, social workers, and teachers be mutually helpful and yet not intrude into each other's professions?

3. Discuss the merit of formal meetings between police administrators and presiding judges, and compare this with the need to change attitudes in these areas of the criminal justice system.

4. Demonstrate that police–community relations is a process, not a product.

5. Discuss how overlapping memberships in various internal and external communities could facilitate both conflict and cooperation.

ONE STEP FORWARD

LAW ENFORCEMENT CODE OF ETHICS*

All law enforcement officers must be fully aware of the ethical responsibilities of their position and must strive constantly to live up to the highest possible standards of professional policing.

The International Association of Chiefs of Police believes it is important that police officers have clear advice and counsel available to assist them in performing their duties consistent with these standards, and has adopted the following ethical mandates as guidelines to meet these ends.**

Primary Responsibilities of a Police Officer

A police officer acts as an official representative of government who is required and trusted to work within the law. The officer's powers and duties are conferred by statute. The fundamental duties of a police officer include serving the community; safeguarding lives and property; protecting the innocent; keeping the peace; and ensuring the rights of all to liberty, equality and justice.

Performance of the Duties of a Police Officer

A police officer shall perform all duties impartially, without favor or affection or ill will and without regard to status, sex, race, religion, political belief or aspiration. All citizens will be treated equally with courtesy, consideration and dignity.

Officers will never allow personal feelings, animosities or friendships to influence official conduct. Laws will be enforced appropriately and courteously and, in carrying out their responsibilities, officers will strive to obtain maximum cooperation from the public. They will conduct themselves in appearance and deportment in such a manner as to inspire confidence and respect for the position of public trust they hold.

Discretion

A police officer will use responsibly the discretion vested in the position and exercise it within the law. The principle of reasonableness will guide the officer's determinations and the officer will consider all surrounding circumstances in determining whether any legal action shall be taken.

Consistent and wise use of discretion, based on professional policing competence, will do much to preserve good relationships and retain the confidence of the public. There can be difficulty in choosing between conflicting courses of action. It is important to remember that a timely word of advice rather than arrest—which may be correct in appropriate circumstances—can be a more effective means of achieving a desired end.

Use of Force

A police officer will never employ unnecessary force or violence and will use only such force in the discharge of duty as is reasonable in all circumstances.

Force should be used only with the greatest restraint and only after discussion, negotiation and persuasion have been found to be inappropriate or ineffective. While the use of force is occasionally unavoidable, every police officer will refrain from applying the unnecessary infliction of pain or suffering and will never engage in cruel, degrading or inhuman treatment of any person.

Confidentiality

Whatever a police officer sees, hears or learns of, which is of a confidential nature, will be kept secret unless the performance of duty or legal provision requires otherwise.

Members of the public have a right to security and privacy, and information obtained about them must not be improperly divulged.

Integrity

A police officer will not engage in acts of corruption or bribery, nor will an officer condone such acts by other police officers.

The public demands that the integrity of police officers be above reproach. Police officers must, therefore, avoid any conduct that might compromise integrity and thus undercut the public confidence in a law enforcement agency. Officers will refuse to accept any gifts, presents, subscriptions, favors, gratuities or promises that could be interpreted as seeking to cause the officer to refrain from performing official responsibilities honestly and within the law. Police officers must not receive private or special advantage from their official status. Respect from the public cannot be bought; it can only be earned and cultivated.

Cooperation with Other Officers and Agencies

Police officers will cooperate with all legally authorized agencies and their representatives in the pursuit of justice.

An officer or agency may be one among many organizations that may provide law enforcement services to a jurisdiction. It is imperative that a police officer assist colleagues fully and completely with respect and consideration at all times.

Personal/Professional Capabilities

Police officers will be responsible for their own standard of professional performance and will take every reasonable opportunity to enhance and improve their level of knowledge and competence.

Through study and experience, a police officer can acquire the high level of knowledge and competence that is essential for the efficient and effective performance of duty. The acquisition of knowledge is a never-ending process of personal and professional development that should be pursued constantly.

Private Life

Police officers will behave in a manner that does not bring discredit to their agencies or themselves.

A police officer's character and conduct while off duty must always be exemplary, thus maintaining a position of respect in the community in which he or she lives and serves. The officer's personal behavior must be beyond reproach.

*Adopted by the Executive Committee of the International Association of Chiefs of Police on October 17, 1989, during its 96th Annual Conference in Louisville, Kentucky, to replace the 1957 code of ethics adopted at the 64th Annual IACP Conference.

**The IACP gratefully acknowledges the assistance of Sir John C. Hermon, former chief constable of the Royal Ulster Constabulary, who gave full license to the association to freely use the language and concepts presented in the RUC's "Professional Policing Ethics," Appendix I of the Chief Constable's Annual Report, 1988, presented to the Police Authority for Northern Ireland, for the preparation of this code.

Source: International Association of Chiefs of Police, Gaithersburg, MD.

BIBLIOGRAPHY

Alex, N. (1969). *Black in Blue: A Study of the Negro Policeman.* New York: Appleton.

Andreotti, D. A. (1971). "Present problems in police–community relations," in C. R. Chromache and M. Hormachea (Eds.), *Confrontation: Violence and the Police.* Boston: Holbrook Press.

Astor, C. (1971). *The New York Cops: An Informal History.* New York: Scribner.

Berkley, G. E. (1969). *The Democratic Policeman.* Boston: Beacon Press.

Bittner, E. (1970). *The Functions of the Police in Modern Society.* Washington, D.C.: U.S. Government Printing Office.

Black, A. D. (1968). *The People and the Police.* New York: McGraw-Hill.

Cole, G. F. (1992). *The American System of Criminal Justice,* 6th ed. Pacific Grove, Calif.: Brooks/Cole.

Critchley, T. A. (1967). *A History of Police in England and Wales, 1900–1966.* London: Constable.

Fischer, R. J. (1981). "Administration in law enforcement: Management in law enforcement viewed as a system of systems," *The Police Chief,* December.

Friedlander, W. A., and Apte, R. Z. (1980). *Introduction to Social Welfare,* 5th ed. Englewood Cliffs, N.J.: Prentice Hall.

Goldstein, H. (1977). *Policing a Free Society.* Cambridge, Mass.: Ballinger.

Greene, J. R. (1989). "Police and community relations: Where have we been and where are we going?" in R. G. Dunham and G. P. Alpert (Eds.), *Critical Issues in Policing: Contemporary Readings.* Prospect Heights, Ill.: Waveland Press.

Lee, M. (1971). *A History of Police in England,* Montclair, N.J.: Patterson Smith. (Originally published in 1901 by Methuen and Co.)

Norgard, K. E., and Whitman, S. T. (1980). *Understanding the Family as a System.* SW 131A. Phoenix, Ariz.: Arizona Department of Economic Security.

Reith, C. (1952). *The Blind Eye of History.* London: Faber & Faber.

School of Police Administration and Public Safety, Michigan State University (1967). *A National Survey of Police and Community Relations.* Washington, D.C.: U.S. Government Printing Office.

Siporin, M. (1975). *Introduction to Social Work Practice.* New York: Macmillan.

Zumbrun, A. J. T. (1983). Manuscript comments, June.

2

THE PUBLIC AND THE POLICE: A CONSORTIUM OF COMMUNITIES

The criminal justice system is, in reality, if not in appearance, a system. . . . You are most likely to accept [it] as a system if you recognize that society is in the process of imposing the system concept on an existing criminal justice apparatus that for years has been loosely tied together. (Chamelin, Fox, and Whisenand, p. 2)

I pick up a guy for car theft; he kicks me and calls me everything but an upstanding citizen all the way to the jail. While I'm still doing the paperwork, he's on his way home, free to steal another car. I don't know why I bother. (A frustrated cop)

In Chapter 1 we stated that "police–community relations are complicated and constantly changing interactions between representatives of the police organization and an assortment of governmental agencies, public groups, and private individuals representing a wide range of competing and often conflicting interests." In these interactions, those communities that are most vocal, like the proverbial squeaky wheel, often receive more attention and wield more influence. Some receive moderate attention and have moderate influence. Still others are seemingly neglected. Due to constant variations within society, the attention given to individual communities by the police and the influence which they have upon the police varies considerably over time.

Within this chapter we focus our discussion of police and community interaction on both the external communities outside the police organization and the internal communities within the police organization. Our primary contention is that successful police–community relations must take into account exchange relationships among community groups located both within and without the police organization (Figure 2-1).

In the following pages we introduce many of the communities, both external and internal, which exert influence upon and are in turn influenced by the police.

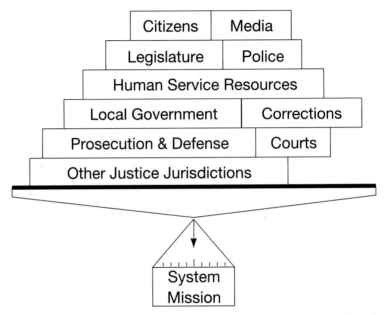

FIGURE 2-1   Achieving the mission of the criminal justice system depends upon the functioning of many external and internal communities.

Understanding the complexity of the interactions between the many communities that comprise the public and the police will enable the reader to better grasp the difficult challenges involved in establishing and maintaining true police–community relations.

STUDYING THIS CHAPTER WILL ENABLE YOU TO:

1. Discuss how relations between the police and the public are in reality complex relations between many overlapping communities.
2. Identify and describe the external communities that comprise the public.
3. Identify and describe the internal communities that comprise the police.
4. Describe how exchange relationships between various communities affect police–community relations.

THE EXTERNAL COMMUNITIES

Ethnic/Racial Minorities

The difficulties that the police and various ethnic groups have had in relating to one another are not of recent origin. Long before the New World was discovered, police forces were being used to control dissident groups. Usually, these groups were comprised of individuals whose homeland had been conquered by another group. The fictional warfare between the Sheriff of Nottingham and Robin Hood was based on actual difficulties that the Normans had with Saxons following their conquest of England. Today, similar difficulties are all too apparent in Israel, Northern Ireland, and Eastern Europe. However, one need not leave the United States to explore this phenomenon.

There are many ethnic minorities within the United States. With the exception of Hispanics (defined by heritage and language), ethnic concerns in the United States focus primarily on racial rather than national, cultural, or religious memberships. Their numbers and the extent of their differentiation from the white majority affects how they are treated within society. Interestingly, discrimination against minority groups is often perpetuated by other minority groups. The worst urban riots that took place in the United States during the 1980s occurred in Miami, Florida and pitted African Americans against Hispanic Americans, and the Los Angeles riot of 1992 produced bitter conflicts between African Americans and Asian Americans.

Regardless of the minority group in question, the primary issues that are faced by police are the same. First, they must provide services to that community in a fair and equitable manner. Second, they must convince the community that they are actually doing so. Often, the second portion of the community relations formula is more difficult to attain than the first. The best means of enhancing relations with minority communities is not slick public relations programs presented by specialized units but the development of police forces that are carefully selected, well trained, highly disciplined, and representative of all communities served (Cox and Fitzgerald, 1992; Radelet, 1986).

Women

Sexism, like racism, has led the police to come into conflict with a sizable portion of the American populace. The treatment of women has differed historically from the treatment of minority groups, in that they were not necessarily the targets of physical brutality or verbal abuse. However, they as a gender group have suffered from discrimination in the forms of condescension and insensitivity on the part of a male-dominated occupation (Cox and Fitzgerald, 1992).

The women's movement and the resulting assertion of women's rights in the work force and the political process have brought about tremendous changes within a relatively short period of time (Radelet, 1986). Male police are becoming highly sensitized to issues that affect females as clients (whether as victims, witnesses, offenders, or concerned citizens) and as colleagues. The increasing numbers of women in law enforcement is accelerating this awareness as police forces become more representative of the community.

Gays

Homosexuals have long experienced discrimination from police officers. Police have zealously enforced laws against homosexuality which have existed in every state. As those laws have been eliminated (or ignored), gays no longer suffer from such blatant persecution but in many areas continue to be treated as second-class citizens (Radelet, 1986). Contempt and derision for the gay lifestyle has led to difficulties in providing the police services to which all citizens are entitled. Confrontations with gay rights protesters have further heightened tensions between police communities and gay communities. This issue is being addressed through training and regulations that promote equitable treatment for gay citizens. Some cities, such as San Francisco, actively recruit gays to join their police forces in order to become more representative of the communities they serve. However, as long as the status of homosexuals in the United States remains unclear, the tensions between gays and police will continue.

Youth

Although most young people never experience any actual difficulties with the legal system, they as a group come into conflict with police at a higher rate than do middle-aged or older people (Walker, 1992). Much of this conflict is nothing more than the age-old dispute that naturally occurs between youth and adults. As young people grow from childhood into adolescence, their potential for conflict increases. Teenagers who are mobile and interested in having fun become even more likely to experience difficulties with police (along with other authority figures). Young adults begin to become more conforming as they mature and find their place within society. The greatest challenge for the police is to allow youth to enjoy being young but to keep them from doing harm to themselves or others.

The Elderly

"Persons sixty-five and older comprise the largest part of the nation's live-alone population, and this proportion is growing steadily" (Radelet, 1986, p. 301). As the number of elderly Americans increases, they are all too frequently becoming the victims of serious crimes. The living conditions of our elderly citizens and their relative susceptibility to crime has caused many to find that their "golden years" are filled with terror. Law enforcement must rise to the challenge of providing services which, along with other governmental assistance, will enrich the lives of our older citizens. Enrichment programs are necessary not only to reduce the victimization of elderly citizens but to halt the increasing numbers of old people engaged in drunkenness, drunken driving, and theft (Radelet, 1986). Public awareness of the needs of the elderly have increased, but there is much to do to alleviate the impact of crime and the fear of it among older Americans.

The Poor

Members of the lower class often view police in a different light than do members of the middle and upper classes. Rather than seeing police officers as protectors of their rights and property, the poor tend to see police as the protectors of other's rights and property. In short, many lower-class people think of the police as their oppressors rather than their defenders. This perspective is easily understood. While the lower class is comprised predominantly of honest and hard-working individuals, it is dramatically overrepresented within the ranks of lawbreakers. People who feel they have been wronged by society have less commitment to the laws of that society.

People who are in desperate situations are more likely to commit desperate acts. And those who feel they have nothing to lose are more willing to risk being arrested.

No matter how fair our society becomes, whether we adopt socialistic programs comparable to those of several European nations, or whether the standard of living for all Americans greatly improves, there will always be a sizable lower class and members of this class will be overrepresented within the criminal community. Therefore, we cannot eliminate conflict between the police and the lower class. But we can reduce the amount of conflict by developing procedures and regulations which ensure that lower-class citizens receive fair and equitable treatment and services from the police.

The Media

The relationship between the police and the media is a complicated one. The police are interested in serving the public and protecting their reputations. The media are interested in serving the public and making profits. The police are obligated at times to withhold information which they feel would be detrimental to the public good (names of victims, case specifics, etc.). The media are obligated to release information which they feel the "public has a right to know." But too often, deciding what information should be released or withheld is based upon self-interest on the part of the media or the police rather than on what is in the public interest (Radelet, 1986).

Because of conflicting views on what is best for the public and because of self-serving motives, the media and the police are often adversaries. How this adversarial relationship is handled is of the utmost importance for the police, the media, and the public. Quite frankly, some secrets must be kept and the media grudgingly realize this. However, the police must also realize that only those secrets that would cause public harm (this does not include embarrassment of police officials or concealment of improper practices) can be legitimately withheld from the media. Therefore, the "relations between media and police personnel should be based upon openness, honesty and availability" (Cox and Fitzgerald, 1992, p. 65). Anything less will only exacerbate an already difficult relationship.

Religious Organizations

The influence of religious organizations may be seen throughout American society. Historically, the United States has been viewed as a Christian country, with most religious disputes occurring between Catholics and the various Protestant denominations. Minority religions were (and are) protected by the U.S. Constitution but were not necessarily tolerated by its peoples. "Blue laws" were passed in many states and communities to force Catholics and non-Christians to comply with Protestant practices. "Heathens" such as Jews, Muslims, Hindus, and Buddhists often found themselves the objects of hatred and intolerance. During the nineteenth century, Mormons were driven out of several states before finding a safe haven in what would become the state of Utah. At that time, also, Native Americans were prevented from practicing their religions.

Today, the relationship between the police and religious organizations are, for the most part, amicable. Most of the traditional religions are supportive of police efforts to provide "law and order" for their community. However, some nontraditional religions are built around practices that might bring them into conflict with law enforcement, and religious organizations are often split on social issues such as civil rights, war, and abortion. In the resulting conflicts, police officials may be placed in the unpopular position of arresting community members who are convinced that they are doing "God's will." As with ethnic minorities, fair and equitable treatment is the key to building and/or maintaining positive relations.

Civic Organizations

Civic organizations such as the Kiwanis, Rotary, Exchange, Civitan, Masons, Shriners, Jaycees, and Lions are less likely to come into conflict with law enforcement than are religious organizations. They, along with the many other reputable organizations dedicated to community service, are often comprised of persons who are thought to be "mainstays" of the community. However, as with any organizations, individual members may engage in unlawful behavior, and local organizations may be created under the guise of civic service which are actually fronts for illegal activities. Police officials should take care to ensure that their membership (or lack of membership) in these organizations does not affect any dealings they may have with them.

Public Service Organizations

Public service organizations are nonprofit associations directed toward accomplishing community goals. The Salvation Army, Goodwill Industries, and American Red Cross are three of the better known charities. The Boy Scouts and Girl Scouts are two of the better known youth development associations. Many local groups that offer family support, crisis counseling, and emergency aid can be valuable allies for the police in rendering assistance to people in need. Police officials need to identify and establish communications with those organizations to enhance their ability to serve the public.

Political Organizations

Politics and policing have been difficult bedfellows for many years. The linkage between politics and police corruption has been a problem not only within the nation's larger cities (Walker, 1977; Reppetto, 1978), but among rural law enforcement as well (Bopp and Schultz, 1977; Johnson, 1988). To "get politics out of the police and the police out of politics" (Walker, 1992, p. 187), has been a goal of reformers for more than a century.

Unfortunately (or perhaps, fortunately) the simple truth is that politics cannot be eliminated from policing or any other governmental agency (Radelet, 1986). Efforts to regulate police membership in opposition parties or to prohibit their involvement in political campaigns have traditionally resulted in abuses on the part of "reformers" (Walker, 1977). As citizens, police officers are entitled to belong to political parties and other political organizations. However, their behavior can be regulated through clear and concise policies and procedures to ensure that their political outlook or activity does not affect their job performance.

Labor Unions

The historical relationship between police organizations and labor unions has been one of hostility and mistrust. The police were frequently used as "strikebreakers" in the labor disputes of the early twentieth century (Reppetto, 1978). Today, the police are prohibited by state and federal laws from violating the rights of striking workers. However, this does not mean that tensions between the police and union members are eliminated. The police are still responsible for the property and safety of industrial management. They must also see that the rights of those workers who do not partici-pate in union activities are protected. Fair and impartial law enforcement is essential.

Economic/Business Organizations

The relations that the police have had with the business community have not been as physically violent as with labor unions, but they have not always been pleas-ant. Often, business leaders have felt that they are "above the law" and should be exempt from police "intrusion" into their affairs. Similarly, many expect preferential treatment when they do need police services. Cooperative relations with business organizations such as the local chamber of commerce, builders' associations, food services, and the trucking industry are necessary. But the neutrality of the police orga-nization in enforcing laws must be stressed.

Community Interest Organizations

The numbers of "watchdog" organizations dedicated to maintaining surveillance over governmental agencies continue to increase. Organizations such as the American Civil Liberties Union and Common Cause are nationally known and respected. Others may consist of only one or two people within a specific community. These organiza-tions may exist for a variety of reasons: to ensure that individual rights are protected; to guard against governmental waste and inefficiency; to protect citizens from haz-ardous conditions; to attract attention to a particular issue; or just to satisfy individual egos. Regardless of their motivation, law enforcement agencies are advised to cooper-ate with them to the extent that departmental procedures, governmental regulations, and state laws will allow.

Clients

The interrelationships between the police community and the external commu-nities that we have discussed are vitally important. However, it should be noted that most individuals hold memberships within several communities at the same time. Fur-thermore, there may be additional factors that influence how they interact with the various police communities.

Many citizens may never have direct contact with police officials. Their percep-tions of the police are based on their memberships within their respective communi-ties. Those perceptions may be reinforced or altered if and when direct contact occurs. A victim who feels that his or her case received only minimal attention from police may be very understanding or very dissatisfied. A victim who feels that he or she was treated with respect and the case handled properly may become an enthusiastic supporter. The same holds true for witnesses, concerned citizens, and sometimes even offenders. Courteous and professional treatment by a police officer can overcome many preconceptions about police. Similarly, one inconsiderate or rude officer can undermine the efforts of many. Once again, fair and equitable treatment of all people with whom the police come into contact regardless of the situation or the person's station in life is the key to good relations.

Governmental Agencies

Law enforcement agencies are but one group out of a myriad number of organizations at all levels of government. The police must interact on a daily basis with representatives of these government agencies: elected officials, top administrators, midlevel bureaucrats, and front-line employees. These agencies may be subunits of the same political entity as the police organization, such as agencies charged with maintaining the streets, utilities, public housing, educational facilities, parks, and public transportation. They may be emergency organizations such as fire departments, ambulance services, and civil defense. They may be local, state, or federal regulatory agencies. Or they may be legislative bodies: city councils, county commissions, state legislatures, or the U.S. Congress which pass laws they are responsible for enforcing and abiding by. In short, the police do not operate in a governmental vacuum (Cole, 1992). They are dependent upon and are depended upon by many other governmental organizations equally dedicated to serving their respective publics.

The Criminal Justice Community

Defining Justice

Police are a part of the formalized structure in our society that is charged with administering justice. Justice, although a topic of great philosophical debate in itself, usually is defined to include the key elements of "impartial adjustment of conflicting claims," and "assignment of merited rewards or punishments" (*Webster's New Collegiate Dictionary,* 1991). Rush defines it as "the process of adjudication by which the legal rights of private parties are vindicated and the guilt or innocence of accused persons is established" (Rush, 1977).

The Mission of a Justice System

The mission of a justice system is to administer justice as society requires. The mission is to be accomplished in a specified manner, by actors in specified roles, based on written (and unwritten) rules, and informed by some basic philosophy of administering justice (and achieving social control). Society's requirements are constantly changing, although the basic components in the system usually remain the same. (Figure 2-2).

This chart seeks to present a simple yet comprehensive view of the movement of cases through the criminal justice system. Procedures in individual jurisdictions may vary from the pattern shown here. The differing weights of line indicate the relative volumes of cases disposed of at various points in the system, but this is only suggestive since no nationwide data of this sort exists.

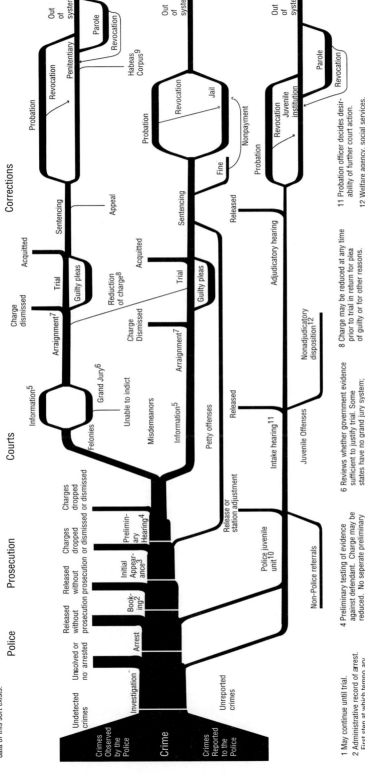

FIGURE 2-2 The criminal justice process. (From the President's Commission on Law Enforcement and Administration, *The Challenge of Crime in a Free Society*.)

1 May continue until trial.

2 Administrative record of arrest. First step at which temporary release on bail may be available.

3 Before magistrate, commissioner, or justice of peace. Formal notice of charge, advice of rights. Bail set. Summary trials for petty offenses usually conducted here without further processing.

4 Preliminary testing of evidence against defendant. Charge may be reduced. No separate preliminary hearing for misdemeanors in some systems.

5 Charges filed by prosecutor on the basis of information submitted by police or citizens. Alternative to grand jury indictment often used in felonies, almost always in misdemeanors.

6 Reviews whether government evidence sufficient to justify trial. Some states have no grand jury system; others seldom use it.

7 Appearance for plea; defendant elects trial by judge or jury (if available); counsel for indigent usually appointed here if not already available. Often not all in other cases.

8 Charge may be reduced at any time prior to trial in return for plea of guilty or for other reasons.

9 Challenge on constitutional grounds to legality of detention. May be sought at any point in process.

10 Police often hold informal hearings, dismiss or adjust many cases without further processing.

11 Probation officer decides desirability of further court action.

12 Welfare agency, social services, counselling, medical care, etc., for cases where adjudicatory handling not needed.

Try Working in This Position

Police fit into this scheme, most directly, as one of the justice components in some specific jurisdiction. The other components are prosecution, courts, and corrections. Each of these components has a decision-making role in the justice process. The complexity of police function requires that officers interact routinely with many other people in their jurisdiction of responsibility, as well as with those who work on other governmental and jurisdictional levels. The governmental level may be federal, state, county, or local. The jurisdictional lines are incredibly more complex; for example, each Indian nation, U.S. Departments of Justice, Defense, and so on, a 1-mile city existing within a large metropolitan community, adult and juvenile, civil and criminal, and many others. Many operational subsystems are established within the larger system, which is the American system of justice. The people who work as a part of the justice process in any of these subsystems become a part of the justice community. How well the entire criminal justice system performs is dependent on the exchange relationships that exist within the subsystems: police, prosecutors, courts, and corrections personnel (Cole, 1992).

Decision making in the justice community is complex by original design. It is further complicated by political and social decisions made by individuals and groups external to the formal justice process.

For Better, for Worse

The concept of system—a set of communities interacting with each other—is imposed on the fragmented, sometimes chaotic and dysfunctional process of justice in which the police are active participants. No one has ever suggested that the justice system works efficiently as a system. As a committee of the American Bar Association observed:

> The American criminal justice system is rocked by inefficiency, lack of coordination, and an obsessive adherence to outmoded practices and procedures. In many respects, the entire process might more aptly be termed a nonsystem, a feudalistic confederation of several independent components often working at cross purposes. (American Bar Association, 1972, p. 7)

Even in a dysfunctioning system, system principles apply. The members of the justice system are interdependent and interrelated in their mission and their functions. If police dramatically increase their arrests, other components of the system will feel the strain. If corrections does not correct, other components of the system will have to process repeat offenders. If police do not investigate thoroughly (sometimes even if they do), their efforts will be wasted because the case will be dismissed. If prosecution is not adequate, even a perfect investigation will be of little benefit. There are times that police might understandably wish for divorce from this system. Even in the case of murder, the crime that is most likely to be reported in our society and for which police are most likely to make an arrest (86 percent of the cases), only 64 percent of those apprehended are actually prosecuted and of those, 43 percent are convicted.

For better or worse, opened or closed, functional or dysfunctional, exchange will occur among the members of this system. Each may declare at times to be an independent agent within the system, owing loyalty and consideration to no one, but this is more an exercise in self-deception than fact. Worse, the deception itself increases the problem of fragmentation. The greater the fragmentation, the less likely system goals will be achieved. Understanding how system principles relate to the justice community will help us to gain a better understanding of this community, assess its needs, and improve its relationships.

THE INTERNAL COMMUNITIES

Police Bureaucracy

The police organization is often viewed by outsiders as a single community of like-minded individuals dedicated to the performance of specifically defined tasks. In actuality, the police organization is a conglomerate of many communities that cooperate in varying degrees in their attempts at accomplishing a variety of complex and ill-defined tasks. These communities are contained within a bureaucratic structure designed to maintain discipline and accountability in the accomplishment of stated goals. Despite decades of managerial fads (Whisenand and Ferguson, 1989), police organizations remain as quasimilitary hierarchies. Efforts to change their organizational structures have met with only limited success. This is because no alternative structure has emerged that can more successfully manage the performance of the many police communities.

Efforts that attempt to restructure the police organization but do not take into account the interaction of the internal communities will produce only short-term benefits. Those communities that feel threatened by proposed changes will undermine such efforts (Walker, 1992). Therefore, proponents of change must fully understand the interactions within the police bureaucracy before they can implement their programs.

Like most large organizations, the police organization is divided into those who perform specific tasks and those who facilitate those who perform the tasks (Gaines, Southerland, and Angell, 1991). Individuals and units assigned to perform specific "police tasks" are categorized as *line* or *operations personnel*. Individuals assigned to facilitate the performance of police tasks (communications, records, training, property, etc.) are categorized as *staff* or *support personnel*. These separate communities are totally dependent on one another. Unfortunately, individuals within the respective communities all too often tend to lose sight of the organizational mission in their concerns with individual or unit goals. When this occurs, mutual cooperation and benefit becomes competition and conflict, which undermine the effectiveness of both the individual units and the overall organization (Sheehan and Cordner, 1989).

Civilian Employees

Demands for enhanced governmental efficiency by taxpayers and community interest groups have affected both the police and other public organizations. One means of increasing police efficiency has been to utilize civilians in those positions that do not require sworn police officers. The vast majority of support services can be provided by civilian personnel (Skolnick and Bayley, 1991). Civilianization may also be extended to many operations duties that can be performed by nonsworn (and less expensive) community service officers.

The use of civilians may be threatening to some sworn personnel, particularly those who occupied positions that have since been "civilianized." In addition, the difference in status between sworn and nonsworn may lead to resentment and conflict (Roberg and Kuykendall, 1990). The importance of all employees, regardless of their assignment or position, to the overall departmental mission must be constantly stressed by management.

Minorities

Initially, minority representatives, regardless of their race or ethnicity, were treated as "tokens" by both police and public (Sullivan, 1989). The few minority officers who were employed often had restricted powers and served only in "their" communities. Since the 1960s, as a result of the Civil Rights Movement, Affirmative Action requirements, federal lawsuits, increased political activities on the part of minorities, and heightened awareness on the part of the white majority, minority representation has increased steadily. Blacks and Hispanics are now well represented within American policing. Other groups, such as Asians and Native Americans, appear to remain underrepresented (Sullivan, 1989).

Despite having achieved more equitable membership within the ranks of the police organization, minorities within supervisory and administrative positions have progressed at a slower rate. This is partially the result of discrimination but is also due to the limited number of management positions that have become available since minorities have been allowed to compete for them. However, progress is occurring. At this writing minority members hold many leadership positions within law enforcement.

Although there has been substantial progress in racial and ethnic representation within law enforcement, it has not been easy or without pain. Resentments have occurred within the police ranks. Charges of discrimination by minorities often have been answered with charges of reverse discrimination by white officers (Roberg and Kuykendall, 1990). Addressing past inequities has created stressful situations for all concerned. These concerns can only be dealt with through organizational policies and procedures that are fair to both minority and majority members.

Gender

Many of the issues discussed in the preceding section are also applicable to women. Actually, female representation in law enforcement has progressed at a slower rate than that of ethnic minorities. It was not until the 1972 Amendments to the Civil Rights Act of 1965 that women obtained the opportunity to choose law enforcement as a profession (Martin, 1989). Prior to those amendments, female representation in law enforcement was minimal and assignments were usually to positions thought to be "properly suitable" by their male supervisors.

Only through legal actions and the perseverance of a group of exceptional pioneers did women break down the barriers within this traditionally male occupation. Today, women have long since proven that they can perform well in all areas of law enforcement. Like ethnic minorities, they have experienced discrimination, resentment, and allegations of preferential treatment. In addition, they have endured the difficulties of sexual harassment from police and public alike. Despite these challenges, women have earned their place in policing.

Sexual Preference

Just as gay men and women have struggled for equitable treatment within the external communities, so have they struggled within the law enforcement communities (Radelet, 1986). Previously gay police officers were required to keep their sexual preferences secret, not only to avoid ostracism but to avoid prosecution for violating laws against homosexuality. As the nation has become more enlightened, laws regulating sexual relations between consenting adults have become more permissive. However, attitudes toward homosexuals have softened only slightly. Whether gays deserve the special protections accorded to ethnic minorities and females is a matter for debate (they are, after all, not recognizable as such unless they indicate their preference). That their private life may be infringed upon by others who may disapprove of their sexual preference is not a debatable issue. Like religion, sexual preference should have no bearing on how people do their jobs or how they are treated while on the job. Gay officers must be accorded the same protections from harassment and discrimination as are accorded heterosexual police employees.

Police Unions

Employee organizations have a variety of names: leagues, fraternal organizations, federations, benevolent associations, and so on, and differing degrees of employee representation (Whisenand and Ferguson, 1989). Yet whatever their name or their affiliation with external employee groups, their mission is to protect and promote the interests of their constituents. While they are categorized as an internal community due to their membership and influence within the police organization, they are often perceived by police administrators as being an external community (Sheehan and Cordner, 1989).

What Are Unions?

A labor union is a legally recognized employee organization that has the authority to bargain with employers on behalf of its membership. Labor unions have existed in this country for nearly two centuries but did not become forces to be reckoned with in policing until the 1960s (Gaines, Southerland, and Angell, 1991). Today, nearly three-fourths of all American police officers are members of unions (Walker, 1992). Despite strong opposition on the part of police administrators and elected officials, police unions have developed in response to desires for better economic benefits, enhanced working conditions, fair treatment, and input into policymaking (Roberg and Kuykendall, 1990).

In addition to collective bargaining, police unions provide representation for individual employees in disciplinary proceedings. They also represent employees who have filed grievances against supervisory actions or administrative policies that are felt to be improper or unfair. Police unions assist in providing legal representation for members. They participate in political campaigns to strengthen the police influence on lawmaking and governmental policies. They lobby local, state, and occasionally, the federal government on law enforcement issues. And they often serve as social organizations that sponsor activities for and on behalf of their memberships.

CONCLUSIONS

In this chapter we have proposed that police–community interaction is not a simple relationship between a police organization and the community it serves but is instead a series of complex and constantly changing relationships between internal police communities and external communities. These communities influence and are influenced by one another on a daily basis. The relationships that exist between various communities are usually competitive, often cooperative, and frequently conflictive.

External communities include ethnic minorities, women, gays, youth, the elderly, the poor, religious organizations, civic organizations, public service organizations, labor unions, business groups, community interest groups, governmental agencies, the courts, corrections, legislative bodies, other law enforcement agencies, the media, citizens directly served by the police, as well as a myriad of other community groupings.

The internal police communities consist of the following: administrative personnel, support personnel, operational personnel, management, civilians, political groups, minorities, males, females, gays, religious groups, college graduates, union members, and other typologies by which individuals and groups may be categorized.

To deal effectively with this complex hodgepodge of humanity, the police organization must be managed in a fair and competent manner that provides equal access and equitable treatment to all communities. Communication is not only the key to the police organizations success in police–community relations but to its survival.

STUDENT CHECKLIST

1. Discuss how relations between the police and the public are in reality complex relations among many overlapping communities.
2. Identify and describe the external communities that comprise the public.
3. Identify and describe the internal communities that comprise the police.
4. Describe how exchange relationships between various communities affect police–community relations.

TOPICS FOR DISCUSSION

1. Identify and describe all the communities of which you are a member. Which could be considered a subsystem of others?
2. Identify and describe all the communities of which a police officer might be a part. Could these overlapping memberships result in conflict for the officer?

ONE STEP FORWARD

Operationalizing the System Concept

Assessing a Local System

This process may be used for assessing either the local justice system, including all key components (see Figure 2-2), or one local agency as a subsystem, or "system within a system" of that larger system.

   I. System Mission
     A. What is the mission of the system?
       1. As defined by legislative and judicial guidelines
       2. As defined by written policy statements
       3. As defined by present agency administrators
       4. As defined by line personnel
       5. As defined by the communities served
       6. As defined by those whose lives are directly affected by the system, the victims and offenders
     B. Assess the mission in system terms.
       1. Is there agreement among these definitions?
       2. If agreement does not exist, what is the nature of the disagreement and where does it exist?
  II. System Components
     A. Identify the key internal system components.
     B. Identify the key functions of each component.
       1. As defined by policy
       2. As defined by procedure
       3. As defined by practice/perception of line personnel
     C. Analyze the ways in which these functions accomplish or undermine system mission.
  III. Interaction in Repetitive Ways
     A. Identify ways that each component interacts with each other.
     B. Identify the written (explicit) rules that guide the interactions of each component with other components.

    C. Identify the unwritten (implicit) rules that guide interactions.

    D. Analyze the ways in which these rules for interaction are constructive or destructive to the system mission.

IV. Structural Variables

    A. Use of power

       1. How is power manifested in the system and in components?

       2. Where is power centered?

       3. What influence do individual components and individuals have on the system?

       4. What sort of leadership evolves from the power structure?

       5. How is power achieved?

       6. How is influence maintained?

       7. How is power balanced among system (or subsystem) components?

    B. Autonomy

       1. How much autonomy (to be self-directing) is given to each component in the system?

       2. How much autonomy is given to each individual?

       3. How is interdependence affected by the autonomy existing in the system?

    C. Coalitions

       1. How do components and individuals within a system form alliances for joint action?

       2. Are the alliances rigid or flexible?

    D. Negotiation

       1. How are agreements made and mutual problems solved within the system?

       2. Is negotiation open and goal oriented?

    E. Syntax: The quality of connections

    (This aspect is difficult to evaluate. Some key questions relating to affect, empathy, respect, and bonding might include the following.)

       1. Is the prevailing mood in an agency or the system trusting, affectionate, hopeful, cynical, depressing?

       2. Do system members demonstrate a willingness to understand the functions and problems of other system members?

       3. Do police extend positive regard to corrections (and vice versa)?

       4. Are emotional bonds among system members strong or weak?

       5. Are existing emotional bonds healthy or destructive?

V. Internal Process

    A. System communication

       1. Permeability

          a. To what degree are system members open to messages from others?

          b. Do system members make certain that messages are mutually understood?

           c. Do system members discount messages from others?

      2. Communication style

           a. Do system members balance consideration of personal needs, the needs of others, and the requirements of the situation?

           b. Is anyone discounted or omitted?

      3. Information processing

           a. Is there congruence in the way different members/components process information?

           b. Are misunderstandings expressed and resolved?

      4. Coherence and flow

           a. Are messages confused in transmission?

           b. Is attention among members focused or scattered?

           c. Does communication flow or is it chaotic and disjointed?

  B. The change process

      1. Impose change, or select an example of imposed change. Analyze the impact on other components of change in one component based on this example.

      2. How do system components deal with change?

  C. Self-esteem

      1. How do members (candidly) value others within the system?

      2. How do members (candidly) value themselves within the system?

VI. External Relationships

  A. The external systems

      1. Identify local systems which impinge on (have major influence on) this system.

      2. What is the function of each as it relates to the system?

  B. The relationship

      1. What is the nature of the relationship of the system/system components with external systems in general (open? closed?)?

      2. What is the nature of the relationship of the system/system components with each external system?

  C. How do system relationships with external systems/individuals affect the achievement of system goals?

VII. Summary of Strengths and Weaknesses

  A. In what ways is this system working effectively as a system?

  B. In what ways is this system working ineffectively as a system?

  C. Given the legal structure, where can change be best applied to effect positive change in the total system?

VIII. System Planning

Robert Cushman (1980) states:

Local criminal justice decision-making should be guided by planning efforts at three levels: criminal justice agency planning, city or county level criminal justice planning, and comprehensive interagency and intergovernmental planning for the criminal justice system as a whole. Planning can help individual criminal justice agencies become more efficient, more productive, and more effective. Planning can help officials of general government—the city mayor, the board of supervisors, and county commissioners—evaluate and make decisions about the criminal justice system and its cost and performance. Many local governments also are finding that comprehensive system-wide planning (interagency and cross-jurisdictional) can help to streamline the entire system of criminal justice, eliminate duplication and fill service gaps, and generally improve the quality of service while minimizing costs.

A. Based on your analysis of the system mission and the reality of systems practice, determine what agencies/individuals should be involved in system planning.
B. Determine an approach to resolving system weaknesses and building on system strengths.

BIBLIOGRAPHY

American Bar Association, Committee on Crime Prevention and Control (1972), *New Perspectives on Urban Crime.* Chicago: American Bar Association, 1972.

Bopp, W. J., and Schultz, D. O. (1977). *A Short History of American Law Enforcement.* Springfield, Ill.: Charles C Thomas.

Chamelin, N.C., Fox, V. and Whisenand, P. (1975) *Introduction to Criminal Justice.* Englewood Cliffs, N.J.: Prentice-Hall.

Cole, G. F. (1992). *The American System of Criminal Justice,* 6th ed. Pacific Grove, Calif.: Brooks/Cole.

Cox, S. M., and Fitzgerald, J. D. (1992). *Police in Community Relations: Critical Issues.* Dubuque, Iowa: W. C. Brown.

Cushman, R. C. (1980) *Criminal Justice Planning for Local Governments.* American Justice Institute, Washington, D.C.: U.S. Department of Justice (LEAA).

Gaines, L. K., Southerland, M. D., and Angell, J. E. (1991). *Police Administration.* New York: McGraw-Hill.

Johnson, H. A. (1988). *History of Criminal Justice.* Cincinnati, Ohio: Pilgrimage Press.

Martin, S. E. (1989). "Female officers on the move? A status report on women in policing," in R. Dunham and G. P. Alpert (Eds.), *Critical Issues in Policing: Contemporary Issues.* Prospect Heights, Ill.: Waveland Press, pp. 312–330.

Radelet, L. A. (1986). *The Police and the Community,* 4th ed. New York: Macmillan.

Reppetto, T. A. (1978). *The Blue Parade.* New York: Free Press.

Roberg, R. R., and Kuykendall, J. (1990). *Police Organization and Management: Behavior, Theory and Process.* Pacific Grove, Calif.: Brooks/Cole.

Rush, G. E. (1977). *Dictionary of Criminal Justice.* Boston: Holbrook Press.

Sheehan, R. and Cordner, G. W. (1989). *Introduction to Police Administration,* 2nd ed. Cincinnati, Ohio: Anderson.

Skolnick, J. and Bayley, D. H. (1991). "The new blue line," in C. B. Klockers and S. D. Mastrofski (Eds.), *Thinking About Police: Contemporary Readings,* 2nd ed. New York: McGraw-Hill, pp. 494–504.

Sullivan, P. S. (1989). "Minority officers: current issues," in R. Dunham and G. P. Alpert (Eds.), *Critical Issues in Policing: Contemporary Issues.* Prospect Heights, Ill.: Waveland Press, pp. 331–346.

Walker, S. (1977). *A Critical History of Police Reform: The Emergence of Professionalism.* Lexington, Mass.: Lexington Books.

Walker, S. (1992). *The Police in America: An Introduction,* 2nd ed. New York: McGraw-Hill.

Webster's Ninth New Collegiate Dictionary (1991). Springfield, Mass.: Merriam-Webster.

Whisenand, P. M., and Ferguson, F. (1989). *The Managing of Police Organizations,* 3rd ed. Englewood Cliffs, N.J.: Prentice Hall

3

PUBLIC RELATIONS
AND COMMUNITY RELATIONS:
A CONTRAST

I think it is important for the police officer who works a beat to be involved in going to meetings of neighborhood associations and civic clubs, getting to know the people so they can know him. It is important for the managers (police supervisors) to do the same thing. Oftentimes there is a historical tendency to have kind of a one-way communications system. It's equally important for the police to receive feedback.
(L. P. Brown, an interview in the *National Centurion,* August 1983)

Police–community relations programs in the United States have been built on already existing public relations programs. Even though community and public relations may be related, they are by no means the same. The differences become especially apparent when the two are compared with reference to their purposes, the activities they involve, and the type of citizen reaction or interest they presuppose. Public relations activities are designed to create a favorable environment for agency operations by keeping the public informed of agency goals and operations and by enhancing the police image; the target is a citizen who *passively* accepts (and approves) what the police department is doing. Community relations, on the other hand, seeks to involve the citizen *actively* in determining what (and how) police services will be provided to the community and in establishing ongoing mechanisms for resolving problems of mutual interest to the community and the police.

STUDYING THIS CHAPTER WILL ENABLE YOU TO:

1. Describe the origin of police–community relations as a separate operational concept.
2. Distinguish between police–public relations and police–community relations.

3. Identify the major purposes of community relations activities.
4. Provide examples of existing programs.
5. Describe community relations issues regarding crime prevention programs.

PUBLIC RELATIONS AND/OR COMMUNITY RELATIONS?

During the short history of police–community relations, there has been little agreement on what it actually is. This lack of agreement among law enforcement professionals has resulted in the development of programs and approaches to community relations that reflect the personal views of local administrators more than they reflect any widely accepted body of knowledge. As a result, considerable confusion exists as to what community relations efforts should accomplish, and how.

It is generally accepted that police–community relations as a separate operational concept originated in the St. Louis Police Department in 1957. Since that time, the community relations concept has experienced sporadic growth throughout the nation. Although the need for community relations is widely accepted today as a crucial part of police administration, its current prominence is of short duration.

The rapid growth of community relations programs resulted from the violent confrontations of the mid- to late 1960s. In larger cities and urban centers, law enforcement administrators realized that they were confronting problems that traditional police tactics were not capable of solving. Administrators in smaller cities, usually on the urban fringes, recognized the possibility that violence might spill over into their communities. In both cases, the creation of specialized units, or the assignment of so-called community relations duties to specific officers, was the response. It was widely felt that such specialized responsibilities could help improve communications between increasingly activist minority groups and the police. In fact, the primary goal of such units at the outset was usually to serve as go-betweens; interpreting the attitudes, desires, and intentions of minority citizens and police agencies to each other.

Over the years, additional duties have been assigned to the community relations specialists. Thus, the community relations function has been variously described as a problem-avoidance methodology (International City Manager's Association), an "art" that is embodied in police administrative philosophy (Earle, 1980), a way of integrating police operations with community needs and desires (Brown, undated), and a way of accommodating the reality that the police are part of the political system (Attorney General's Advisory Commission, 1973). In the early 1980s it was often described as synonymous with police-organized community crime prevention. The concept of *community policing* has now added new meaning to the traditional understanding of police community relations in the 1990s and beyond (Trojanowicz and Bucqueroux, 1990). The community policing philosophy broadens the scope of police–community interactions from a narrow focus devoted exclusively to crime to an examination of community concerns such as the fear of crime, disorder of all types, neighborhood decay, and crime prevention.

These diverse views have resulted in police involvement in remedial educational projects, employment counseling, encounter groups, intensive training in human relations, teaching school, inspecting residences for antiburglary campaigns, organizing block meetings, and dozens of other activities.

This dispersion of effort both reflects and intensifies the lack of agreement on just what community relations is. However, most theoreticians and practitioners agree on one point: what community relations should not be. The President's Commission on Law Enforcement and the Administration of Justice stated that community relations is:

> . . . not a public relations program to "sell the police image" to the people. It is not a set of expedients whose purpose is to tranquilize for a time an angry neighborhood by, for example, suddenly promoting a few Negro officers in the wake of a racial disturbance. (President's Commission on Law Enforcement and the Administration of Justice, 1967)

Despite this warning, and despite the fact that most professionals recognize that community relations must go further than mere image improvement on the part of law enforcement, there is considerable confusion between the concepts of public relations and community relations. Too often the tendency is to regard community relations as:

> . . . public relations, in the traditional sense, i.e., the development of a favorable public impression of a given product—often called "imagery." (Eastman and Eastman, 1971, p. 217)

The Relationship

There is a definite relationship between community relations and public relations. It is important, however, to recognize their differences and to practice both concepts in a way that will meet the needs of the contemporary police agency most effectively. Doing so requires (1) developing an acceptable definition of each, and (2) developing an analytical framework within which they can be examined and measured, no easy task in an area generally considered to be intangible.

Defining Community Relations

We have already noted the problems involved in defining community relations. However, for purposes of the following discussion, it is necessary to construct a definition that includes the most significant characteristics of those definitions discussed earlier. We also need a definition that can generally be applied to a wide range of police efforts. The following definition is suggested by the Attorney General's Advisory Commission:

> Community–police relations is a philosophy of administering and providing police services, which embodies all activities within a given jurisdiction aimed at involving members of the community and the police in the determination of: (1) what police services will be provided; (2) how they will be provided; and (3) how the police and members of the community will resolve common problems.

Such a definition includes the key characteristics of community relations. It must:

- Be a philosophy of police administration and service.
- Integrate police operations with community needs.
- Involve the police and community in problem solving.
- Be reciprocal.
- Be ongoing.

Defining Public Relations

Admittedly, the preceding definition is not too specific. It must be as broad as it is, however, to include the many activities that make up community relations. Any definition of public relations is also broad. It, too, must include the wide variety of operations carried out in its name. For example, *Webster's New Collegiate Dictionary* (1991) defines public relations as "The business of inducing the public to have understanding for and goodwill toward a person, firm, or institution. . . ."

A review of various texts on public relations reveals a variety of definitions. They all have one element in common: each holds that public relations includes those activities that attempt to explain agency goals and operations to the public and to gain public support for those goals and operations.

These two definitions should not lead to the conclusion that either community relations or public relations can be isolated or explained easily. Neither concept is as simple as a basic definition might imply. Rather, the two are complex and can only be understood when several of their individual characteristics are examined.

COMMON FRAMEWORK FOR ANALYZING COMMUNITY AND PUBLIC RELATIONS

Because they are related and both properly part of police activity, the differences between community and public relations should be understood. A useful analytical framework for this purpose focuses on three characteristics of their activities.

1. The *purpose* of the activity.
2. The *processes* involved in the activity.
3. The extent of *citizen involvement.*

The Purpose of the Activity

All police operations have a stated purpose or goal. The purpose of an activity generally embodies the values that the police agency intends to live by. Purpose is an administrative guide. It answers the question: Why has this activity been designed? Purpose, in this sense, is largely philosophical. It describes a hoped-for end. In practice, an activity may serve several purposes. Some activities may be given great administrative importance and others very little.

Why an activity actually takes place and what it accomplishes may have little to do with its stated purpose. Suppose that in an agency, fewer than 7 percent of the agency goals are to "improve the police image," yet some 30 percent of all programs described by the agency fit into a public information category in which most public relations or image-enhancement activities are contained. Officers who participated in the programs probably would rate their programs as highly successful. Their own goals for the programs have been met. The values that the police agency intended to adhere to have not. Understanding the purpose of an activity requires careful observation of what is actually being accomplished versus what was expected.

Public Relations

One common purpose of public relations activities is to develop and maintain a good environment in which to operate. For the police, this involves influencing attitudes in three areas of the environment. They must influence the public, from whom they need support (or, at least, noninterference). They must influence legislators, who are the source of funds. They must influence other elements of the justice community that process those people the police "usher" into the system.

In order to achieve this purpose, the police must minimize obstacles and encourage support. The obstacles result from conscious opposition to what the police have done, are doing, or plan to do. They can include anything from subtle refusal to cooperate to overtly undermining police function. Support for police, on the other hand, could mean anything from passive acceptance to active support and cooperation. Passive acceptance may not be helpful, but neither is it harmful. Active support, such as that required for a campaign to target-harden a residence, is helpful to both the citizen and the police.

In general, the police have employed two ways to achieve their public relations purpose: public information and image enhancement. Public information is perhaps the most routine and widely applied public relations activity in which the police and most other organizations engage. Image enhancement is a logical extension of the public information effort.

Public Information

A strongly held value in our culture is that the informed and educated citizen is the best participant in democratic government. Applied to police performance, the theory is that if people understand why an agency (such as the police), performs as it does, they will be supportive of that performance. Information received by the public, however, often is misinformation, fostered in part by the popular entertainment media, which frequently spotlights and glamorizes the police crime-fighting role.

A check of TV listings for a one-week period in November 1982, revealed that 39 hours of prime time (4 to 10 P.M.) scheduling were dedicated to police or police-related shows. The listings came from four major networks, one independent station, and one pay-TV station. In the 6-hour period covered by the study, at least 1 hour was dedicated to newscasts (sometimes crime drama in themselves, but not counted as part of the 39 hours). Omitting that hour, a person conceivably could have watched police or police-related shows for the entire prime-time period on Saturday, Sunday, Tuesday, and Thursday, and for 4 hours on Wednesday. Mondays and Fridays offered less than 3 hours of this type of material. These shows ranged from serious drama/adventure to light, humorous entertainment programming. A reexamination of TV listings for a one-week period in September 1992 revealed virtually the same results. In a check of TV listings from 5 to 10 P.M., we found that 36.5 hours were devoted to police or police-related shows.

News coverage of police activities focuses on their crime-related duties because these are the most newsworthy. Such emphasis is understandable. Because much public information activity by police is in response to media inquiries about crime, police public information campaigns may underwrite misperception by stressing criminal themes, rather than the totality of the police job (that actually consists mainly of noncriminal responsibilities).

Image Enhancement

Promoting a positive image is a logical extension of the public information activity. Police realize that community-wide respect and cooperation are difficult goals to achieve. There are many negative aspects to the role that society has assigned to the police. Police are charged with seeing that large numbers of people adhere to sometimes unpopular standards, and even the fact that a police force is necessary is distasteful to many citizens. Police need to promote a positive image of themselves whenever possible. In most cases, this is done by stressing the "helping" and "emergency" attributes of the police role. Public information campaigns that focus upon an officer rescuing lost children, capturing armed robbers, and providing assistance at the scene of an automobile accident serve the image-enhancement purpose well.

Community Relations

Community relations programs can (and often do) share purposes and subpurposes with public relations efforts. In this context, however, public relations is a part of a broader, more complex goal. Community relations efforts are geared toward integrating community forces and law enforcement agencies into active partnerships for dealing with the many social and criminal problems assigned to the police. Within this framework, specific objectives of community relations programs are:

- To determine the appropriate range of services the police will provide to the community.
- To determine how these services will be provided (in the sense of appropriate tactics and procedures).
- To identify and define potential problem areas and move to correct them.
- To establish ongoing mechanisms for resolving problems of mutual interest to the police and the community.

The philosophy of community relations stresses the interrelationships and mutual dependencies of police agencies and citizens. The police must depend upon the community as a source of their legitimacy. If they cease to be the "people's police," they no longer achieve their basic mission. Protecting and serving must be defined in terms of the community's needs and wishes in order for the police function to be legitimate. The community is in turn dependent on the police to provide services essential to maintaining an atmosphere of stability. Ultimately, then, community relations serves to create and maintain mutually supportive relationships between police and citizens—something that is needed by both.

PROCESSES INVOLVED IN THE ACTIVITY

Several interesting differences arise when public relations and community relations activities are compared with respect to a set of process questions that apply to both.

1. To what degree are the activities routinized and standardized?
2. Is the activity agency oriented, community oriented, or both?
3. What is the hierarchical level of police agency involvement?
4. What is the direction of information flow?
5. What is the breadth of agency involvement?

Public Relations

Standardization

Public relations activities tend to be routinized and specialized wherever possible. This makes them easier to control, facilitates their repetition, and prevents wasteful duplication or diversion of staff energy from other more highly valued tasks. An excellent example is the agency-initiated press release, the basic tool of the public information function. Preparing such a release is largely a matter of following a standardized form, taking clearly defined steps to obtain administrative sanction, and using regular distribution channels. These steps guarantee a logical, predictable base for the information function.

Agency-Oriented, Community-Oriented, or Both

Public relations activities are agency oriented. They include a range of services designed primarily to serve agency needs. Even services to those outside the agency are designed around the benefits that can be gained by the agency. The agency press release, for example, serves the news media by providing newsworthy information in a readily digestible form. The selection of material and its initial presentation, however, are structured to maximize their image-building or support-gathering potential for the agency.

Information Flow

In public relations activities, information flows outward. This one-way pattern reflects the belief that if those in the agency's environment are properly informed about police operations, they will support them.

Hierarchical Level of Involvement

Because virtually all police agencies are hierarchical in nature, it is relatively easy to pinpoint management responsibility for agency activities once that responsibility has been assigned. Assignment is generally made in direct relationship to the importance given to a specific program by top administration. In other words, if the program is regarded as important, a high-ranking officer will be in charge of it.

Breadth of Agency Involvement

Agency involvement in public relations is narrow. Public relations is a tool of police management, not an essential component of operating philosophy. It is an easily compartmentalized function, even though it attempts to represent all segments of departmental activity. Public relations activities are generally assigned to a specific unit, and they do not require heavy commitments from other elements of the department.

Community Relations

Standardization

In general, community relations activities are difficult to routinize and standardize. Some of their elements may become routine, but the function they are supposed to perform—linking the police to a wide array of publics and interests—usually requires flexibility and capacity for rapid change. Police administrators who prefer the familiar "standard operating procedures" find the concepts of flexibility and capacity for rapid change difficult to understand and accept—and sometimes difficult to permit.

Agency-Oriented, Community-Oriented, or Both

If the function of the police is to protect and serve, then to be community oriented ultimately serves the needs of the agency, too. The aim of community relations is to provide services that are considered important (not by some police administrator but by the people) to the public served. For example, a police storefront center in an urban neighborhood can serve the police by providing information on criminal activity, by functioning as a complaint center, and thereby improving communication with area residents. If it is truly a community relations activity, it also will provide citizens with services that they identify as crucial, such as liaison with other government agencies, assistance in domestic crises, conflict mediation, and referral and counseling services. In this way, an intentional balance of self-serving and citizen-serving processes is achieved.

Information Flow

Two-way information flow is critical to community relations. The communication process must publicize the police point of view, stimulate discussion of issues, and solicit feedback from members of the community or communities involved. In practice, many agencies continue to emphasize the outward flow of messages, sometimes undermining their own community relations efforts.

Hierarchical Level of Involvement

As in the case of public relations, the hierarchical setting of responsibility for community relations activities is so varied that it defies generalization. If community relations activities are specialized, their responsibility would undoubtedly be that of a ranking agency person. But if the activities are expected to pervade the entire organization or involve only specific, line-level units, responsibility might be assigned to lower levels. Each instance is evaluated independently.

Breadth of Agency Involvement

The breadth of agency involvement is a different matter. Although certain aspects of community relations may be assigned to specific departmental units, involvement generally crosses divisional boundaries. This requires a distinction between *specialized programs,* which may have relevance only to a certain geographical or functional unit, and *general practices* aimed at accomplishing community relations objectives department- and communitywide. The former are likely to be successful on a long-term basis only if the latter are part of the department's operating philosophy. Here, a reliable system of internal communication is essential in assuring that the agency presents a "united" community relations philosophy, particularly in areas where news media takes special interest in discovering and publishing contradictions among units of the department.

CITIZEN INVOLVEMENT

Although the police have either assumed or have been assigned responsibility for dealing with many of our more complex social problems, it is folly to think that they alone can solve any of them. In reality, the police are only able to provide limited specialized attention to the most crucial problems, usually in a crisis reactive fashion. Real solutions require much broader efforts by many segments of the community. Even effective crisis reactions often require the involvement of nonpolice resources. In terms of citizen involvement, public relations and community relations activities provide a definite contrast.

Public Relations

In most public relations activities, citizen involvement is kept to a minimum. It is generally passive; the citizens receive information dispensed by the law enforcement agency or utilize services that primarily serve agency purposes. In most cases, citizens are reasons for, but not participants in, the activity.

Community Relations

Community relations activities often rely heavily upon citizen involvement. The citizen is, by definition, an active participant. The police agency does not relinquish responsibility for administering agency programs or practices relating to community relations. It does, however, ensure that citizen resources are properly accommodated, both to provide assistance in accomplishing police goals and to stimulate feedback on issues and problems. Table 3-1 summarizes the characteristics of public relations as compared to community relations.

Why Public Relations Is Not Enough

Public relations activities can and should be a part of a properly applied community relations program, but they cannot substitute for it. The analysis in the preceding section pinpoints some very real weaknesses of public relations programs.

Failing to Provide True Problem-Solving Mechanisms.   Public relations techniques aim to preserve and enhance the department's image, not cope with operating problems. In contrast, community relations programs make a point of identifying problems and working with the community to prevent or resolve them.

TABLE 3-1

CHARACTERISTICS OF PUBLIC RELATIONS AS COMPARED TO COMMUNITY RELATIONS

	Public Relations	Community Relations
Purpose	Attain–maintain good environment	Develop police–community partnership
	Inform public	Integrate community needs with police practices
	Enhance image	
	Minimize obstacles	
	Stimulate support	
Process	Routinized functions comprise activities	Flexible and adaptable functions comprise activities
	Agency-oriented services	Community-oriented services
	One-way (outward) information flow	Two-way information flow
	Responsibility compartmentalized	Responsibility dispersed throughout agency
Citizen Involvement	Consciously kept to a minimum	Actively sought and stimulated

Reaching the Wrong Targets.   Public relations efforts are often directed at intermediaries, usually respected, organized groups whose members are likely to support the agency in any case. For example, providing public speakers is a common public relations device. The department thoughtfully provides informed officers to speak to civic groups, business concerns, clubs, schools, and so on, in basically an educational effort. The target group is generally already supportive of the police. The speaker may talk "at" the audience, answer a few questions, and return to headquarters.

In most instances, everyone is pleased. No dialogue has taken place, however, and the citizens have rarely been encouraged to take an active part in solving police–community problems. The department hopes that group members will act as intermediaries, carrying the department's message to others, thus building support to avert future problems. In contrast, community relations programs are directed both to groups that are supportive of the police and groups that are not. Active citizen assistance and feedback is sought from both.

Alienating Concerned Citizens.   The pure public relations approach alienates concerned citizens by convincing them that the department is merely interested in image building, not in dealing with problems or in effective communication with the community. Similar feelings may disenchant intermediaries with their role. The community newspaper, for example, receiving only superficial news releases that fail to discuss significant issues of concern, will soon refuse to print them. Only limited descriptive material about training courses, medal-of-valor awards, and numbers of arrests made during a month will be printed if real problems of rising crime rates, citizen dissatisfaction with police performance, or similar issues are ignored. Alienating concerned citizens is one of the greatest inherent dangers of a pure public relations concept.

Dealing Ineptly with Crucial Issues.   The purpose of public relations is essentially to change perceptions, not to solve substantive operational problems. Thus, when internal change or real communication between police and community is needed, the superficiality of the public relations approach may simply aggravate matters.

Limited Decision-Making Power.   Public relations is a secondary element of police management, and it is compartmentalized. Those in charge of its activities have little power to influence policy or procedural decisions; their job is merely to secure acceptance of the decisions others make.

How Public Relations Can Strengthen Community Relations

The public relations concept has a distinct and valuable place in agency operations as an element of an overall community relations program when the latter is truly part of administrative philosophy. There are at least five functions that are essentially public relations in thrust but which complement community relations efforts.

Informing the Public About Crucial Issues

The public relations purpose of informing the public can be valuable to both police and citizen if it extends to critical issues. The "whys" of police policies and procedures can be explained to the public. Alternatives to current practice, as seen by the agency, can be explained and any trade-offs outlined. These explanations must be straightforward and honestly portray the police position to inform—not to sell the status quo. This is the point at which the public relations effort supports the community relations effort. Proper performance of police tasks, not public relations techniques, must do the selling.

Developing Community Support

Public relations can work to stimulate active citizen support, including cooperation in crime control and prevention activities. This is a change from the traditional public relations orientation. Generating support must be part of an overall mission of involvement and it must be done with scrupulous honesty. The agency will need to be wary of passive lip service that has characterized purely public relations approaches in the past. Stimulating true citizen involvement can secure the strongest support any criminal justice agency can promote.

Supplementing Agency Operations and Programs

As an outgrowth of a balanced community relations philosophy, police agencies may implement special operations and programs. Public relations techniques can be used to explain the reasons for, and goals of, these activities, stimulate discussion, and elicit feedback about them.

For example, both are useful in initiating a Neighborhood Watch program. Public relations techniques can help to sell the concept and community relations can help to define a specific neighborhood's needs and develop and maintain community feedback and support.

Presenting an Accurate Picture of the Agency and Its Functions

The modern police agency performs a confusing variety of tasks, from catching criminals to providing on-site assistance in serious emotional crises. The mundane and sensational, the dull and controversial, and how they relate to one another, are important aspects of agency function. By presenting an accurate and balanced picture of the police organization, public relations efforts can promote true public understanding of the police role and mission. This is perhaps the most important function that public relations can perform as part of a community relations effort.

Enhancing the Agency's Image

Public relations can continue to perform many of its traditional functions, even when operating in a community relations mode, but these functions become subordinated to the principles of the broader concept. For example, it is unrealistic to ask any bureaucratic organization to abandon its efforts to achieve support for its programs. The realities of competing for scarce operating resources—money, personnel, and material—preclude such simplistic proposals. Nevertheless, the achievement of support, including image enhancement, must be accomplished in accordance with a strict set of guidelines requiring honesty and integrity in the tactics used. Building the agency's image should be a conscientiously controlled means of providing better service, not the ultimate goal of the agency's community relations program.

PROGRAM EXAMPLES

Thus far, this chapter has focused on the differences between the concepts of public relations and community relations as they are commonly applied by the contemporary law enforcement agency. In this final section, attention will turn to examining several public relations and community relations programs. There are few "pure" programs, just as there are few agencies that embody only the characteristics associated with the concept in the preceding pages. Any evaluation of an agency's orientation must be made by examining the total structure of its operations. Some representative examples of community outreach efforts are described in the following pages.

Public Relations Programs

Whether or not a program is purely public relations oriented or is a part of a larger community relations thrust is often determined by its long-range goals and the population it seeks to reach. Although most of the programs listed below as public relations could possibly be incorporated into community relations, they frequently exist for short-term enhancement and reach a population that is already supportive of the police.

Speakers Bureau

Most law enforcement agencies are ready to provide speakers to civic groups, business concerns, schools, and other organizations on request. The speakers usually give a short, informative talk on a topic such as drug abuse, traffic safety, or crime and protection. They may also distribute descriptive literature to the audience.

Ride-Along

Another common program is the citizen ride-along. This program allows members of the general public to accompany a police officer on routine patrol. Although some jurisdictions place few restrictions on the ride-along program, many require that the rider be free of a criminal record or meet requirements of age, occupation, or other significant conditions. The ride-along program does have elements of mutual education for both citizen and police officer, but its primary purpose is to help the citizen "understand" the difficulties of modern police work.

Police Station Tours

Guided tours of police stations have become standard fare for civic organizations and school groups. Depending upon the size and sophistication of the agency, such tours include visiting the jail, crime lab, lineup room, communications center, records center, and various operating bureaus or divisions. Tours are often arranged in conjunction with police week ceremonies.

Safety Lectures

Lectures on traffic laws, crossing the street, and other safety topics—usually geared toward children—are conducted in shopping centers and schools and are often accompanied by films and demonstrations.

Citizen Recognition

Many agencies give awards to citizens who provide particularly helpful services to the police. Such awards may be given for bravery or merely for reporting a suspicious person who turns out to be a burglar or armed robber. In either case, the agency makes a formal presentation of a plaque or some other suitable award to show its appreciation for an informed and involved citizenry.

Programs with a Major Community Relations Focus

Successful community relations programs also serve a public relations function. The following programs were designed as community relations programs. Although they are not universally implemented in ways that realize their optimum effectiveness, the dominant focus of each is community relations.

Rumor Control

The rumor control program is most often used during violent street confrontations, generally between the police and residents of racial and ethnic minority neighborhoods. It involves developing networks for gathering, sorting, and clarifying information. Unfounded or exaggerated rumors are identified and exposed. Facts are provided before the rumors can precipitate disturbances. Local civic leaders such as business people, teachers, and religious leaders usually assist in this process. In some communities, the rumor control operation has been used ineffectively simply to provide information to the community by the police. Where it has been optimally used, however, the control network has developed into a useful forum for discussing common police problems in many neighborhoods.

Storefront Centers

Storefront centers, a well-publicized method of bringing the police officer closer to the people, have been complaint reception centers, mini-precinct houses, and meeting places, and have served many other purposes. Their effectiveness depends on whether they embody the one-way principles of public relations or the two-way principles of community relations.

Neighborhood Team Policing

Community-based teams, under a team commander, have been used to deliver police services to particular neighborhoods. The team has responsibility for deployment, assignments, methods of operations, and other organizational and operational decisions, and offices for team members are located within the policed area. This policing style provides several community relations opportunities. These opportunities include closer, more stable ties with neighborhood residents; citizen participation in planning and delivery of services; and participation and input from all team members with regard to team management and activities. Effectiveness of community-based teams varies widely. Those that are most effective work as a team and consider themselves as part of the community they serve.

Foot Patrol Programs

The reestablishment of foot patrol in many cities has reintroduced a traditional method for intensifying the interaction between citizens and police. A strict reliance on motorized patrol creates a situation where there is little or no face-to-face interaction between citizens and the police and prevents the development of communication and trust. Skolnick and Bayley report that their observations of foot patrol and the research studies of foot patrol reveal four meritorious effects:

1. Since there is a concerned human presence on the street, foot patrol is more adaptable to street happenings, and thus may prevent crime before it begins.
2. Foot patrol personnel may make arrests, but they are also around to give warnings either directly or indirectly, merely through their presence.
3. Properly carried out, foot patrol generates goodwill in the neighborhood, which has the derivative consequence of making other crime prevention tactics more effective. This effectiveness in turn tends to raise citizen morale and reduce their fear of crime.
4. Foot patrol seems to raise officer morale (Skolnick and Bayley, 1986, p. 216).

Physical Decentralization of Command

Many police organizations are decentralizing the police bureaucracy to provide for quality interaction between the police and the community and, as in neighborhood policing, a heightened identification between the police and specific areas. This has led to the creation of fixed substations, ministations, and the creation of additional precincts.

Although these programs share some of the characteristics and objectives of neighborhood team policing, they are quite different, in that they provide for the creation of small autonomous commands and involve the assignment of police personnel to specific areas for long periods of time.

Problem-Oriented Policing

Problem-oriented policing, which includes a number of different programs undertaken in a large number of cities, provides for a new approach to the delivery of police services. In this approach the police go beyond individual crimes and reactions to calls for service and attack the problems that caused them. It moves the police from a reactive response to individual incidents to a proactive approach to citizen concerns.

The police would examine the reasons why particular crimes or calls for service occur in certain locations or at particular times and then map out a strategy for dealing with them. The strategy for dealing with these events would involve active participation by the community members affected. The four features of problem-oriented policing are:

1. As part of their work, officers identify groups of similar or related events that constitute problems.

2. Then they collect, from a variety of sources, information describing the nature, causes, and consequences of each problem.

3. Officers work with private citizens, local businesses, and public agencies to develop and implement solutions.

4. Officers evaluate solutions to see if the problems were reduced (Spelman and Eck, 1986, p. 4).

Crime Prevention: Another Name for Community Relations?

Almost all of the program examples mentioned could be included under a broad crime prevention umbrella, and many others could be added to the list. Several hundreds of millions of federal and local funds have been spent on "crime prevention projects" in recent years (Krajick, 1979, p. 7). There is no doubt that crime prevention is a well-advertised, whether or not a well-executed focus of police function. Citizen demand for crime prevention programs continues to grow. A National Crime Prevention Institute has been established to provide specialized prevention training and consultation (Mellard, 1982, pp. 18–23).

Some of these programs are oriented toward community relations and have become citizen action-centered. In these, citizens and police are involved in defining what crime problems exist in a particular area and population and what actions can be taken to prevent such crime from occurring. Implementation and evaluation are part of the prevention program.

Most programs that are tagged as "crime prevention," however, continue to be, at least in practice if not in original purpose, almost entirely informational—from the police to the citizen. As Krajick states: ". . . in what some crime prevention experts term a 'knee-jerk reflex,' popular programs like brochure distribution and security surveys are picked up by police departments without any study as to whether those programs address a particular problem in their jurisdictions" (Krajick, 1979, p. 7).

Some programs are considered very successful and their success is defined in a wide variety of ways. These include (1) the number of neighborhood crime watch teams formed, (2) number of volunteers in the program, (3) decrease in a particular type of crime in a given neighborhood, (4) number of brochures distributed, (5) number of presentations made, (6) number of households following the security advice of police representatives, and so on.

Some projects have not been successful by the most generous, short-term criteria for success. Even the evaluations of programs in themselves are sometimes suspect either in evaluation design or methodology.

Do successful crime prevention programs also meet long-range community relations goals? The answer is difficult to determine from the short-term rationale used to test for success. Involving the community in an ongoing program of crime prevention requires an underlying community relations perspective. The characteristics of neighborhoods and their problems must be considered. Two-way communication must exist, and a structure must be provided that will encourage continuing involvement of the community.

Even this level of crime prevention will be easier to achieve when working with neighborhoods that already have a positive view of the police. It is much more difficult (and therefore seldom attempted) to build the same relationship in neighborhoods that have had more negative confrontations with police. Police representatives involved in the Neighborhoods Against Crime Program (NAC), a part of a larger crime prevention project under the direction of the Police Bureau in Portland, Oregon, have attempted to reach out to such neighborhoods. In a report of their project they comment on the problems of achieving and maintaining long-range success in such areas.

> Because of the diversity of the neighborhoods with which the coordinators have worked, acceptance of crime prevention concepts and institutionalization of programs varied considerably among areas. For example, Inner Northeast, the center of Portland's Black Community, has a traditionally lower level of trust for the police. Consequently, months of effort to establish programs can be easily undone by negative incidents involving the police and the Black Community. Not surprisingly, efforts to institutionalize have been more slow in that area. The Inner Northeast NAC Coordinator has therefore stressed the need for support from a paid staff person to continue programs in that area. (Portland Police Bureau, 1981, pp. 3–4)

In recent years, many agencies have defined police–community relations in terms of their crime prevention activities. Given the criteria discussed in this chapter for true community relations programs, prevention services would have to be broadly based, meet long-range goals, and be set up to address far more than just "crime-specific" problems to qualify. Rarely is this the case in practice. Therefore where crime prevention has been substituted for community relations, the community relations concept has usually been narrowed. Crime prevention activities can support a total police–community relations effort, but they are only part of it.

Among the most public relations oriented of the crime prevention programs are:

- *Security surveys* in which the police, by invitation or request, visit a home or business and suggest ways in which security can be improved.
- *Clinics* in which individual citizens and businesses are advised how to prevent specific types of crime (e.g., prevention of rape, shoplifting, bank robbery, and burglary).
- *Awareness-alertness programs* in which bulletins about particular crime problems occurring in the community are issued. During the holiday season, many police agencies will issue circulars to business people pointing out various shoplifting techniques. Some agencies also insert burglary prevention messages in public utility billing statements or bank statements. Although these awareness notices often call upon the citizen to help the police by making it hard for the criminal to consummate an unlawful act, they seldom follow up on such requests, nor do they provide any realistic means for helping the citizen to do so.

Under the umbrella of crime prevention are several programs which include both the elements of public relations and community relations. The ultimate impact of these programs depends on the emphasis placed on the various elements and upon the context in which they are applied.

Neighborhood Watch

The many varieties of area watch programs range from those in which residents of a neighborhood are asked to keep an eye on their neighbors' homes for strange activities, to those in which citizens are mobilized into committees to work with local police units in identifying local problems and developing responses to them. In the first instance, the police ask citizens to report any suspicious activities occurring in the neighborhood. The citizen merely becomes an extension of the police patrol apparatus. In the latter instance, the police officer on the beat and the citizen endeavor to perfect their partnership responsibilities in identifying those problems that can ultimately be corrected by police intervention.

Operation Identification

In the operation identification program, police encourage citizens to mark their possessions with their social security numbers or other identification recognizable as belonging to them, in order to discourage theft and to increase the possibility of apprehending the offender and restoring the goods to the original owner. Usually, citizens can bring items to the station for identification marking or they will be provided with an etching tool so that they can mark items in their homes.

Police Auxiliary Volunteers

The elderly are a prime target of crime today. Senior volunteer programs combine police expertise and elderly citizen volunteers, who work together to find ways in which the elderly can assist in preventing crime and in providing support and assistance to elderly victims. Many volunteer auxiliary programs involve citizens of all ages in a broad range of police support activities. (See *One Step Forward* for a discussion of this project.)

Community Crime Watch

In some communities, public utilities, such as telephone, gas, and electric companies have been trained and organized as part of a crime watch team. Because of the extent of their community access and their frequent opportunity for "patrol," employees of such agencies can provide a unique community service. Once trained in what to look for, they become an excellent police support group. If they observe suspicious behavior or circumstances, they are asked not to intervene but to report.

Crime Stoppers

The programs included in this category are known by several names: Crime Stoppers, Crimes Solvers, Secret Witness, Crime Line, and so on. These programs join the news media, the community, and the police in a concerted effort to enlist private citizens in the fight against crime. The program is based on the premise that some citizens who know of or observe crimes will not report them because of apathy or fear but will for a cash reward.

The first Crime Stoppers Program was begun by police officer Greg MacAleese in Albuquerque, New Mexico, in 1976. Since that time the number of programs has steadily increased in this country and in Canada and New Zealand.

CONCLUSIONS

The difference between public relations and community relations is not always clear-cut. The guidelines presented in this chapter can help an observer to make informed judgments about the nature and purpose of police activities, but only if the activities are studied in the context in which they occur. To what extent do primarily self-serving principles and practices affect a police agency's receptivity to community input? The answer to this question ultimately determines whether the agency is operating under a public relations or community relations philosophy.

Public relations by itself can often prove valueless and even harmful to police agencies because its activities are agency-oriented (and thus basically self-serving). Public relations officers are not agents of change and they may gloss over or misrepresent crucial issues. On the other hand, every police agency must rely on public relations to some extent to help assure its position in relation to other forces at work within the community. Public relations activities can play a valuable role in community relations programs provided they follow strict guidelines of honesty and integrity, and make a goal such as image enhancement subordinate to providing better service.

Crime prevention has become a household phrase, although not necessarily a household effort. For crime prevention to be synonymous with police–community relations, crime prevention efforts will need to meet police–community relations goals, something that seldom occurs in practice.

STUDENT CHECKLIST

1. Describe how police–community relations originated as a separate operational concept.
2. Describe the difference between police–community relations and police–public relations.
3. What is the major purpose of police–community relations activity?
4. List three examples of police–public relations programs.
5. List three examples of crime prevention programs.
6. List three examples of programs with a major community relations focus.
7. Describe the characteristics of a crime prevention program that meets police–community relations goals.

TOPICS FOR DISCUSSION

1. Discover what activities and programs your local police agencies participate in. Are these oriented predominantly toward public relations or community relations? Whom do they serve and involve?
2. Devise a community relations project in crime prevention that could be initiated in your community. What are the characteristics that make your project oriented toward community relations rather than toward public relations?
3. What are the disadvantages of community relations programs?

ONE STEP FORWARD[1]

Citizen Volunteers: Making a Concept Work

Philosophical Framework

To achieve its mission, a police agency needs the support and active participation of the citizens served. Such a mission requires that the agency seek to develop:

- A high level of police–community understanding and trust.
- Effective and meaningful two-way communication.
- Increased community awareness of crime problems and ways to reduce the probability of being victimized.
- Alternative resources for the agency that will increase productivity and more effective use of certified officers.

This is the mission of the community relations section of the Pima County Sheriff's Office. Programs developed to fulfill this mission meet nationally recognized criteria for crime prevention practices. They are also unique. They meet the specific needs of the agency and population served. They are innovative in recruitment, training, and utilization of citizen volunteers. The Pima County Sheriff's Office has received national recognition for seeking meaningful participation of citizens in almost every agency function (Figure 3-1).

Specific Projects and Programs

As Lewis and Salem (1981) state: "Community crime prevention strategies prevent crime by altering the relations between the criminal, victim, and environment, reducing the opportunity for victimization." Programs developed seeking to apply these strategies with the help of citizen volunteers in the Sheriff's Office are listed below. Some of these exist in similar form in many communities in the United States. Others are unique to this agency.

[1]Source for Pima County material: Deputy L. R. Sacco, SAV Coordinator, Pima County Sheriff's Department.

FIGURE 3-1 Volunteer auxiliary teams involve citizens of all ages in police support activities. (Courtesy of Pima County Sheriff's Office, Arizona.)

SUSPICIOUS ACTIVITY CARD

SUSPICIOUS PERSON # ONE:			☐ DRIVER		☐ PASSENGER		☐ PEDESTRIAN	
Sex	Race	Hgt	Wgt	Hair	Eyes	Skin	Approx. Age	

SUSPICIOUS PERSON # TWO:			☐ DRIVER		☐ PASSENGER		☐ PEDESTRIAN	
Sex	Race	Hgt	Wgt	Hair	Eyes	Skin	Approx. Age	

Manner of Dress & Identifying Marks (Person # One) ☐ Glasses ☐ Moustache or Beard

Manner of Dress & Identifying Marks (Person # Two) ☐ Glasses ☐ Moustache or Beard

Possible Occupation or Activity of Subject(s)

Location of Suspicious Activity	Sub-Division	Time	Date

Type Veh	Make	Model	Year	Color	Lic No.	State or Color Plate

Additional Information:

Submitted by:	C. Bear #

PIMA COUNTY SHERIFF'S DEPARTMENT, CITIZEN BEARS TEAM
GREEN VALLEY, DISTRICT · GREEN VALLEY, ARIZONA

FIGURE 3-2 Suspicious activity card used by volunteers to report suspicious activity to appropriate agency.

Sheriff's Auxiliary Volunteers
of Pima County, Inc.
P.O. BOX 910 • TUCSON, ARIZONA 85702

INFORMATION FOR ALL NEIGHBORHOOD WATCHES:

The Sheriff's Auxiliary Volunteers has a program in which we Video tape the property inside of your home. This service is free and you are given the tape to be put in safety deposit box or in a safe place.

We also have Home Inspections. An Inspector comes to your home and checks locks, windows, doors, etc.

We have an engraver to loan so you may etch your drivers license number on the TV, microwave, etc.

For more information call the phone numbers listed below.

George Meyers--741-4972
Home Inspections

Isabel Powers--741-4685
Crime Prevention

FIGURE 3-3   Sheriff's Auxiliary Information Sheet.

- *Suspicious activity cards.* All Sheriff's Auxiliary Volunteers participate by documenting their observations that are then routed to the appropriate agency (see Figure 3-2).
- *Business identification program.* Citizen volunteers maintain a cross-indexed file of businesses and their owners or managers, allowing officers quick access to relevant information in the event of a fire or crime on the premises after business hours.
- *Emergency response program.* Certain volunteers have developed additional skills and have Citizen Band radio capability. They have a call-out system devised to put "eyes and ears" into specific areas on request of the department.
- *Neighborhood watch program.* The backbone of community involvement with crime prevention. Neighborhoods are organized into manageable groups that meet four times per year. Members are given initial and follow-up information on prevention techniques. Neighbors are encouraged to be more observant and involved with their areas.
- *Home security survey.* All residential burglary victims are contacted by mail and offered a personalized survey of their home to help prevent being victimized again (Figure 3-3).

- *Operation identification.* Normally included within Home Security checks or Neighborhood Watch presentations. Citizens who demonstrate compliance with suggested procedures receive free Operation Identification stickers (Figure 3-4).
- *Crime watch program.* A minicourse of instruction for nonpolice public officials and private/commercial organizations that have radio-equipped vehicles operating

OPERATION
IDENTIFICATION

A citizen participation
program to prevent
burglary

FIGURE 3-4   Pima County operation identification.

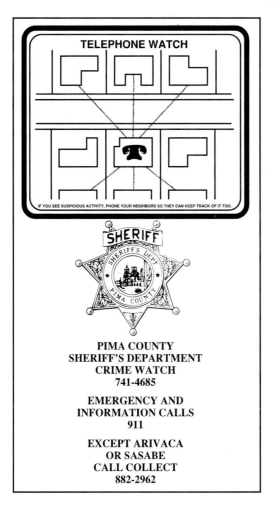

FIGURE 3-5   Pima County telephone watch program.

in the community. The course is aimed at making the operators more efficient observers and reporters of criminal or suspicious activity (Figure 3-5).

- *Inter-departmental people power assistance program.* Many volunteers have provided support to the department by assisting with administrative duties. Help has been provided to records section, burglary detail, auto theft detail, district level administration, and the management services division, which is where the volunteer program is coordinated. The burglary and auto theft units use volunteers to maintain their multi-indexed intelligence files of stolen property.

Public Awareness Programs

The volunteers have participated in various crime prevention awareness shows or programs. They have worked closely with other local crime prevention groups including the Crime Prevention Fair and Crime Resisters. At the crime fair, volunteers staff an informational display. This fair is a highly successful, countywide awareness event held for one week each October. At the annual county fair, held each spring, the volunteers staff and maintain an informational and recruitment display (see Figure 3-1). Volunteers also assist local shopping malls in presenting specific crime prevention themes during weekend expositions. Topics typically include auto theft, burglary prevention, and child safety.

Recruitment

The minimum age for adult citizen volunteers is 18. No upper age limit or restriction exists. A separate county volunteer program exists for teenagers through Explorer Scout posts.

Recruitment is countywide. Both officers and volunteers are involved in recruiting efforts. There are no physical requirements for admission. Screening is thorough. A background check for arrest or prior contact with law enforcement is routine. Prior arrest does not automatically bar an applicant from participation. Circumstances surrounding the event and lapse of time since the offense are considered. The agency seeks responsible volunteers who are sincere in their service goals and who will fulfill the citizen volunteer standard of conduct.

CITIZEN VOLUNTEER STANDARD OF CONDUCT

Members shall conduct their private and professional lives in such a manner as to avoid adverse reflection upon themselves or this department.

Members shall obey all federal, state, and local laws as well as the rules and regulations listed herein.

Members knowing of any other member violating any laws shall report such violation to their District Volunteer Liaison Officer (DVLO) or District Commander.

Members shall treat their peers and associates with respect. They shall be civil and courteous at all times in their relationships with one another.

Members shall make no false reports or knowingly enter or cause to be entered in any departmental report or record any inaccurate or false information.

No member shall willfully misrepresent any matter. Members shall not release any official business of the department without the direct consent of the District Commander or their DVLO.

While acting in an official Sheriff's Auxiliary Team capacity, members shall not recommend to any person the employment of a particular attorney, bail bondsman, towing company, or any other service for which a fee is charged.

Members shall not solicit or accept any personal gift, gratuity, or reward for services rendered in the line of volunteer duty. No member shall purchase, consume, or be under the influence of any alcoholic beverage while acting in the capacity of a Sheriff's Auxiliary Team volunteer.

Members shall not possess or use any controlled substance, narcotic, or hallucinogenic except when prescribed by a physician or dentist.

Members shall keep their liaison deputy informed of any unusual activity, situation, or problem with which the department would logically be concerned.

FIGURE 3-6   Special identification
for auxiliary volunteers.

Training

The foundation of a successful volunteer program is training. In addition to an orientation to the agency and crime prevention (4 to 6 hours), each Sheriff's Office volunteer is trained in basic civil liability; the goals, structure, and procedures of the volunteer programs; introduction to law enforcement systems and agencies; cardiopulmonary resuscitation; basic medical first aid care; identification of criminal or suspicious activity and reporting methods; and traffic accident scene assistance (20 hours).

Advanced skills training is offered in specialized areas. For example, a 44-hour advanced course is required for volunteers who wish to be crime prevention instructors and program facilitators. This training includes: the history and theory of crime prevention and risk management; the concept of creating barriers; security lighting; locks; alarm systems; how to do home security surveys; how to develop neighborhood watch programs; public speaking and instruction skills; how to facilitate citizen emergency response training; and civil liability for instructors.

Class members must demonstrate proficiency through oral board and written examination prior to certification by the department.

Identification

All volunteers who successfully complete the training are issued identification cards which remain the property of the department. Volunteers in specialized support programs may also wear identifying patches when on duty (see Figure 3-6).

Supervision of Volunteers

Effective supervision is critical to program success. Supervision is required to:

- Assure that the skills and interest of the volunteer are matched to departmental needs.
- Facilitate acceptance of the volunteer by departmental personnel.
- Identify any problems early and work toward their solution.
- Encourage cooperation and teamwork among volunteers and between volunteers and agency personnel.
- Effectively coordinate the many volunteer programs and projects.
- Continue to challenge the interest and support of volunteers.
- Maintain the flexibility necessary to meet changing community and departmental needs.

Communication Connections

Information exchange, support, and recognition, always necessary to the success of volunteer programs, are facilitated through a regular newsletter. The Community Connection is published at least bimonthly.

Comments

The Volunteers in Prevention, Prosecution, Probation, Prison and Parole (VIP) division of the National Council on Crime and Delinquency (NCCD) estimates that at least 350,000 volunteers are currently active in direct service juvenile and criminal justice programs. If volunteers in all capacities of criminal justice are included, the total number would be closer to 750,000 volunteers.

Not every justice agency has had the positive experience with volunteer programs that Pima County has had. What are the ingredients that make this and other volunteer programs successful? A study of programs in a variety of justice agencies in the United States suggests that the critical ingredients for success are:

1. Strong administrative commitment to the concept.
2. Clearly defined program goals and functions that relate to community and agency need.
3. Careful screening of volunteers.
4. A strong training program, including ongoing training in specialized areas.
5. Assessment of volunteer interests and skills and assignment of volunteers to meaningful tasks.
6. Sensitivity to the needs and fears of agency personnel regarding volunteer services and early resolution of problems in this area.
7. Development of support of agency personnel for the volunteer concept.
8. Effective supervision of volunteers and monitoring of volunteer activities.
9. Involvement of volunteers in recruiting and supervisory activities.
10. A feedback system that encourages recognition, evaluation, and recommendations for change from volunteers and staff.
11. Sensitivity to the needs of volunteers.
12. A willingness to encourage and accept change within the program necessary for its vitality.
13. Application of group dynamics principles in strengthening volunteer cooperation and coordination.
14. A strong personal commitment on the part of those who supervise the project.
15. Inclusion of line personnel in every phase of the program development and implementation.

BIBLIOGRAPHY

Attorney General's Advisory Commission on Community-Police Relations (1973). *The Police in the California Community.* Sacramento: State of California.

Black, S. (1976). *Practical Public Relations,* 4th ed. New York: Beekman Publications.

Blumenthal, L. R. (1972). *The Practice of Public Relations.* New York: Macmillan.

Brandstatter, A. F., and Radelet, L. A. (1968). *Police and Community Relations: A Sourcebook.* Beverly Hills, Calif.: Glencoe Press.

Brown, L. P. (undated). Police–community evaluation project (unpublished manuscript).

Earle, H. H. (1980). *Police–Community Relations: Crisis in Our Time,* 3rd ed. Springfield, Ill.: Charles C Thomas.

Eastman, G. D., and Eastman, E. M. (1971). *Municipal Police Administration,* 7th ed. Washington, D.C.: International City Management Association.

Edgar, J. M., et al. (1976). *Team Policing: A Selected Bibliography.* Washington, D.C.: National Institute of Law Enforcement and Criminal Justice (National Criminal Justice Reference Service), June.

International City Manager's Association (1967). *Police Community Relations Programs.* Washington, D.C.: ICMA.

Krajick, K. (1979). "Preventing crime," *Police Magazine,* November, pp. 7–13.

Lewis, D. A., and Salem, G. (1981). "Community crime prevention," *Crime and Delinquency,* July, pp. 405–421.

Mellard, R. (1982). "Crime prevention: a workable alternative," *The Police Chief,* March, pp. 18–23.

Myren, R. A. (1972). "Decentralization and citizen participation in criminal justice systems, *Public Administration Review,* Vol. XXXII, Special Issue, October.

Peterson, W., project director; National Sheriff's Association, corporate author (1976). *National Neighborhood Watch Program-Information Packet.* Washington, D.C.: Law Enforcement Assistance Administration.

Portland Police Bureau, Crime Prevention Division (1981). *Institutionalization: A Survey of Community Attitudes Toward Crime Prevention.* Portland, Ore.: PPB, March.

President's Commission on Law Enforcement and the Administration of Justice (1967). *The Challenge of Crime in a Free Society.* Washington, D.C.: U.S. Government Printing Office.

Robinson, E. J. (1966). *Communication and Public Relations.* Columbus, Ohio: Charles E. Merrill.

Skolnick, J. H., and Bayley, D. H. (1986). *The New Blue Line: Police Innovation in Six American Cities.* New York: Free Press.

Spelman, W., and Eck, J. E. (1986). *Problem-Oriented Policing.* Washington, D.C.: Police Executive Research Forum.

Trojanowicz, R., and Bucqueroux, B. (1990). *Community Policing: A Contemporary Perspective.* Cincinnati, Ohio: Anderson.

Webster's Ninth New Collegiate Dictionary (1991). Springfield, Mass.: Merriam-Webster.

4

POLICE ROLE CONCEPT IN A CHANGING SOCIETY

The Policeman is a "Rorschach" in uniform as he patrols his beat. His occupational accoutrements—shield, nightstick, gun, and summons book—clothe him in a mantle of symbolism that stimulates fantasy and projection. (Niederhoffer, 1967)

Variation is basic to all human beings. We might fight less quickly if we looked at it this way and also we might put more energy into finding more harmonious ways to incorporate the differentness. (Satir, 1978, p. 98)

Roles are distinct behavior patterns played in connection with a particular social position. Roles are either ascribed (not under the person's control) or achieved (attained voluntarily). Examples of ascribed roles include male, female, and infant; examples of achieved roles include husband, wife, and teacher. Roles provide us with ways of categorizing and anticipating the behavior of others. They assist us in deciding how to act in relationship to others and help to give order to our world. One person plays many roles, and sometimes these conflict. The Hispanic police officer, for instance, may be faced with role conflict because he is both Hispanic and an officer, and he has difficulty in reconciling the two. Conflict might also occur in other ways: (1) the expectations of others regarding behaviors appropriate to a role may be different from the expectations of the role incumbent; (2) the expectations of others might vary widely, making it very difficult for the role incumbent to be successful in that role; or (3) the "official" and working definitions of the role are contradictory. The police role includes all of these contradictions.

Ask anyone. A police officer is a "crime fighter," or a "human service worker," or "a knight in blue," or "the power arm of the Establishment," or "a dumb cop," or "a competent professional." This chapter identifies and accounts for some of the conflicting perceptions that exist regarding the police role.

STUDYING THIS CHAPTER WILL ENABLE YOU TO:

1. Define *perception* and *role conflict.*
2. Identify and explore conflicting perceptions that exist regarding the role of a police officer in the community.
3. Identify major elements necessary to the success of programs designed to assist officers in achieving realistic role concepts and improved service to and participation in the community.
4. Describe the factors and conditions of change in our society.
5. Identify and describe some of the paradoxes and dilemmas that our changing society creates for the police officer.

GREAT EXPECTATIONS

Police officers in today's society are not only expected to apprehend bank robbers and murderers, but they are also expected to direct traffic, transport the sick and injured to the hospital, help schoolchildren cross streets, patrol polling places on election day, provide shelter and care for drunks and drug abusers, investigate accidents, settle family disputes, locate missing and runaway children, and a host of other things. They must be all things to all people. They are expected not only to enforce the law and maintain order, but to do so in a scrupulously fair manner, no matter what sort of verbal or physical abuse might be directed toward them.

When they gather evidence or apprehend criminals, they must never violate an offender's constitutional rights under penalty of having the evidence suppressed in court. They must be professionally detached from the violence and tragedy that they encounter on their daily tour of duty. They are not only expected to be honest and fair in fact but also to give a constant appearance of honesty and fairness. They must have a professional knowledge of the criminal law in order to ensure that the rights of those they apprehend are protected. They must be prepared to manage conflicts and to deal swiftly and appropriately with almost every manner of crisis society has invented.

The relationship between police and the citizens they are sworn to serve is a close one. As the President's Commission on Law Enforcement and the Administration of Justice observed:

> It is hard to overstate the intimacy of the contact between the police and the community. Policemen deal with people when they are both most threatening and most vulnerable, when they are angry, when they are frightened, when they are desperate, when they are drunk, when they are violent, or when they are ashamed. Every police action can affect in some way someone's dignity, or self-respect, or sense of privacy, or constitutional rights. As a matter of routine policemen become privy to, and make judgments about, secrets that most citizens guard jealously from their closest friends: Relationships between husbands and wives, the misbehavior of children, personal eccentricities, peccadilloes and lapses of all kinds. Very often policemen must physically restrain or subdue unruly citizens. (President's Commission, 1967, pp. 91–92)

Perhaps that is why the officer often is viewed so subjectively. The perception of what the role of a police officer in society is and should be varies considerably depending on who is doing the perceiving and under what circumstances judgment is made.

PERCEPTION

Seeing and Perceiving

Man is not disturbed by events, but by the view he takes of them. (Epictetus)

How often have you heard such statements as these?

Well, this is the way I see it.
I suppose that is just the way he sees it.
I have to respond the way I see it.
I suppose you have to act in accordance with the way you see it.

Perception is more than receiving visual stimulation, or sensing something. It is actually a process of creating meaning out of what we hear, see, smell, taste, and feel (our sensations, or sensory experience) and using that sense which we make of the world as the basis for our actions. The word *see* as used in the examples above, also implies more than a visual sensation. "To see" can mean to believe, to understand, and to make sense of, as well as to view. Sometimes we use the word *see* when we actually mean *perceive*.

Perception Is Personal

It is unlikely that two people, even at a given time and place, will perceive the same event in exactly the same way. Every police officer knows that eyewitness accounts, however sincere, may vary widely and be inaccurate (see also Rodgers, 1982).

Creating meaning from sensations requires a judgment call. Several elements combine to set the context, or the frame of reference, within which a person makes such a judgment call. Attention, knowledge, past experiences, and present motives or needs all help to shape the way a person perceives (or perhaps misperceives). The relatively stable and predictable set of habits by which the person manages day-to-day living under ordinary conditions (personality), influences perception.

Behavior is closely linked to perception. Our actions are based on the world as we believe it to be.

Donna Allen pulls her van over to the curb and steps out to the sidewalk to ask directions from Joan Patrick, who is walking toward her on the sidewalk. Before Joan finishes giving Donna the directions she asked for, both women look up simultaneously and see a huge lion approaching them on the sidewalk. "A lion!" screams Joan, as she turns and runs in the opposite direction down the sidewalk as fast as she can. "Stop!" yells Donna, but Joan is soon out of earshot. Donna then walks to the lion, gently strokes his mane to indicate that all is well, takes the lion to the back of the van, and orders him to leap into the van, which the lion does. Donna then closes the tailgate of the van, climbs into the driver's seat, and continues on her way, regretting that Joan did not take time to give her sufficient directions to reach her destination. She would undoubtedly have to stop again and ask directions, which might make her late for her performance at the circus.

In this example the objective experience of the two women was the same, but they had different perceptual experiences. Objective experience can be standardized and agreed upon by most people. Donna and Joan would agree that they saw an animal approach and the animal was a lion. The lion's appearance on the sidewalk as the two women talked was an objective experience. The perceptual experiences of the two women can be implied by observing their behavior as the lion approached them. Joan saw the lion as dangerous and a threat to her well-being and ran away in fright. Donna did not see the lion as a threat but showed affection toward the lion and concern that the lion might be upset. Her behavior was to comfort the lion, and her most outstanding concern was to get to her destination as soon as possible.

It is possible to analyze this situation in terms of *knowledge, past experience,* and *need.* Donna was acquainted with the lion and, since she was the lion's trainer, she knew that the lion was not dangerous and was no threat to either of the two women. Joan did not have this knowledge and was therefore afraid of the lion. Donna had obviously had experience with this particular lion and perhaps other lions and probably tended to "see" lions in general in a different way than did Joan. Joan's past experience with lions primarily consisted of indirect experiences, such as seeing lions in the zoo, in movies, and on television; in most of those instances the lions that she had seen were portrayed as being dangerous and threatening. Those in the zoo were locked up and those in the movies and on television were always attacking someone or some other animal. Joan had no need in relationship to the experiencing of the lion other than the need for survival. She perceived that her survival was threatened at that moment; thus, her need for survival was really why she chose to run. Donna's most outstanding need of the moment was related to her desire to put on a good performance at the circus and to reach the circus in time for that performance. Consequently, the temperament of the lion was very important to her, so she proceeded to comfort the lion, to load him back into the van, and to drive off as rapidly as she could, hopefully in the direction of the circus.

Richard Bandler and John Grinder theorized how perception comes about. They claim that generalization, deletion, and distortion are psychological processes common to all people. These are ways in which we make sense of and survive in the world. "The processes which allow us to accomplish the most extraordinary and unique human activities are the same processes which block our further growth if we commit the error of mistaking the model for the reality" (Bandler and Grinder, 1975, p. 14).

Generalization is the psychological process whereby a person detaches some part of one model from an original experience and then applies this model to represent an entire category. A common example is experiencing an ice cube. When a person touches an ice cube for the first time, he/she learns that ice cubes are cold. As part of learning about the world, it will be helpful to this person to generalize that other ice cubes are also cold. However, if he/she refused to touch ice cubes after that original experience, generalizing that cold is painful to touch, the generalization could be a hindrance.

"*Deletion* is a process by which we selectively pay attention to certain dimensions of our experience and exclude others" (Bandler and Grinder, 1975, p. 15). People have the ability to filter out experiences while concentrating on a model. The coach, for example, watching the video replay of his basketball team's victory, screens out (deletes) all the activity on the basketball court except the behaviors of the team members and the opponents. He deletes the behavior of the cheerleaders and everyone else in the gym. Although through deletion the coach is able to pinpoint specific information that he might have otherwise missed, he loses the flavor added by the spectators, the band, and the cheerleaders, because he has deleted this dimension of his experience. The coach's perception could get him into trouble when his wife, the band director, asks him later how he enjoyed the victory song played by the band and the coach has no recollection of the experience.

Distortion is the third modeling process, and it allows us to make shifts in our experience of sensory data (Bandler and Grinder, 1975, p. 16). An actress onstage distorts as she exaggerates her movements and sounds. This is a useful form of distortion because it allows the audience to experience the performance in a rich and fantasized fashion. If, however, once offstage, the same actress rushes to the telephone and tearfully reports an exaggerated version of a disagreement between her and her husband to the police, the shift in her experience of sensory data will not be positively useful.

Perception issues exist between police and community groups. In most cases, the officer on the beat perceives the behavior of citizens differently from the way they perceive their own situation, circumstances, and behavior. Citizens may perceive the police officer's role, purpose, and behavior quite differently from the way the police officer does. The factors responsible for such differences in perception are the same as outlined in the previous discussion.

1. Differences in past experience, and sets of habits.
2. Knowledge.
3. Individual needs relative to the situation in question through the modeling processes of Generalization, Distortion, and Deletion.

Consider another example:

John, age 25, has lived all of his life in a suburban area near a large American city. Roy, also age 25, has lived all of his life in an inner-city neighborhood of that same large American city where confrontations between police and youth have escalated to violence several times in the last few years. John and Roy are walking down a sidewalk within the inner-city area together when they see a police officer, on foot, approaching them. As the officer draws nearer, he nods his head in greeting and smiles. John responds, "Good morning officer" and returns his smile. As the officer passes on down the sidewalk, John becomes aware that Roy looks uncomfortable. He recalls that Roy at first did not look at the officer. But after he had said, "Good morning," Roy had looked up at the officer with a tremendous frown on his face and a look of contempt in his eyes. Roy neither spoke to the officer nor returned his smile. John is puzzled; he cannot understand Roy's reaction. To John, the officer was obviously trying to be pleasant. He did not offend John or Roy, and he showed no indication of ill will toward them. Yet Roy finds it very difficult to understand John's behavior because just as Roy was beginning to trust John, John demonstrated to Roy that he was inclined to be friendly with police officers. John feels that Roy now believes John is "not to be trusted"; when the chips are down, John is on the side of the cop.

Is John's perception of Roy in this instance "true"? Or is Roy's perception of John "true"? Whether these perceptions are true or not, the perceptual experiences of the two men in this instance are nevertheless quite real, and capable of affecting their attitudes toward each other, their ability to trust each other, and their method of behaving toward each other in the future.

Another question to be asked is why did Roy and John react differently toward the same objective experience: the approaching of a police officer who greeted them with a friendly smile? First, although the police officer was looking at both of the men when he gave his nod of greeting and smiled, Roy perceived that he was not smiling at him at all. Throughout his life, Roy's only relationships with police officers have been negative ones. Roy has generalized from these experiences to avoid police officers at all costs. He has distorted reality and perceives that "the only purpose of the police is to control, not to protect." Roy perceives that what the police mean by control is to "keep people from the inner-city in their place," "prevent them from expressing themselves," "deprive them of most of the nicer things in life," and so forth. Roy's past experiences with police officers have included their frequent questioning of him about crimes committed—crimes that he knew nothing about. In fact, Roy has never committed a crime in his life. In the past, however, police officers have taken him down to the precinct station and applied pressure to get him to "finger" friends who have been accused of crimes. And, on several occasions, when Roy indicated to them that he knew nothing about whether or not the person involved had committed a crime, he was told that if he did not cooperate, little or no mercy would be shown to him by the police when they caught him in a crime (which they seemed to feel was inevitable).

The police officers who have taken Roy down to the station to question him may be distorting objective reality in much the same fashion that Roy does. The officers may be generalizing from past experience, assuming that Roy's behavior will be similar to the behavior of those in their experience. The officers may be deleting the objective reality about Roy (that he is a law-abiding citizen, for instance) and, instead, be distorting the scowl that appeared on Roy's face when he saw the officers approaching to mean that Roy is guilty. In fact, Roy may be in the process of generalizing from his own past experience about police officers.

Moreover, Roy has never heard any of his friends indicate that they had ever been protected by police officers. His friends always talked about the police as the "enemy." Roy is often afraid as he walks down a street after leaving the movies. He is afraid of other people who might rob or take advantage of persons walking alone on the street late at night. Roy has caught himself on many occasions wishing that there was a police department that would protect him from such hoodlums. Yet, he has never felt that any police officer saw this as his role. Through his own experiences and conversations with his friends, Roy has come to view the police as the most definitive instrument of an oppressing society, deployed not only to protect the rest of society *from* him but to keep him *down* in every way. In contrast to Roy's past experiences with the police, John had always been taught that police officers were his friends. John read about the helpful police in storybooks; police officers came to his schools, and even one of his father's best friends was a police lieutenant who lived in the area. John remembers the time when his family returned from a vacation and discovered that their house had been burglarized. They called the police, and after the house had been searched, it was discovered that the only missing item was $50, which John's mother had placed in an envelope and left on the coffee table before leaving. After the police had talked to John's parents, one of the officers said, "Don't worry, Mr. and Mrs. Jones, we have sufficient evidence. We will get the thief and your $50 will be returned." As John grew up, he became friends with a few police officers, who went out of their way to be nice to him. On occasions, he had been stopped by police officers for speeding or committing some minor traffic violation. But he seldom received a ticket, only a warning which usually ended in, "I'm going to let you go this time, but be careful, we want you to get wherever you are going safely." In general, John has always thought of the police officer as his friend and that the chief role of the police in the community was to protect citizens.

Because of these past experiences, John and Roy responded differently to the smiling policeman as he approached them on the sidewalk. Their differential behavior was obviously based on their differential perception. Their differential perception was in turn based on the differences between them in terms of past experiences with the police, their habits, knowledge of the situation that they were in at the moment, personal needs, distortion, generalization, and deletion.

John and Roy were both reacting to reality as it impinged upon them. Each person's perceptual experience is "reality." Because perceptual experience is not altogether a conscious phenomenon, many individuals would be at a loss if they were asked to explain why they understand life the way they do. In the case of the smiling police officer, Roy could not have readily explained to John why his perception of the officer's behavior was negative. Similarly, John could not have readily explained to Roy why he perceived the officer's behavior to be positive. But each one acted in what he believed to be his best interest, based on his understanding of reality.

There are many differing perceptions of the police function, in the ghetto, the middle- and upper-middle-class suburbs, the political arena, and the police briefing room. Some people see the police as their *personal* instruments for ending or reducing crime on the street to assure their personal safety. Others see police as an *instrument of society,* with the somewhat broader aim of maintaining a degree of harmony, consistency, and peace (whatever the latter has come to mean in today's world). Some people have a more restricted view of the police, seeing them as an agency to suppress underprivileged and minority segments of society. Still others perceive the police as an agency by which dominant society confines and reinforces the boundaries of ghettos and minority groups. The police are also viewed as being so helplessly caught between social class, racial, and political factions that they are utterly stymied in their work but are made the scapegoat for the ills that are inevitable in a society torn by such conflict. It is doubtful that any two people selected at random would completely agree as to what a police officer does (or should do).

ROLE CONCEPT

"A role may be defined as a set of behavioral expectations and obligations associated with a position in a social structure or organization" (Cox and Fitzgerald, 1992, p. 37). These expectations can be framed in an objective, dispassionate manner; a subjective, totally personal manner; or in some modification of these two approaches.

Objectivity as an approach requires the observer to determine, study, and weigh facts in an unbiased, scientific manner, setting aside preconceived notions and personal prejudices and preferences. In this approach, conclusions are drawn from the facts. Any conclusion not borne out by evidence that is objectively based is not acceptable.

Subjectivity, on the other hand, is not concerned with objective fact, and even an awareness by the subjective observer of such fact does not guarantee an objective conclusion. Facts are redefined by the observer in terms of his/her personal life, biases, assumptions, dreams, and fears. His/her judgment is based on how he/she feels about what they see and how the person believes what he/she sees relates to him or her. Although others may consider his/her view unrealistic, given the world as he/she understands it, his/her expectations are logical. Most expectations held by most people are, to some degree, subjectively derived.

THE POLICE OFFICER'S ROLES

Crime Control

> Ask a retiring officer to tell you about his best memories. He'll probably recall stories of high speed pursuits, shoot-outs, fights or chasing someone on foot. Ask a new rookie what he likes about being a cop and he'll say things like "putting the bad guys in jail." The fact is, most officers see their role as a crime fighter. (Trautman, 1991, p. 16)

Very few, if any, would argue with the statement that a core mission of the police is to control crime. The police do have, and we expect them to perform, a crime control role. However, the police and the public often see crime control as the total responsibility of the police. Furthermore, the police and the public see the crime control role of the police as the only role the police should perform. This myopic view of the police and their role has a significant impact on policing as an occupation and upon the performance of individual officers as actors in the criminal justice system.

The exclusive image of the crime control role of the police embodied in the "crime fighter image" has serious consequences on the police and their behavior. Crime and its control are not the sole responsibility of the police. The police did not create nor can they control the social conditions that create crime. At best, the law and the criminal justice system is a poor controller of human behavior. As long as we see crime control as the primary role of the police, we fail to recognize that crime is a social phenomenon and that crime prevention is the responsibility of society, communities, and a host of other social institutions. In addition to creating unrealistic expectations about the police's ability to contend with crime, this narrow view prevents an informed analysis of the other important roles assigned to the police (Walker, 1992).

Order Maintenance

The crime control role involves all those functions of arrest and detection of law violators as well as those behaviors devoted to crime prevention (preventive patrol, etc.). However, as Wilson (1968, p. 4) pointed out, less than one-third of all police radio calls involve criminal matters which may result in an arrest and only about 5 percent of all cases actually result in an arrest. It is the order maintenance role which is more central to the modern police officer's job than any other aspect of his/her behavior. Most recent studies support the assertion by Wilson that the role of a patrol officer "is defined more by his responsibility for maintaining order than by his responsibility for enforcing the law" (Wilson, 1968, p. 16).

Order maintenance activities may consist of officers simply being seen so as to provide a sense of security or as an aid in promoting the public peace. It may consist of monitoring the activities of individuals engaging in behavior which if allowed to "get out of hand" could result in inconvenience or annoyance for other citizens. It can involve restoration of order to disorderly or potentially disorderly situations. And it can be the actual intervention into disputes between individuals or groups which if unchecked could lead to serious violations of the law. Most of these activities do not involve actual enforcement of laws. Those situations in which legal conditions for arrests do exist are dealt with through mediation or warnings in lieu of arrest (Barker, Hunter, and Rush, 1994).

Service

In addition to their crime control and order-maintenance roles, the police spend a great deal of time performing service activities. This role is second only to order maintenance in importance. The duties and responsibilities that fall within this category include many activities which may appear to be only peripherally related to the direct police services of patrol, investigations, traffic control, and the police mission of preventing crime and disorder (Barker, Hunter, and Rush, 1994). Providing emergency rescue services, working traffic accidents, unlocking locked cars, jump starting stalled vehicles, and helping people in distress are but a few of the many services routinely provided by the police.

Many of the services performed by the police are not inherent to the police mission but have become police services by default. Because the police are available 24 hours a day and no one else has emerged to perform a specific task, that task may come to be seen within a particular community as a police responsibility.

Other Roles

In addition to the three roles discussed above, other duties are also performed by the police (Table 4-1). Whereas Cordner (1989) argues that information gathering could legitimately be classified as a law enforcement duty, others argue that it is more appropriately a service or even an order-maintenance function. Still others (Barker, Hunter, and Rush, 1994) consider information gathering to be a separate role that falls partially within all three. Since the majority of police reports are taken primarily for insurance purposes, we will classify information gathering as a distinct role.

Yet another police role that is contained partially within the duties of crime control, order maintenance, and service is that of protection of individual rights. The police in the United States and other democracies are responsible not only for protecting society from individual behavior but ensuring that the constitutional rights of all citizens are upheld (Barker, Hunter, and Rush, 1994).

TABLE 4-1
WHAT POLICE DO (POLICE WORKLOAD IN WILMINGTON, DELAWARE, 1988)

Type of complaint	Total hours	Percent of hours	Collapsed code[a]
Officer in trouble	17	0.02	C
Suspicious person/vehicle	1,732	2.46	C
Crime in progress	1,783	2.53	C
Order maintenance—In progress	5,678	8.07	O
Alarm	2,430	3.45	C
Investigate—not in progress	10,625	15.09	C
Animal complaint	41	0.06	O
Noise complaint	426	0.61	O
Service-related	2,977	4.23	S
Serve warrant/subpoena	1,805	2.56	C
Assist other police	157	0.22	C
Park and walk	71	0.10	F
Traffic accident investigation	3.787	5.38	T
Parking problems	786	1.12	T
Motor vehicle driving problems	2.887	4.10	T
Traffic control	31	0.04	T
Fire emergency	467	0.66	T
Medical emergency	1,394	1.98	M
Clear	20,660	29.35	F
Unavailable	3,614	5.13	U
Meal break	4,569	6.49	A
Report writing	15	0.02	A
Firearms training	1	0.00	A
Police vehicle maintenance	873	1.24	A
At headquarters	2,386	3.39	A
Court-related	814	1.16	A
At corrections institution/other police agency } At local hospital } At state hospital/medical examiner }	253	0.36	M
Total UAF District car time	70,396	100.00	

Source: J. R. Greene and C. B. Klockars, "What police do," in C. B. Klockars and S. D. Mastrofski (Eds.), *Thinking About Police: Contemporary Readings.* New York: McGraw-Hill, 1991.

[a]A, administrative activity; C, crime-related activity; F, free patrol; M, medical-related activity; O, order-maintenance activity; S, service activity; T, traffic-related activity; U, unavailable for assignment.

POLICE ROLE CONFLICT

In the preceding section we discussed the various roles assigned to police officers within a typical police agency. The extent to which these complex and often contradictory roles are carried out varies considerably among police agencies, due to their nature, tradition, size, location, mission, and the orientation of the community served. In addition, there is considerable variation within agencies due to different role outlooks among individual officers. As discussed in Chapter 1, the police are affected by both external and internal groups. Individual perceptions and political ideologies also influence the behavior of police officers (Walker, 1989).

Traditionally, the literature on policing has focused on four individual styles that were derived from Wilson's (1968) departmental roles. This typology consists of: "crime fighters", "social agents", "law enforcer", and "watchmen" (Berg, 1992). The "crime fighter" or "cowboy" is an officer who views himself/herself as primarily a serious crime investigator. Lesser offenses and noncriminal duties are seen as trivial and not worthy of police attention. The "social agent" views policing as a combination of crime control, order maintenance, and provision of services. Law enforcement duties are considered an important but only a minimal portion of their overall duties. The "law enforcer" or "legalist" is similar to the crime fighter in that he/she tends to emphasize crime control. However, the "law enforcer" differs from the "crime fighter" in that all statutes, ordinances, and regulations are felt to be important and require strict enforcement. The "watchman" is dedicated to preserving social and political order within the community. He/she will enforce the laws to the extent necessary to maintain the peace.

The four categories discussed above are not felt by many police scholars to adequately present the variations among individual officers in regard to role perceptions. In response to such criticisms, Broderick (1987) has developed a classification scheme that attempts to categorize officers based on personality type rather than on a particular police style. The product is a typology which is useful in assessing individual behavior patterns but is less rigid in predicting performance. Broderick's categories include enforcers, idealists, realists, and optimists.

Enforcers are concerned primarily with keeping the streets "clean" and ensuring that citizens behave properly. They see themselves as protecting the "good people" from the "bad people." Most enforcers would be considered authoritarians who perceive citizens as either hostile or apathetic toward them. *Idealists* are committed to the law and the rights of citizens. They see themselves as professionals who better serve the public than do their more authoritarian and/or less dedicated colleagues. Frustration with the "system" often drives these individuals into other careers or causes them to become realists. *Realists* tend to be cynical and dissatisfied with society and the criminal justice system. As a defense mechanism, they have stopped caring about their role as police officers and generally do only that which is required to stay out of trouble. Realists often seek transfers to assignments where they can "hide out" and be left alone by both the public and other police officials. *Optimists* see themselves as service providers who are performing an important societal function. They view themselves, their colleagues, and the public in a positive manner. Although aware that they alone cannot change the world, they are willing to do their part. Officers often do not fit in any one of these categories and may occasionally shift categories during their careers.

As if the contradictory perceptions on the part of individual officers were not complicated enough, debates regarding the role of the police in a democratic society confuse the issue further. As seen by Roberg and Kuykendall (1993, pp. 43–50), these debates include: "Do rigid bureaucratic rules or responsiveness to political demands best serve the public interests?", "Should police be concerned with preserving community norms or strict compliance with laws?", "Is the police occupation a professional activity or a craft?", "Are officers to emphasize their duties as crime fighters or social service workers?," "Should the police be more concerned with crime prevention or the apprehension of criminals?", and finally, "Should police activities be of a proactive or reactive nature?". The manner in which public officials, community leaders, and police officials resolve their differences in regard to these debates influences the organization's values and goals and determines those tasks and activities which will be emphasized by that police agency.

As may be seen, the consequences of contradictory views on the part of individual police officers, police administrators, public officials, and community leaders leads more to confusion (and often conflict) than to consensus in regard to the role of the police.

FORMATION OF ROLE CONCEPTS

The Sources of Role Concepts

Role concepts have their sources in needs and past experiences. Because both of these can vary widely from group to group and individual to individual, so can role concepts.

Three major factors affect the way individuals and groups in society perceive the role of the police officer.

1. The individual's or group's specific needs and problems.
2. The individual's or group's personal experiences with police officers.
3. The image of police officers created by various media.

If expectations are unrealistic, so is the role concept, and it will become further distorted if the unrealistic expectations are repeatedly unmet.

Some people, for instance, have often experienced oppression by the police. If a particular neighborhood has a severe crime problem and the police are not solving it, residents will conclude that police either cannot or do not want to fulfill the community's needs. In other words, unfulfilled needs and past experience have induced the community to expect little of the police. Based on that expectation, they may withhold community cooperation from law enforcement, thus compounding the problem and further strengthening the negative role concept.

Lack of Information

Sometimes, lack of accurate citizen information regarding police efforts can lead to unreasonable expectations on the part of an individual or a group in the community. For example, an area of a city might be plagued with assaults and robberies. The police in that area may respond by increasing routine patrol, increasing foot patrol in business areas, and generally focusing most of their efforts on that current problem. Personnel shortages may prevent ideal service to other, less immediate problems, such as juveniles racing cars in the streets. The citizens may not be aware of the increased efforts of the police in the assault and robbery areas. When complaints are made about juveniles racing cars in the streets, the citizens may conclude that the police are negligent if they take longer than usual to respond to the call.

How Police Respond

To understand the problems involved in creating and maintaining positive role expectations for the police, consider the three possible outcomes when a law enforcement problem arises.

1. *The problem is confronted and solved.* This creates the expectation that the police will do so again, if and when necessary. Note, however, that in one familiar area, enforcing traffic laws, the police often attain a negative role concept by effective actions.
2. *The problem is confronted, but not solved.* Naturally, this often has negative impact on the police role concept, but the police may have no way of preventing certain problems (ranging from murder to domestic arguments); citizens who believe otherwise have unrealistic expectations.
3. *The problem is not confronted.* The usual reason is that the problem (e.g., trash removal, street and light maintenance) is the responsibility of some other agency. Nevertheless, the citizen may feel it is police failure to resolve the need for personal service.

Thus, in at least two of the three cases just described, observers are likely to experience a negative role concept of the police, even though the expectations on which that concept is based are unrealistic or mistaken.

THE MEDIA AND ROLE CONCEPTS

Today in this country, the media play a very important part in forming expectations about the police. Thus, many people evaluate the actions of police officers against criteria formed by TV or movie scriptwriters. If preconceived ideas regarding the police role are challenged by a reality that contradicts what people believe to be true, will they choose to believe the reality? Unfortunately, the answer is not always yes.

The police officers of Hollywood lore are fictional images of police stereotypes that have been exaggerated to provide entertainment to a bored public. That public (and indeed, the police themselves) tend to accept the images created by scriptwriters and portrayed by actors and actresses who have little or no knowledge of what police officers actually do. The result is the creation of mythical police roles that have only a limited basis in reality.

Holden (1992) identified six police stereotypes that have either been created or perpetuated by the entertainment media. The first and perhaps oldest media image of the police is that of the "buffoon". This characterization began in early movies such as *The Keystone Kops* and continues in present-day television and movie depictions. A second image is not as extreme as the "buffoon" but tends to present police officers as slow-witted and unprofessional "dullards" who need the guidance of smart citizens (à la Sherlock Holmes, "Mrs. Columbo," or Jessica Fletcher of "Murder, She Wrote") in order to solve crimes. A third type, the "sadist," abuses his/her police authority to perpetuate evil acts. Such characters were aptly portrayed by Richard Gere in *Internal Affairs* and Ray Liotta in *Unlawful Entry*. A fourth image is that of the "hero" who fights the bad guys (and often police superiors and the criminal justice system) to protect the innocent from evil. Mel Gibson in the "Lethal Weapon" series and Bruce Willis in the "Die Hard" series exemplify such heroes. A fifth character is the "wizard," a supercop who solves challenging cases utilizing his/her superior intellect and/or technical expertise. "Kojak" and "Columbo" exemplify these images. Finally, we are presented with the "harassed professional" who is highly competent but overworked and underappreciated. The characters of "Cagney and Lacey" would fall within this category.

In addition to the foregoing roles depicted by the entertainment media, the public are influenced considerably by the news media. Media attention (TV, newspapers, radio, magazines) comes to police agencies for the police crime-fighting role rather than their service role (it makes better copy). Depicting the police negatively as misusing deadly force, police prejudice, or police corruption is also newsworthy. The amount of emphasis given to police actions and the media's interpretation of those actions as either proper or improper has a tremendous effect on the public's perception of the police. It has been argued that media coverage can transform a local incident into a national crisis (Cox and Fitzgerald, 1992, p. 108). We doubt that anyone watching the media coverage of the 1991 beating of black motorist Rodney King by white Los Angeles police officers and the subsequent events in several areas of the nation would challenge that assertion.

FACTORS AND CONDITIONS OF CHANGE

Reassessing the Dimensions

Traditionally, obedience to the law, ethical behavior, and moral decisions have been bound and intertwined into an absolute adherence based on extremes of legal versus illegal, good versus bad, and right versus wrong. Situations were black and white, or at least they appeared to be. In small rural, agriculturally based communities a police officer could make decisions based on the relatively fixed value system of the majority. It was not that minorities did not exist, but rather that they were usually not vocal and, for the most part, not counted separately.

Since the end of World War II, however, the continuing struggle between tradition and change, between fixed values and no values, and between simple lives and complex living has seen tradition slowly dying. At the same time, people have not been able to adapt as quickly as the technology surrounding them. They are somewhat bewildered by a growing shrinkage of space and time and a negative relationship between the two. They find the so-called knowledge and information explosions threatening to overwhelm them. They find that the emergence of electronic controls creates what might be called "electronic amorality." The struggle for survival takes on new dimensions, and fixed value systems are seriously questioned and sometimes abandoned.

Never before have philosophers and peace officers, politicians, and the public been so carefully and sincerely reexamining the dimensions and limits of liberty, freedom, and democracy as living entities. Some years ago, George Orwell stated:

> The point is that the relative freedom which we enjoy depends on public opinion, the law is no protection. The governments make laws, but whether they are carried out, and how the police behave, depends upon the general temper of the country. If large numbers of people are interested in freedom of speech, there will be freedom of speech even if the law forbids it; if public opinion is sluggish, inconvenient minorities will be persecuted, even if laws exist to protect them. (Orwell, 1963)

A philosopher and commentator on man in a democracy, Milton Mayer, in his *Liberty: Man Versus State* has commented on the many perceptual facets of liberty: "Plainly, what one man calls justice another man calls expropriation; and one man's security is another man's slavery, one man's liberty is another man's anarchy" (Mayer, 1969, p. 41). Mayer wonders if in our time the rule of law is not becoming the enemy of liberty.

Values have become relative to one another and to situations. "Policies" help to "bend" the law, and social conditions tend to confuse and confound the search for simple solutions and answers. From a quiet, relatively simple rural life with fixed values we have moved to an involved, complex urban community where any sense of common union is difficult to find and where all groups wish to be counted. Increasingly in the last several decades many of the formerly powerless groups in our society (African Americans, Hispanic Americans, Asian Americans, Native Americans, women, the elderly, and gay rights groups, to name a varied few) have demanded that their wants and needs be addressed. (Figure 4-1.) The influences of minority groups upon policing are in evidence both within and without police organizations. Although most of the media and public attention regarding the police and minorities focuses on external relations, advocacy groups representing the views of minority officers are becoming commonplace.

In determining the will and consent of the people, all of these factors must be considered in a given community, and absolutes are very difficult to find.

FIGURE 4-1   Officer in Chinatown. (Courtesy of the New York City Police Department.)

A World of Infinite Choices

A new era of development is occurring in the world. Changes are overwhelming and rapid, much like the science-fiction fantasies we once read. This has been dubbed the Information Age, and it is developing out of television, cable networks, micro-computers, satellites, and other related information and entertainment resources. In many ways it has been the tiny microprocessor (a silicon chip), that is at the center of the storm. Every field of human endeavor and most leisure time activities have been or will be affected by it. Combined with various other scientific advances (particu-larly biomedical) this new era promises to move us into a world of choices of which we have never even dreamed.

Those who attempt to predict the future disagree on whether the greatest impact of this new age will be positive or negative. Everyone agrees, however, that it will be great . . . perhaps greater than any revolution we have yet known.

Life is already being changed by these new technologies, and with change comes new opportunities and new problems. Some jobs are disappearing and others appearing as industries computerize. Social isolation, already a problem in our society, may be a by-product of our changed life-styles as more work is done without ever leaving home. Intense interaction with machines is new to most of us. It will be a very different kind of communication. Some people will find the promised increased leisure time satisfying, whereas others may find it boring. Boredom can bring about new frustration, anger, and depression.

Biomedical advances have changed our lives for better—and in the opinion of some—for worse. Artificial organs, prosthetic devices, birth control pills, test-tube babies, genetic engineering, microsurgery of DNA all move us toward the twenty-first century.

New ethical problems must be confronted. When does life begin and end? What is quality of life? What limits are appropriate on creating and ending human life? How can we protect rights to privacy in an information age? Who is to monitor information systems? Can we prevent the dehumanization effect that so many people fear? Will private and governmental monitoring of our lives and activities take away or add to our freedom? What values are we modeling as the TV screen becomes an all-purpose display, and even two-way communication instrument? What values do we wish to model?

These changes can make the job of police officers easier and more scientific. They can also bring new cooperation and integration among members of the justice community. Already new technologies have made it possible for officers to predict where and at what time crime will occur, match crime characteristics to offender characteristics quickly, increase the information that can be gathered and used from a crime or crisis scene, improve surveillance techniques, record calls and responses, and benefit from research in all areas of criminal justice training and function.

These same advances are changing the nature of the role of the police officer and the skills that an officer needs on the job. Improved skills in sorting and using the available information, problem solving, knowledge of the new technologies and new resources may be just the beginning (Bennett, 1990; Mastrofski, 1990; Barker, Hunter, and Rush, 1994).

Although important to effective police function, technological sophistication cannot take the place of daily, one-on-one interactions between officers and the citizens they serve. As the trend toward computerization increases, police administrators will need to assure that positive police–community relations in the form of daily interaction between officers and the citizens they serve, continue to be a departmental priority.

THE PARADOXES OF POLICE PRACTICE

Individuals involved in our criminal justice system have to face paradox after paradox: They are very often confronted with situations in which they are "damned if they do and damned if they don't." This paradox is illustrated by the fact that society is just starting to recognize the contradictions and burdens placed on the police. They are expected to represent heritage in a changing time. They are expected to represent the controls of authority and the controls of tradition, yet they are faced with a hierarchy of ethical decisions in which they often must decide which law they may or may not allow the individual or criminal or the youngster to break or not break. The police are faced with the ethical problem of how far one can bend the law before it will break. In keeping with these paradoxical concepts, we find that police are expected to have a definite, if somewhat vague, role in society—a role tainted and tinged by stereotyping, prejudice, and an aura of unreality concerning this stressful profession.

Within this framework, in which police are considered to be on the side of our heritage and yet are expected to cope with change, we find that there is not just one "police officer"—a person involved in various aspects of law enforcement. Rather, we find that there are many "police officers" and that there are many emerging roles, styles, and skills involving the police. These include the police officer as a counselor, as a human services representative and a member of the human services team, as a human relations expert, as a decision maker, as an agent for change; and as a trust builder between police agencies on the one hand and the various increasingly hostile segments of society on the other. The police officer is not only expected but is mandated to transmit, carry forward, control, and enforce those aspects of human existence that individuals, society, nations, and civilization have considered worthwhile, and which they have put into a code of laws.

COMMUNITY RELATIONS: RESIDUE FROM THE PAST

Often compounding the individual officer's problems is the police department's problem of poor community relations. Looking back into the recent history of policing, we can find many practices that were seemingly brutal and abusive, but which had the open or silent approval of most of the members of the community. Even though these practices of misconduct have been eliminated or greatly curtailed, the residents of the community may still have a tendency to view their police as somewhat less than sensitive; unfair, oppressive, and perhaps even unaware of social needs and changes.

New officers who rid themselves of prejudicial attitudes, or master their personal prejudices so that they do not affect their jobs are still perceived by the community as being insensitive, unfair, oppressive, and unaware of social needs and changes. The members of the community respond only to their perceptions of the uniform. As a group, they generally do not consider any officer's professional attributes. Members of the community may therefore act in a hostile manner, regardless of the individual officer's professional behavior. Some community members apparently have been conditioned to the concept that everyone who wears the uniform has certain prejudicial attitudes. Because the new officer is responded to with what he/she considers to be hostility, he/she is not given a chance to demonstrate to the community that he/she is an unbiased professional. Older officers will warn the new officer that his/her professional considerations are not the appropriate response for dealing with certain groups or individuals in the community, and that "there's only one way to handle those people." The typical response for the new officer is to become more and more like the experienced officers.

The chance the police department had of beginning a new era of excellent community relations is then stifled. The incoming officer is socialized to the standards of the past. Thus, the cycle of poor police–community relations seems to continue unbroken, even when the department has been fortunate enough to recruit an officer who did not bring unfavorable attitudes with him or could control the negative attitudes he did have.

TOWARD A REALISTIC ROLE CONCEPT

The Police Officer's Working Personality and Reality

Skolnick's analysis of the police officer's "working personality" (discussed in greater detail in Chapter 5) highlighted three elements of the officer's task: danger, authority, and efficiency. According to Skolnick, these elements in turn generate three personality characteristics: suspiciousness, feelings of isolation, and police solidarity (Skolnick, 1975, p. 44). This context is supported by the paramilitary structure of the police organization which discourages innovation and flexibility and encourages dependency (Auten, 1981). As the rigidity of the structure increases, the degree to which these characteristics are emphasized also increases.

If over 80 percent of the officer's time is spent in service-related duties, role concepts that stress danger, authority, and efficiency should be joined or replaced with one more in keeping with the service function.

Service Versus Crime Fighting

Clearly, role concepts based on crime fighting and on the service model of police work will be quite different. Some of the most important contrasts are given below.

Crime Fighting	*Service*
Specialization	Decentralization
Strong hierarchical authority	Neighborhood involvement
High mobility	Foot patrol
Strict procedures	Wide discretion
Close surveillance and readiness to make arrests	Tolerance and willingness to handle problems by means other than by arrest

Which model is more appropriate for police work? Many citizens and police officers would choose the crime-fighting model. Yet the objective realities of police work suggest that the service model must be given at least equal emphasis.

TOWARD A CONGRUENT ROLE

Police role must be defined within the legal limits of authority and in relationship to the needs of the public. The National Advisory Commission recognized the following list of functions that police agencies perform:

- Prevention of criminal activity.
- Detection of criminal activity.
- Apprehension of criminal offenders.
- Participation in court proceedings.
- Protection of constitutional guarantees.
- Assistance to those who cannot care for themselves or who are in danger of physical harm.
- Control of traffic.
- Resolution of day-to-day conflicts among family, friends, and neighbors.
- Creation and maintenance of a feeling of security in the community.
- Promotion and preservation of civil order (National Advisory Commission on Criminal Justice Standards and Goals, 1973, p. 72).

How much emphasis each function should receive is often a matter of controversy, and varies from jurisdiction to jurisdiction. In every instance, however, working out the optimum mix of functions and priorities will require the active cooperation of local government, the police, and the community.

ELEMENTS OF CHANGE

The police–community relationship is vital to obtaining a realistic and mutually satisfactory role concept for police officers. For their part, police administrators must take steps to overcome the distrust and misunderstandings of the past and to develop internal and external programs that help officers to (1) serve the community more effectively, (2) view their own role in more favorable terms, and (3) participate in developing community relations. This will require sound planning based on the following elements.

1. Absolute commitment on the part of the police organization.
2. A law enforcement philosophy which recognizes that about 80 percent of police activity involves noncriminal matters.
3. Attempts to instill a professional service concept in existing personnel and in new recruits.
4. Proper balance between the academic and practical aspects of police education and training.
5. Using nonpolice personnel to teach police wherever appropriate (e.g., in areas such as sociology, psychology, and criminal law).
6. An organizational philosophy based on a behavioral approach to law enforcement goals (i.e., on modifying attitudes and behavior).
7. A reevaluation of recruitment methods.

8. Use of such methods as problem simulation, role playing, and group work to modify attitudes and behavior.

9. The realization that change is lasting only if it occurs at all organizational levels.

CRITERIA FOR CHANGE

The following criteria can be used to evaluate police education and training programs. These must be designed to promote needed change.

1. The education and training process should be lively and creative, an arena where ideologies, ideas, and points of view may clash and compete.

2. Attention must be given to a wide range of personal and institutional behavior. Being an effective and professional police officer involves at least:
   a. A sophisticated understanding of the moral, social, political, and legal framework of the society.
   b. An intensive understanding of the community—its values, aspirations, difficulties, needs, and resources.
   c. Considerable personal strength, autonomy, and self-understanding.
   d. The ability to understand, empathize, and communicate with others.
   e. A deep commitment to the basic ideals of justice and freedom within our society.
   f. A deep understanding and knowledge of the policies and practices of law enforcement organization.

3. Stress should be placed on the development of programs designed to give insight into the personal, social, legal, and cultural context of law enforcement service. The education and training function should be able to develop more sophisticated mechanisms for field training and greater articulation between the classroom and the real world.

POLICE IN A CHANGING SOCIETY

The conditions that affect society have their potential effect on the police officer as an ethical practitioner and as a human being. Police officers are not immune to the situations they must face. They are influencers and controllers of the situations. Whether they are facing problems of deadly force, problems of mixed ethical decisions, or problems involving the fundamental privacy of individual citizens, it all rubs off on them.

The alienation resulting from loneliness, inadequacy, despair, and helplessness found among many of the persons with whom they are in contact every day is bound to have its effect on the personality and psychological stability of every police officer. Many police officers sense that they are becoming withdrawn and distant because of the situations they have to face. There is no greater irony in law enforcement than to find attrition in the ranks of competent police officers as they paraphrase the adage, "We have faced the enemy and he is us."

Yet if this is a time of growing public and private cynicism and changing values, it is particularly challenging for people in law enforcement to avoid attempts to manipulate and distort daily police practice. Indeed, now more than ever before, it is essential for those sworn to represent and uphold the law to do exactly that.

The police officer is, for most people, their only contact with the law. What the officer says, thinks, and does reflects on the total community. A successful police department must be attuned to and have the respect and support of the community. The misuse of office or denial of justice to even one person, like ripples on a pond, spread wider and wider until all are touched.

The National Advisory Commission's assessment of the situation remains as relevant today as it did in 1973:

> The communities of this Nation are torn by racial strife, economic chasms, and struggles between the values of the old and the viewpoints of the young. These circumstances have made it difficult for the policeman to identify with and be identified as part of a community of citizens. As communities have divided within themselves, there has been a breakdown in cooperation between the police and the citizens.
>
> The problem is particularly acute in large urban population centers. Here, the fibers of mutual assistance and neighborliness that bind citizens together have grown precariously thin. (National Advisory Commission, 1973, p. 72)

The prescription recommended for improving the situation described is cooperation between police and community. As an essential element of cooperation the police agency must constantly seek to improve its ability to determine the needs and expectations of the public, to act upon these needs and expectations, and to inform the people of the resulting policies developed to improve the delivery of police services.

On the other side of the relationship, the public must be informed of the police agency's roles so that it can better support the police in their efforts to reduce crime (p. 72).

CONCLUSIONS

Law enforcement often becomes the object of animosity against the establishment. Because of the police officer's traditional role, this may be an expected sociological or psychological occurrence. It seems clear that if new methods of reducing tensions are not found, an increased polarization in society will take place, which can only lead to more violence and retaliation. In an atmosphere of fear and distrust, the problems themselves lose proportion and cooperative solutions become impossible.

Police agencies generally reflect the community. If the community is progressive, its police agencies become progressive. If the total community is belligerent, police agencies become belligerent. If a community has racist tendencies or is indifferent to the plight of minority groups, police agencies will almost always reflect the same tendencies. If the community is apathetic, police agencies become apathetic.

The police must make every effort to understand the needs and aspirations of all members of the community. There is also a great need for the public to understand the proper role to be played not only by police agencies but also by the entire criminal justice system within the community in our changing society. Such an understanding is impossible to achieve if it is forgotten that the police are essentially a service agency.

If progress is to be made, changes must be sought and initiated by all segments of the community, including the police. The progress of change always seems to begin with small things. Change must be based on an understanding of the community and an appreciation of what the community can be tomorrow and the day after.

STUDENT CHECKLIST

1. Define the terms *perception* and *role concept.*
2. How does a citizen's perceptions of the police affect the way that the citizen acts toward a police officer?
3. List three factors responsible for differences in perception.
4. Describe the processes of generalization, deletion, and distortion.
5. Describe objective and subjective approaches to framing role expectations.
6. Identify and account for some of the conflicting perceptions that exist regarding the role of a police officer in the community.
7. Name several factors and conditions of change in our society.
8. Identify some of the paradoxes and dilemmas our changing society creates for the police officer.
9. What are some of the elements necessary to the success of programs designed to assist officers in achieving realistic role concepts and improved service to and participation in the community?

TOPICS FOR DISCUSSION

1. What is your perception of the police in your community? What life experiences have brought you to that perception?
2. From your own community, suggest some specific examples of destructive perceptions between police and citizens (individuals or groups) that lead or could lead to poor police–community relations.
3. Suggest some ways to modify these destructive perceptions. (See topic 2.)
4. Survey students in the class individually as to their concepts regarding the role of police officers. Is there a consensus of views? To what degree are the concepts subjective? Objective? Are the views expressed representative of the views of identifiable groups in your community?

ONE STEP FORWARD

An Exercise in Role Clarification

This exercise is based on a role analysis technique (RAT) that is often used in team development (see Tansik and Elliott, 1981). It is designed to be used by students as a classroom exercise. It may also be used as an intra- or inter-agency exercise by administrators, units, teams, sections, or other identifiable groups to clarify the roles of group members.

Supplies

Several large sheets of butcher paper, several large markers, and a chalkboard

Step I: Establishing Groups

Divide the class into police teams of 4 to 6 members. Each team will be designated Group A, B, or C. Assign (or allow group members to choose) a role to every member by title only from the titles in their group below:

Group A: Police Chief, Police Lieutenant in charge of Support Services, Police Sergeant supervising Community Relations Programs, Traffic Officer, Detective in charge of Special Problems, Field Patrol Officer.

Group B: Community Relations Officer, SWAT Team Officer, Police Psychologist, Traffic Officer, Field Patrol Officer, Citizen Police Volunteer.

Group C: Community Relations Officer, Police Psychologist, Corrections Officer, Field Patrol Officer, Social Worker, Police Chief.

Step II: Independent Listing of Duties and Responsibilities

Each person lists on paper (independently of others in the group) the responsibilities and duties of his/her job.

Step III: Focal Role Analysis

One person is chosen to begin. That person's role is then referred to as the "key role." That person shares his/her list with the group and discusses the difference between what he/she believes is done compared with what should be done. Group members contribute additional duties (and recommend deletion of duties) from the list based on their perceptions. Discussion continues until a list of duties can be agreed upon.

Step IV: Obligations of Other Group Members

The person in the key role lists his/her expectations of all other team members in relationship to his/her role. Again, input from other members is invited. Discussion continues until consensus is reached.

Step V: What Is Needed from the Key Role Incumbent

All other team members in turn state what they believe they will need (or want) from the key role incumbent in order for them to meet their obligations (see step IV).

Step VI: Repeat the Process

Repeat the process until every group member has been chosen as the key role incumbent and steps III, IV, and V have been repeated for each one.

Step VII: New Job Descriptions

Based on the results of the process, each group member makes a new list of his/her own responsibilities and duties. As a result of this process, every group member should have a better understanding of his/her own role and the roles of others in the group. Used in an interagency or intra-agency context this exercise can help increase cooperation among group members.

BIBLIOGRAPHY

Auten, J. H. (1981). "The paramilitary model of police and police professionalism," *Police Studies,* Summer.

Bandler, R., and Grinder, J. (1975). *The Structure of Magic,* Vol. I. Palo Alto, Calif.: Science and Behavior Books.

Barker, T., Hunter, R. D., and Rush, J. P. (1994). *Police Systems and Practices: An Introduction.* Englewood Cliffs, N.J.: Prentice Hall.

Bennett, G. (1990). "Cultural lag in law enforcement: Preparing police for the crimewarps of the future," *American Journal of Police,* Vol. XI, No. 9, pp. 81–126.

Berg, B. L. (1992). *Law Enforcement: An Introduction to Police in Society.* Boston: Allyn and Bacon.

Broderick, J. J. (1987). *Police in a Time of Change,* 2nd ed. Prospect Heights, Ill.: Waveland Press.

Cordner, G. W. (1989). "The police on patrol" in D. J. Kenney (Ed.), *Police and Policing: Contemporary Issues.* New York: Greenwood Press.

Cox, S. M., and Fitzgerald, J. D. (1992). *Police in Community Relations: Critical Issues.* Dubuque, Iowa: Wm. C. Brown.

Greene, J. R., and Klockars, C. B. (1991). "What police do," in C. B. Klockars and S. D. Mastrofski (Eds.), *Thinking About Police: Contemporary Readings.* New York: McGraw-Hill

Holden, R. N. (1992). *Law Enforcement: An Introduction.* Englewood Cliffs, N.J.: Prentice Hall.

Mastrofski, S. D. (1990). "The prospects of change in police patrol: A decade in review," *American Journal of Police,* Vol. XI, No. 9, pp. 1–79.

Mayer, M. (1969). *Liberty: Man versus State.* Santa Barbara, Calif.: Center for the Study of Democratic Institutions.

National Advisory Commission on Criminal Justice Standards and Goals (1973). *A National Strategy to Reduce Crime.* Washington, D.C.: U.S. Government Printing Office.

Niederhoffer, A. (1967). *Behind the Shield.* New York: Doubleday.

Orwell, G. (1984). New York: Harcourt Brace Jovanovich.

President's Commission on Law Enforcement and the Administration of Justice (1967). *The Challenge of Crime in a Free Society.* Washington, D.C.: U.S. Government Printing Office.

Roberg, R. R., and Kuykendall, J. (1993). *Police and Society.* Belmont, Calif.: Wadsworth.

Rodgers, J. E. (1982). "The malleable memory of eyewitnesses," *Science,* Vol. 82, June, pp. 32–35.

Satir, V. (1978). *Your Many Faces.* Millbrae, Calif.: Celestial Arts.

Skolnick, J. H. (1975). "A sketch of the policeman's working personality," in *Justice Without Trial,* 2nd ed. New York: Wiley.

Tansik, D. S., and Elliot, J. F. (1981). *Managing Police Organizations.* Monterey, Calif.: Duxbury Press.

Trautman, N. (1991). *How to Be a Great Cop.* Dallas, Texas: Standards and Training, Inc.

Walker S. (1989). *Sense and Nonsense About Crime,* 2nd ed. Pacific Grove, Calif.: Brooks/Cole.

Walker S. (1992). *The Police in America: An Introduction,* 2nd ed. Pacific Grove, Calif.: Brooks/Cole.

Wilson, J. Q. (1968). *Varieties of Police Behavior.* Cambridge, Mass.: Harvard University Press.

5

COPING WITH THE HUMAN EXPERIENCE OF BEING A COP

... a good officer doing his job is a textbook example of burnout in progress ...
(Daviss, 1982, p. 14)

A good police officer is like the transmission of a fine highway tractor—10 speeds forward, 3 in reverse, with a clutch that makes it possible to move from one to another smoothly and virtually at will. (Delattre, 1981)

A career in law enforcement can be exciting, challenging, and rewarding for those who are people oriented and committed to public service. Yet it can also be devastating for those who are not prepared for its rigors. Thousands of well-meaning, dedicated individuals who thought that police work was the career for which they were destined have discovered that the mental, physical, social, or economic costs of continuing such a career were too high. Many others have persisted within the field but at considerable expense to them and to others.

Police work is a hazardous craft that requires strong, caring individuals who can consistently deal with stressful situations. Over time, the impact of the dangers and stressors inherent to policing affects individual police officers differently. Some, perhaps most, go through their entire careers without suffering personally in any unusual or specific way. For others, policing appears to take a special toll on their lives. The sense of community isolation, the potential dangers, and the unique police lifestyle all seem to work together to adversely affect certain officers' physical, mental, and social well-being.

STUDYING THIS CHAPTER WILL ENABLE YOU TO:

1. Identify and discuss factors that make it difficult for police officers to cope with change.
2. Discuss how the police working personality contributes to community isolation.
3. Identify and discuss the social hazards of police work.
4. Identify and discuss the health hazards of police work.
5. Identify and discuss strategies for reducing the stressors of police work.

CHANGE AND THE POLICE

Some of the changes of recent years that have had especially strong impact on police work have been discussed in some detail in previous chapters. They include:

- Unprecedented advances in technology.
- Biomedical advances.
- Rethinking of moral issues.
- Erosion of the sense of community or neighborhood solidarity.
- Breakdowns in traditional social roles and institutional arrangement (especially those involving the family).
- Demands for a more just distribution of wealth and civil, social, and political rights.
- High unemployment, unpaid mortgages, and a sluggish economy.

The police frequently are caught in the middle between those who want change and those who want to preserve the status quo. Individual police officers feel the conflict daily. The officer who is attacked by a group of angry youths as he attempts to arrest one of them for speeding understands the problem of being caught in the middle. So does the officer who, in a time of high unemployment, must serve an increasing number of eviction notices to families who cannot make mortgage payments on their homes, and supervise an auction of the family's possessions.

WHAT POLICING DOES TO THE POLICE

The Working Personality

Jerome Skolnick presented an analysis of how certain features (that he identifies in the police officer's environment) interact with the paramilitary structure of the typical police organization to produce what he calls a *working personality* (Skolnick, 1975, pp. 42–70). The danger present in the police officer's environment makes police officers suspicious people. They must respond to reported assaults against property and persons. As a result of their preoccupation with violence, they develop a stereotyping "perceptual shorthand" to identify "symbolic assailants": for example, "black equals danger." The individual police officer's suspiciousness does not necessarily result from personal experience. It may develop through identification with fellow officers who may have been victims of violence in the line of duty. They may feel socially isolated from a community that may consider them to be similar to occupation troops in an occupied country, as in the case of ghetto sections of a city. The police band together with a solidarity surpassing that found in most occupational groupings.

The authority invested in the police further isolates police officers from a public that resents their direction in such activities as traffic and sports events or their regulation of public morality. Police officers are further charged with hypocrisy. Officers are presumed to have taken part in some of the activities (as drunkenness) that they are called upon to suppress.

Since Skolnick's working personality of the police officer was first presented, the subject of the police personality has been discussed and analyzed from several different perspectives. Much of the literature tends to support, expand, and/or clarify elements of Skolnick's original thesis (Burbeck and Furnham, 1985; Alpert and Dunham, 1992).

Selection or Socialization

Policing has great impact on those who choose it as a career. Some authors suggest that people who choose police work as a career are in a sense "predisposed" toward formulating a police personality. In other words, they may exhibit personality traits that are particularly accepted and possibly rewarded in a law enforcement occupation.

This predispositional viewpoint may be interpreted in two different manners. The first interpretation is that those who seek to enter police work are authoritarian personalities who desire to have power and control over other citizens. This view or "myth" (Berg, 1992) now receives little support from police scholars. A second predispositional interpretation is "that the behavior of a police officer is primarily explained by the characteristics, values and attitudes that the individual had before he or she was employed" (Roberg and Kuykendall, 1993, p. 161). An example of this interpretation is Holden's (1992, p. 164) argument that police values are for the most part the lower-middle-class values that the majority of police officers bring into police work.

A police behavioral perspective which competes with predispositional theory is that of socialization. Socialization theory holds that police behavior is learned from interactions with other police officers. Proponents of this view argue that as new police officers learn the "skills of policing" they also adopt the attitudes and values of their peers (Bayley and Bittner, 1993). In fact, those interested in a career in policing may actually begin to acquire police values and beliefs prior to entering police work (Roberg and Kuykendall, 1993). Socialization is thought to occur as a result of the formal police organizational structure with its rigid rules and discipline, the informal "police subculture" into which the new officers are gradually assimilated, and from the inherent nature of police work.

If one assumes, as do the authors, that human behavior is a product of lifelong learning experiences, an integrated perspective that considers the effects of socialization both prior to and after entering police service provides a more satisfactory explanation of police behavior. The values and beliefs that the individual officer takes into police work may or may not be compatible with those held by other officers. The new officer must then reassess his/her personal viewpoints to determine whether or not to adopt what appears to be "police norms." It is the view of the authors that the extent to which police officers accept or reject these norms is determined by the influence of the various community groups (discussed in Chapter 1) to which they belong.

THE SOCIAL HAZARDS OF POLICING

Alienation from the Public

The police officer's role in society tends to alienate the officer from society as a whole. Police are given considerable authority by society to protect life and property and to keep public order; they are expected to risk their lives if necessary to discharge these duties. However, the police feel that they receive little prestige and support for such actions. Only recently has compensation in terms of salary increases and fringe benefits begun to be more closely commensurate with the responsibility and authority of the police, and these increases have not occurred uniformly throughout the United States or even from agency to agency in a given state or community.

Isolation and rejection of the police from society results in a sense of alienation. This pressures the police to develop their own subculture with norms that provide them with a basis for self-respect independent to some degree of civilian attitudes. Thus, many police officers look upon themselves as an oppressed minority, subject to the same kind of prejudice as other minorities.

Police as a Minority Group

A minority is a social group whose members experience, at the hands of another social group, various disabilities in the form of prejudice, discrimination, segregation, or persecution (or any combination of these). People tend to exclude police from their circle of friends because of the nature of the law enforcement occupation and its responsibilities. Such social discrimination is illustrated by the comments of a police officer to one of the authors.

Example

The business where my wife works recently had a picnic. My wife and I attended. I joined several other men at the barbeque pit to assist with the cooking. As we drank a beer or two, the discussion drifted to what occupations were represented in the group.

I said that I was a police officer. One person turned to me and asked: "What kind? A detective?" I replied, "No, a traffic officer."

The other man then became very interested. "What do you think of the new law that requires you to take away an individual's license when they have an accident until they can prove liability coverage?"

I replied that it was a step in the right direction, but not enough. He exclaimed: "AHA!!! See, guys, what I told you! These guys are all alike. Give them a badge, a gun, some authority and it goes to their head. They want to play storm troopers and abuse citizens!"

By this time a larger group had gathered because the man had become very loud and argumentative. I told him quietly: "Listen, I don't want an argument. You asked for my opinion. Let's drop it. I just came over for some fun. I don't want any trouble." But he wouldn't stop.

I walked over to my wife, informed her we were leaving. We spent the evening in our own backyard eating hamburgers that we had picked up on the way home. The evening was ruined for both of us. I'm not sure it is worth the trouble we have to go through just to be sociable.

Police are more likely to isolate themselves than to be isolated by others. Neighbors and friends have difficulty separating the person from the badge. When guests at a party discover there is a police officer present, they typically tell about the "crooked cops" they knew or how unfairly a friend of theirs was treated by a police officer. Most veteran officers grow weary of defending the police and withdraw into close associations with other officers. Given a choice, they would prefer to relax in the company of their fellow officers. In addition, the irregular hours created by shift work makes it difficult for police to mesh their off-hours with those of neighbors who have "normal" occupations. A police officer is never "off duty." Many departments require an officer to carry a gun when not working and make arrests in outstanding cases.

Discrimination also affects the police officer's spouse and children.

Example

After I joined the force, the department started a program which allowed the officers to take their vehicles home. Since this program began, I have been asked on several occasions to speak to neighborhood youth who were racing up and down the street on dirt bikes. Everyone in the neighborhood now knows that I am an officer.

Since beginning to bring the unit home, I have had my mailbox torn down several times. Excrement has been placed in it. Obscene phone calls are made frequently to my home. Beer bottles and empty cans have been thrown on my property. Trash cans have been turned over and the contents spilled on the ground.

We are avoided by our neighbors, even though the neighborhood in which I live is a fine, so-called middle-class area.

My family is very unhappy. We are considering moving to another area—one where other police officers live. There we can have some peace and an opportunity to socialize without problems.

A sense of community isolation then emerges as the result of the job and the socialization process that takes place in becoming a police officer. Police officers and their families develop strategies to cope with isolation from the community which tends to lead to further isolation. They withdraw into the police subculture, which provides "protective, supportive, and shared attitudes, values, understandings and views of the world" (Inciardi, 1990, p. 227). The product of this withdrawal is the exclusion of nonpolice associates, which leads to the development of a myopic (and therefore hazardous) view of society which Barker, Hunter, and Rush (1994) define as "blue blindness."

Isolation from the Family

All too often, policing becomes a disruptive influence for the family. The potential for danger, the authoritarian nature of the job, around-the-clock shifts, constantly changing shifts, and accommodations that must be made in family life all work together to increase tension in the law enforcement family. As a result, many believe that marital problems are endemic to law enforcement.

A high divorce rate is often linked to the police occupation itself (Terry, 1981). However, when policing is compared with other occupations and professions, it is found that the divorce rate is not that high (Alpert and Dunham, 1992). In many cases, the divorce rate among police officers is lower than anticipated (Niederhoffer and Niederhoffer, 1978).

In some cases this lower rate may be the result of more women involved in policing; there are now more two officer families. In other cases, the spouse (particularly the wife) may have grown up in a police household and hence be familiar with the strains attributable to policing. Finally may be the fact that police families simply cope as well as or better than nonpolice families (Elliott et al., 1991). Further, when there is a divorce in a police family, it probably is for the same reasons that divorce occurs in any other family and not because of "the job." In divorce, as with many other aspects of policing, all too often the job gets blamed when the cause is elsewhere.

Salary Limitations

Before accepting or rejecting law enforcement as a career, the person should carefully weigh the pros and cons of other occupations for which he/she might qualify. Although there are many other issues to consider in selecting one's life work, financial considerations cannot be ignored. If one's goal in life is to accumulate great wealth, he/she should not become a law enforcement officer! Despite their education, training, and professionalism, unless they rise to top administrative positions, become corrupt, or win the lottery, they will experience a lower-middle-class existence.

Significant progress was made in the area of law enforcement wages and benefits during the 1980s, especially in large departments. Despite this, inadequate pay remains a problem for law enforcement officers nationwide. In performing their duties, officers believe that they are performing an important role in the community (i.e., protecting life and property). They also believe, especially in light of the dangerous nature of their work, that they should be paid commensurate with it and with the benefits they are providing to society. Overall, officers are simply frustrated at not being paid what they feel they are worth (Aynes and Flanagan, 1990, p. 14).

Career Limitations

Yet another issue that should be considered in pursuing a law enforcement career is: Where does a person expect to be at the peak of his/her career? Everyone cannot become the chief of police in a large metropolitan agency. Nor will all those who wish to become supervisory federal agents do so. Whether one's career is successful depends on how one defines success. There are many officers who have spent their entire careers as patrol officers in small or midsized law enforcement agencies who are rightly proud of their accomplishments. Similarly, there are many frustrated individuals (at all ranks and levels of policing) who feel that they never received a fair chance. They might have felt this way no matter what occupation they chose. As in any job, perseverance and a good work ethic help things to happen.

Liability Issues

In a democratic society the police are limited in what they can do. The public has both civil and criminal recourse to protect against police abuses. In addition, police bureaucracies have administrative processes that regulate the behavior of police personnel. Failure to act in a manner that is felt to be consistent with proper law enforcement procedures could result in a minor reprimand. More serious violations could result in more severe disciplinary actions, such as suspensions, compulsory transfers, demotions, or even terminations. Violations that are felt to have infringed on the legal rights of others could result in costly civil litigation at the state or federal levels. Violations thought to constitute criminal actions could result in arrest, conviction, and imprisonment at either the state or federal levels. Whether they are convicted or subsequently acquitted of all charges, the economic impact of legal costs and career damages can be devastating to officers and their families.

HEALTH HAZARDS

Violence

Danger is an inherent part of police work, and this danger is reinforced by the element of authority. Police are required to enforce laws, laws that are often either more conservative or more liberal than the area or person against whom it is being enforced. Notes Bittner (1991, p. 37), "the policeman is always opposed to some articulated or articulable human interest." In addition, police are almost always interacting with individuals in a moment of crisis. Thus the police are, more often than not, perceived more as adversaries than as friends.

All too often the scenario described above results in an act of violence in which the police officer is either the victim of violence or is forced to use violence to defend himself/herself or others. During the years 1981 through 1990, 762 law enforcement officers were feloniously killed within the United States (FBI, 1991, p. 15). While the number of officers slain in the line of duty does not reach the proportions depicted by the American entertainment industry, the potential of being murdered is a real threat with which police officers and their loved ones must contend.

While the potential for violent death is relatively low for American law enforcement officers, the possibility of being injured due to violence is not. Within 1990 alone, 71,794 state and local officers, and 1154 federal officers were assaulted (FBI,

1991, pp. 41, 49). From those assaults, 26,031 state and local officers and 289 federal officers received injuries.

The threat of death and injury due to violence as well as the psychological impacts of possibly having to cause death or injury to others is a fact with which law enforcement officers must contend. The keys to coping with these hazards are personnel selection and training (Miller and Allard, 1991). Law enforcement personnel must be rigorously screened to obtain people who can be taught how to respond properly to dangerous situations. This must be followed by extensive training and education of officers as to the potential threats they will face and the proper responses to those threats (Garner and Clemmer, 1986).

Accidents

Law enforcement officers have about an equal potential to lose their lives due to accidents rather than homicides. For example, in 1990 sixty-five officers were murder victims but sixty-seven were killed in accidents that took place while performing their duties (FBI, 1991, p. 4). Automobile accidents, motorcycle accidents, aircraft crashes, being struck by vehicles, accidental shootings, falls, and drownings tend to be the more common causes for accidental deaths among officers. The number of officers who are injured due to accidents is not readily available, but it is not unrealistic to suppose that several thousand occur each year. Broken bones, burns, animal bites, abrasions, back injuries, and any number of other physical maladies are incurred by officers on a daily basis.

As with threats from violence, accident prevention depends on education of law enforcement officers as to potential threats and proper solutions. In particular, training in pursuit driving and emergency responses (emphasizing the dangers of such actions to the officers and the public, as well as the need to limit such pursuits to life-threatening situations that justify the risks) is imperative. Additionally, traffic direction techniques, animal control techniques, and proper responses to hazard situations such as fires and chemical spills are necessary.

Contagious Diseases

During the latter half of the twentieth century, police officers had relatively little to fear from contagious diseases. Some of the more common communicable diseases, such as gonorrhea, herpes, and syphilis, would hopefully not be contracted while on duty. Outbreaks of the old horrors of earlier times—diphtheria, polio, tetanus, smallpox, and whooping cough—were being controlled through vaccinations. Meningitis, mononucleosis, scarlet fever, salmonellosis, and tuberculosis remained as threats along with a variety of childhood diseases, such as mumps, measles, and chickenpox, but the possibility of infection was rare.

During the 1980s police officers became aware of a threat that was not only highly communicable but also lethal. Most citizens felt that AIDS (acquired immune deficiency syndrome) was a disease that only threatened gays, prostitutes, and drug users. While learning that there were indeed "high-risk groups," police officers also learned that the potential to contract the human immunodeficiency virus (HIV) which causes AIDS was there for anyone who might somehow exchange bodily fluids with an infected person. Since the demands of police work not only place officers in contact with high-risk individuals but also in situations in which bodily fluids could be exchanged (contact with open wounds, blood, saliva, etc.) it is imperative that officers be informed as to the facts and fictions regarding AIDS and the proper precautions that should be taken (Blumberg, 1993). Table 5-1 contains responses to law enforcement concerns regarding AIDS. As with other communicable diseases, common sense and knowledge from proper training are the best defenses.

TABLE 5-1
RESPONSES TO AIDS-RELATED LAW ENFORCEMENT CONCERNS

Issue/concern	Educational and action messages
Human bites	Person who bites usually receives the victim's blood; viral transmission through saliva is highly unlikely. If bitten by anyone, milk wound to make it bleed, wash the area thoroughly, and seek medical attention.
Spitting	Viral transmission through saliva is highly unlikely.
Urine/feces	Virus isolated in only very low concentrations in urine; not at all in feces; no cases of AIDS or AIDS virus infection associated with either urine or feces.
Cuts/puncture wounds	Use caution in handling sharp objects and searching areas hidden from view; needle stick studies show risk of infection is very low.
CPR/first aid	To eliminate the already minimal risk associated with CPR, use masks/airways; avoid blood-to-blood contact by keeping open wounds covered and wearing gloves when in contact with bleeding wounds.
Body removal	Observe crime scene rule: Do not touch anything. Those who must come into contact with blood or other body fluids should wear gloves.
Casual contact	No cases of AIDS or AIDS virus infection attributed to casual contact.
Any contact with blood or body fluids	Wear gloves if contact with blood or body fluids is considered likely. If contact occurs, wash thoroughly with soap and water; clean up spills with one part water to nine parts household bleach.
Contact with dried blood	No cases of infection have been traced to exposure to dried blood. The drying process itself appears to inactivate the virus. Despite low risk, however, caution dictates wearing gloves, a mask, and protective shoe coverings if exposure to dried blood particles is likely (e.g., crime scene investigation).

Source: Hammett, 1987, p. 6.

Emotional Distress

Due to the hazards that are inherent in law enforcement, *all* officers will, on occasion, experience emotional distress. While other occupations may be far more dangerous, the constant exposure to stressful stimuli makes policing one of the most difficult occupations (Anson and Bloom, 1988). The threat of violent death and injury, the constant exposure to human tragedies, the responsibility for others, the feelings of alienation and helplessness, the demands of shift work, the limited career opportunities, and the lack of input in administrative decision making all combine to create stress for even the most stable and well-adjusted persons (Kroes, 1985; Smith, 1982).

The impacts of stress can be temporary depression, extreme anguish, paranoia, cynicism, authoritarianism, denial, or just about any other means by which human beings try to cope with their feelings. Despite what some may think, police officers are human beings with the same frailties and weaknesses as other human beings. When the amount of stress to which they are exposed becomes too heavy, police officers will become emotionally distressed (Colwell, 1988; Bryant, 1990). How they cope with this distress may be positive (seeking counseling, recreation, relaxation, etc.) or negative (denial, withdrawal, abuse of alcohol, fits of temper, etc.).

It is of vital importance that law enforcement administrators and their employees realize the sources and consequences of stress. Before officers can learn to cope with the stress that is inherent in policing, they must first be taught to overcome the "John Wayne mentality," which refuses to acknowledge any weaknesses (Darrow, 1988). Once officers have learned to acknowledge the existence of stress, they can be taught how to identify and neutralize those stressors with which they as individuals must contend (Territo and Vetter, 1981).

The best means for officers to learn to cope with stress is for their agencies to develop programs that promote mental wellness. These may include providing counseling services for employees and their families, and developing peer counseling programs, enhanced training programs, and enlightened management policies. The following additional stress reduction techniques have been suggested to reduce stress or as means to cope with stress.

1. More efficient pre-employment screening to weed out those who cannot cope with a high-stress job.
2. Increased practical training for police personnel on stress, including the simulation of high-stress situations.
3. Training programs for spouses so that they can better understand potential problems.
4. Group discussions where officers and perhaps their spouses can ventilate and share their feelings about the job.
5. A more supportive attitude by police executives toward the stress-related problems of patrol officers.
6. A mandatory alcoholic rehabilitation program.
7. Immediate consultation with officers involved in traumatic events such as justifiable homicides.

8. Complete false arrest and liability insurance to relieve the officer of having to second-guess his decisions.

9. The provision of departmental psychological services to employees and their families (Territo and Vetter, 1981, p. 272).

Mental Illness

If the distress discussed in the preceding section is not dealt with appropriately, it may escalate into behaviors that threaten the welfare of the officer and/or others. The individual officer may come to suffer from relatively mild emotional disturbances that require only counseling and reassurance, or he/she may be plagued by severe mental disorders that are career threatening or even life threatening in nature.

Law enforcement agencies must not only have assistance programs designed to help officers contend with emotional distress but must also develop strategies to aid those whose problems become too severe for continued police service. Medical pensions, extended health coverage, and family support services are only fair for those who have paid too high a price for their police careers.

Suicide

Being a police officer is also thought to increase one's risk of falling victim of suicide. Preliminary studies (Lester, 1983; Wagner and Brzeczek, 1983) identified higher levels of suicide among police officers than among other occupations. One study suggested a rate of three times as high as the general population (Violanti, Vena, and Marshall, 1986). In Chicago, alcohol abuse was linked to 60 percent of the police suicides (Wagner and Brzeczek, 1983). Although these higher rates have been challenged by a more recent study suicide among Los Angeles officers (Josephson and Reiser, 1990), increases in officer suicides were noted.

Given the general nature of police work, many officers who feel suicidal are either afraid or have no one to turn to in discussing their feelings. This leads to an even greater sense of isolation, with many believing suicide to be the only way out. Fortunately, programs in stress reduction, marital and mental health counseling and wellness are aiding many departments in addressing this concern. Unfortunately, suicide is expected to remain higher for law enforcement personnel than within the general populace (Berg, 1992).

Substance Abuse

Police administrators frequently report that alcohol is a severe problem with officers and often report the existence of alcohol-related behavioral problems (Alpert and Dunham, 1992). As early as 1972, Skolnick reported that officers drink heavily and with other officers. Fifteen years later, Carson (1987) found that officers involved in cases of excessive force and use of firearms drank more than officers who avoided such activities. Farmer (1990) found that alcohol use was an acceptable coping mechanism for both male and female police officers. In another study, both male and female officers reported drinking more alcohol than the general population (Pendergrass and Osgrove, 1986).

The use and abuse of alcohol among police officers is apparently one way of coping with the problems inherent in "the job" (Violanti, Marshall, and Howe, 1985). Alcohol is the only and best coping mechanism some police officers believe they have. Clearly, then, with this belief system at work police officers are at a high risk for alcoholism.

Although alcohol is the "drug of choice" among police officers, caffeine and nicotine are also extremely popular. It is not unusual for officers to drink several cups of coffee, glasses of tea, or soft drinks during their workday. Similarly, many officers use tobacco products while on duty. In addition to being chemically addictive, these drugs are also psychologically addictive in that they often develop as means of killing time during periods of tedium.

The drugs mentioned above are not the only ones with which officers might experiment. The use of illicit drugs may also develop (or be continued). Dealing with these abuses is problematic because they are not only considered to be physically and psychologically harmful, they are also unlawful to possess or use. The abuse of such drugs by officers is not only potentially harmful to the officer but to the reputation of the law enforcement agency as well.

As with the hazards discussed in the preceding section, substance abuse is best dealt with by departmental programs designed to inform officers of the dangers involved, the policies and regulations of the department in regard to those issues, and the types of assistance available for those who seek help.

Physical Wellness

In addition to substance abuse, a number of other health hazards exist for police officers. Stress, poor nutrition, and lack of exercise also contribute to poor physical health. Terry (1981) has documented numerous physiological effects of police stress. These problems include headaches, indigestion, ulcers, lower back pain, and high blood pressure. In addition, Norvell, Belles, and Hills (1988) have found that police officers have a higher risk of mortality associated with cancer, diabetes, and heart disease than do nonpolice. It is evident that a strong relationship exists between job-related stress and physical illnesses.

In addition to physical hazards attributed to stress, police officers are noted for having poor eating habits. Fast-food diets and limited exercise result in poor conditioning, which over time leads to obesity and/or other physical ailments. In combination with stress, these health problems can range from minor irritants to life-threatening illnesses.

The role of the police agency in providing for the physical health of its employees is crucial. Just as programs have been developed that assist in providing for the mental health of law enforcement officers, so are programs needed to promote physical wellness. Education as to proper nutrition, and recreational needs must be provided. Whenever possible, incentives should be provided to encourage employees to maintain physical fitness. Assistance should be readily available for those seeking help from chemical dependency. In addition, these programs should be available to family members.

COPING WITH BEING A COP

In recent years law enforcement administrators have increasingly recognized that they must do more to protect their employees from the hazards described previously. The results have been better selection procedures, more extensive training, and the development of employee programs designed to aid both sworn officers and nonsworn police personnel in coping with the challenges inherent in contemporary law enforcement (Figure 5-1). In the following sections we highlight some of the procedures that are being utilized by progressive police agencies.

FIGURE 5-1   A law enforcement officer who leads a full life in addition to his/her police duties is less likely to succumb to the social and health hazards of police work. One such example is Deputy Roy Turman, who leads a busy, challenging, and balanced life. (*Courtesy* of Deputy Roy Turman, Calhoon County, Alabama Sheriff's Department.)

Selection

Since the days of August Vollmer, police reformers have called for the use of selection criteria to screen out those persons who were "unfit" for police work. Initially this procedure consisted of eliminating applicants who had criminal records and/or histories of violence. As policing has become more complex and demanding, the need for effective employee screening procedures has become even more important. A modern police officer must be intelligent, articulate, diplomatic, and compassionate. He/she must be sensitive to the needs of individuals and groups, yet be forceful and direct when circumstances dictate intervention. They must be dedicated to serving their community and enforcing laws. They must be able to use their considerable discretion in a fair and unbiased manner. They must be adaptable to any situation that might arise, and they must be able to endure the continuing stressors of police work. Choosing such a person is no easy task.

The task of selecting qualified officers is complicated by the need to make police forces more representative of the community being served. Height and weight requirements that were supposed to ensure physical competence were found to have little validity and were discriminatory toward women and Hispanics (Martin, 1993). The requirement of a college education was thought to discriminate against African Americans and other minorities (Sapp and Carter, 1992). Other screening procedures, such as psychological testing, were also feared to be biased (Alpert, 1993). The product of these conflicts has been the gradual development of selection procedures designed to eliminate gender or ethnic bias while ensuring that competent individuals are employed.

Currently, progressive police agencies use a variety of selection procedures, such as written examinations, oral interviews, physical agility tests appropriate for both males and females, medical examinations, polygraph examinations, situational testing, background investigations, and psychological profiling. The emphasis is to eliminate the truly unfit without being biased against particular individuals or groups. Many agencies also use educational requirements which are now considered to be less discriminatory as more minorities obtain college education (Carter and Sapp, 1992) (Table 5-2).

TABLE 5-2
EDUCATION LEVELS BY RACE/ETHNICITY

	Average Level of Education (years)	Percent completing:		
		No College	Some Under-graduate Work	Graduate Degree
Black	13.6	28	63	9
Hispanic	13.3	27	68	5
White	13.7	34	62	4
Other	13.8	19	73	8

Source: Carter and Sapp, 1992, p. 11.

While these techniques are useful, perhaps the best means of obtaining competent officers is aggressive recruiting, developing attractive financial packages and retirement benefits, providing for career development, and establishing a reputation of concern for employees. These strategies, in conjunction with sound supervision, extensive training, and support programs, not only assure that qualified applicants will compete for the available positions but that most of those selected will remain with the organization.

Training

Traditionally training has been an area of weakness within police organizations. Police officers were sworn in and immediately put to work. They learned the job through trial and error, by observing other officers, and by listening to "war stories." Since the early 1970s recruit training or "basic training" has become the norm throughout the United States. This training is provided at police academies which are either run by or comply with standards mandated by state police training commissions. The type of curriculum and hours required varies considerably from state to state. Initially, the focus of police academies was to teach recruits the technical knowledge required for police work (legal requirements, report writing, first aid, defensive tactics, and firearms proficiency). In recent years the curriculums have been lengthened to include a broader spectrum of subjects relative to the needs of modern police officers. Communication skills, sensitivity to cultural and ethnic diversity, conflict management, and liability concerns inherent in providing police services are now being taught in addition to the traditional "law enforcement" topics.

In addition to academy training, new police officers in many departments now receive additional training in a field training officer (FTO) program. The "rookie" rides with an experienced officer who has been carefully selected and trained to become an FTO. Over a period of several weeks (and frequently several months) the FTO teaches the rookie how to apply his/her academy training to handle real-world situations. As the rookie is being taught, his/her progress is monitored and evaluated. A person whose performance within the program is consistently unsatisfactory will be terminated. Those who complete the FTO program successfully are assigned to a regular patrol shift. They will continue to be closely monitored by senior officers and supervisors throughout their probationary period (usually one year from time of employment). The benefits of the FTO programs are not only in preparing new officers for a demanding job but are also seen in improved community relations and enhanced morale within police organizations (Gaines, Southerland, and Angell, 1991).

Yet another area of training that is of benefit to both the police and the community is in-service training. Too frequently, the needs of veteran officers have been ignored by police organizations. By developing periodic in-service training programs, all police personnel can be kept abreast of changes in laws and changes in departmental procedures, be taught new police skills and techniques, be prepared for career development, be informed of community concerns, and be reassured in regard to their importance to the organization.

Family Programs

Police departments have also instituted programs to assist officers experiencing marital or family problems. An example of one such program may be found in Tallahassee, Florida, where a mental health counseling program in which departmental members (sworn and civilian) and their families may anonymously participate has been operating for several years. It is the view of the Tallahassee Police Department's administration that any stress inducers (personal or familial) that could affect their employees well-being are legitimate concerns. Therefore, not only police employees but their spouses and dependents are eligible for free counseling at a mental health facility with whom the city of Tallahassee contracts.

In addition to family counseling programs as exemplified above, many departments provide support groups for the spouses and families of departmental employees. Periodically, their employees and their families are offered seminars on such topics as nutrition, stress, reduction, physical fitness, and financial planning. A number of other activities designed to promote family-member inclusion within the organization and their understanding of the work that their loved one performs may be found within many police organizations. These include but are not limited to: ride-along programs, departmental dinners and banquets, and recreational associations. In some agencies, spouses are even allowed to participate in portions of recruit training in order to better understand what their spouses are going to be involved in.

Wellness Programs

In addition to the programs discussed in the preceding section, many agencies have also started treatment programs for officers with substance abuse problems, along with suicide intervention and stress reduction programs. The mere fact that agencies are now recognizing these problems and offering assistance rather than ignoring them or terminating employees is a major step. In addition, many departments have undergone "smoke-free" environments or have instituted preventive health programs to assist officers who wish to get in better physical condition.

Community Policing

Community policing (discussed in detail in Chapter 13) is yet another attempt at having police officers become more involved with the community they serve. By seeking to become a part of the community, attending community meetings, talking to residents, seeking community input into police decision making, and so on, it is hoped that the community will become more accepting of police officers and that officers will feel less isolated from the community.

CONCLUSIONS

All of the aforementioned programs and others being developed are designed to help deal with whatever problems might affect the officer. These traumas of police work are real regardless of the officer's gender, race, or age. They do not affect all officers—perhaps not even a majority—but for those that are affected, the consequences are enormous, for the officer, for the department, and for society. To keep and maintain a solid, well-trained police force, departments and individuals alike must be aware of the potential for problems, identify existing problems, and seek out or provide adequate treatment. To do any less is unacceptable. Police officers are human beings first, facing the same problems that anyone else might face, indeed having a greater propensity for some than other occupations. Fortunately, departments and officers are recognizing this and taking steps to prevent or deal with such problems.

STUDENT CHECKLIST

1. Describe the factors that make it difficult for police officers to cope with change.

2. Identify and describe job stressors of police work and their consequences for police officers.

3. Describe some ways in which stress can be reduced.

4. Describe the social hazards of police work.

5. Describe the health hazards of police work.

TOPICS FOR DISCUSSION

1. How does the working personality contribute to community isolation?

2. What is the primary cause of police officer deaths?

3. What are some effects of stress on police officers?

4. What is the primary substance abused by police officers? Does gender play a role in its abuse?

5. How are police agencies dealing with the hazards of police work?

6. What is meant by career limitations, and what does it mean for police work?

ONE STEP FORWARD

A novel approach to enhanced police–community relations may be found in Columbia, South Carolina. There, city police officers are encouraged to find homes for sale (particularly in low-income, high-crime neighborhoods) which need at least $5000 worth of structural repairs. The city of Columbia then offers the officers the chance to purchase the homes, with no money down, lends the amount needed for repairs, and puts all costs into a 20-year mortgage at 4 percent interest. The city's purpose is twofold, "We want to promote home ownership for our police officers and we want to establish a police presence in neighborhoods to try to keep those areas from going downhill" (Ryan, 1992, p. 33). The products of this innovative program is that the officers involved not only police the community but become a part of the community.

BIBLIOGRAPHY

Alpert, G. P. (1993). "The role of psychological testing in law enforcement" in R. G. Dunham and G. P. Alpert (Eds.), *Critical Issues in Policing: Contemporary Readings,* 2nd ed. Prospect Heights, Ill.: Waveland Press, pp. 96–105.

Alpert, G. P., and Dunham, R. G. (1992). *Policing Urban America,* 2nd ed. Prospect Heights, Ill.: Waveland Press.

Anson, R. H., and Bloom, M. E. (1988). "Police stress in an occupational context," *Journal of Police Science and Administration,* Vol. 16, No. 4, pp. 229–235.

Aynes, R. M., and Flanagan, G. S. (1990). *Preventing Law Enforcement Stress: The Organization's Role.* Washington, D.C.: National Sheriffs' Association.

Barker, T., Hunter, R. D., and Rush, J. P. (1994). *Police Systems and Practices: An Introduction.* Englewood Cliffs, N.J.: Prentice Hall.

Bayley, D. H., and Bittner, E. (1993). "Learning the skills of policing," in R. G. Dunham and G. P. Alpert (Eds.), *Critical Issues in Policing: Contemporary Readings,* 2nd ed. Prospect Heights, Ill.: Waveland Press, pp. 106–129.

Berg, B. L. (1992). *Law Enforcement: An Introduction to Police in Society.* Needham Heights, Mass.: Allyn and Bacon.

Bittner, E. (1991). "The functions of police in modern society," in C. B. Klockars and S. D. Mastrofski (Eds.), *Thinking About Police,* 2nd ed. New York: McGraw-Hill, pp. 35–51.

Blumberg, M. (1993). "The AIDS epidemic and the police: An examination of the issues," in R. G. Dunham and G. P. Alpert (Eds.), *Critical Issues in Policing: Contemporary Readings,* 2nd ed. Prospect Heights, Ill.: Waveland Press, pp. 208–219.

Bryant, C. (1990). "Law enforcement stress: 'I need help,'" *FOP Journal,* Spring, pp. 10–11, 57–58.

Burbeck, E., and Furnham, A. (1985). "Police officer selection: a critical review of the literature," *Journal of Police Science and Administration,* Vol. 13, pp. 58–69.

Carson, S. (1987). "Shooting, death trauma and excessive force," in H. More and P. Unsinger (Eds.), *Police Managerial Use of Psychology and Psychologists.* Springfield, Ill.: Charles C Thomas.

Carter, D. L., and Sapp, A. D. (1992). "College education and policing: Coming of age," *FBI Law Enforcement Bulletin,* January, pp. 8–14.

Colwell, L. (1988). "Stress: A major enemy of law enforcement professionals," *FBI Law Enforcement Bulletin,* February, pp. 11–14.

Darrow, T. L. (1988). "Addressing stress," *Police,* December, pp. 46–49.

Daviss, B. (1982). "Burn out," *Police Magazine,"* Vol. 5, pp. 9–18.

Delattre, E. J. (1981). "The police: From slaying dragons to rescuing cats," *FBI Law Enforcement Bulletin,* November, pp. 17–18.

Elliott, M., Bingham, R. D., Neilsen, S. C., and Warner, P. D. (1991). "Marital intimacy and satisfaction as a support system for coping with police officer stress," *Journal of Police Science and Administration,* Vol. 14, No. 1, pp. 40–44.

Farmer, R. (1990). "Clinical and managerial implications of stress research on the police," *Journal of Police Science and Administration,* Vol. 17, pp. 205–218.

Federal Bureau of Investigation (1991). *Law Enforcement Officers Killed and Assaulted, 1990.* Washington, D.C.: U.S. Department of Justice.

Friedman, P. (1967). "Suicide among police," in E. Schneidmann (Ed.), *Essays in Self-Destruction.* New York: Science House.

Gaines, L. K., Southerland, M. D., and Angell, J. E. (1991). *Police Administration.* New York: McGraw-Hill.

Garner, J., and Clemmer, E. (1986). "Danger to police in domestic disturbances: A new look," *NIJ/Research in Brief,* November.

Hammett, T. M. (1987). "AIDS and the law enforcement officer," *NIJ Reports,* Vol. 206, pp. 2–7.

Holden, R. N. (1992). *Law Enforcement: An Introduction.* Englewood Cliffs, N.J.: Prentice Hall.

Inciardi, J. A. (1990). *Criminal Justice,* 3rd ed. San Diego: Harcourt Brace Jovanovich.

Josephson, R. L., and Reiser, M. (1990). "Officer suicide in the Los Angeles Police Department: a twelve-year follow-up," *Journal of Police Science and Administration,* Vol. 17, pp. 227–229.

Kroes, W. H. (1985). *Society's Victims: The Police,* 2nd ed. Springfield, Ill.: Charles C Thomas.

Lester, D. (1983). "Stress in police officers: an American perspective," *The Police Journal,* Vol. 56, pp. 184–193.

Martin, S. E. (1993). "Female officers on the move? Status report on women in policing," in R. G. Dunham and G. P. Alpert (Eds.), *Critical Issues in Policing: Contemporary Readings,* 2nd ed. Prospect Heights, Ill.: Waveland Press, pp. 327–347.

Miller, G. I., and Allard, R., Jr. (1991). "Death data: Analyzing statistics for tactical awareness," *Police Marksman,* March/April, pp. 36–38.

Niederhoffer, A., and Neiderhoffer, E. (1978). *The Police Family: From Station House to Ranch House.* Lexington, Mass.: Lexington Books.

Norvell, N., Belles, D., and Hills, H. (1988). "Perceived stress levels and physical symptoms in supervisor law enforcement personnel," *Journal of Police Science and Administration,* Vol. 16, pp. 75–79.

Pendergrass, V., and Osgrove, N. (1986). "Correlates of alcohol use by police personnel," in J. Reese and H. Goldstein (Eds.), *Psychological Services for Law Enforcement.* Washington D.C.: U.S. Government Printing Office.

Roberg, R. R., and Kuykendall, J. (1993). *Police and Society.* Belmont, Calif.: Wadsworth.

Ryan, M. (1992). "When the police move in," *Parade Magazine,* May 24, pp. 32–33.

Sapp, A. D., and Carter, D. L. (1992). "Police and higher education" in R. N. Holden (Ed.), *Law Enforcement: An Introduction.* Englewood Cliffs, N.J.: Prentice Hall.

Skolnick, J. (1975). *Justice Without Trial,* 2nd ed. New York: Wiley.

Smith, D. (1982). "Sources and consequences of stress for the police," *American Journal of Police,* Vol. 1, No. 2, pp. 114–148.

Territo, L., and Vetter, H. J. (1981). "Stress and police personnel," *Journal of Police Science and Administration,* Vol. 9, No. 2, pp. 195–207.

Terry, W. C., III (1981). "Police stress: The empirical evidence," *Journal of Police Science and Administration,* Vol. 9, No. 1, pp. 61–75.

Violanti, J., Marshall, J. R., and Howe, B. (1985). "Stress, coping and alcohol use: The police connection," *Journal of Police Science and Administration,* Vol. 13, pp. 106–110.

Violanti, J., Vena, J., and Marshall, J. R. (1986). "Disease, risk and mortality among police officers: new evidence and contributing factors," *Journal of Police Science and Administration,* Vol. 14, pp. 17–23.

Wagner, M., and Brzeczek, R. (1983). "Alcoholism and suicide: A fatal connection," *FBI Law Enforcement Bulletin,* Vol. 52, pp. 8–15.

6

THE COMMUNICATION PROCESS

More powerful than mace, the night stick, or the gun, effective rhetoric is an officer's most useful tool in the field. (Thompson, 1982)

Communication is basic to the world we know. We transmit and receive information in our world, often without even being aware that we are doing so. Because communication is a process that is shared by everyone and that is constantly with us, it is easily taken for granted. Communication skills supposedly just "come naturally."

Yet it is faulty communication that generates misunderstanding and helps to build social barriers between and among people. The result of poor communication can be anything from poor job performance to war. Effective communication encourages healthy relationships between two people, within a family, between the police and the community, between employer and employee, among nations, and so on.

It is the function of this chapter to define and describe the process of communication in action and to identify some specific ways through which a person can increase the effectiveness of his or her own communication with others.

STUDYING THIS CHAPTER WILL ENABLE YOU TO:

1. Define the communication process.
2. Contrast modes of communication.
3. Demonstrate effective listening skills.
4. Describe the communication process in police practices.
5. Identify several common blocks to effective communication in police–community relations.

COMMUNICATION IN ACTION

Communication is a process through which messages are exchanged. It is effective only when these messages are mutually understood by the sender and receiver.

Communication operates on many dimensions. The most commonly recognized are intrapersonal, interpersonal, and person-to-group. Because the nature of the work in the administration of justice process requires volumes of written reports (many of which will become legal records of the system), we include an additional dimension in this chapter: official communications.

Intrapersonal communication takes place within the person. We "talk to ourselves" as we solve problems or perform tasks. We may even write messages to ourselves. The academic community has just begun to speculate about the intrapersonal communication of criminal justice professionals. What happens to the thinking processes of the new recruit? Some suppose that the stresses of the occupation may distort the intrapersonal process, resulting in cynical, tough patrol officers, high divorce rates, and even illness.

Interpersonal communication is literally person-to-person. Whether or not we are able to form and maintain caring connections with others depends largely on our effective interpersonal communication skills. Police officers may stop or start fights, increase or decrease tension, gain or lose the cooperation of a witness, victim, or suspect through the exercise of their interpersonal communication skills. This is the dimension to which most discussion regarding communication skills is addressed and to which definitions of the communication process most directly refer. This dimension will be a major focus of this chapter. Much that is said in this context, however, can be generalized to other dimensions of communication in action.

Person-to-group communication implies a structured situation in which one person addresses a group on a predetermined subject. Public speaking engagements, a witness before a jury, and a minister before a congregation are all examples of person-to-group communication.

Some specific skills concerning group dynamics, presentation, and public speaking are related to this dimension of communication. To the extent that a group response is sought and received, people in the group reflect a group identity as they hear and respond to the message sent. In addition to this group dimension, however, every individual-group communication is also a person-to-person communication. The speaker is actually communicating individually with each person in the group, and the message received by one person will differ to some degree from the message received by any other person. This is true even though group consensus regarding some of the elements of the message may exist, and group response may provide feedback to the sender that the message sent was (or was not) received.

Official communication is usually written and can appear to be person-to-person or person-to-group. Actually, however, it usually is a "public" documentation of policy or procedure, or the official report or evaluation of events. It may be an in-house memo or a formal communication with other agencies. Lack of effectiveness in this dimension of communication has a sometimes subtle but very high cost. Administrators may lose the cooperation of staff members; agencies and individual officers may lose community support; prosecutors may lose convictions in court; and children and adults may be mislabeled, misdiagnosed, and mistreated. Official communication is an important part of communication in action. Some of the specific basic writing skills involved in this dimension of communication are not within the scope of this chapter. Official communication is discussed here in the context of effective police–community relations.

THE PROCESS OF COMMUNICATION

The Elements of Communication

The process of communication, as described in Figure 6-1, begins with a *source* who has an idea (meaning) that he or she wishes to transmit to the *receiver.* The idea cannot be transmitted as an idea. It must be encoded into symbols (spoken or written words, gestures, pictures, etc.). Once encoded, the message is transmitted and received. The receiver must decode the message (the symbols) into meaning. The receiver's response, or feedback, to the source is based on the receiver's perception of the meaning of the message sent. Feedback is encoded, transmitted, and decoded, and so the process continues.

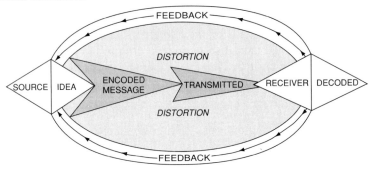

FIGURE 6-1   Process of communication.

Sources of Distortion

Distortion can occur at any and all stages of the process. Perhaps the symbols used were not mutually understood. Perhaps the message sent was confused at the source. Perhaps the receiver received only a part of the message or, because of distorted perception, was not open to receive a clear message.

Because messages are sent and received in some situational context, other elements outside the source and the receiver may contribute to or distort the message. A noisy room, a crowd of people, poor lighting, interruptions in the sending or receiving elements of the process, and even the passage of time (particularly if the message is written) all can affect what is sent and received.

A Continuing Process

Communication has no beginning or end; it is a continuing process. As we analyze the process and provide its "elements" with names and functions, we may sometimes give the false impression that the communication process does have a beginning and an end and that only one message is dealt with at any given time. As a matter of fact, communication in action does occur in sequence but never so simply as it may appear in a diagram. Messages are received and sent simultaneously. Messages from other sources are received in addition to the message received from the identified source, and these other messages may influence the transmission or reception of the original message.

A single message may be received by one receiver, by several individual receivers (some of whom neither the source nor the receiver knew were receiving), or by a group receiving as a group and/or as individuals. Several messages may be sent at once by one source and received as one or many messages by all or some of the above-mentioned receivers. Considering the opportunities for distortion of the message and the number of messages bouncing around at any given time, it is a miracle that we are able to communicate effectively with one another at all (see Figure 6-2).

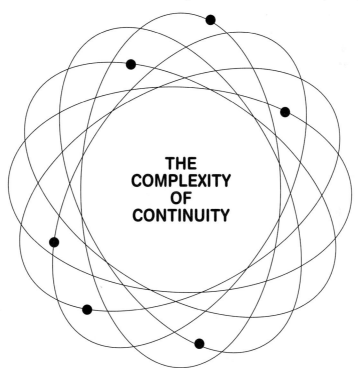

FIGURE 6-2   With so many messages bouncing around at once, effective communication is a miracle.

MODES OF INTERPERSONAL COMMUNICATION[1]

There are three interpersonal channels or modes of communication: *verbal, nonverbal,* and *symbolic. Verbal* communication refers almost totally to the words and

[1]Material in this section is based in part on Institute of Government, *Interpersonal Communication,* University of Georgia, Athens, Ga., 1970.

combinations of words used in the message transmitted (or in feedback, which may again be a message transmitted). Words have no meaning in and of themselves. Meaning is derived from the person and from the context in which words are used.

The *nonverbal* mode can be divided into three subgroups: paralanguage (vocal characteristics), kinesics (body language), and proxemics (personal and social space). Paralanguage includes such elements as diction, the rate and pitch at which a person is speaking, the loudness or softness of speech, and changes in these characteristics during communication (Table 6-1). Proxemics becomes a mode of communication in the manner in which personal space is used. Space may become a territorial issue, an intrusion into privacy. How it is used can increase or decrease social distance. Kinesics includes gestures, body positioning, facial expressions, movement, and the like.

TABLE 6-1
TONE, RHYTHM, AND TEMPO[a]

Statement	Meaning
"I don't care what you do."	Personally, I don't care.
"I *don't* care what you do."	I really *don't*.
"I don't *care* what you do."	Just do as you please, will you.
"I don't care *what* you do."	You have the choice, do what you want.
"I don't care what *you* do."	It doesn't matter to me what you do, but I care about what others do.
"I don't care what you *do*."	It's what you don't do that I'd like to talk about. Just get out of here and leave me alone.

Source: Adapted from materials developed by Cynthia Roed, Tucson, Arizona.

[a]Tone, rhythm, and tempo of speech provide nonverbal cues to the listener as to the meaning being expressed by the speaker. The same words may have a wide variety of meanings.

Symbolic communication, which is often included as a category of the nonverbal mode rather than as a separate channel of communication, occurs continuously at a passive level. We send and receive symbolic messages that we are not always aware of. We make judgments regarding other people based on symbols to which we have assigned meaning and which may have nothing to do with the individual observed. Because symbolic communication is passive, judgments are based on symbolic data that are seldom checked out for their validity. Almost anything can be a meaningful symbol to an individual, but usually symbolic communication includes messages relating to style of dress, place of residence, place (and type) of employment, type of car driven or transportation preferred, jewelry worn (or not worn), and so on (he wears a beard; all persons who wear beards are . . . ; therefore, he is . . .).

VERBAL AND PARALANGUAGE CUES

Articulation

Emerson wrote, "I learn immediately from any speaker how much he has already lived, through the poverty or the splendor of his speech." Lazy speech can be corrected. Pronunciation depends primarily on correct articulation. Articulators are the teeth, tongue, lips, and hard palate. Sounds to pay particular attention to are f,p,b, and v. These sounds are hard to pronounce correctly. As our society becomes more educated, police begin to deal with a larger population possessing a certain standard of pronunciation. Each of us lapses into an occasional "yeah," and there may be situations in which more casual diction or word usage would be appropriate. However, as a norm, sloppy articulation can be annoying, and it is extremely unprofessional. "Kinda," "jist," "gonna," "cause," or "dere" or sentences filled with "you know," "and uh," or "sorta" are examples of sloppy articulation that can be easily corrected if the speaker is aware of the problem. As students in a captive audience, we notice these patterns in an instructor, but it is more difficult to examine our own speech habits objectively and to change them.

Volume and Rate

Everyone has an "Aunt Maude." When she calls, you hold the telephone 6 inches from your ear, and every word is still clearly audible. Coupled with a military uniform, a loud voice will prolong the "redneck cop" stereotype. What is your reaction to a raised voice? If you are like most people, you raise your own. But the police officer has the power to declare a citizen's raised voice disorderly conduct. What if the police officer begins a transaction with a louder tone than normally used socially, and the situation escalates into a shouting match? Is the citizen really at fault?

Our society equates fast speech with excitement. Fight narratives delivered in a staccato nonstop rate add excitement to even a dull match. For police officers, consideration of this fact makes the rate of their speech all-important. As an example, consider this hit-and-run accident. The victim's motorcycle was demolished, and the victim lay sprawled in the middle of rush-hour traffic, bleeding profusely from the head. Despite the obvious necessity for speed, the veteran sergeant on scene communicated slowly and calmly with witnesses before calling in a report. Therefore, he did not heighten an already excited situation. He slowed down the witnesses' rate of speaking and increased the intelligibility of the communication he was receiving. Rate of speech can also be too slow, in which case, words may sound disconnected. When this occurs, the listener may lose both interest and the trend of the thoughts expressed.

Language

Human beings have the almost unconscious ability to turn thoughts into words. The words we choose and how we string them together to express our thoughts are very important to effective communication. Meanings are in people not in the words themselves. Unless the people involved in interpersonal communication have common meaning for the language used, the message will not be mutually understood. Language, then, can become a barrier to communication as well as a tool for effectively achieving it.

Language and its meaning vary from culture to culture. Traditionally, to say that a person is multilingual has meant that the person can communicate in several languages such as Spanish, English, Chinese, or German. Today we also include sign language and computer languages in this list. We also recognize (painfully some-times) that Spanish is not Spanish nor English, English. Meaning and phrasing vary from locale to locale, profession to profession, street to agency, children to adults.

Jargon, the special or technical language used by a group or discipline, probably impedes communication more often than it helps. Officers who employ police jargon when communicating with citizens are likely to confuse and annoy them. They may even create problems for themselves at home. Erma Bombeck chose the topic of "Flu-ent Law Enforcement" for one of her columns. She humorously envisions the follow-ing conversation begun by a wife as she greets her police officer–husband at the door:

> "Hi, honey, dinner will be ready in a few minutes. Who was that I saw you waving to?"
>> "The white Caucasian adult, approximately 62 inches tall, weighing 119 pounds, green eyes, brown hair, and no visible distinguishing marks?"
>> "That's the one."
>> "She has been identified tentatively as our new neighbor, but we'll have to check it out. By the way, where is 11-83?"
>> "I wish you'd stop referring to our son as the code number for 'accident.'"
> (Excerpt from column quoted in *Vanguard,* August 1982, p. 16)

Profanity can be useful for gaining attention or expressing verbal hostility but, in the final analysis, it reduces the user's power to negotiate. Those who want their profanity to upset hearers (or readers) should remember that the more they use a pro-fane expression, the less shocking it is.

Research has shown that the use of profanity by police officers occurs almost exclusively during interactions with certain citizens or categories of citizens (e.g., racial and ethnic minorities, lower-and working-class citizens and other powerless and devalued persons). The use of such language is likely to be restrained and con-trolled in the presence of persons of power and influence (White, Cox, and Basehart, 1994). The use of such language is deliberate and represents previously learned tactics and strategies for the performance of their duties with such categories of people. White, Cox, and Basehart point out that simplistic explanations of officer profanity such as "lack of verbal skills" or "loss of personal control" do not fit reality because it is inconceivable to believe that a police officer would use profanity or obscenities dur-ing a deposition or in court testimony when tensions, stress, frustration, or anger-provoking conditions are high (White, Cox, and Basehart, 1994).

There are at least three interactive contextual dimensions in which the officer might use profanity in his/her dealings with citizens. The first is a personal dimension. That is, an officer uses profanity or obscenity to satisfy his/her own psychological or personal agenda. The officer may build up tensions, frustrations, and anger on the job and find catharsis in verbal expressions. A second dimension is a situational one. Offi-cers use profanity or obscenities as a means of dealing with a variety of stressful situ-ations, such as perceived danger, provocation, and resistance.

The third dimension involves the socialization experiences of the officers. It may be that the socialization experiences of the officer, including his/her training, provides formal and informal definitions of persons or groups as deserving of less than civil treatment. Van Maanen (1978) suggested that some citizens are labeled as "assholes" by the police and treated accordingly.

Intercultural distortion of words can cause great harm. In Spanish *tu madre* means "your mother." In colloquial (street) Spanish it is an offensive phrase. A better choice of terms would be "mama" (Quintanilla, 1983, p. 5). There are many other similar examples. Perhaps the best distortion example involves the Japanese response to our warning in 1945 that we possessed a powerful new weapon, the atomic bomb. The response contained the word *migugostu,* which can mean either abrupt dismissal or "we shall consider it." The American interpreter read it as a rebuff, perhaps wrongly, with tragic consequences for Hiroshima and Nagasaki.

Tone of Voice

In situations where communication is repetitive, it is easy to present a bored, monotonous tone. This insulates the speaker from other people and produces a feeling of coldness. Clergymen repeating the same ritual each week encounter this, as do actors in a long run of a play.

Television viewers can affirm that there are many tones of voice in which the Miranda rights can be delivered. The police dispatcher sighing, "Yesss, lady," into the telephone communicates a very clear but nonverbal message to her.

If we feel depressed, angry at the world, or "hung over," our voice patterns will reflect our feeling in inflection and intonation of words. A professional police officer deals largely with a "captive" clientele. However resistant clients may feel, they must relate in some way to the officer. What the officer expresses in paralanguage may not be reported to superiors, but may have great impact on the police department's image in the community.

Telephone Cues

Victor Strecher, discussing police conduct on the telephone, states, "Voice, diction, reaction to the citizen's call, approach to the problem, and basic etiquette are the criteria of judgment. Here again, negative evaluations cannot be reversed. The police telephone response can easily predispose a complainant to a favorable or unfavorable reception of the radio car officers who later respond to this request. Those who neglect telephone courtesy will not overcome the deficiency in police image through the correctness of their uniform and their approach to service calls" (Strecher, 1971, p. 104).

Listening to one's own voice over a tape recorder is effective feedback for analyzing presentation. Objective self-criticism is difficult but necessary. Just as officers must check their uniforms and equipment, a periodic evaluation of voice is equally important It is a matter of training the ear to hear what is and is not of value.

The telephone voice characterized as bad is expressionless, mechanical, indifferent, impatient, and inattentive. Although the officer may come across as "tough" in the station, the receiver of the communication in turn, may come across as a bristly, hostile citizen the next time he or she encounters an officer. The police officer seeking information by phone might find citizens more receptive to providing it, if positive telephone communication techniques are used by the officer.

Following are the basic rules of police telephone conduct:

1. Be courteous at all times, especially when things are a mess.
2. Avoid slang.
3. Be brief, but clear and concise. Use complete sentences. Organize your thoughts in advance, particularly if you are initiating the call.
4. Speak clearly in as relaxed a voice as possible, directly into the mouthpiece.
5. Do not eat or drink when making a phone call to a client or receiving one.
6. Picture the person at the other end of the line sympathetically. Talk to that person, not to the telephone.
7. Keep the receiver close to your ear, and listen to what is being said verbally and nonverbally.
8. If you must consult with someone, put the client on hold if such equipment is available. Nothing is more aggravating, nor presents a more unprofessional image, than monitoring a shouted conversation.
9. Letters and numbers will obviously play a crucial part of police phone communication. Take care when pronouncing them, thus avoiding incorrect spelling, misunderstanding, and repetition. Effective enunciation requires that every sound be given its proper value.
10. As much as humanly possible, refrain from interrupting the other person; allow the person to finish what he or she wants to say. However, emergency phone calls that involve agitated citizens may require firmer guidance to get the proper information.

KINESICS AND PROXEMICS CUES

Correct interpretation by officers of cues communicated by suspects through body language and use of social and personal space has saved many police lives and prevented many crimes. Without the use of such cues, a major police function that is sometimes taken for granted—directing traffic—could not be accomplished.

Best-seller lists have featured several books on nonverbal cues. These books concentrate primarily on three concepts: body motion and positioning (kinesics) as a communication device; the use of personal and social space (proxemics); and the influence of certain clothing (symbolic) on ourselves and on others. Much of how we perceive ourselves is modeled in these ways.

Body Language

Julius Fast, author of *Body Language,* notes that sometimes our body cues reinforce our words, and at other times they may contradict one another. For example, a calm, emotionless face that is accompanied by active arms, hands, legs, and feet is a distinctive feature of deception no matter what is said (Broughman, 1992, p. 16). The human body is the least controllable nonverbal channel of communication.

The Kinesic Interview Technique, taught at seminars throughout the country; the U.S. Army Military Police School at Fort McClellan, Alabama; numerous police academies; and law enforcement agencies at the local state and federal levels, relies on unconscious verbal and nonverbal behaviors to reveal deception (Link, 1993). The first rule of this technique is to watch for breaks in eye contact as an indication that the interviewee is lying. This body language cue is hard to control when one is talking to another.

The Meaning of the Message

Stress is often demonstrated in nonverbal ways, particularly in body language. Anger, too, denied verbally, may be "clearly" stated in kinesics (and proxemics) through clenched fists, muscle tautness, abruptness of manner, perspiration in the palms, and shaping of personal space (e.g., becoming very "turf"-centered, pacing back and forth, etc.). Many interrogators and polygraph examiners suggest that some of the same symptoms may occur in the person who is lying—willingly and knowingly relating something other than the truth. They also describe other changes in physiological and biological processes, such as change in pulse rate, perspiration flow, change in skin color, and so on (Abrams, 1989).

Although changes in body language do have meaning, the meaning is not always apparent. What may seem to be evidence of a lie may be concern for a loved one; what may appear to be staggering and falling from drunkenness may instead be caused by a physiological disorder. We may accurately recognize a symptom, but not correctly assess what it is a symptom of. Lie detection through the use of the polygraph is supported by psychophysiologist David Raskin and challenged by psychologist David Lykken. Both agree, however, that in verifying the truthfulness of innocent subjects, "the lie detector turns up more innocent people found guilty—false positives—than guilty people found innocent" (Meyer, 1982, p. 26). As discussed in earlier chapters, what we see, hear, and smell is personalized through our perception process. Officers should be very aware of kinesics but also very cautious in drawing conclusions regarding the meaning of messages received without checking out their hunches through other feedback options.

The Officer's Message

In addition to being aware of messages received through the body language of others, police officers need to be very aware of the messages transmitted through their own body language. Police officers may express boredom, interest, disgust, disrespect, anger, frustration, acceptance, authority, nervousness, and any number of other emotions through body language alone. An officer's body language may calm or ignite a situation. A youth gang member may act on what he interprets in an officer's body language cues to be an insult. It is a rare veteran offender who does not guess, before any words are exchanged, who the new police officers and correctional service officers are, and proceed to test those people.

Personal Space

A Territorial Imperative

Nonverbal cues are probably displayed most prominently in Western peoples' use of proxemics, personal space. People tend to establish, or stake out, their own territory. Robert Ardrey (1966) traced this concept to biological inheritance, examining how animals establish certain territories. Fast (1981) relates a delightful anecdote in his book in which he experiments with a friend in a restaurant by moving his silverware and dishes, piece by piece, as if inadvertently, into the other man's table space. His friend became noticeably upset. Establishing territorial space is also illustrated by the behavior of students in the classroom: After high school, the "assigned-seat-alphabetical-order" arrangements cease, but notice how students tend to occupy the same territory in college classrooms. You may find yourself slightly irritated when someone occupies "your space."

Identifying Territory

We identify territory as ours by spreading our books or dishes over a table, putting our pictures on the wall, putting our name on the mailbox, or graffiti on a neighborhood boundary. Even on the job, we attempt to maintain a work area that is ours. If it is not respected, we are uneasy, somewhat confused, and at least mildly annoyed.

Territory in police work is identified in many ways: jurisdictional boundaries, district boundaries, the agency's organizational structure, job description, and so on. Territory can also be defined in the sense of level of discretionary decision making, or which car an officer drives.

The very need for territory sometimes interferes with the need for change. Change can be viewed as territorial infringement, and it may require that new boundaries be set. The issue of territory and change may become a major problem of police–community relations. It can be an issue for an individual officer or team, for two warring youth gangs, or for a neighborhood threatened by new freeway construction.

Interpersonal Space

Generally, the rules that "regulate" our use of personal space are implicit. Formal business requires a different use of distance than does friendship. What is comfortable and acceptable may depend both upon the nature of the activity and the relationship. Hall (1966) identified four basic personal space zones:

1. *Intimate distance,* extending to about 18 inches from the skin. This is reserved space. Intimate activities include lovemaking, cuddling, massaging.
2. *Personal distance,* about $1^1/_2$ to 4 feet from the body. Interactions with friends and people we care about are allowed in this space.
3. *Social distance,* about 4 to 12 feet. Impersonal and casual business is conducted at this distance.

4. *Public distance,* more than 12 feet. Formal interactions, lectures, and speeches take place at this distance.

The Message of Proxemics

Police officers violate, or invade, a person's space, sometimes deliberately and sometimes without intending to, causing the invaded person to move away or become (sometimes act) defensive. Brougham (1992, p. 16) reports that successful police interviewers create a high level of anxiety in a suspect by beginning an interview in a comfortable distance when they are discussing general information. Then the inter-viewer will move closer to the suspect when questioning on key points and back off during desired responses. He states that this practice serves to program a person to cooperate with the interviewer's line of questioning.

Physical obstacles may prevent effective communication. The authority figure sitting behind a desk places an obstacle between self and client. This use of proxemics says, "You must obey me. I am your superior." As Fast (1981) observed: "We learn certain tricks of domination to control a situation. We can arrange to be higher than our subordinates, or we can allow our boss to be higher than we are. We can be aware that we dominate our children when we hover over them" (p. 90). The act of stopping a vehicle is structured to place the police officer in an authoritative position. The citi-zen remains seated in his or her car, while the officer occupies "territory" over the individual.

Movement across social distances in our culture also distorts communication and causes feelings of anxiety. Huseman and McCurley (1972), in a study of police communication behaviors, found that police officers experience most of their prob-lems in communicating with minority groups.

SYMBOLIC CUES

From birth we are taught to attach great importance to symbolic cues. A symbol is something that stands for something else. They carry a meaning that is recognized by members of a culture (Macionis, 1993, p. 65). Virtually all interaction between human beings involves the use of symbols. We are constantly looking for "clues" about the appropriate behavior in social situations.

The criminal justice system makes use of a number of symbols. The scales of justice convey the meaning that the system is blind to personal distinctions as it goes about evaluating evidence and judging guilt or innocence. The blue or red lights sig-nal the presence of an emergency vehicle. Traffic signs present various symbols that tell us what to do as we drive. Police officers use a variety of socially understood sym-bols, uniforms, nightsticks, other weapons, badges, and so on.

Generally speaking, the police uniform is a symbol of authority. In situations where the officer is regarded as the person who can take command of a situation and solve a crisis, the uniform speaks positively in the police–citizen interaction. In situa-tions where the officer is regarded as the enemy or as the scapegoat, the uniform becomes a negative symbolic cue, interfering with positive interaction between the officer and citizen. A veteran officer in a police–community relations class remarked, "If I approach a citizen to give a ticket, and push my hat back on my head, hook my thumb in my belt buckle and smile, I'm in for trouble."

Realizing that the uniform itself is sometimes a negative symbolic cue to citizens, some departments have experimented with dressing officers in blazers, thus softening their image. Although studies regarding the practice have been inconclusive, interviews with police administrators indicate that street experience in most areas has led them to vary the use of the blazer and uniform depending upon a number of factors. Key factors mentioned include (1) type of activity, and (2) characteristics of citizens involved (age, level of initial hostility to police).

OFFICIAL COMMUNICATION

Verbal, nonverbal, and *symbolic cues* have relevance in the dimension of official communication. Awareness of language, its usage, and its impact are very important in written communications. The opportunity to gain immediate feedback (and therefore to determine whether or not the message received was the one sent) is not available. Certain words carry more importance than others in writing.

Paralanguage, the power of what is not said, is also critical in official communication. Written word is read without the sender's inflection. It should be reviewed carefully by the sender for any unintended ambiguity and fragmented statements.

Proxemics, in the sense of social space, may be expressed or challenged implicitly or explicitly in official communication. Territorial issues may be generated or resolved in intradepartmental memos. Reports may make positive or negative use of jurisdictional power and limitations.

Symbolic meaning is attached to whether or not official communication is written on letterhead (or on which letterhead), in a proper format, length of the document, quality of paper, original or copy, by whom it is signed, and so on.

ACHIEVING EFFECTIVE COMMUNICATION

Communicating effectively requires ongoing effort in sharpening skills. It does not happen by chance, nor is it something that can be tucked away in a uniform pocket and pulled out at the appropriate opportunity. Skills learned must be applied in many different ways and in as many different situations. What works best in one situation may not be the best choice in another.

One thing is certain, however. Effective communication is essential to positive police–community relations. Its power can scarcely be overestimated. Its success is incredible; its failure disastrous.

EFFECTIVE LISTENING

Listening as a Mental Exercise

Hearing is the act or power of perceiving sound. Hearing with normal ears is an automatic process, but listening is a mental exercise. Radio and television broadcasters are continually concerned with how many people are hearing their programs. However, the question, Does anybody listen? seems immaterial to them. This is a radically different question. It asks: Does anyone understand my idea, my intention, my message? Does anybody care?

Americans are not effective listeners. In general they talk more than they listen. As one theorist states, "It is really not difficult to learn to listen—just unusual." Many of us, while ostensibly listening, are actually preparing a statement to "stun" the company when we gain the floor. A good relationship between listener and speaker is necessary in a conversation—in fact, an effective *listener* leads the conversation. John F. Kennedy was famous for the incisive questions he asked and the way he listened to replies. Robert Saudek, who conferred with him at the White House while producing "Profiles in Courage" for television, later told friends, "He made you think he had nothing else to do except ask you questions and listen—with extraordinary concentration—to your answers. You knew that for the time being he had blotted out both the past and the future. More than anyone else I have ever met, President Kennedy seemed to understand the importance of *now*." We all crave good listeners. Sporadic or half-attentive listening are easily detected through nonverbal feedback cues received by the source.

Effective listening is important in any occupation. However, it is especially important in police–community relations. Miscommunication between citizens and police officers can have disastrous, if not fatal consequences.

Nonjudgmental Listening

Carl Rogers outlined the idea of nonjudgmental listening in his book, *On Becoming a Person:* "I would like to propose, as an hypothesis for consideration, that the major barrier to mutual interpersonal communication is our very natural tendency to judge, evaluate, to approve or disapprove the statement of the other person or the other group" (Rogers, 1961, p. 328). Rogers goes on to state that real communication occurs when one listens with understanding, trying to place himself in the other person's position. This is most difficult in highly emotional situations—the kinds of situations criminal justice personnel often deal with. When a police officer encounters similar situations, such as quarrels in the same family over and over again, the officer may have a strong desire to "tune out." It is precisely that behavior which is ineffective.

In many Wisconsin communities, suburban police departments employ a "court officer" who serves as liaison between the district attorney and his department. One such officer encountered continued friction with a fellow officer over the matter of ticket dismissals. "The law is the law," the second officer adamantly stated. It did not matter to him whether or not the defendant had good reason for clemency from the judge; he would not listen to explanations but merely delivered lengthy tirades. Suddenly the duty roster rotated the men, and this officer became—you guessed it—the court officer. In a few weeks his entire attitude changed completely. He learned to listen to complete explanations.

Weaver summarizes, "All this really means is that in order to understand a verbal message well, you must understand the talker to some degree. This makes communicating with a total stranger somewhat difficult when you get above the level of asking or giving directions or talking about the weather" (Weaver, 1972, p. 88). In *Future Shock*, Toffler (1970) spoke of the increasing number of short-duration relationships, particularly in service occupations, and pointed out the difficulty of a professional attempting to listen and communicate with increasingly large numbers of people.

Listening Efficiency

Tests on listening show repeatedly that people have an average listening efficiency of only 25 percent. (This varies—some people can retain up to 70 percent and others, only up to 10 percent.) Listening is not an easy, passive process. It is hard work, characterized by faster heart action, increased circulation of the blood, and a small rise in body temperature.

Most people talk at a speed of about 125 words a minute. Strong evidence exists which indicates that if thought were measured in words per minute, most of us could think easily at about four times that rate. It is extremely difficult to slow down thinking time; thus we normally have about 400 words of thinking time to spare during every minute a person talks to us. What do we do with that excess thinking time while someone is speaking?

In interpersonal relationships we too often prepare our next comment; in formal situations, as the speaker bores us, we become impatient and turn our thoughts to something else. Soon the side thought trips become too enticing, and when we attempt to return to the speaker, we are lost. Effective listeners use their thought speed to advantage, not side trips. They constantly apply their spare thinking time to what is being said.

Some Effective Listening Facilitators

1. Be prepared to listen. Rid yourself of as many distractions as possible.
2. Be an attentive listener. Observe the speaker for verbal and nonverbal cues that will increase your understanding of the speaker and the subject.
3. Be willing to risk becoming involved as a participant in, not just as an observer of, the communication.
4. Avoid prejudging what is being said and interrupting to offer criticism or advice.
5. Genuinely accept the other person's feelings and recognize his or her right to have views that differ from yours.
6. Offer feedback to the speaker, not in the form of judgments as to the "rightness" or "wrongness" of what was said, but in the form of a restatement and clarification of what was said both in terms of objective reality and in terms of the speaker's perceptions of and feelings about that reality (What I am hearing is . . .), (Are you saying that . . .).

THE EMPATHIC QUALITY

The squad car is repeatedly cited as the great insulator in police work, as are heavy caseloads for probation and parole officers. Given the police officer in the squad, the changing nature of neighborhoods, and the sheer numbers of people dealt with in human relations occupations, people in these professions will need to develop high degrees of trust quickly, as will society. In reply to a questionnaire, one police officer answered, "I do my work impartially and without emotion."

Imagine that you are an elderly woman. Your only income is your social security check, which is very small. As you are walking to the grocery store, a man attacks you from behind and takes your purse, containing the only money you have. You are knocked to the ground. You sit there, dazed and bewildered. Someone calls the police, and soon two officers arrive. They begin immediately to fill out their report. They take information from you, asking you short and specific questions. The officers are doing their job impartially and without emotion. They are not sharing themselves with you, and were they to take the time to understand your feelings, they would not only have to spend more time with you but they would also have to deal with their own feelings. The method used by the police officers insulates them from their own emotional involvement with you and is expeditious and efficient. But how are you feeling about their humaneness?

People entering the criminal justice profession need to possess a very special communication quality. Unlike the development of voice or listening skills, this concept has a rather vague aesthetic nature. It is called empathy, and theorists maintain that those entering people-oriented professions need to have large amounts of it. It is a caring attitude, the developed capacity to understand another, and to comprehend another's feelings, attitudes, or sentiments.

In its most extreme example, those persons who are unable to comprehend another's feelings, attitudes, or sentiments are sociopathic or psychopathic personalities. They are incapable of experiencing normal amounts of love or empathy (Levin and Fox, 1985, pp. 71–72). Psychologists speculate that some people become sociopaths because they have been rejected in their family relationships and cannot form social bonds. They often engage in various forms of misbehavior, cheating, lying, and for the most severely effected, rape and murder (Ressler, Burgess, and Douglas, 1988).

BLOCKS TO EFFECTIVE COMMUNICATION

When community relations efforts fail, at least one of the following blocks has contributed to that failure: (1) community distrust of the police; (2) police distrust of community members; (3) poor training of police; (4) the organizational structure of the police agency; and (5) scapegoating.

Community Distrust of Police

If the citizens do not trust the police, they will not talk to them: They will avoid police contact. Therefore, if distrust causes avoidance and failure to communicate, the implications for the police organization are very dramatic. Citizens will not report crime; they will not give statements to officers who are investigating crimes; and they will not testify in court. The result is inefficiency and an unsafe community.

Police Distrust of Community

If the police view the community or some geographical part of the community they have sworn to protect as dangerous and full of people who are hostile to them, police will react in a negative way. They will not feel free to communicate with the community and will be guarded and cautious when they come in contact with those they are protecting. As a result, police officers will contribute to widening the gap between themselves and the rest of the community. Their belief system will be reinforced by negative community contacts. Eventually police officers will become fearful and hostile toward the very people they are supposed to be protecting and serving.

Poor Training

The training of police officers has significantly improved in recent years. However, the training curriculum of most police academies is heavily weighted on those skills necessary to perform the law enforcement task. This law enforcement task occupies a small portion of the officers' time. A recent study of recruitment, selection, and probationary training in major U.S. police departments (over 500 officers) found that only two of the 80 police departments surveyed devoted 20 percent or more of the initial training time to interpersonal skills (Strawbridge and Strawbridge, 1990). The majority of the time was spent on police procedures, law, weapons training, driver training, self-defense, and first aid. Conflict management and sensitivity were two of the areas mentioned under interpersonal skills, but these were not taught in all academies, even those that offered numerous interpersonal skills hours.

Consequently, dedicated and responsible officers may be placed on the street unprepared for the experiences they will face. They do not have a clear understanding of the true attitudes of the public they are policing. They may not have an appreciation of the historical factors that shaped the larger community and its neighborhoods. They may not understand the sources of the fears and prejudices of the people in the community, including themselves. They may not be trained in the techniques necessary to defuse dangerous situations with finesse or to seek alternatives to arrest. Unfortunately, they are too often taught to respond to threats or hostility with force.

Lack of training in such subjects as introduction to social theory, basic psychology, human development and behavior, minority history, constitutional law, ethnic studies, interpersonal relations, and communication skills allows communication blocks to remain intact.

Organizational Structure

The majority of America's police departments are paramilitary organizations. There are "chains of command," defined areas of responsibilities, volumes of rules and regulations, and a clear hierarchy of memberships. Police organizations have chiefs, deputy chiefs, captains, sergeants, and patrol officers, and many large organizations carry the military tradition even further, using the ranks of colonel, major, and corporal in the organizational structure.

The results of the paramilitary structure being used for a police service organization are well described by Egon Bittner:

> Another complex of mischievous consequences arising out of the military bureaucracy relates to the paradoxical fact that while this kind of discipline ordinarily strengthens command authority it has the opposite effect in police departments. This effect is insidious rather than apparent. Because police superiors do not direct the activity of officers in any important sense, they are perceived as mere disciplinarians.
>
> Contrary to the army officer who is expected to lead his men into battle—even though he may never have a chance to do it—the analogously ranked police official is someone who can only do a great deal to his subordinates and very little for them. For this reason supervisory personnel are often viewed by the line personnel with distrust and even contempt. (Bittner, 1970, p. 59)

An even more important consideration is that the paramilitary organizational structure not only blocks effective communication within the organization because of the superior/subordinate relationship, but the same working relationship inevitably is transferred to contacts between patrol officers and citizens.

Scapegoating

Allport (1954) defined scapegoating as "a phenomenon wherein some of the aggressive energies of a person or a group are focused upon another individual, group or object; the amount of aggression and blame being either partly or wholly unwarranted."

In more specific terms, police have often focused their attention on particular groups or individuals when such attention was really unwarranted.

There are a number of steps that precede scapegoating. If we are aware of the progression, we will be able to spot the danger signs and take action before a serious problem occurs. These steps are (1) simple preferences, (2) active biases, (3) prejudice, (4) discrimination, and (5) full-fledged scapegoating.

Simple Preferences

We all have preferences—we like people who agree with us, who have similar backgrounds, and who share our value system. Our socialization process in many overt and subtle ways teaches us to prefer spaghetti to curry, gefilte fish to soul food, blondes to brunettes, or Cadillacs to Fords. This simple preference for one food or one type of person to another is both natural and inevitable. A technical term for this simple preference is predilection.

Active Biases

Here the simple preference turns stronger. People state their preference in negative terms, instead of saying, "I prefer spaghetti to curry." The statement might be "I don't like curry," or "I don't like Jewish food." An active bias is the stepping-off point toward a closed mind, an ineffective person, and an uninformed person. It immediately precedes a full-blown prejudice.

Prejudice

Many people have prejudices, which means that they have a tendency to prejudge certain groups, persons, or events. It is a prejudgment that is rigid and inflexible. Although a prejudice does no great social harm as long as it is not acted out, in the case of people involved in public service, it is extremely difficult not to let a prejudice affect judgment.

Discrimination

This is an act of exclusion prompted by prejudice. The most commonly accepted examples are discrimination against blacks and Hispanics by white society. This discrimination has manifested itself in different ways: employment, housing, health care, and other social institutions. Although significant progress has been made, discrimination is one of America's most significant social problems and a problem that profoundly affects American police and their level of professionalism.

Racial and ethnic groups have, in the past, been systematically excluded from police service and from promotional appointments. Affirmative Action programs have had an impact on this systematic exclusion. According to a study commissioned by the Police Executive Research Forum (PERF), the estimates of blacks, Hispanics, and other racial/ethnic groups in 486 police agencies serving populations of 50,000 or more are very close to the current Census Bureau estimates for the population (Carter, Sapp, and Stephens, 1989, p. 39). Although this is cause for optimism, it does not signal an end to discrimination in the hiring practices of police agencies or discriminatory behavior on the part of individual officers. There are still police officers who look upon minorities as being unworthy, unwanted, and unacceptable as human beings. The Rodney King beating in Los Angeles once again raises the specter of police discrimination against minorities.

Full-Fledged Scapegoating

Scapegoating manifests itself after all the preceding steps are fulfilled. It consists of concentrated aggression in both word and deed. The victim is abused both physically and verbally. The persons or group being scapegoated are often given credit for astounding power and evil, as in the following examples: "The Jews are ruining America"; "Ship all blacks back to Africa and crime will stop"; "Wetbacks (Mexicans) are responsible for all of California's labor problems"; and "All teenagers are inherently lazy." When such statements are seen in print they are easily identified by anyone with average intelligence as simplistic statements. Yet many people make these statements day after day and, unfortunately, they believe what they are saying.

Why Scapegoating Occurs

Allport (1954) identifies a number of reasons for the phenomena of scapegoating. Among them are: "tabloid thinking," self-enhancement, peer pressure and conformity, fear and anxiety, and displaced aggression. Some of these are discussed more fully on the following pages.

Tabloid Thinking

This is the process in which people simplify a problem by blaming a group or class of people. For example, some people blame crime on illegal drug abuse; they feel that most crime is committed by drug-dependent people trying to get money to feed their habit. Although these people do commit crime, in reality they are responsible for only a small percentage of the crime rate. This tabloid-thinking process allows people to overlook real issues while they focus on the wrong object.

Illegal drugs are sometimes "the wrong object." Illegal drugs are those that we frequently define as dangerous substances. These substances include heroin, cocaine, LSD, angel dust, marijuana, certain prescription drugs, and many others. These represent a wide assortment of substances with many different sources, prices, and resulting behaviors. The most damaging, commonly abused drug in our society is not included in the list; it is alcohol. Under most circumstances it is not illegal to use. In tabloid thinking, it is not even recognized as a drug.

Considering the extent of the problem, efforts to prevent the crime, injury, and death caused by alcohol are very limited in the United States, with the exception of a recent tightening of laws relating to DWI/DUI (Driving While Intoxicated/Driving Under the Influence) behavior. We are more likely to use our resources fighting illegal drug use. Tabloid thinking is a type of tunnel vision, that by omitting all the facts, may encourage us to focus all our energies on the wrong battle.

Self-Enhancement

Some people have inferiority complexes. People who are experienced in interviewing police applicants often discover individuals who want to join the police department because they feel that having a badge and a gun will make them something they are not; that is, strong, more respected, or allowed to exercise control or authority over other people. Such applicants are serious liabilities to the police profession if they slip through the screening process. They will cause many communication blocks with the community through their scapegoating of others to cover their own inferiority. This type of person is also dangerous because he or she is often afraid; this personal fear often results in the use of excessive force. The use of such force when it is not warranted leads to a breakdown in communication between the police and the community.

Peer Pressure and Conformity

The need to belong to a group or organization is very strong in most people. New officers who join an organization that engages in scapegoating will find themselves joining with their fellow officers just so they can be part of the group. This is particularly evident when a new officer is coupled with an "old-timer." Too often the officer ends up acting like the trainer.

STRATEGIES OF CHANGE

Toward Achieving Mutual Respect

Mutual respect is achieved best in an atmosphere in which everyone counts. If I make promises that I cannot keep, or make decisions that affect your life without considering your needs or your views, I am discounting you. If you treat me as if I am a category rather than a person, you discount me.

Strategies for overcoming blocks in the area of mutual respect include establishing programs that encourage honest, open exchange and positive personal contact between citizens and officers. Some of the options include:

- Increasing the number of walking police beats.
- Decentralizing functional police units.
- Implementing police–community projects in which shared decision making actually occurs.
- Assuring that ride-along programs involve not only the youth and adults who already have respect for the police, but those who are distrustful.
- Establishing and supporting creative educational liaison projects.
- Initiating projects that survey citizen input and make changes based on the results of the survey.
- Participating in a community communication network designed to decrease problems with rumors and misunderstandings.
- Participating in a proactive social service action program.
- Involving volunteers in most areas of the police process.
- Assisting individual officers to increase their skills in analyzing the factors existing in each situation and selecting an interpersonal communication approach that is most congruent with existing needs.

Improving Training

Police training is an intense experience which has improved immensely in the last 20 years. Ways in which training can change to improve effective communication in police–community relations include:

- Building the academy and in-service training content on a basic humanistic philosophy.
- Incorporating the teaching of more effective communication skills in ongoing workshops for officers.
- Placing a greater emphasis and more academy hours on service concepts and issues.
- Encouraging educational goals of officers, especially in seeking professional and liberal arts and sciences degrees.
- Assuring that street training experience for new officers supports the philosophy and content of the academy.

Rethinking Police Organization

Realistically, reorganization in police agencies is traumatic, and it is difficult to conceive, achieve, and retain. Some communication blocks seem inherent in the organizational structure. Small system changes, however, can help to reduce the number and influence of these blocks. Suggestions include:

- Requiring management training seminars for all key management personnel.
- Using noncertified personnel in some key positions.
- Developing a reward system that places a high agency value on individual effective communication efforts.
- Increasing opportunities for exchange between line officers and top administration.
- Incorporating a "quality circle" concept into the organization to assure that all personnel are valued in the organization.
- Committing the organization to a single (rather than contradictory) philosophy that encourages personal growth and community service.

Preventing Scapegoating

Efforts that increase mutual respect also will help to decrease scapegoating. Humanistic training efforts help to prevent the problem, sometimes by screening out recruits whose actions already demonstrate discrimination and scapegoating attitudes. Organizational changes that encourage personal growth and community service help to discourage scapegoating. Other strategies that focus on the individual officer might include:

- Providing opportunities for the officer to become more self-aware.
- Increasing opportunities for personal values clarification.
- Rewarding actions that demonstrate a lack of bias.
- Providing counseling opportunities.
- Providing opportunities for the officer to experience exceptions to stereotypes.

CONCLUSIONS

The quality of police–community relations depends on the quality of police–community communication, and vice versa. This chapter has focused on the continuous, ongoing communication process and the possible blocks to this process. Communication occurs on many levels. It is intrapersonal, interpersonal, person-to-group, and written. It includes the elements of sender, receiver, and message in a situational context.

There are three basic modes of interpersonal communication: (1) verbal; (2) non-verbal (paralanguage, kinesics or body language, and proxemics or communication through the use of personal or social space); and (3) symbolic (the messages conveyed by style of dress, personal appearance, one's possessions, etc.). Cues exist for each mode that an effective communicator must learn to recognize and use. For example, a police officer who wants to use language and paralanguage well must pay attention to articulation of words, volume and rate of speech, tone of voice, choice of language, and (when necessary) telephone manner. The officer must also be aware of the effect of body positions, use of space, clothing, and personal appearance on communications.

An effective communicator is someone who not only sends but also receives messages well. Unlike hearing, listening is a mental exercise. People can "think" words much faster than they can speak or listen to them; effective listeners are those who apply their spare thinking time to what is being said—and who try to place themselves "in the speaker's shoes" in a nonjudgmental way.

Effective communicators are aware of themselves and others in a situational context. They determine what message(s) is appropriate to send and then couch it in an approach that they feel will most effectively achieve their goals. A communication quality that is especially important in the administration is empathy. Free, open communication with other members of the community is possible only for the person who can empathize with others.

In this chapter we have also explored five common blocks to effective communication in police–community relations: community distrust of the police, police distrust of the community, poor training, police organizational issues, and scapegoating. We have also identified strategies for change that can eliminate or lessen these blocks to communication. Many of these strategies will be further explored in later chapters.

STUDENT CHECKLIST

1. Identify and describe three levels of communication.
2. Define and diagram the communication process.
3. Identify and give examples of the modes of communication.
4. What is effective listening?
5. What is the role of empathy in communication?
6. List the blocks to effective communication most frequently encountered in police–community relations.
7. List the strategies for change that could eliminate or lessen the blocks to effective police–community communication.

TOPICS FOR DISCUSSION

1. Why is nonjudgmental listening an important skill for police officers to have?
2. When would it not be useful to be an effective listener?
3. How can you be assured of getting feedback in the communication process?
4. Discuss the common blocks to effective communication between police and citizens mentioned in this chapter in relationship to your own community.

5. What programs identified in strategies for change might remove the blocks to effective communication that exist in your community?

6. Discuss the difference between active bias and simple preference.

ONE STEP FORWARD

Is It a Fact or an Inference? A Communication Game[2]

A *statement of fact* is an observation that is verifiable. An *inference* is a conclusion or opinion; a subjective evaluation. Both are a necessary part of police work. Some of our greatest problems occur when we confuse the two. This exercise will help you learn the difference between statements of fact and inferences and gain a better understanding of the way in which inferences are made.

In this game, you will read three reports and answer questions about them. Then you will have an opportunity to check your answers.

Directions: Read each report twice. Then answer the questions that relate to that situation.

Situation A

John and Betty Smith are awakened in the middle of the night by a noise coming from the direction of their living room. Smith investigates and finds that the door opening into the garden, which he thought he had locked before going to bed, is standing wide open. Books and papers are scattered all over the floor, around the desk in one corner of the room.

Situation B

A businessman had just turned off the lights in the store when a man appeared and demanded money. The owner opened a cash register. The contents of the cash register were scooped up, and the man sped away. A member of the police force was notified promptly.

Situation C

Members of the 12th Street Gang are planning an assault on the 4th Avenue Gang. Two days ago a 4th Avenue Gang member was in 12th Street territory. Tires on a car were slashed.

Testing Your Skills

Directions: After reading each report twice *and without returning to the report for review,* answer the questions related to that situation below by circling the correct

[2]This exercise is based on a game entitled "Inference Versus Observation," in *Interpersonal Communication: A Guide for Staff Development.* Athens, Ga.: Institute of Government, University of Georgia, 1974.

response. Mark "T" if the statement is definitely true on the basis of the information given in the report. Mark "F" if the statement is definitely false. Marking a "?" means that you cannot be certain on the basis of the information given in the report. If any part of the statement is doubtful, mark "?".

Statements About Situation A

T F 1. Mrs. Smith was awakened in the middle of the night.
T F 2. Smith locked the door from his living room to his garden before going to bed.
T F 3. The books and papers were scattered between the time Smith went to bed and the time he was awakened.
T F 4. Smith found that the door opening into the garden was shut.
T F 5. Mr. Smith did not lock the garden door.
T F 6. John Smith was not awakened by a noise.
T F 7. Nothing was missing from the room.
T F 8. Mrs. Smith was sleeping when she and Mr. Smith were awakened.
T F 9. The noise did not come from their garden.
T F 10. Smith saw no burglar in the living room.
T F 11. Mr. and Mrs. Smith were awakened in the middle of the night by a noise.

Statements About Situation B

T F 1. A man appeared after the owner had turned off his store lights.
T F 2. The robber was a man.
T F 3. The man did not demand money.
T F 4. The man who opened the cash register was the owner.
T F 5. The store owner scooped up the contents of the cash register and ran away.
T F 6. Someone opened a cash register.
T F 7. After the man who demanded the money scooped up the contents of the cash register, he ran away.
T F 8. Although the cash register contained money, the report does not state how much.
T F 9. The robber demanded money of the owner.
T F 10. The report concerns a series of events in which only three persons are referred to: the owner of the store, a man who demanded money, and a member of the police force.
T F 11. The following events were included in the report: someone demanded money, a cash register was opened, its contents were scooped up, and a man dashed out of the store.

Statements About Situation C

T F 1. One of the boys from the 4th Avenue Gang was in 12th Street territory.

T F 2. The 4th Avenue Gang is a youth gang.

T F 3. The leaders of the 12th Street Gang are planning an assault.

T F 4. Three tires on a car were slashed.

T F 5. The car in the story was in 12th Street Gang territory.

T F 6. One of the 12th Street Gang members was in 4th Avenue territory.

T F 7. The tires were slashed by a 4th Avenue Gang member.

T F 8. The car belongs to a 12th Street Gang member.

T F 9. The 12th Street Gang is a youth gang.

T F 10. The slashing of the tires was a deliberate attack on the 12th Street Gang.

T F 11. The member of the 4th Avenue Gang was in 12th Street territory to challenge the 12th Street Gang.

BIBLIOGRAPHY

Abrams, S. (1989) *The Complete Polygraph Handbook.* Lexington, MA: Lexington Books.

Allport, G. W. (1954) *The Nature of Prejudice.* New York: Doubleday.

Ardrey, R. (1966) *The Territorial Imperative.* New York: Atheneum.

Bittner, E. (1970) *The Functions of the Police in Modern Society.* Bethesda, Md.: National Institute of Mental Health.

Bombeck, E. (1982) "He Spoke Fluent Law Enforcement," in *Vanguard,* Official Publication of the San Jose Peace Officers Association II, August: 16.

Brougham, C. G. (1992) "Nonverbal Communication: can what they don't say give them away?" *FBI Law Enforcement Bulletin,* July: 15–18.

Carter, D. L., Sapp, A. D., and Stephens, D. W. (1989) *The State of Police Education: Policy Direction for the 21st Century.* Washington, D.C.: Police Executive Research Forum.

Fast, J. (1981) *Body Language.* New York: Pocket Books.

Hall, E. T. (1966) *The Hidden Dimension.* Garden City, N.Y.: Doubleday.

Huseman, R., and McCurley, S. (1972) "Police Attitudes Toward Communication with the Public," *The Police Chief 39,* December.

Institute of Government, (1970) *Interpersonal Communication: A Guide for Staff Development.* University of Georgia, Athens, Ga.

Levin, J. and Fox, J. A. (1985) *Mass Murder: America's Growing Menace.* New York: Plenum Press.

Link, F. (1993) *The Interrotec® Kinesic Interview Technique: A Short Course in Detecting Deception Behaviorally,* February 27 seminar at Ft. McClellan, AL.

Macionis, J. (1993) *Sociology,* 4 ed. Englewood Cliffs, N.J.: Prentice Hall.

Meyer, A. (1982) "So Lie Detectors Lie?" *Science 82,* June: 24–27.

Quintanilla, G. (1983) "Cross-cultural Communication: An Ongoing Challenge," *FBI Law Enforcement Bulletin,* February: 1–8.

Ressler, R. K., Burgess, A. W. and Douglas, J. E. (1988) *Sexual Homicide: Patterns and Motives.* Lexington, Ma.: Lexington Books.

Rogers, C. (1961) *On Becoming a Person.* Boston: Houghton Mifflin.

Strawbridge, P. and Strawbridge, D. (1990) "A Networking Guide to Recruitment, Selection and Probationary Training Department of the United States of America." New York: John Jay College.

Strecher, V. (1971) *The Environment of Law Enforcement.* Englewood Cliffs, N.J.: Prentice-Hall.

Thompson, G. J. (1982) "Rhetoric, an Important Tool for Police Officers," *FBI Law Enforcement Bulletin,* April: 1–7.

Toffler, A. (1970) *Future Shock.* New York: Random House.

Van Maanen, J. (1978) "The Asshole." in Manning, P. K. & J. Van Maanen (eds). *Policing: A View From the Street.* Santa Monica, CA: Goodyear Publishing Co.

Weaver, C. H. (1972) *Human Listening: Processes and Behavior.* New York: Bobbs-Merrill.

White, M. F., Cox, T. C. and Basehart, J. (1994) "Theoretical Consideration of Officer Profanity and Obscenity in Formal Contacts with Citizens," in Barker, T. & Carter, D. L. (eds.) *Police Deviance,* 3rd ed. Cincinnati, Ohio, Anderson.

7

POLICE DISCRETION AND COMMUNITY RELATIONS

Attached to our democracy by the glue of necessity is a continuous and pervasive delegation of authority which empowers man to use his best judgment in governing others. (Reed, 1980, p. 54)

The exercise of discretion in the administration of justice is inevitable and, within bounds, desirable. It has existed in every legal system in history (Davis, 1970, pp. 58–59).

Discretion occurs at every decision point in the justice process. How it is exercised by members of one component in the justice system affects how it can be exercised by members of other components. The exercise of discretion by police and citizens helps to shape what occurs throughout the entire process.

Police, through their discretionary judgments, are street interpreters of law. In a practical sense, police selectively determine what and how law is to be enforced. They determine what services they will offer and under what circumstances and to whom they will offer them. Police discretionary decisions are most frequently street decisions, directly affecting individual citizens and neighborhoods. Conversely, discretion exercised by those same citizens affects what is reported to police, whether or not witnesses will testify, and how much support and cooperation the police will receive. Mutual respect and support between the police and the community they serve are often defined in how fairly, objectively, and impartially police discretionary judgment calls are made.

In this chapter we address:

- The role of discretion in the justice system.
- The nature of selective, and sometimes discriminatory, law enforcement.
- Factors influencing decision making.
- Justifications and legal authority for selective enforcement.
- Dangers of selective enforcement.
- Strategies for structuring discretion.

STUDYING THIS CHAPTER WILL ENABLE YOU TO:

1. Define *discretion* and its role in the system.
2. Explain some of the justifications for selective enforcement.
3. Identify the legal authority for selective enforcement.
4. Describe some of the dangers inherent in selective enforcement.
5. Demonstrate a strategy for structuring discretion.

THE ROLE OF DISCRETION IN THE SYSTEM

Our society is based on freedom of choice, and that freedom requires the exercise of discretion. Against a backdrop of government by laws and equality of all people under the law, one of the most perplexing problems confronting the administration of justice is that of discretionary, or selective, enforcement of laws.

For a system of justice to function humanely, flexibility and discretion must exist within the system. The more flexibility in the system, the greater the possibility that individualized justice may be served—and the more the system is vulnerable to abuse. According to Atkins and Pogrebin (1978):

> The invisible system of justice that lies beyond the formal scriptures of the law derives its energy from the failure of statutory law or any administrative code of regulation to specify all contingencies of decision-making. The essential problem becomes that of discovering the elusive balance between structuring decisions and providing for individualized justice." (p. 2)

Defining Discretion

Discretion is an exercise of individual choice or judgment. The range of choices may be limited by certain legal, administrative, or ethical bounds, or it may appear to be limitless. Discretion requires discerning or distinguishing among options. And as the Commission on Accreditation for Law Enforcement Agencies (1987) points out:

> Because the concept of discretion defies rigid codification, officers should be trained in how to exercise the broad discretionary authority they have been granted (1.1).

The Elements of Discretion

Discretion is *personal,* which means that individual experience, education, style, goals, and ethics are all involved in the decision-making process.

Discretion requires *judgment,* which means that some choice is made among perceived options.

Discretion often grants both *personal autonomy* and *personal influence* over the lives of others.

The ability to discriminate, in the sense of discerning or distinguishing among options is a part of the exercise of discretion. To discriminate, as we commonly use the term, or in other words to treat differently or favor on a basis other than individual merit, is an abuse of discretion.

Exercising Discretion in the System

The exercise of discretion in one part of the justice system affects all other parts. A few of the discretionary choices available to system members are as follows:

Police, many times during the working day, will make decisions that in effect, suspend or modify statutory laws. Sometimes police administrators informally and unofficially institute policies that involve selective enforcement. Yet this use of discretion—although well known to prosecutors, judges, legislators, and some members of the public—is rarely acknowledged openly by police. The power of the police is great as a practical interpreter of the law. Police officers also have much discretionary power in their public service and order maintenance roles. In fact, every situation confronting the officer requires the use of discretion (Barker, Hunter, and Rush, 1994).

Citizens can choose whether or not to report crimes; whether or not to testify in court; whether or not to press charges; whether or not to support the police. Citizens determine through their discretionary judgment what level of crime will be tolerated.

Defendants and their attorneys can choose whether or not to cooperate with others in the system; what strategies will be employed in the defense.

Prosecutors choose whether or not to file; what charges to bring; what bargains are reasonable; what strategies to employ in the prosecution.

Judges determine legal questions; review cases and reports; sentence offenders.

Corrections officials choose to a large degree what happens to the convicted offender in terms of custody and treatment so long as the offender is in their jurisdiction.

THE NATURE OF SELECTIVE AND DISCRIMINATORY ENFORCEMENT

A Modern Tightrope

The modern police officer walks a tightrope between the right of the community to be protected and the right of the individual to be left alone by government. Our legal justice system is based on the concept that most people voluntarily obey the law and police themselves. In a free society, every citizen is responsible for his or her own behavior, and the police are considered to be agents of the citizenry they serve, enforcing laws and maintaining order in the interest of "liberty and justice for all." This is a humanitarian ideal. In this context, law applied without discretion may actually conflict with justice.

Our burgeoning urban population centers are composed of many different cultures and subcultures with many different views as to how laws should be enforced. This factor makes the process by which police try to match selective law enforcement decisions with priorities of the public served increasingly complex.

The police officer's judgment on whether or not a violation of law has taken place is not the major topic of our discussion in this chapter. Certainly, there are many occasions on which a patrol officer must decide whether to take action to enforce the law (i.e., whether an act of omission has occurred, is occurring, or will occur). The activity that concerns us most in this chapter, however, is perhaps an even more controversial one with direct and ongoing impact on community relations. It involves the decision *not* to enforce laws when there is no doubt that a violation occurred.

The Administrative Choice

Police organizations rarely make explicit policies that require selective enforcement of laws. Yet, on occasion, they do sacrifice "strict enforcement" to other values or principles, and police officers soon learn of unstated departmental policies to this effect. James Q. Wilson, in *Varieties of Police Behavior,* describes the development of departmental policies through weighing strict enforcement against accommodations that will serve other values. He suggests that at times a department may have to sacrifice strict application of laws to achieve the values of "order" and "service giving," that are also part of the police mission (Wilson, 1968).

Even though they may not be subject to direct disciplinary action for failing to adhere to these policies, officers who disobey them will undoubtedly find themselves receiving less direct, but very displeasing penalties (lost opportunities for promotion, undesirable work or shift assignments, letters of reprimand, etc.). In this way, administrators can make informal or unofficial policies as binding as formal, official ones.

Operational-Level Choices

The Police Officer as Legislator, Prosecutor, and Judge

In day-to-day contact with citizens, police officers have discretion to "bend" the law—or even fail to enforce it altogether—as they see fit. In particular, they can play three important roles.

As legislators they can specify what enacting legislatures stated in general language; they can establish classes of exceptions that are not specifically provided for in statutory law.

As prosecutors, they may decide not to proceed against a suspect in exchange for cooperation that may have a value for law enforcement.[1]

---

[1] In most jurisdictions there are immunity statutes that the prosecutor may invoke. The effect of these statutes is to allow a citizen to testify before an investigative body without subjecting himself to the peril of having the information that he divulges subsequently used against him in a criminal proceeding. A grant of immunity almost always requires judicial approval. An example of such a statute is the Federal Immunity Act, which provides that a U.S. attorney may move for immunity on behalf of anyone he wishes to call as a witness, but who he believes will refuse to provide information under his privilege against self-incrimination (Section 6000-3, Title 18, U.S. Code).

It should be noted that the prosecutor may also have power to terminate a pending matter through the plea of *nolle prosequi*. This procedure is usually subject to the approval of the courts (see Rule 48, Federal Rules of Criminal Procedure).

There are many situations, however, where the prosecutor is in a position to use his or her discretion not to proceed in an arbitrary manner. See *Challenge of Crime in a Free Society,* President's Commission on Law Enforcement and the Administration of Justice (Washington, D.C.: U.S. Government Printing Office, 1967), p. 133. But we would argue that, in an operational sense, the extent of the prosecutor's discretion is not nearly as great as that of the patrol officer.

As judges, they may determine that a suspect deserves a "suspended sentence" (i.e., release with a warning) or some on-the-spot punishment at the officer's own discretion (e.g., confiscation of contraband, participation in a social program).

The Invisibility of the Police Officer's Choices

When a police officer chooses to act as legislator, prosecutor, or judge, few people ever learn about or review the decisions. There is no record for supervisors to review. The suspect is unlikely to say anything, especially if the officer has been lenient. And in those cases where the officer does not work alone, the officer's partner (who is usually at the same level of authority) will remain silent unless some very severe abuse occurs (Barker and Carter, 1994).

FACTORS INFLUENCING DECISION MAKING AT AN ADMINISTRATIVE LEVEL

Considering the quantity and breadth of laws they are supposed to enforce, police administrators sometimes conclude, quite reasonably, that they do not have the budgetary or personnel resources to enforce all laws fully. Consequently, they have to find some basis for choosing which laws to enforce.

Finding the Optimum Law Enforcement Level

When resources and/or personnel are limited, a sensible way to decide which laws to enforce is to find the mix that provides the most law enforcement with the officers, funds, and material available. But working out the optimum mix is not easy. First, there are some laws that every administrator will want to enforce, regardless of cost. With regard to other laws, the administrator can make decisions about which ones to enforce and how strictly to enforce them—after determining the time, effort, funds, and personnel that different options would entail. In matters such as these, however, which touch the public so deeply, basing decisions purely on cost and efficiency considerations is impossible.

Community Input

No administrator can afford to ignore public opinion when deciding which laws to enforce. For one thing, on purely practical grounds, laws opposed to the community are likely to be far more expensive to enforce than those that are not. Moreover, trying to enforce them may lead to lack of cooperation in other enforcement efforts (Reiss, 1971, pp. 68–102).

But who is the "community" or the "public"? Sometimes, the police are going along with the general sentiments of the population of a neighborhood. At other times, they are bowing to the desires and interests of the powerful, the vocal, or some other segment of the community.

As Wilson (1977) noted:

The administrator becomes attuned to complaints. What constitutes a "significant" citizen demand will, of course, vary from city to city. In some places, a political party will tell the police whom to take seriously and whom to ignore; in other places, organized community groups will amplify some demands and drown out others; in still other places, the police themselves will have to decide whose voices to heed and how to heed them. Whatever the filtering mechanism, the police administrator ignores at his peril those demands that are passed through. (p. 70)

Administrators will not always choose the policy that produces the greatest amount of successful law enforcement effort at the lowest unit cost. They may determine instead that the cost of losing support of some community groups because of police efforts may be compensated for in the value of enforcement to the larger community. An example is a strong enforcement campaign directed against drug dealers. The campaign might alienate the community of drug users and be much more expensive to maintain than an intensified effort against parking ticket scofflaws. On the other hand, value to the larger community in terms of property crime reduction and general community support resulting from the reduction in drug activities would likely outweigh the cost of enforcement.

Bargaining and Law Enforcement

The politically powerful residents of the community may not want selective enforcement of laws but may instead prefer that the laws be applied only in limited situations. Thus, parking laws may be strictly enforced in some areas, but during holiday shopping seasons the police may adopt a policy of "forgiveness" in areas surrounding shopping centers. Selective enforcement also occurs in the application of laws against prostitution. For example, police arrests of prostitutes and their clients may cause business convention planners to avoid some cities. When convention business is lost as a result of strict enforcement of vice laws, members of the business community may exert considerable pressure on police officials to relax enforcement of these laws. At the same time, the police administrator may recognize that there is strong support in the community as a whole for laws against prostitution; if this were otherwise, the legislature would have changed the law. The result of these opposing pressures upon the administrator may lead him to adopt law enforcement policies that limit prostitution to a controlled level of practice. Prostitution flourishes, but it becomes hidden from the public view. Therefore, it is not likely to cause mobilization of citizens who would favor full suppression. The police administrator's objective in adopting a selective enforcement policy would be to strike a bargain with the citizens who support limited prostitution in exchange for their support of "more important" law enforcement objectives.

A hidden danger to law enforcement in this kind of balancing act is loss of integrity in the public eye. General public knowledge of selective and discriminatory patterns of law enforcement will produce, at the very least, an attitude that justice can be negotiated.

The Rule of Silence

Police administrators rarely issue orders or make public statements listing the criteria for selective law enforcement policies. Administrators expect subordinates to develop the "right" kinds of priorities without specific direction. This method of operation is undoubtedly reinforced by the fact that legislators, courts, and prosecutors rely on the police to use discretion when applying laws. These assumptions, although never formally stated, bear an important relationship to the laws that will actually be enforced in the community. There have been exceptions to the administrative level "rule of silence" on selective enforcement policies.

Exceptions to the Rule

Written policy guidelines sometimes set standards for the use of alternatives to arrest. Under such standards, people who could be charged with drunk and disorderly offenses are sometimes referred to clinics where treatment can be offered. Recently, a county sheriff, concerned about the already overcrowded local jail, requested publicly that both city and county officers stop arresting people for misdemeanor offenses. He recommended that violators be cited instead of arrested.

Although in the instance above no public comments of support or concern were forthcoming from other police agencies, public statements encouraging selective enforcement may receive much criticism from other agencies, especially if local community support is divided or uncertain. When Connecticut State Police Commissioner Cleveland Fuessenich announced a policy that would allow his officers to use discretion in determining whether an arrest should be made in cases involving the possession of small quantities of marijuana in 1971, other Connecticut police chiefs reacted with criticism. Their comments reflect a conventional public position: "The law says a crime has been committed. . . . Who is to say which law will be enforced?". . . "It is the court system which has the discretion over cases brought before it . . . the system should remain that way." . . . "It is not the job of the law enforcement agency to pick out which laws shall be enforced and for which people" (*New Haven Register,* Dec. 2, 1971, p. 1). Support for such a policy would vary with time and place. Today possession of small quantities of marijuana has been decriminalized in many jurisdictions.

FACTORS INFLUENCING DECISION MAKING AT AN OPERATIONAL LEVEL

Police officers are charged with responding directly to the citizens' requests for service and to public safety and order situations on the streets of the community. In most cases, they decide what action to take. They may observe an event, consider several alternative courses of action, and make a decision without recording it or doing anything that anyone else could report. For example, a police officer might observe a motorist drive through a red traffic signal and decide not to give chase. In this sort of situation, not even the citizen knows that he or she has been the focus of law enforcement discretion. This kind of decision is among the least visible of the criminal justice processes.

When being observed by a suspect, a complainant, a fellow police officer, or a supervisor, the officer will be very aware of the observer's expectations as he or she chooses a course of action. The literal interpretation of the law to the situation might only be of secondary importance.

Operational level decision-makers' judgments are governed by the same kinds of influences that affect the decisions of higher level administrators. But, because officers operate within a much smaller political sphere, they find their relationships with the more limited community potentially more intense. The reciprocal impact of both officer and community becomes clearer. It is easier to "bargain" within these more intimate relationships.[2]

Community Input

If citizens do not report crimes to the police or summon an officer when service is needed, police will intervene only in those situations that they personally observe. Witnesses and victims who do not cooperate with the police limit police discretion.

A common reason why citizens do not report auto accidents or burglaries to the police is that their insurance might be canceled or their rate increased if the report is made. Conversely, they might report if they believe such a report is necessary in order for them to collect on insurance. The relationship between the victim and offender and the attitude of the citizen toward police also have a great influence on the willingness of the citizen to report (Reiss, 1971, pp. 42–43). In a sense, the community members express their expectations to police in their interactions with them. The clearer the statement, the better police can structure their discretion to meet the community's needs.

Situational Factors

Several studies have found specific situational factors to be influential in discretionary decision making. Major factors include the attitude and appearance of the offender, political factors such as community attitudes, pressures, and biases. As mentioned earlier, who else is present (victims, witnesses, other officers) also may influence decision making (Senna and Siegel, 1993; see also Goldman, 1963; Cicourel, 1968; Piliavin and Briar, 1964).

Another important factor is whether the situation is on view (one that the officer has seen and in which he or she intervenes without invitation) or is one to which the officer was summoned by citizens. Wagner reports that more complaints occur against officers who intervene in on-view situations than against those who intervene at citizen request. Officers in two-officer vehicles also appear to be more susceptible to citizen complaints (Wagner, 1980).

Environmental Factors

Senna and Siegel (1993) suggest that certain environmental factors influence discretionary power, including (1) personal values, (2) pressure of police supervisors and peers, and (3) personal perception of what alternatives to arrest are available

---

[2]One police officer interviewed during the course of the Wilson study reported that when he was instructed to tell the priests in his area that they would have to close down their bingo and carnival concessions, he was fearful of being excommunicated (Wilson, 1968, p. 107).

(pp. 284–288). An officer who grew up in a conservative environment may find decision making in a liberal environment uncomfortable. Routinely, the officer will be required to "assess cultural norms accurately and to be, in effect, the cultural and social engineer at that moment" (Greenlee, 1980, p. 51). Lester (1981), in his discussion of police use of deadly force, points to an apparent correlation between attitudes of violence in a community and use of deadly force. Where high rates of police violence existed, he found high rates of citizen against citizen and citizen against police violence also. He suggests that often police attitudes toward violence may reflect those of the community (pp. 56–57).

Educational and Experiential Factors

Carter, Sapp, and Stephens (1989) found that college-educated police recruits were slightly more likely to choose alternatives to arrest. Their findings suggest that education does have some effect upon discretionary decision making. Finckenauer (1976) found that the primary factor which characterized all the situations that seemed to influence how discretion was exercised was the desire of the police to maintain a certain public image of the police role. Experience too, in the sense of "street wisdom" seemed to influence discretionary decision making (Finckenauer, 1976, pp. 92–93).

JUSTIFICATIONS FOR SELECTIVE ENFORCEMENT

Justification by Administration

Police administrators justify selective enforcement generally by arguing that they do not have the personnel, financial support, nor support from the community or the criminal justice system to enforce the laws strictly. As we have discussed, selective enforcement in itself may be justified, and indeed be desirable, so long as reasonable boundaries of discretion are established that help to prevent abuse.

Justification for keeping selective enforcement policies secret, on the other hand, may serve to increase abuse and community distrust, and lower officer morale. Administrators commonly offer five arguments for secrecy. Each is considered in terms of police–community impact.

1. *"If the policies were stated, administrators would have to defend the quality of their decisions."*

The statement is true. Responsible police administrators owe the community explanations for decisions that directly affect it. It follows then, that if an administrator's decisions are indefensible, they should be changed, not hidden.

2. *"Acknowledgment of such decisions would cause police administrators to lose the image of impartiality."*

Perpetuating a false image of impartiality is of little or no positive value to the police–community relationship. In fact, once discovered, deluding the public creates a sense of distrust that may be very difficult to overcome.

3. *"Statutory law prohibits the development of such policies."*

The force of this argument is that the policies may be needed, even though the law forbids them. But it is the policies, not the secrecy, that the law forbids. As noted earlier, legislatures and courts recognize that police officers make discretionary selective decisions about the law. If administrators state their policies and the reasons for them openly, the chance of accommodation by legislators and courts is great.

4. *"Discretion breeds corruption."*

If so, discretion would tend to breed corruption, whether open or secret. In fact, officially developed and publicly defended policies, together with procedures to review and control the use of discretion, could minimize corruption.

5. *"There is a danger that stated policy, not statutory enactment, would become the limit of the law."*

The inference here is that citizens might argue that the law is suspended by discretionary policy. According to most authorities, however, this defense in individual cases is appropriate only if citizens can show that imposition of policy resulted in an obvious injustice. Such defense would be available whether the policy is stated or unstated. (See the final sections of this chapter for further discussion of this point.) The issue, then, is whether the policy is justly applied, not whether it is stated or unstated.

Justification by Officers

A Question of Injustice

Selective enforcement decisions are justified by police officers most frequently by the statement: "Strict enforcement of the law could result in injustice." It is instructive to discuss some of the ways in which police officers believe this result might occur.

1. *"The legislature did not intend for some laws to be applied literally; the law was intended to apply only to the situation where wrong occurs."*[3]

---

[3]The problem that faces legislators in writing laws so that they are usable was discussed by Justice Frankfurter in his dissenting opinion in *Winters* v. *U.S.,* 333 U.S. 520 (1948) at 515–15: "Unlike the abstract stuff of mathematics, or the quantitatively ascertainable elements of much of natural science, legislation is greatly concerned with the multiform psychological complexities of individual and social conduct. Accordingly, the demands upon legislation and its responses are multiform. That which may appear too vague and even meaningless as to one subject matter may be as definite as another subject mater permits, if the legislative power to deal with such a subject is not to be altogether denied. . . . If a law is framed with narrow paticularity, too easy opportunities are afforded to nullify the purposes of the legislation. If the legislation is drafted in terms so vague that no ascertainable line is drawn in advance between innocent and condemned conduct, the purpose of the legislation cannot be enforced because no purpose is defined."

As a matter of fact, legislatures cannot make each law specify every case or situation to which it applies; it is just not practical. A police officer might conclude from this fact that the legislature assumes that those who enforce the law will exercise reasonable judgment in doing so. Given this view, the officer believes that he is really carrying out the legislative mandate when he decides that someone who violates the letter of the law has not violated its "spirit," and thus has done nothing wrong.

2. *"The statute in question is out of date; to apply it to a contemporary situation would work an injustice."*

Over the years, many states have accumulated laws that do not apply to the realities of modern life, but they have never been repealed. Were police officers to enforce them, people in the community would be outraged.

3. *"Sure, the behavior violates the law, but if I arrest the perpetrator, the official system will not handle the matter justly."*

This position is argued when the officer feels that the person who committed a violation is not "really" a criminal, and therefore should not undergo the trauma of being processed through the criminal justice system or bear the stigma of a criminal record. The officer may administer a reprimand of some form of corrections (e.g., doing some "good deed," making restitution of some kind, seeking counseling).

4. *"If an arrest is made, the official system will not treat the offense seriously enough."*

Police officers may feel that the criminal justice system (especially the courts) is too "soft" on criminals and affords them too many protections. Instead of arresting certain offenders, then, police may feel that confiscating contraband, repeatedly stopping the offenders for questioning, and imposing other forms of harassment are more effective ways of enforcing the law.

5. *"The community does not support enforcement of the law in some cases."*

Police officers sometimes feel that the neighborhood they serve has a greater tolerance for certain types of behavior than does the community at large. For example, an officer may believe that assaults between two citizens residing in a barrio are both common and acceptable forms of social contacts within that community. The officer may also believe that the assault complaint made by a wife in this neighborhood against her husband is similar to the complaint that a wife in a more affluent neighborhood might take to a family counselor. Consequently, the police officer may overlook an assault case that would almost certainly result in arrest in another area.

The reasoning above is dangerous, and it may be the source of disharmony between a community and the police. Studies conducted in many ethnic neighborhoods echo the findings of a 1968 study by the National Advisory Committee on Civil Disorders. Lack of satisfaction by black ghetto communities with the level of services they received from police was voiced in their concern: "The police maintain a much less rigorous standard of law enforcement in the ghetto, tolerating there illegal activities like drug addiction and prostitution and street violence that they would not tolerate elsewhere" (*Report of U.S. National Advisory Committee on Civil Disorders,* 1968, p. 161).

One study of child abuse cases has revealed that the police were more likely to report child abuse cases involving white families than those involving black families (Willis and Ward, 1988). They believe that the officers in their research took this action because (1) police officers view a situation involving a white victim as more deserving of official action than a situation involving a black victim, or (2) police officers may hold negative stereotypes of black family life, which includes the notion that violence and abuse is normal.

On the other hand, a decision not to raid a poker game in the basement of a citizen's home or not to arrest juveniles "tossing quarters" in the alley may be accurate personal interpretations of community norms. Accurately or not, police reasoning usually follows this pattern:

1. The activity in question is prevalent.
2. The community does not view the activity as wrong.
3. The community would view enforcement of the law in relation to the viewed activity as wrong. Enforcement may elicit negative responses from the community in the form of: political pressure to cause the officers to be either reprimanded or transferred; social ostracism from the community and treatment with great incivility; lack of cooperation in other aspects of the police mission; and physical threats to their well-being.
4. The value of enforcement against the observed activity may be outweighed by the general loss of police effectiveness to render law enforcement services in higher priority areas; this loss of effectiveness results when the community withdraws its support.

Four Other Common Justifications

In addition to asserting that strict enforcement of the law could result in injustice, police officers note at least four other common justifications for selective enforcement.

1. *"The community may want laws to be applied discriminatorily against 'objectionable' persons whose general conduct and presence are not illegal."*

Occasionally, a community may expect police to enforce infrequently used laws against specific individuals or groups. Officers are expected to overlook violations committed by other community members against these same individuals or groups. In this situation, the selective enforcement and nonenforcement of law becomes an expression of community bias.

2. *"Other parts of the criminal justice system have suspended the operation of some laws."*

If a supervisor complains about an officer's attempts to enforce a given law, or if a judge or district attorney feels that certain offenses are trivial or perhaps should not be offenses at all (especially regarding so-called victimless crimes such as gambling), then the police officer will feel little motivation to enforce the laws in question. In this way, discretionary judgment made by a judge or district attorney can have a great impact on the discretion of others in the system—in this case, the police.

3. *"There may be a 'trading' advantage of law enforcement value in the decision not to enforce the law."*

In many cases, police can "bargain" with an offender after apprehension. Officers might treat the offender leniently and even fail to arrest if the offender will, in turn, help to solve a more important case or apprehend a more important offender. Skolnick's study of criminal investigators found that burglary detectives often permitted informants to commit narcotics offenses, whereas narcotics detectives allowed informants to steal (Skolnick, 1975, p. 129).

Undercover techniques must be innovative and yet not corrupt, but the line between the two is sometimes blurred for police and offenders. Undercover techniques, by necessity, include deception, trickery, temptation, and coercion. Informants are a major part of the process and they are often able to use the system to personal advantage. For example, informers in the ABSCAM case were able to exploit their roles. One swindled West Coast businessmen. (The FBI did nothing to stop him until ABSCAM was publicized.) Another informant acknowledged publically that he has made over $200,000 from his activities and an advance for a book regarding his exploits (Marx, 1982, pp. 179–180).

4. *"It may be inconvenient to enforce the law."*

Officers may hesitate to enforce the law if it might involve personal inconveniences such as losing a day off, working overtime, or missing a meal.

THE QUESTION OF PROFESSIONALISM

The claim to professionalism made by police officers requires an assumption of the obligations of a profession. Reiss (1971) says that an attribute of a profession is "the making of decisions that involve technical and moral judgments affecting the fate of people" (p. 123). Police make these kinds of decisions. As Reiss suggests, if the police do not develop adequate discretionary guidelines, external controls will be developed to govern the police use of discretion. Should this occur, professionalism would be negatively affected. Mark (1976) points out that

> The public acceptance of police discretion . . . is crucial to professional growth. The public served must see the need for police discretion and acknowledge the competency of the practitioner to use discretion constructively and in the public interest. It is largely

by the level of public acknowledgment of the police practitioner's competency to exercise discretion for the public good that one may sense the real impact of and progress toward true professionalization. (p. 361)

LEGAL AUTHORITY FOR SELECTIVE ENFORCEMENT

What the Law Says

Statutory law is usually clear on the duty of police officers when they are confronted with what they believe to be a violation of the law. For example, Section 16-1-3 of the Official Code of the State of Georgia (*Georgia Criminal Justice and Traffic Law Manual,* 1991) states:

(11) "Peace Officer" means any person who by virtue of his office or public employment is *vested with a duty to maintain public order or to make arrests for offenses,* whether that duty extends to all crimes or is limited to specific offenses. [italics added]

The Georgia statute is representative of most state statutes that prescribe a peace officer's duty. The officer is not given any authority to discriminate between cases that appear to fall under the literal terms of a statute. An exception to this rule would be where an officer has knowledge of a court decision holding a portion of a statute or ordinance to be unconstitutional or in some other way limiting its literal application. If the law allows for tempering its application with mercy or with any other quality, it does not appear that statutory law provides the police officer with the authority to do it. The California statute is an exception to this rule, however. It appears to direct peace officers to use judgment to discriminate between apparent violations of the law.

"The rule of the common law, that penal statutes are to be strictly construed, has no application to this code. All its provisions are to be construed according to the fair import of their terms, with a view to effect its objects and to promote justice" (California Penal Code, Section 4). In California Penal Code (CPC) 836 the so-called "Law of arrest" states that a "peace officer *may* make an arrest . . ." *May* is a term that provides for discretionary judgment; in contrast, *shall* is a term that allows for no choice.

In the police officer's world, the essence of the arrest process is judgment (Wilson, 1989). The situations that the police encounter are not all alike and the people involved also vary. Therefore, the officer on the street must decide within certain often ambiguous statutes whether or not to make an arrest or take some other action (see Figure 7-1).

What the Courts Say

Acknowledging that discretion is exercised at all is important, but it is only the first step in the reform of selective enforcement decision-making policies. Even though the legal duties of police may be clearly stated, numerous documentable instances of selective law enforcement at both the administrative and operational levels of policing exist in every jurisdiction. Furthermore, the courts have carefully avoided responding to any reference to these kinds of practices. A defendant is not

---

LEGAL GUIDELINES

16-11-41 Public Drunkenness

(a) A person who shall be and appear in an intoxicated condition in any public place or within the curtilege of any private residence not his own other than by invitation of the owner or lawful occupant, which condition is made manifest by boisterousness, by indecent condition or act, or by vulgar, profane, loud, or unbecoming language, is guilty of a misdemeanor.

40-6-95 Pedestrian Under Influence of Alcohol or Drug

A person who is under the influence of intoxicating liquor or any drug to a degree which renders him a hazard shall not walk or be upon any roadway or the shoulder of any roadway. Violation of this Code section is a misdemeanor and is punishable upon conviction by a fine not to exceed $500.00.

A police officer in Georgia was presented with this set of circumstances. He encountered a person who was so intoxicated that he could not stand or walk without assistance. The man was not loud, profane, or boisterous, in fact; he was too intoxicated to talk. Therefore, he did not fall within the definition of public drunkenness statute 16-11-41; however, the man's condition certainly falls within the parameters of a hazard under statute 40-6-95 (Figure 7-1). Unfortunately, for the officer and the man, this took place in an open parking lot some 25 feet from the roadway. Therefore, the officer could not arrest the man for being a pedestrian under the influence of alcohol or drugs. The end result was that the officer did not arrest this severely intoxicated and incapacitated person and his alternative to arrest was inappropriate for the circumstances and is the basis for a wrongful death action in federal court.

FIGURE 7-1   Guidelines for public drunkenness arrests in Georgia.

ordinarily allowed to raise, in his defense in a criminal prosecution, the fact that authorities knowingly ignore hundreds of similar violations. The issue, if raised, is usually treated as being irrelevant to the question of the defendant's guilt. Clearly, the question of whether or not the defendant committed certain acts is not answered by the assertion that other persons may have done the same thing.[4]

In relation to fact-finding in the individual case, it would appear that the court's treatment of such matters is reasonable. But important issues are avoided. Does the "law," as it is applied to a given community, appear to single out particular people and their acts? And does this method of applying laws result in unequal protection of citizens, in violation of the Constitution? Setting the legal issues aside, it is

---

[4]Discretion, as exercised in the diverting of some offenders from the criminal justice system at the point of apprehension or arraignment, appears to be gaining support of police, prosecutors, and judges if it is handled on an individualized basis and is specifically approved by the prosecutor. New laws in several states, however, appear to be aimed at limiting judicial discretion and eliminating disparities in sentencing of felony offenders and recidivists.

fundamentally unfair for any agency to reserve statutes for application only to unlucky people who fall into a special, but not legally defined, class. The U.S. Supreme Court has attempted to deal with the issue of unequal protection under the law raised by discriminatory law enforcement. The case of *Yick Wo* v. *Hopkins* (118 U.S. 356, 1886) is the most frequently cited case in this area. It dealt with the situation of Chinese laundry operators who were subjected to regulations that apparently were never enforced against Caucasians. The regulations in question did not provide for differentiation by race, but patterns of enforcement over a period of several years made the discrimination obvious. The Court said:

> Though the law itself be fair on its face and impartial in appearance, yet, if it is applied and administered by public authority with an evil eye and unequal hand, so as practically to make unjust and illegal discrimination between persons in similar circumstances, material to their rights, the denial of equal justice is still within the protection of the Constitution.

Although the *Yick Wo* case would appear to provide for the victim of discriminatory law enforcement, it has been used in the courts in a very narrow manner. *Yick Wo* is generally held to be applicable only to situations where a contending party can show that there has been a systematic program of discrimination focused specifically on him or persons easily identifiable with him as members of the same class. This is an almost impossible fact for a defendant to prove in most cases, and it would not apply to the many discriminatory law enforcement decisions that are made by individual police officers every day. In another case, the Supreme Court avoided dealing with the issue of discriminatory enforcement of a vagrancy ordinance against the defendant when there were many other violators present at the time of his arrest. The defendant alleged that he was arrested not so much for vagrancy but because his previous public statements were unpopular with the police officers present (*Edelman* v. *California,* 344 U.S. 357, 1953).

WRITS OF MANDAMUS

In addition to defendants in criminal cases, other citizens may also be concerned with the problem of selective law enforcement. The only way they can correct selective law enforcement policies they do not like is through the political system. Some effort to use *writs of mandamus* have been made. *Mandamus* is available by statute in most American jurisdictions. It is an action that can be brought against a public official to compel the official to perform specified ministerial acts that are directed by statute. Because *mandamus* is generally held applicable to ministerial acts that do not involve the use of judgment by the party that it is directed to, courts have been unwilling to use the remedy to tell police departments how to conduct their business. The courts will not involve themselves in supervising the operation of the function of policing, which requires continuous attention and the exercise of judgment.

Other attempts have been made to seek court orders compelling police to do their duty. These efforts have failed, for the most part, because the courts are unwilling, except in the most abusive cases, to substitute their judgment for that of an agency under the executive branch of the government.

DANGERS OF SELECTIVE ENFORCEMENT WITHOUT APPROPRIATE GUIDELINES

Abuse of Power

If a practice that represents a major portion of police work is not recognized as existing, it is excluded from police academy and inservice training programs. The officer is left to make decisions without guidance. This fact alone increases the possibility that decisions will vary widely and often will be made arbitrarily on subjective factors, without the benefit of adequate information. Decision making of this sort is most likely to reflect bias and favoritism. The officer is in effect given increased power to abuse power. The lack of guidelines also inhibits an agency's ability to deal with substantial questions of corruption and the abuse of citizens.

Particularly in undercover work a potential for problems exists. Illegal activity may be committed by police agents; privacy may be unduly invaded.

Lack of Support for the Officer

If police administrators make secret policies and if individual officers are called upon to tailor justice on a daily basis, officers, for lack of clear policy, can only guess what their supervisors want them to do. In most instances, they improvise; they are in a very ambivalent position. When officers make selective enforcement decisions, their confidence in their own integrity may be undermined by the feeling that they are part of an illicit conspiracy. Believing that they should make exceptions in the application of laws, they are unable to act openly because special accommodation is not supposed to be made. The necessity that all must be unspoken taints the contact of the officers with citizens and even with fellow officers. Also, officers may feel that no matter what they decide, they will be wrong. Should they make an unpopular decision, they may face the consequences alone. Because they acted "independently of written policy," they may not have agency support.

Impact on Public Image

A conspiracy of silence presents to the public a negative image of the entire system. Evasiveness and defensiveness on the part of the agency undermines credibility.

STRATEGIES FOR STRUCTURING POLICE DISCRETION

Recognizing Discretion in Law Enforcement

The American Bar Association, experts on law enforcement such as James Q. Wilson, and others have urged the importance of open recognition by all parties (legislatures, the courts, the public and, most important, police agencies themselves) that selective law enforcement is a fact. Of course, the public (and others) implicitly know this already; professional law enforcement officers should now admit it and develop controls over its use (American Bar Association, 1972, pp. 13, 116–144; Wilson, 1968, pp. 83–88; Barker, Hunter, and Rush, 1994).

Enforcement Policy Boards

One approach to providing discretionary guidelines for police was suggested by Stephen Schiller. He recommended that police departments establish enforcement policy boards to develop selective policies where needed. Statements of the policies, together with the reasons for them, would be made public and given to line personnel along with their training materials (Schiller, 1972).[5]

Composition of the Board

The presiding officer of the board would be the chief of police. It seems clear (even though Schiller did not suggest it) that the board might also include civic or community representatives, and that some procedures would be set up for citizen input. The board would not get involved with individual citizen complaints, however; these would be handled by the courts or police internal affairs units.

Policy Implementation Units

Every board would have a policy implementation unit to collect data on the use of policy at the operational level, to record inquiries by police officers, and to record difficulties in understanding policies in operational settings. These data will guide field personnel in interpreting policy in particular cases, and they would be reviewed periodically by the board.

The Courts

What functions should the courts play in implementing openly selective law enforcement policies? First, if a citizen is charged under a statute that is subject to the policy, the courts should decide if the statute really applies to the defendant under the policy (and the prosecution will have the burden of proving that it does).

---

[5]At this point many would argue that such an undertaking by a police agency, even given express direction by the legislature to form a board to develop policy for selective law enforcement, would constitute an usurption or an illegal delegation of legislature authority. As a practical matter, the so-called nondelegation doctrine is no longer workable. The courts have recognized that the complexities of regulatory needs make such a doctrine totally unfeasible. K. C. Davis in his *Administrative Law Treatise—1970 Supplement,* in sections 200–200–4, demonstrates through decided cases that the doctrine has lacked vitality from the time of its inception. A rule of nondelegation cannot be operationally implemented without tremendous cost in the quality of public regulation. Davis, in section 200–5 of his *Treatise,* suggests that the focus should not be on nondelegation but on controls and safeguards against abuses of delegation. Also see K. C. Davis, *Discretionary Justice* (Baton Rouge, La.: Louisiana State University Press, 1979), p. 44.

Second, the courts might also determine whether or not a policy is arbitrary. If it is ruled arbitrary, the policy should be nullified (although the policy board should have the right to appeal the ruling to a reviewing court).

Review

Internal Review

A police internal review unit should be available to answer citizen complaints about nonenforcement or selective enforcement of laws. Where appropriate, the policy implementation unit would determine whether the complaints indicate violations of departmental policy. The policy implementation unit should collect and review data on all reported incidents to see if a policy is meeting the expectations of the policy board. If it is not, the unit should recommend that the board review the policy.

Legislative Review

Once selective law enforcement policies have been stated by the police department, legislators can act on them, clarifying any misunderstanding through committee proceedings or more definitive statutes. If the legislature rejects the law enforcement agency's interpretation of a statute, the agency must follow suit, even though it disagrees. Out of this disagreement, however, may come a clearly developed issue for review by the electorate.

The Community

Police have a great deal of legitimate coercive power and influence in the community. As Finckenauer suggests, such coercive influence can be legitimate only if it is consistent with community expectations. "It is therefore incumbent upon the community and its representatives to make known to the police what their expectations are" (Finckenauer, 1976, p. 94). (Figures 7-2 and 7-3 illustrate established guidelines for police discretion in traffic stops and in taking juveniles into custody.

It is not sound police policy to apply the statutes literally by authorizing officers to stop any car they want to. It wastes manpower and needlessly irritates the stopped motorist.

The sound police policy is to stop motorists only in those cases where

a. A motor vehicle violation has been observed by the officer.

b. There is reasonable ground to suspect that another offense had been committed so as to allow a stop under [other stop/frisk/arrest] criteria.

c. A general checkpoint has been authorized by higher authority, usually for temporary purposes such as obtaining statistics of compliance.

Source: L. B. Schwartz and S. R. Goldstein. *Law Enforcement Handbook.* St. Paul, Minn.: West Publishing Co., 1980.

FIGURE 7-2   Traffic stop guidelines, an example of police discretion.

STANDARDS FOR THE ADMINISTRATION OF JUVENILE JUSTICE

2.23 Decisions to Take a Juvenile into Custody

2.231 Criteria for Taking a Juvenile Into Custody—Delinquency. Whenever practicable, an order issued by a family court judge should be obtained prior to taking into custody a juvenile alleged to have committed a delinquent act.

An order should not be issued nor a juvenile taken into custody without an order unless there is probable cause to believe that the juvenile falls within the jurisdiction of the family court over delinquency described in Standard 3.111, and it is determined that issuance of a summons or citation would not adequately protect the jurisdiction or process of the family court; or would not adequately protect the juvenile from an imminent threat of serious bodily harm; or would not adequately reduce the risk of the juvenile inflicting serious bodily harm on others or committing serious property offenses prior to adjudication.

In making this determination, the family court judge or law enforcement officer should consider:

a. The nature and seriousness of the alleged offense;

b. The juvenile's record of delinquency offenses, including whether the juvenile is currently subject to dispositional authority of the family court or released pending adjudication, disposition, or appeal;

c. The juvenile's record of willful failures to appear following the issuance of a summons or citation; and

d. The availability of noncustodial alternatives, including the presence of a parent, guardian, or other suitable persons able and willing to provide supervision and care for the juvenile and to assure his/her compliance with a summons or citation.

Written rules and regulations should be developed to guide custody decisions in delinquency matters.

Source: National Advisory Committee for Juvenile Justice and Delinquency Prevention, U.S. Department of Justice, Office of Juvenile Justice and Delinquency Prevention. Washington, D.C.: U.S. Government Printing Office, 1980.

FIGURE 7-3   Police discretion with juveniles: guidelines.

LOOKING TOWARD TOMORROW

Some Recommendations

Presidential commissions, state advisory groups, and several distinguished scholars agree on the need for official police recognition of selective law enforcement policies, but they have not always agreed on exactly what this would involve. How-ever, the following projects can be recommended.

1. Statutory revision so that the description of the peace officer's duty indicates that he or she is to arrest "if the circumstances are such as to indicate to a rea-sonably prudent person that such action should be taken." (Other phrasing could be used so long as it indicates a recognition that the officer has discretion in enforcing the law.)
2. Structures within the department for policy articulation and policy implementa-tion; both should be open and make provision for getting input from and report-ing to the public. Discretionary limits will need to be clearly defined and updated as necessary to meet changing public need.
3. Police selection, training, and supervisory models that reflect the place of selec-tive law enforcement in police work.
4. Articulation with other decision makers in the justice system to assure that plan-ning, implementation, and evaluation occurs in the context of the whole system rather than just the police component.

A Lesson from the Past

Police secrecy and indecisiveness about the issue of selective law enforcement is reminiscent of the way issues of abuses in interrogating suspects were handled by police in the past. Instead of developing guidelines and controls to prevent these abuses, the police did little to correct them. Finally, it fell to the U.S. Supreme Court—notably in the decision in *Miranda* v. *Arizona* (384 U.S. 436) and others—to correct abusive police practices. The lesson can be applied to the selective law enforcement issue. If professional law enforcement officers do not deal with impor-tant policy issues such as selective law enforcement in an open and straightforward manner, others will do it for them.

CONCLUSIONS

Police administrators rarely admit the existence of selective law enforcement policies, yet they often implement such policies without stating them officially or acknowledging them publicly. The very nature of law and our criminal justice system gives operating police officers wide discretion in deciding when and how the law should be enforced. On both the administrative and the operating levels, there are often very good reasons for selective law enforcement (e.g., budgetary constraints on what can feasibly be done, the existence of outdated statutes) and, on occasion, some very bad reasons (e.g., bias against a segment of the community).

To prevent abuses, selective law enforcement policies should be formulated and implemented in an open, orderly manner. The means for accomplishing this exists. Such action would benefit both the police and the community, and would increase the positive nature of their ongoing relationship.

STUDENT CHECKLIST

1. Define discretion and its role in the justice system.

2. Explain some of the administrative and operational justifications for selective enforcement.

3. Identify the legal authority for selective enforcement.

4. Describe some of the dangers inherent in selective enforcement.

5. Based on the strategies discussed in this chapter, develop a strategy for structuring discretion in a police agency. Describe its strengths and weaknesses.

TOPICS FOR DISCUSSION

1. Debate the use of selective law enforcement.

2. What will happen if police agencies are open in regard to their use of selective and discriminatory law enforcement?

3. How do the police agencies in your community (1) define policy regarding discretionary decision making, and (2) provide controls to eliminate abuse?

ONE STEP FORWARD

Making a Decision

Stage One

You are dispatched to 3321 N. Maryvale Road to the Janns's residence. The dispatcher says that a family fight is reported to be in progress. Upon arrival, you hear yelling and screaming coming from inside the residence. You are joined by Deputy Slick. The two of you go to the front door and request permission to come inside. Mrs. Debra Janns invites you inside the residence.

As you step inside, Mr. Paul Janns, age 30 years, yells at his wife and you. He says to you and Deputy Slick: "Get the hell out of my house! I didn't call you and you don't belong here."

At this point:

1. What is your primary goal?

2. What are your options for accomplishing this goal?

3. Looking at each option, were you to act on it, what would be the probable outcome (both short term and long term)?

4. Which option will you choose and how will you act upon it?

Stage Two

Because at least one of your immediate goals would be to defuse the volatile situation you might do the following:

In a calm, even voice you ask Mr. Janns to calm down and either to step outside or go into another room with you to talk about the situation. Mrs. Janns, at this point, yells at her husband: "Get out of here! I don't ever want to see you again." Mr. Janns says he isn't leaving. He turns to you and Deputy Slick and says that he and his wife can solve this problem without your help.

Should you:

1. Leave? Why or why not?
2. Arrest him? Why or why not?
3. Arrest them both? Why or why not?
4. Try another calming approach? Why or why not?
5. Do you have as many options as you did at Stage One?

Stage Three

You place a hand on Mr. Jann's arm. He pulls away from you. Deputy Slick quickly steps in. He orders Mr. Janns to step outside. Mr. Janns says: "I don't want to go. I don't have any place to go."

Mrs. Janns says that she would like to file a complaint against her husband for assault. At this statement, Mr. Janns begins yelling again. He lunges at his wife.

1. What is your goal at this point?
2. Is the goal different from the one you expressed at Stage One?
3. What are your options for achieving it?
4. Are your options more limited at this point than in Stage One and Two? Why or why not?

Stage Four

Hopefully, you will have avoided this very common outcome to this scenario:

You and Deputy Slick move quickly to restrain Mr. Janns physically, because that seems to be your only remaining option. You arrest him, read him his rights, and take him into custody.

1. Did you have other options at this point?
2. What would you recommend to officers as guidelines for discretion in such situations?
3. How do the guidelines you suggest protect both you and the family and encourage solution at Stage One or Two?
4. Compare your suggested guidelines with those established for a law enforcement agency in your community.

BIBLIOGRAPHY

American Bar Association (1972). *The Urban Police Function.* New York: Institute of Judicial Administration.

Atkins, B., and Pogrebin, M. (eds.) (1978). *The Invisible Justice System: Discretion and the Law.* Cincinnati, Ohio: Anderson.

Barker, T., and Carter, D. L. (1994). *Police Deviance,* 3rd ed. Cincinnati, Ohio: Anderson.

Barker, T., Hunter, R. D., and Rush, J. P. (1994). *Police Systems and Practices.* Englewood Cliffs, N.J.: Prentice Hall.

Carter, D. L., Sapp, A. D., and Stephens, D. W. (1989). *The State of Police Education: Policy Direction in the 21st Century.* Washington, D.C.: Police Executive Research Forum.

Cicourel, A. (1968). *The Social Organization of Juvenile Justice.* New York: Wiley.

Commission on Accreditation for Law Enforcement Agencies (1987). *Standards for Law Enforcement Agencies.* Fairfax, Va.: CALEA.

Davis, K. C. (1970). "Discretionary justice," *Journal of Legal Education,* Vol. 23, pp. 58–59.

Edelman v. California, 344 U.S. 357 (1953).

Finckenauer, J. (1976). "Higher education and police discretion," *Journal of Police Science and Administration,* Vol. 3, pp. 450–457.

Finckenauer, J. (1976). "Some factors in police discretion and decision-making," *Journal of Criminal Justice,* Vol. 4.

Gardiner, J. (1969). *Traffic and the Police.* Cambridge, Mass.: Harvard University Press.

Georgia Criminal Justice and Traffic Law Manual. (1991). Charlottesville, Va.: The Michie Company.

Goldman, N. (1963). *The Differential Selection of Juvenile Offenders for Court Appearance.* New York: National Council on Crime and Delinquency.

Goldstein, H. (1963). "Police discretion: The ideal vs. the real," *Public Administration Review,* Vol. 23.

Goldstein, H. (1977). *Policing a Free Society.* Cambridge, Mass.: Ballinger.

Greenlee, M. R. (1980). "Discretionary decision making in the field," *The Police Chief,* February, pp. 50–51.

Lester, D. (1981). "An alternative perspective: The use of deadly force by police and civilians," *The Police Chief,* December, pp. 56–57.

Mark, J. A. (1976). "Police organizations: The challenges and dilemmas of change," in A. S. Blumberg and A. Neiderhoffer (Eds.), *The Ambivalent Force: Perspectives on the Police,* 2nd ed. Hinsdale, Ill.: Dryden Press.

Marx, G. T. (1982). "Who really gets stung? Some issues raised by the new police undercover work," *Crime and Delinquency,* April, pp. 165–193.

New Haven Register (1971), New Haven, Conn., December 2.

Newman, D. J. (1978). *Introduction to Criminal Justice,* 2nd ed. Philadelphia: J. B. Lippincott.

Piliavin, I., and Briar, S. (1964). "Police encounters with juveniles," *American Journal of Sociology,* Vol. 70, p. 206.

Reed, B. (1980). "Issues and trends in police discretion," *The Police Chief,* November, pp. 54–59.

Reiss, A. J., Jr. (1971). *Police and the Public*. New Haven, Conn.: Yale University Press.

Report of U.S. National Advisory Committee on Civil Disorders (1968). Washington, D.C.: U.S. Government Printing Office.

Schiller, S. A. (1972). "More light on a low visibility function," *Police Law Quarterly*, Vol. 6. See also October 1972, January 1973, and April 1973 issues.

Senna, J. J., and Siegel, L. J. (1993). *Introduction to Criminal Justice*, 10th ed. St. Paul, Minn.: West.

Skolnick, J. (1975). *Justice Without a Trial*, 2nd ed. New York: Wiley.

Smith, W. F. (1983). "Undercover operations: Essential to combat public corruption." Excerpted from an address by the attorney general at a public forum sponsored by the Association of the Bar of the City of New York. Printed in *Justice Assistance News*.

Wagner, A. E. (1980). "Citizen complaints against the police: The accused officer," *Journal of Police Science and Administration*, Vol. 8, pp. 373–379.

Willis, C., and Ward, R. (1988). "The police and child abuse: An analysis of police decisions to report illegal behavior," *Criminology*, Vol. 26, pp. 695–716.

Wilson, J. Q. (1968). *Varieties of Police Behavior*. Cambridge, Mass.: Harvard University Press.

Wilson, J. Q. (1977). *Thinking About Crime*. New York: Random House.

Wilson, J. Q. (1989). *Bureaucracy: What Government Agencies Do and Why They Do It*. New York: Basic Books.

8

THE MEDIA LINK

Relations in the community . . . are a direct product of police activities in the jurisdiction. But, all too often, we tend to overlook that they are also a product of perceptions and opinions formed by public contact with the mass media.
(Speir, 1977)

The media represent a principal link between police agencies and the public they serve. Media impact on virtually every citizen is enormous, and crime news is a major media topic. Except for the relatively few people who become directly involved with the police, private citizens learn of police activity, of crime prevention, of the pursuit and apprehension of criminals and their disposition in the courts by what they read in their newspapers and see and hear on television and radio. True or not, positive or negative, what a citizen reads, hears, and observes in the local media largely defines the citizen's perception of the police.

Efforts of the press to transmit the truth as they see it may help or hinder the efforts of the police. They may endanger an individual or group, increase public fear, the intensity of riots, and the credibility of terrorists, and according to some observers, create a criminal environment. They may invade privacy or defame character of individuals. They may interfere with the rights of defendants to a fair trial. On the other hand, efforts of the press may uncover crime and criminals, exonerate those convicted unjustly, protect the public from corruption in public service, encourage public involvement in crime prevention and other special emphasis programs, decrease danger to individuals or groups, and allay excessive public fear, usually through education.

STUDYING THIS CHAPTER WILL ENABLE YOU TO:

1. Overview media commitment to the reporting of crime news.
2. Contrast the responsibility of the press and the police.
3. Justify the need for guidelines in reporting.

4. Establish police–media guidelines for routine information release, crisis situations, and hostage situations.

5. Identify ongoing blocks to positive police–media relations and strategies for resolving them.

6. Contrast individual constitutional rights and the public's right to know.

MASSIVE MEDIA IMPACT

The crucial importance of the media to local police departments can be emphasized by considering the media environment with its numerous technological choices that we live in as we go about our daily activities. For example:

> We awaken to the alarm of a clock radio in the morning, listen to the news as we comb our hair, watch the "Today" show as we eat breakfast, hear our favorite singer on radio show which is interrupted by local and national news, telephone and teleconference with others at work, connect with the traffic world on our CB as we drive home in the evening, relax after dinner by watching the evening news on television. Late that night, we might watch a sports event or movie on television. (Adapted from Silvestri, 1991)

The problem with this media technology is that it acts as a "go-between" or gatekeeper which selects and heightens certain kinds of information. Therefore, the "reality" of the media information may not be the reality of the real world. As Silvestri (1991) suggests, media consumers always run the risk that they may accept media choices as the only "real" ones. This is especially likely when one considers that 98 percent of all households have television sets.

A COMMUNITY RELATIONS CONTEXT

In Chapter 7 we concentrated on police discretion and selective enforcement of law, something that is often hidden from public eye. In this chapter we address police–media relations, something that is rarely hidden from the public. Some references approach police–media concerns in a narrow public information or public relations context. We approach it, instead, in the broader context of community relations because the nature of the police–media relationship in a community is integrally related to the nature of the larger police–community relationship.

A COMMITMENT TO CRIME COVERAGE

Statistics on massive media impact would be of little interest to police if it were not for the fact that media commitment to crime coverage is great. Some difference of opinion exists as to how much news about murder, robbery, rape, and larceny the public really wants or demands. But there can be little doubt that, with or without clear public demand, maximum coverage of crime is offered. Recent surveys have placed the proportion of crime news to total newspaper space at anywhere from 3 to 10 percent. In an individual issue, crime news may represent 30 to 35 percent. Moreover, this news often is given priority space.

The Subjectivity Factor

Papers can emphasize crime (grossly overemphasize, the critics of the press argue) by the placement of stories on page one, by large, black, and often lurid headlines, and by other attention-getting devices. "In weighing the effect on justice," Lofton, author of *Justice and the Press,* wrote, "The play and the slant of crime news are even more important than the amount of space allotted to the subject. . . . The large and dramatic headline on the front page gets more attention from readers than a small, unprovocative item buried on the back pages" (Lofton, 1966). In large city newspapers in particular, sensational crimes are often given more space than significant news of national and international events. The story of a $15 robbery in a small community often occupies more space in the local newspaper than the expenditure by the local government of hundreds of thousands of dollars.

Some people question whether or not a news story can ever be totally objective. Paul Harvey, the well-known radio commentator, was asked on ABC television's "Good Morning, America," why he chose to call his newscasts commentaries rather than news reports. He explained that news reports are assumed to be objective, yet, realistically, all such reports include some elements of subjectivity (in what is reported and omitted, what is accented, the tone in which it is reported, etc.). Saying that a report is objective, then, may be misleading. Paul Harvey would rather not mislead his listeners. Because news commentary makes no claims to objectivity, and is, by definition, a subjective comment on the news, Mr. Harvey stated that he feels more comfortable with that format (March 1983).

An Argument for Restricting Coverage

Although some media sources choose individually to restrict crime coverage in some specific category of crime for a specific period of time, rarely has a general policy to restrict crime coverage been made and adhered to.

In the 1930s, Curtis H. Clay, editor of the La Salle, Illinois *Post-Tribune* made such a policy. Although crime news was not entirely omitted from the newspaper, it was relegated to less than front-page priority for a period of two or three years. Ownership of the paper has changed. It is now called the *Daily News-Tribune,* and this policy no longer exists (Hames, 1983). Mr. Clay's rationale for his restrictive policy is instructive, however:

> The intelligent criminal enters his career deliberately, with eyes open to chances of beating the law. He believes he is smarter than the police. Publicity encourages him; he likes to see his name in the headlines. He laughs at the "dumb cops" and continues his outlawry, glorying in his notoriety. If and when he gets caught, he is ready to face the music. Wasn't his name on the front page for weeks, months? . . . Publicity can't stop him. It will not injure his reputation. It will enhance it. (MacDougall, 1964, p. 389)

An Argument for Heavy Coverage

Using Al Capone as his central character, Thomas S. Rice, a student of the press, argued an opposite view—that of sensationalizing crime in order to fight it:

> It is far, far better for the safety of our citizens and their families that we should have too much crime news instead of too little. . . . Every improvement in police administration and methods has followed newspapers playing up crime. Constant harping on Al Capone, with the definite object of bringing him to book, was not making a hero out of him. The Chicago newspapers which led the fight against that contamination of their city had the definite purpose of causing his fall. . . . Capone and other lawbreakers have come to grief from systematic sensationalizing of their personalities as well as their deeds until the public rose in revolt. (MacDougall, 1964, p. 391)

Rice claimed that what he called "systematic sensationalizing" led not only to Capone's downfall but to the creation of the Chicago Crime Commission, which helped improve the administration of criminal justice in that city. Similar "sensationalizing" by newspapers, Rice said, led to the creation of similar commissions in Cleveland, Baltimore, and Philadelphia.

Certainly the press often can cause public outrage which, in turn, will bring about political pressures needed to motivate appropriate police action (Barker and Carter, 1994).

EXPLOITATION OF CRIME NEWS

Whatever one thinks of the relative merits of the conflicting arguments of Clay and Rice, it is the latter's views that are practiced by virtually all publishers, editors, and reporters of the daily newspapers of America. Newspaper coverage that followed the 1946 arrest of a 17-year-old Chicago youth, William Heirens, for several brutal murders was reasonably typical: The five Chicago newspapers gave, in total, much more coverage to the Heirens case, from arrest to sentencing, than to critical national events. A study of 85 issues of Chicago newspapers during that period revealed 62 banner headlines for the Heirens case, 11 to the operations of the Office of Price Administration (which affected the pocketbooks of virtually every person in America), and only 4 to atomic bomb tests.

Whether or not the readers of American newspapers share this preoccupation, a favorite topic of the media, newspapers in particular, is violent crime. And although the degree of sensationalizing in American newspapers has diminished in the last 50 years, there is more than enough evidence that the press relies heavily on crime news. There is also evidence to suggest that some newspapers exploit what they claim to be public interest in crime in order to sell their newspapers. Ed Murray, managing editor of the Los Angeles *Mirror,* wrote of the Marilyn Sheppard murder case: "This case has mystery, society, sex, and glamour," thus explaining the massive coverage American papers gave to an event that was really a rather ordinary homicide (Lofton, 1966, p. 182). Herbert H. Krauch, editor of the Los Angeles *Herald and Express* (2000 miles from the murder and trial site) said of the trial of Sam Sheppard: "It's been a long time since there's been a murder trial this good" (Sandman et al., 1972, p. 369).

There are other editors who, like Murray and Krauch, are convinced that crime news sells. And there is evidence to support them. In 1956, for example, two sisters were raped and murdered and the resultant stories boosted total circulation of the city's daily newspapers by 50,000 copies. One year later when a rapist ran wild in San Francisco, that city's four newspapers had a field day. The *Chronicle* called the attacker the "Torture Kit Rapist" (the victims had been manacled and tortured by the rapist who had used a knife, adhesive tape, manacles, and scissors). The *News* called the murderer the "Fang Fiend" (because he had been described by one would-be victim as having "canine teeth, which protruded fang-like over his lower lip"). A 23-year-old warehouse clerk was arrested as the rapist-murderer; when another man confessed, the press abandoned the case. But the coverage had been profitable, for during each day of the almost two-week coverage of the case, each San Francisco newspaper sold about 15,000 more copies than normal.

Competition today is greater in television news than among newspapers in many areas. Although there may be a minimum of four local channels (NBC, ABC, and CBS affiliates and a local independent station) competing for the "best" coverage of the evening news, there may be only one evening newspaper.

PUBLIC REACTION TO MEDIA COVERAGE

Much has been said about the impact of television programming—sometimes including the news—particularly on young members of the viewing public. This impact is behind the recent move of the television networks to restrict the amount of violence shown on TV. This voluntary movement by the television networks came about because Congress was going to examine the issue. The average American child watches more than 20 hours of TV a week, and studies have shown that youths exposed to violence and aggression on television and in the movies are more likely to copy that behavior (Senna and Siegel, 1993). Controlled laboratory studies have not confirmed this link, however; there is a need for more research on this issue.

The press, particularly television, has been criticized by citizens, acting independently of these organizations, for what the citizens have perceived as exploitation of crime coverage. For example, a television documentary on the life of Gary Gilmore, the convicted murderer who made national news for choosing to be executed, was angrily denounced by many as a poor use of air time. It was suggested that the time and money spent developing and airing such a product could be better spent on documentaries about people who had made positive contributions to our civilization.

NBC's 1983 program called "Special Report" generated even more anger among many citizens. "Special Report" was actually a work of fiction realistically portrayed on television, using NBC's "Special Report" format. The story was a modern version of H. G. Wells's *The War of the Worlds*. It ended depicting massive destruction by terrorists in South Carolina. Although disclaimers were broadcast frequently, many people believed that the story was a special news report. The anger directed at the network, however, was for what citizens viewed as network irresponsibility in presenting a realistic model for terrorists to follow.

Coverage by media of the Tylenol poisonings in Chicago in 1982 received mixed reviews by the public. Some people seemed to feel that the coverage sensationalized events and encouraged "copycat" crimes. Others expressed an appreciation of the coverage, calling it restrained and geared toward the protection of the public (because the cause of the problem was not immediately apparent).

Recently, the Pepsi tampering scare led to more than 50 complaints in 23 states within days of the first complaint in Tacoma, Washington. By the end of the first week many of these complaints had been exposed as hoaxes and at least a dozen people had been arrested. Forensic psychiatrist Park Dietz, consultant to the FBI, states that "each nationally publicized incident generates on average 30 more seriously disruptive crime," and asks that news organizations limit their coverage of tampering (Toufexis, 1993). N. G. Berrill, a psychologist with the New York Forensic Health Group, states that the classic tamperer is an angry, antisocial person who "gets a real sense of power from devising a plan and seeing it blossom in the media" (Toufexis, 1993).

When ABC undertook its 1983 "Crime in America" series, the network demonstrated awareness of crime coverage issues by taking great care to avoid sensationalism. The series was presented with documentation and reserve. Balance was provided by presenting issues from many points of view. The current interest in such shows as "Unsolved Mysteries," "America's Most Wanted," and "Cops" would be open to charges of crime exploitation, especially when they portray actual victims and witnesses, if it were not for their crime-fighting credentials.

CONFLICT BETWEEN MEDIA AND POLICE

It is clear that accounts of sensational, violent crimes sell newspapers and draw attention to radio and television news. But do attempts by the media to report crime help or hinder police efforts to fight crime? The record does not supply a clear answer.

A Hindrance and a Help

From the point of view of the police, overcoverage and sensationalizing of crime may not in themselves produce law enforcement problems. Occasionally, however, the press works at cross-purposes with the police, and law enforcement is hindered. This is particularly true in kidnapping cases, where the relationship between press and police is the most critical; the safety of the victim often depends upon the cooperation given by the press to the police. Former FBI Director J. Edgar Hoover once compiled a list of cases in which he claimed the media had seriously hindered the work of his agency. One such case cited by Hoover was the Mattson kidnapping. Newspapermen prevented contact with the kidnappers of young Charles Mattson by refusing to leave the neighborhood of the Mattson home in Seattle. The boy's father received a letter from the kidnappers containing a newspaper picture of reporters around the house and said there would be no contact until they left. The Mattson boy was later found dead, obviously murdered by the kidnappers. In another case, the Peter Levine kidnapping, a reporter, trying to verify rumors that the boy was missing, phoned the boy's father who, caught off guard, admitted that his child was missing and said that he was willing to pay ransom. Warned by the kidnapper to prevent publicity, the father tried to persuade the newspapers to suppress the story, but the papers refused. Later, the headless body of the kidnapped boy was found floating in Long Island Sound.

But, in other cases, the press has shown restraint and cooperation with the police. In the Lindbergh kidnapping case, the press voluntarily suppressed the contents of the original ransom note and the fact that the Treasury Department had sent the serial numbers of the bank notes used as ransom to banks across the country. The press also refrained from following Lindbergh on his futile trips to meet the kidnapper and deliberately misled the kidnapper by publishing false information about police activity. Such cooperation did not save the Lindbergh infant. It eventually led to the capture, trial, and execution of Bruno Richard Hauptmann for the kidnapping and murder of young Lindbergh.

Generally, the press has become more sensitive in kidnapping cases. In 1954, a 60-hour "conspiracy of silence" by all San Francisco newspapers, wire services, and broadcasters was credited with saving the life of a kidnapped real estate operator. A year later, however, the New York *Daily News* was widely, and properly, condemned by police and others for failing to go along with other New York area newspapers that had refrained from publishing accounts of the kidnapping of one-month-old Peter Weinberger (MacDougall, 1964, p. 395). Frightened by the crowd at the site selected for the transfer of the ransom money, which had been reported in the *Daily News,* the kidnapper killed the baby.

The press has occasionally thwarted police work in nonkidnapping cases as well. By reporting detailed clues discovered by the police or announcing the time and place of a planned investigation, the press can—and in some cases actually does—tip off the criminal, who may destroy the evidence and avoid capture. But again, the record of the press is mixed, for persistent, imaginative reporters have helped the police to solve crimes and, in some cases, have solved the crimes themselves. The brutal murder of Bobby Franks in Chicago in 1923 was solved by the detective work of two reporters of the Chicago *Daily News,* whose suspicions led to the arrest and conviction of Nathan Leopold and Richard Loeb. In 1930, the Kansas City *Star* solved the murder of Mrs. A. D. Payne by her husband. Ku Klux Klan leader D. C. Stephenson went to prison for the murder of Madge Oberhalzer as a result of the investigative efforts of the Indianapolis *Times* and the Vincennes *Commercial.* The Chicago *Daily News* won a Pulitzer Prize for uncovering the stealing of millions of dollars from the Illinois State Treasury by the state auditor, Orville Hodge.

Other media exposés include the Watergate findings that ended the presidency of Richard Nixon and brought charges against his aides.

The complete list of similar exposés of crime is long, evidence that the press and police are not necessarily natural adversaries.

Champions of the Innocent

The press has not only uncovered crime and criminals, but it can point to a long record of exonerating people already convicted of crime. In 1932, Joe Majczek was sent to prison for life for a murder he insisted he had not committed. Twelve years later, a series of articles in the Chicago *Times* revealed that he had been convicted largely on the testimony of a witness who had been threatened with prosecution for violating the Prohibition law unless she identified Majczek as the murderer. Majczek thereupon was freed from prison, fully pardoned, and compensated by the state for his 12 years in prison. The same year that Majczek was freed, a young, inarticulate black, Willie Calloway, was sentenced to life imprisonment for murder. His case came to the attention of reporter Ken McCormack of the Detroit *Free Press* who wrote a series of articles that helped to exonerate Calloway. Calloway was then released after eight years in prison for a crime he did not commit.

A CLEAR NEED FOR GUIDELINES

The Background

Essentially, police and the media have different functions, and the difference can bring them into conflict. The police task is to prevent crime, maintain law and order, protect the citizens of the community, and apprehend lawbreakers and bring them to justice. The media in a free society have an obligation to seek out and report the truth, even though the truth may embarrass or hinder the police. The information becomes a product that they package and sell in competition with other media. Nevertheless, the Society of Professional Journalists has had a Code of Ethics since 1926 (see Figure 8-1). This code does not specifically cover all the incidents that may arise in the reporting of crime-related information (e.g., protection of rape victims, juveniles, hostage and terrorist incidents, etc.).

Competing Rights

Conflict between police and media often arises because the police are caught in the crossfire of competing rights under two key amendments to the U.S. Constitution. On one hand, the First Amendment guarantees an almost absolute right to print virtually anything, free of legal restraint. The Sixth Amendment, however, guarantees every person the right to a fair trial, which means a trial by peers who have not been influenced by prejudicial publicity before or during trial. Individuals in our society have a right to privacy and, within limits, not to have their character defamed (see Appendixes for text of Amendments). How can these competing rights be resolved fairly?

According to the U.S. Supreme Court in *Branzburg* v. *Hayes* [408 U.S. 665, 682–685, 92 S.Ct., 2646, 2657–2658, 33 LEd 2nd. 626 640–642 (1972)], "Newsmen have no constitutional right of access to the scenes of crime or disaster when the general public is excluded and they may be prohibited from attending or publishing information about trials if such restrictions are necessary to assure a defendant a fair trial before an impartial tribunal."

Recognizing the Need for Guidelines

The necessity for developing guidelines for resolving or controlling conflicts involving the responsibilities or rights of the media, the police, and citizens (victims and defendants), has not always been recognized. However, three sensational cases were largely responsible for spotlighting or demonstrating this need.

FIGURE 8-1   Code of Ethics of the Society of Professional Journalists.

SOCIETY of Professional Journalists, believes the duty of journalists is to serve the truth.

We BELIEVE the agencies of mass communication are carriers of public discussion and information, acting on their Constitutional mandate and freedom to learn and report the facts.

We BELIEVE in public enlightenment as the forerunner of justice, and in our Constitutional role to seek the truth as part of the public's right to know the truth.

We BELIEVE those responsibilities carry obligations that require journalists to perform with intelligence, objectivity, accuracy, and fairness.

To these ends, we declare acceptance of the standards of practice here set forth:

I. Responsibility:

The public's right to know of events of public importance and interest is the overriding mission of the mass media. The purpose of distributing news and enlightened opinion is to serve the general welfare. Journalists who use their professional status as representatives of the public for selfish or other unworthy motives violate a high trust.

II. Freedom of the Press:

Freedom of the press is to be guarded as an inalienable right of people in a free society. It carries with it the freedom and the responsibility to discuss, question, and challenge actions and utterances of our government and of our public and private institutions. Journalists uphold the right to speak unpopular opinions and the privilege to agree with the majority.

III. Ethics:

Journalists must be free of obligation to any interest other than the public's right to know the truth.

1. Gifts, favors, free travel, special treatment or privileges can compromise the integrity of journalists and their employers. Nothing of value should be accepted.

2. Secondary employment, political involvement, holding public office, and service in community organizations should be avoided if it compromises the integrity of journalists and their employers. Journalists and their employers should conduct their personal lives in a manner that protects them from conflict of interest, real or apparent. Their responsibilities to the public are paramount. That is the nature of their profession.

3. So-called news communications from private sources should not be published or broadcast without substantiation of their claims to news values.

4. Journalists will seek news that serves the public interest, despite the obstacles. They will make constant efforts to assure that the public's business is conducted in public and that public records are open to public inspection.

5. Journalists acknowledge the newsman's ethic of protecting confidential sources of information.

6. Plagiarism is dishonest and unacceptable.

IV. Accuracy and Objectivity:

Good faith with the public is the foundation of all worthy journalism.

1. Truth is our ultimate goal.
2. Objectivity in reporting the news is another goal that serves as the mark of an experienced professional. It is a standard of performance toward which we strive. We honor those who achieve it.
3. There is no excuse for inaccuracies or lack of thoroughness.
4. Newspaper headlines should be fully warranted by the contents of the articles they accompany. Photographs and telecasts should give an accurate picture of an event and not highlight an incident out of context.
5. Sound practice makes clear distinction between news reports and expressions of opinion. News reports should be free of opinion or bias and represent all sides of an issue.
6. Partisanship in editorial comment that knowingly departs from the truth violates the spirit of American journalism.
7. Journalists recognize their responsibility for offering informed analysis, comment, and editorial opinion on public events and issues. They accept the obligation to present such material by individuals whose competence, experience, and judgment qualify them for it.
8. Special articles or presentations devoted to advocacy or the writer's own conclusions and interpretations should be labeled as such.

V. Fair Play:

Journalists at all times will show respect for the dignity, privacy, rights, and well-being of people encountered in the course of gathering and presenting the news.

1. The news media should not communicate unofficial charges affecting reputation or moral character without giving the accused a chance to reply.
2. The news media must guard against invading a person's right to privacy.
3. The media should not pander to morbid curiosity about details of vice and crime.
4. It is the duty of news media to make prompt and complete correction of their errors.
5. Journalists should be accountable to the public for their reports and the public should be encouraged to voice its grievances against the media. Open dialogue with our readers, viewers, and listeners should be fostered.

VI. Mutual Trust:

Adherence to this code is intended to preserve and strengthen the bond of mutual trust and respect between American journalists and the American people.

The Society shall—by programs of education and other means—encourage individual journalists to adhere to these tenets, and shall encourage journalistic publications and broadcasters to recognize their responsibility to frame codes of ethics in concert with their employees to serve as guidelines in furthering these goals.

Code of Ethics (adopted 1926; revised 1973, 1984, 1987).

FIGURE 8-1   (continued)

The Bruno Hauptmann Trial

Before 1935, there was comparatively little concern for the rights of suspects and defendants, some of whom were badly treated by the police or the press, or by both. Then came the trial of Bruno Hauptmann for the kidnap-murder of the Lindbergh infant. The press, which had shown such commendable restraint before Hauptmann's capture, treated the trial at Flemington, New Jersey, as a combination circus and passion play, as did the prosecution, the defense, and the public itself. The prosecutor told a reporter that he "would wrap the kidnap ladder around Hauptmann's neck," a threat that was duly carried in the newspapers of the day. The defense counsel ordered stationery for Hauptmann to answer his "fan mail"; the letterhead carried a facsimile of the kidnap ladder. The press allied itself with the prosecution, charging once that the defendant was making "senseless denials" and, on another occasion, with being "a thing lacking in human characteristics." Although photographs had been forbidden in the courtroom, not only still pictures but motion pictures as well were taken and displayed to the public.

It was the Hauptmann trial that first compelled the organized bar to consider the need for a code of conduct that might prevent the improprieties and excesses of that trial. An 18-member committee of newspaper reporters, broadcasters, editors, publishers, and lawyers agreed on a general code of conduct to guide prosecutors, defense counsel, and the press in future criminal trials. The code drawn up by this committee was accepted by the American Bar Association but, except for Canon 35 (which prohibited photographs in the courtroom), the guidelines were generally ignored until two events many years later—the assassination of President John F. Kennedy and the Supreme Court decision in the Sam Sheppard case.

The Assassination of President Kennedy

The aftermath of the Kennedy assassination did more than anything since the Hauptmann trial to spur new remedies for the injustices of pretrial publicity. "From the moment of his arrest until his murder two days later," the American Civil Liberties Union concluded, "Lee Harvey Oswald was tried and convicted many times over in the newspapers, on the radio, and over television by the public statements of the Dallas law enforcement officials. Time and time again, high-ranking police and prosecution officials stated their complete satisfaction that Oswald was the assassin. As their investigation uncovered one piece of evidence after the other, the results were broadcast to the public" (Lofton, 1966, p. 130). The Warren Commission reached similar conclusions in its 1964 report and also criticized District Attorney Henry Wade and Police Chief Jesse E. Curry for their statements to the press which, the commission believed, were potentially harmful to both the prosecution and the defense. The commission criticized, too, the press for its lack of self-discipline, which created general disorder in the police and court buildings in Dallas. The events in Dallas that weekend, the commission said, "are a dramatic affirmation of the need for steps to bring about a proper balance between the right of the public to be informed and the right of an individual to a fair and impartial trial" (Lofton, 1966, p. xii).

The Trial of Dr. Sam Sheppard

But the need for definitive guidelines did not become critical until 1966 when the Supreme Court, in the Sam Sheppard decision, told the bench, the bar, the police, and the press that every defendant in a criminal case was entitled to a trial unpolluted by prejudicial pretrial publicity. It is widely held that the 1955 trial of Dr. Sheppard is one of the most flagrant examples of irresponsible behavior, not only by the news media but by the judiciary and law enforcement officials as well. The Supreme Court, in reversing Sheppard's conviction, agreed.

In its Sheppard decision, the Court offered explicit guidance on how trial courts and police should seek to preserve the defendant's right to a fair and impartial trial, preventing interference by the press. Many of these strictures were incorporated into guidelines that were later drawn up by joint bench-bar-press committees in various states, although many of the Supreme Court "rules" were already contained in such guidelines established prior to 1966.

Complicating Issues

Concerns of Victims and Witnesses

Publication of a victim's name and address may increase potential danger to that person and lessen his or her ability to resolve the personal emotional trauma related to the event. This is especially true for rape victims. There are times when witnesses too may be endangered in much the same way by media coverage. Publication restraint in these areas requires media guidelines. Only recently have these concerns of victims and witnesses been considered in any organized way by the media.

The highly publicized 10-day rape trial of William Kennedy Smith in 1991 raised two issues concerning media coverage: the use of TV cameras in the courtroom and media protection of the privacy rights of the rape victim. The legal community was deeply divided over the issue of TV coverage (*USA Today,* 1991). Nevertheless, TV coverage was allowed in this trial and the privacy issue became a source of controversy. CNN News covered the face of the alleged rape victim, but it was not long before she was identified. The same issues were raised in the highly publicized 1992 rape trial of heavyweight champion Mike Tyson. The state of Indiana, which normally does not allow courtroom TV coverage, allowed the use of closed-circuit TV to accommodate the more than 100 news organizations which covered the trial (Senna and Siegel, 1993).

It is easy to imagine the horror of learning of the death of a loved one by way of the media news. Because the news may be broadcast or published before next of kin can be notified of the death of a family member, guidelines for release of the name and address of the deceased are necessary.

Crisis Situations

Disturbances and Unrest

The advent of militancy in the 1960s, urban guerrilla warfare, student unrest and demonstrations, civil rights protests, riots, and fire bombings have created new problems for the police. Effective working arrangements with the mass media in these situations are critical.

One commentator said: "Nothing, but nothing, ever happens the same way after you put a television or movie camera on it." Television, with its capacity for instantaneous reporting, has often incited violence, usually unintentionally, by attracting those who seek attention. Both rioters and police have been known to perform for the media. And occasionally the media has manufactured the news. During the riots in Newark, New Jersey, for example, a newspaper photographer from a New York newspaper was seen urging, and finally convincing, a young black boy to throw a rock for the benefit of the cameras. In Chicago in the late 1960s, a television camera crew was seen leading two "hippie" girls into an area filled with National Guardsmen. As the cameras started rolling, one of the girls cried on cue: "Don't beat me, don't beat me!" Virtually all the media outlets have their own rules against this sort of staging, but occasionally the rules tend to be forgotten during a major upheaval.

A less violent confrontation was described by an observer in the 1960s after a three-man television crew arrived at a labor picket line. Although the crew chief was disappointed because, from a pictorial standpoint, it was not much of a demonstration, he decided to film it anyway ("We may as well get it."). As the observer related: "The light man held up his 30-foot lamp and laid a 4-foot beam of light across the picket line. Instantly, the marchers' heads snapped up, their eyes flashed. They threw up their arms in the clenched fist salute. Some made a 'V' with their fingers, and they held up their banners for the cameras." The event was transformed into something substantially different than it would have been had not the television crew arrived to record it.

Immense damage can result during a civil disturbance as a result of a lack of restraint by press or police, by inaccurate reporting, by journalistic sensationalizing, by police overreaction, or by a breakdown in communication between the press and the police. A false rumor that police had killed a black cab driver in Newark, New Jersey, and an unfounded report of the killing of a seven-year-old boy in Plainfield, New Jersey, fanned major disturbances in those cities. In Tampa, Florida, a deputy sheriff died in the early stages of a riot that intensified after both the Associated Press and United Press International reported that he had been killed by rioters when, in actuality, he had suffered a heart attack.

Much concern was expressed by the media and the public regarding a man who "performed" a suicide for the camera. Many observers believed that no suicide would have taken place if the media had not covered the "event." Some local television stations, acknowledging that "acting" for the camera during disturbances adds to existing problems, use unmarked units on the scene, and thus maintain a low profile. (Figure 8-2).

Although television coverage does provide incentive to violence, police should realize that coverage can also have the opposite effect. No one, including demonstrators, wants his or her unlawful acts recorded on camera (Figure 8-3). The presence of cameras can also have a restraining influence on overzealous police authorities; during the late 1950s and early 1960s, the Justice Department encouraged media coverage of civil rights demonstrations in the belief that it would inhibit violence by unsympathetic police in the Southern states.

Except in the rare instance when police intend to engage in improper conduct, it is in their interest to have reporters present. In Chicago in the 1960s, comedian Dick Gregory complained that police had been "brutal" in arresting him. Station WMAQ-TV carried Gregory's statement without comment, then reran the film showing

FIGURE 8-2   How could press coverage help or hinder police efforts in resolving this crisis? (From the *Tucson Citizen,* Tucson, Arizona.)

Gregory being arrested, a film that did not bear out his claim. The Chicago police were grateful.

Media representatives have long been aware of their grave responsibilities during riot situations. As far back as June 1963, in anticipation of confrontations at

FIGURE 8-3   Although television coverage of scenes of potential disorder may provide an incentive to violence, it may also deter violence, since neither demonstrators nor police wish to have unlawful acts recorded on camera. (Courtesy of Dan Walsh/The Picture Cube.)

Selma, Alabama, Richard Salant, president of CBS News, sent a memorandum to his news personnel at Selma. He warned of "the unsettling effect on a stimulated crowd that the TV camera has," and requested that personnel and equipment be as unobtrusive as possible and that cameras be turned away or covered when there was any danger that their presence might aggravate tensions. In the 1980s in Miami, Florida, the media helped both to increase and decrease tensions in that already tense community.

In December 1979, Arthur McDuffie was involved in a high-speed chase with the police in the streets of Liberty City, a ghetto area of Miami. When he was stopped, a struggle ensued from which McDuffie emerged in a coma. He died four days later from massive skull injuries. Four officers were charged with his death and were acquitted in May 1980. In the riot that followed this decision, 18 more deaths occurred in the Liberty City ghetto. The media in this instance helped to increase the tensions in Liberty City. The case became a major national media event, and many officials believe that the coverage contributed to the problems that already existed (Katzenbach, 1980). In contrast, in early 1983, when blacks were again prepared to riot over another incident, media coverage helped to prevent more violence. Leaders were televised advising restraint. Community administrators were covered promising investigation which was forthcoming.

Hostage and Terrorist Activity

Of growing concern is the disturbing frequency of hostage and terrorist activity involving mass media and local police in almost free-for-all, three-sided confrontation. This has been exacerbated by technological advances in communications such as satellites, microwave relays, and portable cameras and recorders. Most disturbing of all is the occurrence of the "media events" that are staged by various terrorist groups or simply lone psychotics solely to attract mass public attention to their particular demands or problems. A particularly disturbing event of this nature took place in Berkeley, California in 1990. Mehrdad Dashti held 33 hostages in a hotel bar while he made a series of barely coherent demands and statements defining his propose. Even though there was a television set in the bar, TV crews broadcast the event live and reported on what the police were doing outside. The hostage situation was finally resolved with eight hostages shot, one fatally, and Dashti shot dead by the police. This event resulted in a debate over media disclosures of police operations (Goodman, 1990).

Vetter and Perlstein (1991) state that the 1977 Hanafi Muslim Siege in Washington, D.C. is a good example of how the media can be used to make a big story out of a minor terrorist incident. On March 9, 1977, Hamaas Abdul Khaalis, a Hanafi Muslim leader, and 12 members of his religious sect seized 134 hostages. Khaalis demands were that the murderers of his family members (rival religious sect) be handed over to him so that he could exact justice. He also wanted the movie *Mohammed, Messenger of God,* banned in America because it was blasphemous. Television reporters began broadcasting live from the scene and journalists tied up telephone lines by interviewing the terrorists. According to Schmid and DeGraaf (1982) during the three days of the incident NBC spent over 53 percent of its evening news on the story, CBS spent over 31 percent, and ABC spent 40 percent. One news reporter, seeing the police bringing food to the terrorists, reported erroneously that the police were preparing to assault the building. Another reporter called Khaalis and told him that the police were trying to trick him.

More recently, the entire world was mesmerized by the siege of the Branch Davidian compound in Waco, Texas and the deaths of four federal officers during the initial siege. There are allegations, which are under investigation at this time, that the cult members were tipped off about the assault by media representatives.

Of major concern and frustration to the police in these events is the apparent erosion of police control over the situation as a result of the presence of an aggressive, emotion-charged press corps. At times, the terrorist–media contact becomes more amiable than the police–media contact. The obvious presence of physical danger to hostages, police, and others heightens the frustration felt by police.

Since the 1977 Washington, D.C. situation occurred, many attempts have been made to resolve differences between police and press. Negotiations have begun in many cities between news media and police in an effort to establish workable guidelines for both "sides," should such crisis occur in their city. It is not possible to tell in advance, however, how closely police and press will cooperate in the future to guarantee complete and orderly dissemination of information to the public and to preserve the safety—and rights—of all involved.

Studies of prison hostage situations indicate that the amount of violence occurring in the situation is directly related to the degree of media coverage.

SETTING GUIDELINES

Information Release

Guidelines—or statements of principles, as they are called in some states—do exist. Some examples include: in Oregon, a Bar-Press-Broadcasters Joint Statement of Principles; in Massachusetts, a Guide for Bar and News Media; in Kentucky, a Press Association Statement of Principles for Pretrial Reporting; in New York, a Code on Fair Trial and Free Press of the New York County Lawyers Association; and in Philadelphia, a Statement of Policy of the Philadelphia Bar Association. In 1965 the Department of Justice adopted rules, later to be known as the Katzenbach Guidelines (after the then attorney general), which dealt with release of information relating to criminal proceedings by police personnel of the department and its agencies, such as the Federal Bureau of Investigation.

Most such guidelines, particularly as they apply to police, are basically similar. The following discussion is of two sets of guidelines. The first was developed in 1968 by the Wisconsin Advisory Commission on Pretrial Publicity (including a local police chief, a county sheriff, a district attorney, newspaper reporters and broadcasters, several academicians, and a trial judge). The second set, was first developed in 1975 by the Professional Standards Division of the International Association of Chiefs of Police, with input from Public Information Officers from all regions of the United States (Figure 8-4). These are relatively typical of those developed by other states and in local communities.

The Wisconsin Guidelines

These guidelines acknowledged that the media have the right to publish, and the public the right to have, the truth about the administration of criminal justice. On the other hand, law enforcement officials have the right and responsibility to protect the individual's right to a fair trial. The guidelines, therefore, were to aid these officials in deciding what information should or should not be released.

What Can Be Released. *After arrest,* the police can make public the following information under the Wisconsin guidelines.

- The text or substance of the charge.
- The name of the investigative and arresting agency.
- The length of the investigation.
- The defendant's name, address, age, employment, and marital status.

In most states, the police cannot by law release the name of a juvenile defendant. *During an investigation,* the police can release photographs of suspects

FIGURE 8-4   IACP Guidelines for Release Information.

Before Arrest

Information Released

1. A description of the exact offense, including a brief summary of events.
2. Location and time of the offense.
3. Amount taken, injuries sustained, or damages resulting from the action.
4. Identity of the victim, except for a sex crime victim.
5. Whether or not there are suspects.
6. Information about unidentified suspects, such as physical description, vehicle description.
7. Identification of fugitive suspects for whom a warrant has been issued.
8. Criminal background of fugitive when the public should be alert to danger.
9. Method of complaint (officer observation, citizen, warrant, indictment).
10. Length of investigation and name of officer in charge of investigation.

After Arrest

1. Time and place of arrest.
2. Defendant's name, age, residence, employment, marital status, and similar background.
3. The exact charge.
4. Facts and circumstances relating to the arrest, such as resistance, pursuit, possession or use of a weapon, description of contraband discovered.

5. Identity of the agency or unit responsible for the arrest, including the name of the arresting officer.
6. The name of the arresting officer, unless there are unusualy circumstances where it is felt the officer would be jeopardized.
7. Duration of the investigation.
8. Pre-trial release or detention arrangements (including amount of bond, location of detention).
9. Scheduled dates for various stages in the judicial process.

Information Not Released

1. Identity of suspects who are interviewed but not charged.
2. Identity of witnesses, including a victim who can positively identify an assailant.
3. Identity of sex crime victims. (The information should be general—race, sex, age.)
4. Identity of juveniles when specifically restricted by state law.
5. Exact identifying information about the weapon or other physical evidence.
6. Any information that could be known only to the guilty party.
7. Information about valuable items not stolen.
8. Conjecture about suspects or fugitives.
9. Misleading or false information.

After Arrest

1. Comments about the character or reputation of the defendant.

2. Information about the existence or content of a confession, admission, or statement by the accused.

3. The refusal of an accused to make a statement.

4. The refusal of an accused to submit to tests or examinations.

5. Results of any examinations or tests.

6. Description or results of laboratory examination of physical evidence.

7. Re-enactment of the crime.

8. Revelation that the defendant directed investigators to the location of a weapon, contraband or other evidence.

9. Any remarks about the assumed guilt or innocence of the defendant.

10. Comments about the credibility of testimony.

11. If the information for the arrest was derived from an informant.

Source: Reprinted by permission of International Association of Chiefs of Police, Gaithersburg, Md.

FIGURE 8-4 (continued)

"wanted" posters, and other information deemed necessary to the investigation or the apprehension of suspects.

What Cannot Be Released. The Wisconsin guidelines advise that the police not release the following kinds of information.

- Any confessions, admissions, or incriminating statements by the suspect.
- The results of investigative procedures (e.g., polygraph tests, fingerprint identification, ballistics tests).
- Any statement by police officers that might reflect on the credibility of witnesses and expected testimony.
- Any expression of opinion by police officers regarding the character or the guilt or innocence of the accused.

Problem Areas. On some matters guidelines have been somewhat difficult to formulate, and different codes take different positions on what is to be done.

1. *Interviews.* Under the Wisconsin guidelines (and most others) the police will allow the media to interview a defendant only if the person in custody requests it and has been advised of the right to counsel. If the defendant already has an attorney, that attorney must be advised of the request for interview.

2. *Photographs.* Should the police grant media requests to photograph or televise suspects while in custody? The Wisconsin position is that the practice should neither be encouraged nor discouraged. The police should not deliberately pose the suspect, but they may give out a current photo of the suspect.

3. *The circumstances of arrest.* Like most guidelines, those in Wisconsin allow the

police to make a *factual, unadorned* statement of the circumstances surrounding an arrest (e.g., possession of contraband or weapons, resistance to arrest).

4. *Previous criminal record.* The appearance of a suspect's prior record in the press could influence a potential juror; on the other hand, the record is supposed to be public. The Wisconsin guidelines (and most others) resolve the dilemma by instructing police not to *volunteer* the information, but to make it available on *specific inquiry* about it.

Police Operational Response

Who Should Observe the Guidelines?

Guidelines like those adopted in Wisconsin indicate what information should or should not be released to the media, but they do not indicate who in police agencies should make the relevant decisions. Nevertheless, the following rules seem sensible.

1. Statements relating to crime should be made by the ranking member of the department who is present before representatives of the media.
2. If no ranking officer is present, the police officer at the scene of the crime should be entitled to supply "basic and unelaborated information."
3. Where there is doubt as to whether information should be released or withheld, police officers should always choose to withhold it. (If the decision proves wrong, it can be corrected later; a decision to release, on the other hand, cannot be corrected later.)

Voluntary Guidelines

Measures to restrict the flow of prejudicial pretrial publicity may be implemented as a result of statute or court order. The police, press, and members of the bar, however, are free to take such measures on their own. Of course, such voluntary guidelines are not legally binding; nevertheless, by properly disciplining violators, a police agency can ensure that members of the department observe the guidelines.

Advantages of Guidelines to Individual Police Officers

In criminal cases police officers at all levels may face a great deal of media or public pressure to release information that should be withheld. If joint press–bar–police guidelines are in effect, they relieve pressure by pointing to what the police and the press have both agreed to. If only the police have adopted the guidelines, the individual officers can still take themselves "off the hook" by emphasizing that they are only following "policy."

Crisis Guidelines for the Media

As a result of evidence that the presence of the news media, especially television, can encourage violence, the National Advisory Commission on Civil Disorders urged news organizations to develop guidelines for responsible coverage of riots.

Some of the results are listed below. (The initials used indicate the three major networks—NBC, CBS, and ABC.)

1. Use of unmarked or camouflaged cars and equipment (NBC and CBS).
2. Extreme care in using inflammatory words and phrases (e.g., "police brutality," "angry mob," "racial," "riot") and in estimating the size and intensity of crowds (all three networks).
3. Prohibitions against giving the exact location of disturbances or specifics about weaponry; "capping" cameras and lights if they seem to be contributing to disorder or interfering with the police (all three networks).
4. No "live" coverage of disturbances (ABC and CBS).
5. Agreement that media representatives would ask for police protection when needed and that the police are entitled to ask for special credentials from press representatives (all three networks).

Local stations and network affiliates may have individual policies that vary from these guidelines. Police officials need to work closely with local media.

Some suggestions made by a committee of the Northern California Chapter of the Radio and TV News Directors Association fill some of the gaps in the network codes:

1. Competition between broadcasters should continue, but the focus should be changed from dynamic impact to calm reporting of vital information to the public, with maximum assistance in reestablishment of control as the primary goal.
2. Police authorities should take necessary steps to ensure that adequately informed staff members will be on duty at command posts and be available to supply properly identified broadcast newspeople with pertinent information about the disorder.
3. Reports should be calm and objective and should present the overall picture. They should be devoid of sensationalism, speculation, and rumors that could incite or further extend disturbances or stir news breaks.

A Common Interest

The interests of the police and the media sometimes conflict, but they both want to see order restored as quickly as possible in riot situations. The media need the police to get the facts, and the police need the help and the restraint of the media. Thus, they have a second basis for cooperation and for working out, together, plans for dealing with disorders.

A Proposal for Hostage–Terrorist Situations

The following specific guidelines were first suggested by District of Columbia Police Chief Maurice J. Cullinane in 1977 after several major incidents. These suggestions give increased authority and discretion to the police negotiator.

The Media Link   187

1. Live minicamera broadcast should be limited to distance shots.
2. Media should remain in a special "broadcast area" apart from the police line where they could receive briefings from police. (The police negotiator might allow the press into the command center where negotiations are conducted, if circumstances allow.)
3. Telephone calls to people holding hostages should be banned.
4. Live broadcasts showing police stationed around a hostage situation would be barred.

ONGOING PROBLEMS

When in Crisis, React

Because guidelines may be needed only in times of crisis, they may actually be forgotten in the urgency of the moment. If they had been needed on a regular basis, they would be more likely to be a part of common experience and more readily brought to the emergency. They become, then, an untapped resource.

Gathering Dust

Guidelines that gather dust also fail to be updated with changing needs. They exist; they are "on file" but no one knows exactly what they say nor where they are.

Feedback and Updating

The use of guidelines helps to make them practical. If they are tested, reviewed, and evaluated, they become practical and therefore useful.

STRATEGIES FOR THE FUTURE

Regular Police–Media Meetings

The simplest way to ensure effective police–media communication is to *schedule regular meetings between police and media representatives.* One meeting could take place at police headquarters, and the next at a newspaper office or radio or TV station; this alternating pattern would be good from a psychological point of view.

Local police departments would appoint a public information officer or a community relations officer to represent the agency at these meetings, where he or she would work toward clearing up misunderstandings and exploring ways of improving police–media relations.

In addition, the police agency needs to maintain a regular, predictable process for providing crime news to the press. The agency can make offense face sheets ("blues") and police activity résumés available at announced intervals during the day.

Police agencies are not required to provide this information and the press privilege could be withdrawn. However, police efforts to meet the needs of the press for information encourage mutual trust and positive police–press relations (Walsh, 1983).

Press Councils

Background

Several communities in California, Oregon, Illinois, and elsewhere have set up press councils made up of working journalists and members of the public. Their purpose is to review community complaints about the press. With police cooperation, however, they could also help establish liaison between the police and the media. Thus, the police could suggest that a member of the department be a council member, and even that such a council be set up if none exists.

A Proposal

In many places, a specialized press council that would concentrate on crime news might be worthy of consideration. It could consist of 11 persons—five from the media, an attorney or judge, a police official, and four members of the public. Most of the council's work would involve investigating complaints and issuing public reports on its findings. Its only power to effect changes would come from the publicity its findings give problems or abuses, but that is often all that is required to change things for the better.

The Newspaper Ombudsman

The term *ombudsman* refers to a type of official who, in Sweden, deals with citizen complaints against government agencies. Several newspapers in the United States have appointed an ombudsman to deal with citizen complaints about the press (e.g., that a particular crime has been sensationalized, inaccurately reported, or underreported).

Where a newspaper or radio-television ombudsman exists, the police can use this person to register their own complaints and build better police–media understanding.

Mutual Education

This is perhaps the most important approach to improving relations between police and the media. Essentially, it involves giving both sides new insights into the rights and responsibilities of those on the other side. A study by Lazin (1980) of the attitudes of 69 white ethnic and minority police cadets indicated that almost 90 percent lacked confidence in the veracity and objectivity of the press. They perceived newspapers as partisan and political (p. 158). If this perception is actually a dominant view of police cadets and is not addressed, mutual respect and cooperation between police and media will be undermined.

Media Initiatives

Many people in the media have become aware of deficiencies in the way crime is reported. Their remedy is to use trained experts to handle crime news. They can either hire former lawyers to do it (as the *New York Times* does) or arrange seminars and other educational programs designed to give experienced reporters a better understanding of crime and law enforcement.

Police Initiatives

Police personnel could benefit from educational programs dealing with the methods and operations of the mass media. Such programs might be provided by a national police training institute or by local educational institutions. Courses in press law and press relations for police officers, workshops or seminars in media concerns can be sponsored by the local press and/or police agencies.

What Police Officers Should Know About Media

"Police officers should never allow themselves to forget that they are not censors" (Walsh, 1983). With that as a guiding premise, they need to educate themselves about local media. Among the topics which police need to address are:

- How local media function in terms of techniques and personnel.
- The relationship between editors and reporters and the problems posed by deadlines and mechanical limitations.
- How decisions are made about placement and emphasis of new stories, especially those about crime.
- The laws of libel as they affect crime news.
- When and how to go "off the record" with reporters, when to give the press what it wants and when to refuse, and how to refuse with tact and diplomacy.

The Role of the Police Information Officer

A police public information officer (PIO) is supposed to maintain liaison with the media, thus relieving department administrators of some of the burden of working with reporters. This person's skill is a critical factor in moving the agency from an adversary position to one of cooperation. The PIO is also the ideal person to set up internal training programs in press relations.

The National Association of Public Safety Information Officers (NAPSIO), set up by PIOs in 1974, became a major forum for exchanging ideas and programs. NAPSIO has conducted training workshops in all facets of professionalizing police–press liaison and maintains a network of correspondence among PIOs throughout the country, with beneficial results.

NAPSIO no longer exists as an organization. PIOs now are associated through the Public Information Office Section of International Association of Chiefs of Police (IACP) and through that affiliation have worked together to develop international standards for police–media relations.

NEW MUTUAL GOALS

Crime Prevention Projects

An increasingly popular joint project by police and media is the use of mass media as a channel of communication for dissemination of crime prevention information. It is possible to provide both general crime awareness and specific risk-reducing skills to audiences in this way. Such programs have a variable pattern of success, however. Drawing from much of the research on public impact of such programs, Sacco and Silverman (1982) note that the following factors are related to campaign effectiveness.

1. The campaign information must be readily available to the members of the audience.
2. The themes must be interesting, important, or relevant to the audience.
3. The information provided must not conflict with other major audience information sources, or it may increase resistance.
4. The goals of the project should be realistic and clearly defined.
5. The course of action desired of the audience must be clearly stated. Fear-arousing appeals may actually produce outcomes which are not sought and may be counterproductive to project goals (pp. 257–269).

Police Education

Using a satellite hookup, LETN (Law Enforcement Television Network) has been making daily news, training, and other law enforcement information available to its subscribers since 1989. LETN is a subsidiary of the Dallas-based Westcott Communications, well known in the growing private satellite television industry.

Public Opinion Surveys

Radio and television have become popular media for surveying public opinion. Surveys may be taken through these resources on a variety of police-related issues, providing prompt citizen–police feedback opportunities.

Teleconferences

Teleconference communication is available for closed circuit as well as general audience broadcast. This type of conference can bring police administrators closer to the community, and sometimes to their own officers as well. Teleconferences provide an exchange of information by people at many different locations. In most teleconferences, the participants are able to see one another on the video screen, and thus communication can be personalized.

CONCLUSIONS

The media represent a principal link between police agencies and the public they serve. Media impact on virtually every citizen is enormous, and crime news is a major media topic. Except for the relatively few people who become directly involved with the police, private citizens learn of police activity, of crime prevention, of the pursuit and apprehension of criminals and their disposition in the courts by what they read in their newspapers and see and hear on television and radio. What a citizen reads, hears, and observes in the local media largely defines the citizen's perception of the police.

Easy generalizations about whether the media help or hinder law enforcement and "heat up" or "cool off" civil disorders should be avoided: It is too easy to cite evidence on either side of the issue. However, both the police and members of the media have an interest in the security of all citizens and the preservation of order. The American system has a built-in conflict between the freedom of the press guaranteed by the First Amendment to the Constitution and the right to a fair trial guaranteed by the Sixth Amendment; there is often accurate information that could prejudice jurors if it were known to them. The police are in the center of this conflict, and therefore should develop—with or without the cooperation of the media—guidelines for disseminating information about crime.

During the crisis situations (e.g., riots, demonstrations, terrorist actions) that have become so characteristic of life today, the police and the media have sometimes found themselves working at cross purposes; here again, guidelines are needed so that neither party tramples on the rights or responsibilities of the other. Fortunately, several means exist for improving police–media relations, including regularly scheduled police–media meetings, press councils, working with a press or radio and TV ombudsman, mutual education programs, and mutual projects and goals.

The police–media–community link is a critical one. The nature of a community's police–media relationship helps to define police–community relations in that community.

STUDENT CHECKLIST

1. Overview media commitment to the reporting of crime news.
2. Contrast the responsibility of the press and the police.
3. Justify the need for guidelines in reporting.
4. Establish police–media guidelines for routine information release, crisis situations, and hostage situations.
5. Identify ongoing blocks to positive police–media relations and strategies for resolving them.
6. Contrast individual constitutional rights and the public's right to know.

TOPICS FOR DISCUSSION

1. Should there be a code of conduct for all the media, not just professional journalists? Support your answer.

2. What things, in your opinion, should police not volunteer to the media about a crime?

3. How responsible is the press in your community?

4. How is information disseminated to the press by police agencies in your community?

ONE STEP FORWARD

Public Information and Community Relations[1]

54.1 Public Information

54.1.1   *A written directive states that the agency is committed to informing the community and the news media of events within the public domain that are handled by or involve the agency.*

Commentary: To operate effectively, law enforcement agencies must obtain the support of the public they serve. By providing the news media and the community with information on agency administration and operations, the agency can foster a relationship of mutual trust, cooperation, and respect. (Mandatory for all agencies)

54.1.2   *A written directive establishes a public information function, to include:*

*   *assisting news personnel in covering routine news stories, and at the scenes of incidents;*
*   *being available for on-call responses to the news media;*
*   *preparing and distributing agency news releases;*
*   *arranging for, and assisting at, news conferences;*
*   *coordinating and authorizing the release of information about victims, witnesses, and suspects;*
*   *assisting in crisis situations within the agency; and*
*   *coordinating and authorizing the release of information concerning confidential agency investigations and operations.*

Commentary: The agency's written directive should address how the agency will handle potential situations in which the news media are interested in agency operations, as well as situations in which the agency wishes to generate media interest. (Mandatory)

54.1.3   *A written directive specifies a position in the agency responsible for the public information function.*

[1]From the Commission on Accreditation for Law Enforcement Agencies (1991, pp. 54-1 to 54-3).

Commentary: The intent of the standard is to ensure that the agency has a point of control for disseminating information to the community, to the media, and to other criminal justice agencies.

In smaller agencies these activities may be assigned as part-time responsibilities; in larger agencies the activities may be assigned to a full-time public information officer or component.

The directive should also establish procedures to guide the actions of the public information officer in daily operations as well as at the scene of crimes, catastrophes, special events, and unusual occurrences. (Mandatory)

54.1.4 *A written directive establishes the procedures for press releases, to include:*

- *frequency of press releases*
- *subject matter*
- *media recipients*

Commentary: The agency should have procedures that address the criteria to be used in determining (1) the need for press releases on a daily or weekly basis, or as necessitated by specific occurrences in the agency's service area and (2) the content and the extent of coverage of agency activities.

The directive should also include policy on disseminating material in such a manner to ensure that first-release information is equally available to all news media. Press releases may be issued in bulletin form or through tape-recorded messages, as long as the agency has addressed the equal-access issue. (Optional)

54.1.5 *A written directive identifies—by name or position held—those within the agency who may release information to the news media:*

- *at the scene of an incident;*
- *from agency files;*
- *concerning an ongoing criminal investigation; and/or*
- *at any time that the public information officer is not available.*

Commentary: Situations may arise when the agency's public information officer is not available or events at the scene of an incident or other fast-breaking event require an immediate agency spokesperson. (Mandatory)

54.1.6 *A written directive establishes criteria and procedures for issuing and revoking credentials to news media representatives.*

Commentary: Because of the unique relationship between agencies and news media personnel, agencies should develop procedures governing the issuance and the revocation of credentials, as well as criteria for the conduct of news media representatives. The agency policy should not attempt to limit the number of credentials issued but should make media representatives aware of their obligations and responsibilities as they cover daily assignments and special events. Credentials should be revoked only when the criteria governing conduct have been violated. If credentials are revoked, a statement should be sent to the concerned individual's employer citing the specific violation. (Optional)

54.1.7 *A written directive governs the access of news media representatives, including photographers, to the:*

- *scenes of major fires, natural disasters, or other catastrophic events; and*
- *perimeter of crime scenes.*

Commentary: News media representatives should not be in a position to interfere with law enforcement operations at the scene of an incident. The guidelines for news media access, including access by photographers, to the scene should be communicated to the media to help ensure their cooperation. (Mandatory)

54.1.8 *A written directive establishes procedures for involving the news media in the development of changes in policies and procedures relating to the news media.*

Commentary: By allowing media representatives to participate in the process of developing policies and procedures relating to the news media, agencies can demonstrate that they value good rapport with the media and appreciate the problems such persons confront in their daily work. (Optional)

54.1.9 *A written directive specifies the information held by the agency regarding ongoing criminal investigations that may be released to the news media.*

Commentary: The intent of the standard is that the agency provide specific guidance to personnel regarding the release of information about (1) the prior criminal record, character, or reputation of the accused; (2) mugshots of the accused; (3) the existence of any confession, admission of guilt, or statement made by the accused or the failure or refusal by the accused to make a statement; (4) the results of any examinations or tests conducted or refusal by the accused to submit to any examinations or tests; (5) the identity, testimony, or credibility of any prospective witness; (6) any opinion of agency personnel regarding the guilt or innocence of the accused; (7) any opinion of agency personnel regarding the merits of the case or quality of evidence gathered; (8) personal information identifying the victim; (9) information identifying juveniles; and (10) information received from other law enforcement agencies without their concurrence in releasing that information. (Mandatory)

54.1.10 *A written directive requires that information released under standard 54.1.9 be reported to the agency's public information officer as soon as possible.*

Commentary: The person responsible for the public information function should not have to rely on the media to be informed of newsworthy events involving the agency that occur within the agency's service area. Moreover, such information should be conveyed in a timely fashion. (Optional)

54.1.11   *A written directive establishes agency procedures for releasing information when other service agencies are involved in a mutual effort.*

Commentary: The word "agencies" as used above is meant to refer to all public service agencies (e.g., fire departments and coroners' offices). In instances in which more than one agency is involved, the agency having primary jurisdiction should be responsible for releasing, or coordinating the release of, information. (Optional)

BIBLIOGRAPHY

Barker, T., and Carter, D. L. (1994). *Police Deviance,* 3rd ed. Cincinnati, Ohio: Anderson.

Commission on Accreditation for Law Enforcement Agencies (1991). *Standards for Law Enforcement Agencies.* Fairfax, Va.: CALEA.

Goodman, W. (1990). "How much should t.v. tell and when? *New York Times,* Oct. 29.

Hames, H. (Ed.) (1983). *Daily News Tribune,* LaSalle, Ill., Interview, April.

Katzenbach, J. (1980). "Overwhelmed in Miami," *Police Magazine*, September, pp. 7–15.

Lazin, F. A. (1980). "How the police view the press," *Journal of Police Science and Administration,* Vol. 8.

Lofton, J. (1966). *Justice and the Press.* Boston: Beacon Press.

Lyle, S. (1979). "Police and media cooperate to fight vandalism in Odessa, Texas," *The Police Chief,* July, pp. 63, 80.

MacDougall, C. D. (1964). *The Press and Its Problems.* Dubuque, Iowa: W. C. Brown.

Sacco, V. F., and Silverman, R. A. (1982). "Crime prevention through mass media: Prospects and problems," *Journal of Criminal Justice,* Vol. 10, pp. 257–269.

Schmid, A. P., and DeGraaf, J. (1982). *Violence as Communication: Insurgent Terrorism and the Western News Media.* Beverly Hills, Calif.: Sage.

Senna, J. J. and Siegel, L. J. (1993). *Introduction to Criminal Justice,* 10th ed. St. Paul, Minn.: West.

Silvestri, V. N. (1991). *Interpersonal Communication: Perspectives and Applications.* Boston: American Press.

Speir, W. E. (1977). "News media relations: A key ingredient in developing community involvement," *The Police Chief,* April, pp. 18–19.

Toufexis, A. (1993). "A weird case baby? Un huh," *Time* June 28:41.

USA Today (1991). "Smith trial offers mixed message about date rape," Editorial, December 12, p. 10A.

Vetter, H. J., and Perlstein, G. R. (1991). *Perspectives on Terrorism.* Pacific Grove, Calif.: Brooks/Cole.

Walsh, M., Vice-Chairman, Public Information Officers Section, International Association of Chiefs of Police (1983). Interview, April/May.

9

THE YOUNG, THE ELDERLY, AND THE POLICE

Reaching old age with a measure of dignity and a sense of well-being is difficult in contemporary society. (National Association of Social Workers, March 1982, p. 37)

His [the adolescent's] delicate masculinity is at stake. He must save face and prove himself to his companions. (DeSanto and Moore, 1981, p. 49)

Every day, every minute, police are first on the scene. They must decide if a child is in imminent danger of abuse and needs to be removed from his or her surroundings. They must comfort the elderly woman or man whose spouse has died. They must search for the child or elderly person who has wandered away from home and is in danger. They must confront a teenager who held up a convenience store at gunpoint, bludgeoned a blind 79-year-old, crippled woman to death, or ran away from an intolerable home situation. They must confront a 60-year-old man who molests children, and arrest an elderly woman who has somehow survived a failed suicide pact. After being called every name known to man, police officers must maintain their composure and act in the best interest of the youth who is insulting them.

It is a police responsibility to help the child and elderly person to protect themselves from crime and yet to protect them from themselves and from the sense of isolation and alienation that comes with the fear of being victimized and that is detrimental to quality of life.

Community relations efforts, especially crime prevention programs, often target the needs of these two groups. Even efforts considered successful often do not reach the populations they purportedly seek to reach. Many are undermined by individual officers in personal interactions with young and elderly persons. Existing problems also may be escalated by officers who are poorly trained in working with these populations. Sometimes understanding is misunderstanding, because myths regarding the young and elderly in our society are common. These myths act as barriers to positive police relations with two major segments of the community.

196

Information in this chapter is designed to debunk some of the myths and to increase understanding of needs of the young and the elderly in our society. Strategies for increasing the effectiveness of community relations efforts are suggested.

STUDYING THIS CHAPTER WILL ENABLE YOU TO:

1. Identify how the young and the elderly in a community pose special problems for the police.
2. Describe some of the developmental characteristics of adolescence and how they impact interactions of the young with police.
3. Describe some of the developmental characteristics of maturation and aging and how they impact interactions of the elderly with police.
4. Contrast the needs of the young and elderly.
5. Identify the major elements that contribute to resolving or compounding the problems of the young and elderly.
6. Suggest several ways through which the effectiveness of services to the young and elderly might be improved.

SPECIAL PROBLEMS FOR POLICE

The young and the elderly represent two major groups in society for whom the police must provide specialized services. Both need the protection of police, sometimes even from members of their own families, each other, and themselves. The young and the elderly are more vulnerable to almost all types of abuse than other age groups in our society. Estimating conservatively from the findings of national studies, over one million children (birth to 18) and another million elderly people (65 and over) are abused yearly in the United States. No one knows for sure how many die from abuse and neglect.

Youths between the ages of 11 and 18, more than any other age group, confront and are confronted by police. Over half of the arrests made by police are of people under the age of 18. Most police-youth contacts do not result in arrest. In fact, were police to formally act upon every police-youth contact that legally could be said to involve a juvenile offense, the number of arrests would more than double.

Studies suggest that young peoples' future attitudes and behavior toward police and the law are influenced by the way police handle encounters with them. A discretionary decision by the officer to divert a child to other resources or make a field adjustment (although not legally granted to police in some states) is exercised at some level in every state. Such decisions are often made based on the following factors: the officer's confidence in the local juvenile court; the seriousness of the offense; circumstances surrounding the offense; the attitude and demeanor of the child; the presence of clear evidence; and the wishes of a complainant (Black and Reiss, 1970; Lundman, Sykes, and Clark, 1976; Senna and Siegel, 1993, p. 664). Departmental policy and attitude of parents are also influential in such decision making. Such a decision is difficult to make under the best of circumstances. Prejudice, lack of understanding of youth, and any number of other factors could negatively influence the outcome.

By the year 2000, people aged 65 and over in our society will represent almost 32 percent of the total population. Police must deal with increasing numbers of crimes by and against the elderly[1] and offer protection, patience, and resolution of what may be the most serious problem of all to the elderly—fear. How to best develop and use resources on the behalf of the elderly requires an understanding of the problems of the elderly and of the strengths and limitations an elderly person can bring to the problem and its solution.

UNDERSTANDING THE YOUNG

The First 10 Years

Interactions between police and children who are 10 or under are for the most part positive. Children move through several developmental stages during this period, as they gain new skills, independence, and learn about a "bigger world." From infancy, in which they are totally dependent on others to meet their needs, through the toddler stage, when they gain a greater sense of autonomy and more self-awareness, their world is relatively small because most of their interactions are with family and close friends. As they reach preschool age, however, they interact with more people outside the family group and increase their range of experiences. They are curious and imaginative during this time. They like to imitate and observe.

Middle childhood, the period from about 7 to 11 years of age, builds on the previous ones. The primary people in the children's lives are at home, in the neighborhood, and at school. If children have been encouraged to be imaginative, curious, and to observe, they can learn good work habits. The world of these children is much larger and the range of their experiences greater than ever before.

Meeting Basic Needs

For many children, police can be a role model, a powerful authority figure, a protector, an adult friend, a hero, and an avenue to adventure and excitement. Relationships between police officers and children are important (Figure 9-1). "Clancy the talking police car," "Officer Friendly" programs, station house tours, bicycle safety, crime prevention poster competitions and other projects target preschool and elementary school children for safety and crime prevention information and guidance, and to establish police as a positive force in society. Programs such as these are important ones. They are most successful when conducted by officers who are patient, have a sense of humor that young children can appreciate, and who understand and like children. Other programs designed to prevent child abuse and to help children to recognize danger and protect themselves from abuse (or further abuse) are also very useful

---

[1]The increase is apparent in volume but not necessarily in rate of crime. Much disagreement exists as to whether or not the rate of crimes committed by the elderly has actually increased.

FIGURE 9-1   DARE Program, Birmingham, Alabama.

for school-age children. Special training for officers is mandatory for properly conducting such programs.

The Teenage Years

Much of the potentially negative interaction between young people and police occurs between the ages of 11 to 17, because this is the period during which most delinquency and incorrigibility takes place. If we were to search for one word to describe the youth developmentally, the word would have to be *change*. This is a period of transition from child to adult, from dependence to independence. No two children proceed through this period and deal with these changes in exactly the same way.

A Time of Rapid Change

"Human development is defined as physical, emotional, and social changes in structure, thought, or behavior which are functions of biological and environmental influences" (Mayhall and Norgard, 1983, p. 67). Adolescence is the final stage before adulthood in human development and it is probably more than one stage. It is a time of rapid changes in all areas of development. It begins with the onset of puberty, which for most people occurs between 11 and 13 years of age, and is marked by physical and sexual maturing.

Mental ability changes during adolescence. Piaget suggests that it becomes more operational. The youth gains the capacity (but not necessarily the practical experience or the information) to reason in more formal ways, analyze problems, sort through possible outcomes or consequences, make complex moral analyses, and arrive at reasonable solutions and moral judgments (Piaget, 1968). Relationships with family members may become more distant and relationships with peers, both male and female, become closer.

Development Tasks

Havighurst (1972) suggests the following as the developmental tasks of the adolescent:

1. Achievement of new and mature relations with age mates of both sexes.
2. Achievement of masculine or feminine social roles.
3. Acceptance and effective use of one's body.
4. Achievement of emotional independence from parents and other adults.
5. Preparation for marriage and family life.
6. Preparation for a career.
7. Acquisition of a set of values and an ethical system.
8. Acquisition and utilization of socially responsible behavior.

In the view of many, and sometimes of themselves, teenagers are "too" almost everything—too emotional, too calm, too big, too little, too sexually interested or disinterested. They are concerned with "body image" and with the opinion of their peers. They seek ways of testing changes, physically, emotionally, and socially. They act on the need to test new strength, new maturity, new freedom, and to "prove" knowledge and toughness, especially for the benefit of peers. If unresolved in other arenas, their conflicts between authority and freedom, dependence and independence seem to be a natural source of police–youth confrontations. As youth take risks and act in disrespectful ways, they set up power struggles with authority figures who need to "teach them a lesson." Power struggles decrease goodwill and increase distrust. They underscore mutual self-esteem issues. If enough encounters with police end negatively, outright mutual hatred may result and tensions in a community increase.

Meeting Basic Needs

Programs for youth are often designed to divert youth from the juvenile justice system (as police-social work teams, mental health and social service referral projects, crisis hotlines, runaway houses, time-out programs, drug and alcoholism diversion projects); to encourage positive behavior in juvenile gangs and programs that are geared to change juvenile attitudes toward police and teach youth about police organization and function (such as station house tours, junior police, youth ride-along programs).

The most difficult questions facing police officers regarding teenagers often are not addressed by these programs: How can the officer deal with youthful misbehavior

WHAT WOULD YOU DO?

Situation: Deputy Hernandez, on routine patrol, observed a white Chevy traveling at high speed and driving into oncoming traffic. Hernandez activated her emergency equipment and, finally, stopped the vehicle. *Time:* noon.

Deputy Hernandez walked over to the vehicle on the driver's side and, in an angry tone, told the driver to get out of the car. The driver was slow to react and appeared to be drunk. The deputy opened the car door and pulled the driver out of the car. She told the youth, Joe Garcia, age 16, to show his driver's license. After much fumbling the youth found the license.

Deputy Hernandez administered a physical sobriety test to Mr. Garcia, it indicated that he was intoxicated. The deputy told Joe Garcia that he was under arrest. As the deputy attempted to place handcuffs on the youth, the youth resisted, and a fight ensued. Finally, Joe Garcia was subdued and taken to the county juvenile detention facility.

At the facility, the youth continued to be belligerent, and detention officers were advised of his previous conduct. When the handcuffs were removed, Joe began fighting again. The officers restrained him. He was again handcuffed and taken to the county hospital for treatment of scrapes and bruises received in the scuffle. Later, he was returned to the detention home.

As the officer, how could you have handled this situation differently?

FIGURE 9-2   Case study.

in a way that both protects the public, discourages the behavior, and yet does not negatively label the youth unnecessarily? How can an officer help a youth to solve the tasks of adolescence and encourage maturity? How can the officer help a youth to satisfy the need for excitement and risk and "proving" him or herself in positive, constructive ways? These are the problems that programs for youth must address (see Figure 9-2). They are also the problems that every officer who encounters youths on a regular basis must personally solve.

UNDERSTANDING THE ELDERLY

A Profile

Between 1900 and 1980 the percentage of people in the United States age 65 and older nearly tripled (White House Conference on Aging, 1981). By the year 2000 close to one third of the U.S. population will be over 65. Currently, more than 60 percent of the elderly in the United States live in metropolitan areas. Many reside in high crime areas because rents are lower and fixed incomes stretch further, which may actually add to the isolation of the elderly. Crimes committed by the elderly, once considered to be almost nonexistent, are increasing. Although the increase is occurring in many crime areas, the greatest problem appears to be petty larceny offenses, such as shoplifting. In one Florida city, for example, 44 percent of the shoplifting cases against people over 60 involved theft of food items (valued less than $10) (National Institute of Law Enforcement and Criminal Justice, 1981, p. 2). This increase is not due to a "geriatric delinquent" class. As the U.S. population becomes older, we can expect greater increases in their crime involvement over the next several decades (Schmalleger, 1993, p. 60).

Transitions into Late Adulthood

There is no "typical" older person developmentally, socially, or economically. Although we have "discovered" finally that development does not stop with becoming an adult, we are just beginning to learn about the subtleties of the aging process. Many factors are involved in aging, and most are complex. Environment, biology, diet, life-style, and any number of other factors vary the process of aging. (Women generally live longer than men; some people are more susceptible to disease than others, etc.)

Parent (1977) suggests that people must solve three developmental tasks in the transition into late adulthood. (1) completion of one's life goals; (2) evaluation of one's life performance and the resolution of conflict about one's failures and disappointments; and (3) preparation for decline.

According to Peck (1968, pp. 88–92), the transition into late adulthood is the retirement process: Integration versus despair; ego differentiation versus work-role preoccupation; body transcendence versus body preoccupation; and ego transcendence versus ego preoccupation. (Figure 9-3).

An elderly person has relinquished a parental role, lived through loss of many family members and friends, confronted in some ways the successes and failures of his or her life thus far, and practically prepared for old age. This preparation is usually by simplifying lifestyle, preparing for future financial security, arranging for physical care, etc. On an emotional level the elderly person becomes more aware, consciously, of death.

What factors help to ease the transition? Golan (1981) states, regarding women, ". . . psychologists feel that the critical variable is ego strength or emotional autonomy, while sociologists tend to believe that social connectedness or ties to a network of social relationships are most likely to help. For some women, the two factors may be mutually reinforcing; for others, one set may serve as the substitute for the other" (p. 211).

Facts About the Elderly

Physical Facts

Generally older people are more affected by chronic disease than by acute illness. The most prominent health conditions are heart disease, arthritis, and diabetes. Physical limitations and reduced functioning are generally present, and the aged are more prone to accidents than younger people. Crisis tends to precipitate debilitating accidents.

FIGURE 9-3   One of New York's finest giving assistance to elderly.

The physical changes in the elderly have created a serious problem with health care fraud (Ford, 1992). Health care is the second-largest U.S. industry, next to education. Ford states that every level of this health care system is affected by fraud—from a doctor who charges exhorbitant fees and authorizes unnecessary tests, to a hospital or nursing home that overbills Medicare, to pharmacists who dispense generic drugs at brand-name prices (Ford, 1992, p. 2) (Figure 9-4).

Emotional and Functional Facts

Functional disorders most frequently observed in the elderly center around depression. Physical and mental health are usually closely related. Organic disorders,

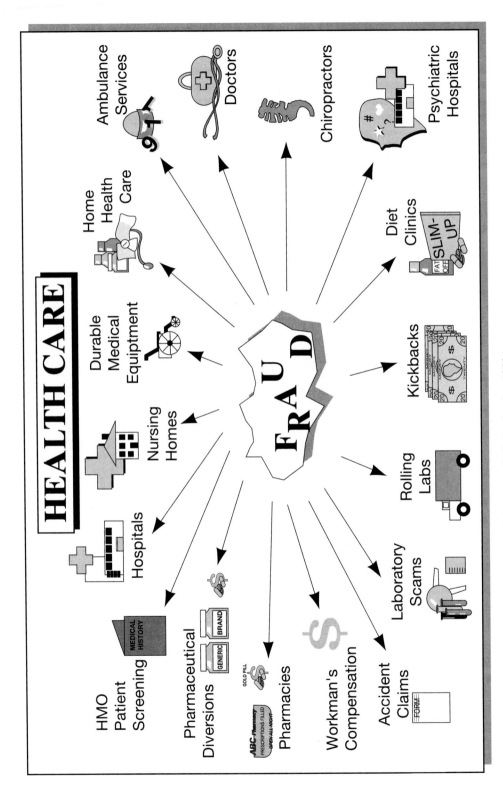

FIGURE 9-4   Health care fraud. (From *FBI Law Enforcement Bulletin*, October 1992.)

often because of strokes (blocking of brain tissue), may cause a wide range of behavioral symptoms from irritability and confusion to paralysis.

Although declining health is a fact of late adulthood, level of function depends largely upon "the individual's determination to remain active in order to retain his functioning and on the availability of medical and social service resources in the community that can support this level of functioning" (Golan, 1981, p. 219). Other important considerations are nutrition as an integral part of health care, living areas that meet the needs of the older person, social interaction, and meaningful work or activity. These are very important considerations as programs for the elderly are planned by police.

Ms. Patricia Moore, a noted gerontologist, over a three-year period traveled throughout the United States and Canada disguised as a woman in her eighties. She reported on her findings in 1988 at a national symposium on "Violent Crime Against the Elderly," co-hosted by the American Association of Retired Persons (AARP), the International Association of Chief's of Police (IACP), and the FBI (Lent and Harpold, 1988). The thesis of her argument was that there is a need for better services and programs to facilitate a better future quality of life and that the law enforcement community needed to become involved in this movement.

Meeting Basic Needs

Helping the elderly to meet their basic needs may require a wide range of programs including federally funded public housing, local city-county funded special needs transportation, housekeeping and visiting nurse services, increased medical assistance through Medicare and Medicaid, and supplemental programs, Meals on Wheels (a program that provides hot meals to elderly people), and reduced senior citizen rates for prescription medicines. Police projects might include programs for crime prevention and citizen safety, and should also focus on programs that offer opportunities for the elderly to participate in their own behalf and also in behalf of police projects (victim-witness advocacy programs and police volunteer organizations) (see Figure 9-5).

YOUTH AND THE ELDERLY: SOME SHARED PROBLEMS

Dependency Issues

Although the symptoms may vary dramatically, there are some intriguing similarities in the experience of being young and the experience of being elderly. The most immediately apparent of these is that a large percentage of the population of both groups is dependent upon other persons or on social agencies for most or all of their basic needs. The young are dependent upon their parents for food, clothing, shelter, discipline, and training. As they grow, they are dependent also upon schools, over which they have little or no control, for their continued socialization and education. In some families, children gain increased decision-making power as they develop, and thus gain increased power over their own lives. In other families, however, the power is retained by parental figures, courts, and/or other external decision makers.

FIGURE 9-5 Protection-prevention lectures and demonstrations provide the elderly with advice on how to avoid being victimized. (Courtesy of Tom Mulligan.)

The elderly are dependent, in varying degrees, on their children, on social security payments, and often on various welfare agencies for food, clothing, shelter, and general health care. They, too, often seem to have little control over many of the decisions made in their behalf.

Both groups, according to the degree of their dependence and/or vulnerability (openness to victimization), require special protection from the justice system. All persons have the right to a safe environment and to have their life and property protected. This has always been one of the primary justifications for the existence of government. The elderly have the legal and human rights of any citizen and may have been very active in exercising these rights in the past. As dependence on others increases, however, the ability to exercise rights, independently, decreases. The young are sometimes not aware that they even have rights, nor do they understand the appropriate avenues for exercising them.

> The child is a citizen of the State. While he "belongs" to his parents, he belongs also to his State. Their rights in him entail many ties. Likewise the fact the child belongs to the State imposes upon the State many duties. Chief among them is the duty to protect *his right to live and to grow up with a sound body*, and to permit no interference with that right by any person or organization. (*In re* Sampson, 317 N.Y.S. 2nd 611) [Italics added]

The constitutional rights of a child to due process in juvenile court proceedings were clarified in *In re Gault* (1967). *Parens patriae*, the court acting in the best interest of the child, can no longer be interpreted as a means of depriving a child of these express rights. Other recent court decisions have extended and clarified the rights of children in a number of other areas, including their right to receive treatment for venereal disease and treatment for the use of dangerous drugs without parental knowledge or consent.

Although many protections for the young and the elderly exist, intervention on the part of others in their behalf (advocacy) is necessary in order for their rights to be protected.

Dependency, vulnerability, and protection are all terms that infer a limit on the ability of a person to choose for himself, to have charge of life decisions. The more limited the choices a person feels he has, the more powerless a person believes himself to be. A child who is removed from his own home and "in his best interest" is placed in a series of foster homes, none of which he chose or was invited to participate in the choice of, is in a position of increased powerlessness (Figure 9-6). In a similar position is the elderly woman, accustomed to driving her own car, who has to admit that she can no longer drive and must depend on others for transportation. Her choices have been limited and her powerlessness increased.

Personal Identity Issues

When the young or the elderly (or even people in between these ages) feel powerless, this feeling is often acted out in one of the following ways: (1) the person defers to the powerlessness and agrees to be helpless; or (2) the person finds ways of publicly asserting power (e.g., through power struggles with parents and/or teachers, riots, gang confrontations, murder, rape, vandalism, and so on).

Where Do I Fit?

The young and the elderly often wrestle with opposite sides of the same identity problem: Where do I belong? How can I fit into society or the community? The young are seeking ways to increase their independence while retaining, with or without their consent, a part of their dependence. They wish to have an independent place in the world but are not prepared to give up the security they have in the family system. Parents contribute to the ease or difficulty with which this problem is resolved, but much of the burden rests with the youth.

Self-Image and Self-Esteem

The elderly struggle to retain a part of their independence while their dependency needs increase. As with youths, the frustration of the struggles is compounded by the fact that many of the changes they experience occur, to a large degree, without their voluntary consent. The issue in both instances is one of personal identity. It is an issue of self-image and self-respect, and it is resolved (or unresolved) on an individual basis.

The young and the elderly share another experience. Often both are treated "like children" in society. They are talked at, talked about, and planned for, but often they are not included in the decision making that takes place about their lives. Sometimes they are "taken care of" so well that their dependence upon others increases without their consent or realization.

Even more than for other children, society has a responsibility along with parents for the well-being of foster children. Citizens are responsible for acting to insure their welfare.

Every foster child is endowed with the rights inherently belonging to all children. In addition, because of the temporary or permanent separation from and loss of parents and other family members, the foster child requires special safeguards, resources, and care.

Every Foster Child Has the Inherent Right:

Article I. To be cherished by a family of his own, either his family helped by readily available services and supports to reassume his care, or an adoptive family or by plan, a continuing foster family.

Article II. To be nurtured by foster parents who have been selected to meet his individual needs and who are provided services and supports, including specialized education, so that they can grow in their ability to enable the child to reach his potential.

Article III. To receive sensitive, continuing help in understanding and accepting the reasons for his own family's inability to take care of him, and in developing confidence in his own self-worth.

Article IV. To receive continuing loving care and respect as a unique human being—a child growing in trust in himself and others.

Article V. To grow up in freedom and dignity in a neighborhood of people who accept him with understanding, respect and friendship.

Article VI. To receive help in overcoming deprivation or whatever distortion in his emotional, physical, intellectual, social and spiritual growth may have resulted from his early experiences.

Article VII. To receive education, training, and career guidance to prepare him for a useful and satisfying life.

Article VIII. To receive preparation for citizenship and parenthood through interaction with foster parents and other adults who are consistent role models.

Article IX. To be represented by an attorney at law in administrative or judicial proceedings with access to fair hearings and court review of decisions, so that his best interests are safeguarded.

Article X. To receive a high quality of child welfare services, including involvement of the natural parents and his own involvement in major decisions that affect his life.

Source: Committee of National Action for Foster Children. Ratified in Congress Hall, Philadelphia, April 28, 1973.

FIGURE 9-6   Bill of Rights for Foster Children.

In acting as the parental authority for these persons, we achieve the following:

1. We strip them of a part of their independence and their self-respect.
2. We increase their vulnerability and encourage the assumption that these persons are unable to choose for themselves.
3. We decrease, even more than necessary, their right to make decisions for themselves and their responsibility for their own actions.
4. We increase their feelings of powerlessness.
5. We fail to provide positive ways in which they can experiment with decision making.

Essentially, if police act like the authoritative parent, they encourage others to act like children. "Children" have license to pout, complain, defer decisions, feel persecuted, and blame the consequences of their actions on others. The likelihood of "misbehavior" is increased.

Stereotyping Issues

There is at least one more experience that the young and the elderly share in our society. Perceptions about them are seldom based on their individual characteristics. Instead, they are based on some generalized perception that has become the stereotype of their group. Often this perception is based on a negative, disabling stereotype. Elsewhere in this book, we have discussed in much detail the problems created by stereotyping and destructive or negative perception. Certainly all of these apply to stereotyped perceptions of the young and the elderly. Hostility invokes hostility and also perpetuates stereotyping (see Figure 9-7).

FIGURE 9-7   Stereotypes about the young and the elderly lead to reinforcement of myths. What myth seems to be reinforced or refuted in each of these photos? (Courtesy of Travis L. Mayhall.)

(Courtesy of Michael X. Shannon, Medical Photographer.)

FIGURE 9-7 (continued)

Myths About Youth

Myth 1: All Teenagers Who Commit Delinquent Acts Are Going to Be Adult Criminals

Actually a very small percentage of all youths who are referred to juvenile courts for delinquent acts become adult criminals. When it is considered that most (if not all) youths commit at least one delinquent act (whether or not they are caught and/or referred), that small percentage is significantly reduced.

Myth 2: All Teenagers Have Severe Adjustment Problems During Adolescence

Some teenagers are better able to adjust to adolescence than others. Most are not referred for delinquency or incorrigibility. Many are school, church, and community youth leaders and move without major disruption into adulthood.

Myth 3: Teenagers Cannot Be Trusted

As with all people, teenagers are individuals. Treating teenagers with respect encourages trustworthy behavior.

Myth 4: All Teenage Groups Are Gangs

Gangs, by definition, have some specialized features. They are organized, have a leadership, symbols, common goals, and criteria for membership. Thus far in this definition, the Boy Scouts, Campfire Girls, 4-H Clubs, and church groups would all qualify as gangs. What separates gangs from other organizations is usually the nature of their goals, and their illegal and sometimes violent activity. However, many modern-day juvenile gangs are separated even further.

In the past, young people joined gangs for a sense of personal identity; however, many gangs today are motivated by financial interests. They are in the business of acquiring and selling stolen goods or drug trafficking and they apply ruthless violence to protect their illicit enterprises. Some members of large-city gangs have ready access to semiautomatic weapons and submachine guns. The largest number of current gang members who fall into this category belong to the "Crips" and the "Bloods," two juvenile gangs organized around drug trafficking who got their start in Los Angeles.

Myths About the Elderly

Myth 1: People over 65 Are More Often Victimized by Crime than the Rest of the Population

Persons over 65 are not necessarily victimized by crime any more than the rest of the population. They do tend to be frequent victims of certain types of personal larceny crimes, such as purse-snatching, pocket-picking, consumer fraud, and con games. Also, older people, when victimized, are more vulnerable to physical and psychological harm than people in other age groups, and the loss of what might seem to be a minimal amount of money or property might create a greater hardship on the elderly than on other groups.

Myth 2: Women over the Age of 65 Are Frequently Rape Victims

Actually, the opposite is true. In fact, only about 1 percent of all known rape victims are women who are over 50 years of age. Fear of rape and of other violent crimes, however, may create a sort of "self-imposed" isolation of an elderly person and may restrict that person's life-style dramatically.

Myth 3: The Elderly Are Totally Dependent on Others for Their Care and Offer No Contribution to Society

The elderly are an oft untapped resource of information and service in our communities. They may serve as consultants to business and industry and to the criminal justice system. They are often skilled and conscientious volunteers in the system. They are some of the best community relations links that an agency can have.

Myth 4: The Elderly Cannot Enjoy Sex Because of Physiological Difficulties

A person's attitude toward sex and the availability of a sexual partner are by far the most important factors influencing presence or absence of a continued and gratifying sex life (Masters & Johnson, 1966, pp. 241–242).

Myth 5: Intelligence Reaches a Peak in the Twenties and Declines at a Steady Rate

So long as health is generally good, research indicates that intellectual stability and growth can be an important part of middle and old age. Where problems occur they are usually caused by illness or marked inactivity (Colarusso and Nemiroff, 1981, pp. 110–115; see also Botwinick, 1977, and Horn, 1975). In fact, recent studies suggest that the adult brain may not really be a "finished product" after all. It may continue to be capable of structural change, or a sort of "rewiring," or the formation of synapses in the case of some forms of damage. Current findings are based only on laboratory animal studies (Lund, 1978); however, as Colarusso and Nemiroff (1981) observe, this evidence does "raise the distinct possibility that our current concept of the adult brain as static and slowly degenerating may be as dated as the idea that the earth is flat" (p. 115).

THE CONTRASTS BETWEEN YOUTH AND THE ELDERLY

Interactions with the Criminal Justice System

Although an increasing number of elderly people are encountering the criminal justice system as offenders, most interact with this system as victims of/or witnesses to crime. A larger number of youths interact with the system as juvenile offenders. Those who encounter the system as victims are usually victims of abuse and neglect rather than victims of other types of crime. (However, because teenagers are even more reluctant than the elderly to report crimes committed against them, this statement may simply reflect a reporting bias.)

Maturity and Life Experience

The elderly, although faced with problems of declining health, increasing vulnerability, and dependence, and possible lack of self-esteem, possess a level of maturity and life experience that the young do not yet have. Their resources may be greater. They have also had the opportunity to plan for this period in their life and may in fact therefore be prepared for some of the difficulties they may encounter. In contrast, the very immaturity and impulsiveness of youth and their lack of experience contribute to adjustment problems.

Looking Toward the Future

The young and the elderly see life and its opportunities from two different views—one in anticipation and one in review. Health issues are different; health problems of the young are usually acute; those of the elderly, usually chronic. Differences in health and life perspective also influence decision making.

THE PROBLEMS WITH PROGRAMS

Knowledge of Resources Available

Resources are usually available in areas of recreation, public assistance, information resources, counseling, crime prevention, and support services. Often the difficulty in finding a program that might match the needs of a young or elderly person is not that they do not exist, but that the officer is not aware of the resource. Police–community relations must include knowledge, use, and constant updating of available community resources.

Some Do Not Reach the Population They Hope to Serve

Obviously, there is a great variety of programs available to provide services to young and elderly persons. In practice, however, many of these programs do not reach the population they purportedly serve, even though they appear to be successful programs. Sometimes the difficulty lies in the fact that they are time-limited or funding-limited projects, which may be "phased out" before many people know that they exist. Other times the problem is the degree of enthusiastic commitment on the part of the provider. Many programs responding to the same need for services never reach and involve the youths who needed them most. The same is true, although in a different context, with programs for the elderly. Because of a poor knowledge of the population served, inadequate information dissemination, a lack of transportation services, and financial limitations, a number of persons who most need to be involved in prevention-protection programs:

1. Are not aware that they exist.
2. Have no means of transportation to and from the location where the programs are being made available.
3. Are afraid to hear any more about crime because they might not be able to sleep at night ("If I ignore it, maybe it will go away").
4. Do not feel the program applies to them.

SAV

**SHERIFF'S
AUXILIARY VOLUNTEERS**
of Pima County, Inc.

AN ACTIVE, HANDS-ON TEAM
working with the
PIMA COUNTY SHERIFF'S DEPARTMENT
Tucson, Arizona

CLARENCE W. DUPNIK, Sheriff

FIGURE 9-8   A community involvement program.

As discussed in the previous section, there is even a danger in some of the ways in which we choose to meet the needs of young and elderly persons. We may actually contribute to new problems in our approach to solving the old ones.

A NEW APPROACH

With this new information and a different perspective, perhaps it is possible for us to approach the young and the elderly differently. The content of the programs we provide for both groups may be valid, although sometimes not dynamic nor far-reaching enough. *The greatest problem is in how service is provided.*

It is important that a young person or an elderly person be approached:

1. As an individual.

2. With respect for that individual, no matter what his needs or views.

3. In a way that involves the person being served in the assessment of the need to be addressed, in the planning of the action to be taken, and in the action itself.

Without such an approach, our programs will fall short of their potential. Worse, we may compound the problems of the people we intended to help and, as a result, compound the problems of the police and the community.

An innovative program started by the Fort Myers, Florida Police Department addresses the needs of the elderly and the young. The program called G.R.A.M.P.A. (Getting Retirees Actively Motivated to Policing Again) Cops uses retired police officers to work in the schools with school resource officers (SROs) in drug prevention programs (Spurlin and Schwein, 1990). These G.R.A.M.P.A. Cops also assist in other programs, such as bicycle safety or child molestation. According to Spurlin and Schwein, the program has benefited both the police department and the schools. It has allowed experienced police officers to reenter the police profession and decreased operating expenses for the department, which no longer has to assign regular police officers to the schools. It has also allowed the police department to double its budget for school resource officers.

CONCLUSIONS: KEYS TO OPTIMUM SERVICE

Many resources are available to help police meet the needs of the young and the elderly. Some may be used intact; others will require change to meet specific needs. New resources will be developed. The agency that truly wishes to meet the needs of the young and the elderly successfully will need to address the following areas when planning and delivering services:

1. Increased training of officers in developmental issues of the young and elderly, in self-awareness, and in strategies for meeting the needs of even difficult-to-reach individuals in these populations.

2. Ongoing awareness of community resources.

3. Planning and implementation of programs that actively involve youth and elderly and foster their input and interaction in a meaningful way in all stages of development and delivery.

4. Planning and implementation of programs that do not increase fear and reduce quality of life.

5. Increased efforts on the part of all officers to build interpersonal relationships with individual youths and elderly members of the community, and the groups to which they belong.

STUDENT CHECKLIST

1. Identify how the young and the elderly in a community pose special problems for the police.

2. Describe some of the developmental characteristics of adolescence and how they impact on interactions of the young with police.

3. Describe some of the developmental characteristics of maturation and aging and how they impact on interactions of the elderly with police.

4. Contrast the needs of the young and elderly.

5. Identify the major elements that contribute to resolving or compounding the problems of the young and elderly.

6. Suggest several ways through which the effectiveness of services to the young and elderly might be improved.

TOPICS FOR DISCUSSION

1. Are the basic human rights of young and elderly persons different from those of other persons?

2. How do suggestions made in this chapter for increasing the effectiveness of programs for the young and elderly compare with suggestions made for increasing effectiveness in police–community relations?

3. What is your perception of the needs of young and elderly persons who live in your community? How can you ascertain whether or not your perception is correct?

ONE STEP FORWARD

DRUG FREE ZONES FOR SCHOOLS

I. DRUG FREE ZONES

The new Washington State law, RCW 69.50.435, provides for *double* penalties to anyone convicted of selling *illegal drug* substances within a 1000 feet radius of any public or private *school property.*

While specific sentences for selling illegal drugs vary based upon an individual's criminal conviction record, dealers who sell near schools now risk much more time in jail. The sentencing law has been amended to add jail time to the standard sentence for dealers convicted of selling drugs within a Drug Free Zone.

To serve as evidence for the prosecution, a map is adopted as an official record by the City Council, indicating the 1000 foot zone boundaries. Signs will be posted by the Department of Engineering clearly indicating the areas designated as Drug Free Zones throughout the city.

II. THE DRUG FREE ZONE PROGRAM

In order to best take advantage of this new law, Seattle's public and private schools, K through 12, the community and the City/County agencies will develop ways to: 1.) educate 2.) inform 3.) find alternatives to drug use *including treatment resources* 4.) more effectively report drug activity to law enforcement.

To facilitate this effort the Seattle Police Department's Crime Prevention Division provides a Program Coordinator to assist in the formation of local organizing groups around the schools (684-7555). Every school in Seattle will eventually be assisted in developing projects and improving programs in its area, through a partnership with agencies, professionals, citizens, parents, and students, working together to provide a healthier and safer environment for all our children and families.

Because of the broad-based nature of this effort, the following phone numbers can be used for assistance, information, and referral:

DRUG & ALCOHOL HELPLINE - 24 HOURS   722-3700
(Crisis intervention/information/education)

PUBLIC SCHOOL EDUCATION/COUNSELING   298-7050

COMMUNITY SERVICE OFFICER (7am - midnight) 684-4790

REPORTING DRUG ACTIVITY (including suspicious   9-1-1
activity, Narcotics Activity Reports-NAR)

SEATTLE POLICE DEPARTMENT
PERSONAL SAFETY FOR CHILDREN

Family Rules

Establishing a system of "family rules" about personal safety can be a good way to teach children to distinguish between safe and non-safe situations. Many families already have rules about bedtime, TV watching, chores, etc. By adopting rules about personal safety, parents can teach good habits through reinforcement and repetition without generating excessive fear. The following are suggestions for personal safety rules that can be incorporated into a family routine.

Inside rules

Kids should know their complete home address, telephone number including area code and parents' first and last names.

If kids are old enough to answer the phone they should know how to call police 9-1-1. Practice with receiver button taped down.

Kids should be taught never to reveal any personal (their name, school, age, etc.) or family information over the phone unless permission has been given by parent.

If kids are home alone and answer a phone call for the absent parent, they should say "she can't come to the phone right now," and take a message or tell the caller to try later—don't make excuses, they sound phony.

It's OK not to answer the phone, or to work out a code (ring twice, hang up and call again) so a parent can check on a child that is home alone.

Kids are old enough to answer the door when they are old enough to check the identity of the person at the door WITHOUT opening it.

Kids should help their parents make sure doors that should be locked are locked.

Outside rules

Establish a system of accountability. Learn the full names of your kids' friends, their parents' names, addresses and phone numbers. Check to verify the accuracy if you get the information from your kids. When your child is at a friend's home, who else is present? parents? older kids? other neighbors? no one?

Know your child's routes to and from school, play and errands. Insist they stick to the same route—no shortcuts! If you have to look for them, you will know where to begin.

Kids should be taught never to go anywhere with anyone without parental permission. This includes getting permission a second time if plans change and calling to check before going from one friend's home to another location.

Kids should never play in isolated areas of parks or playgrounds, and should avoid public restrooms, building sites and dark or lonely streets.

Teach kids alternatives; if they are bothered or followed on the playground, walking to friends' home, school or store, where do they go? Walk these common routes with your child and look for choices. Can they go back into the school, in a store or business (kids are reluctant to enter a strange store or business unless you give them permission,) into a fire station or approach someone doing yard work?

Knocking on the door of a stranger is a last resort. If they have no other choice they should look for a house with a light on (at night) or toys in the yard if possible and ask the homeowner to "Please call the police, someone is bothering me," but not to go inside the house.

Kids' best defenses are their voices and their legs. Teach them to run away from someone who is bothering them while yelling to attract as much attention as is possible.

Teach kids not to approach cars that stop to ask for help. Most legitimate adults would not ask a young child for directions anyway. If the car follows them or the driver gets out they should run away and yell.

Bad Guy Rules

Teach kids that "bad guys" can be anyone; society teaches kids bad guys are always ugly, mean and scary, and look like monsters. Bad guys are almost always portrayed as strangers.

Remember, a stranger is someone who is not known by the child. A friend of parents, a friend of the child's friend or a neighbor can be a stranger. And a stranger can be a good guy or a bad guy.

Some bad guys act nice, friendly and attractive. Some bad guys play tricks on kids. Typical bad guy tricks include bribes (money, toys, games, or promises of those things), lies (your mother told me to pick you up at school), requests for help (my puppy ran away, can you help me find him?) or threats (if you don't come with me I'll hurt your mom).

Teach kids that a bad guy is someone who asks them to violate family rules, e.g. someone who says they don't need permission to accompany them.

Develop a family "code word". If someone other than a parent is going to pick up a kid at school, that person should repeat the "code word" first before the kid agrees to leave the safety of the school grounds. The code word should remain a secret and be changed should others learn of it.

BIBLIOGRAPHY

Anon. (1982) "Law related education emerges as useful tool to deter delinquency," *Street Law News,* Spring.

Black, D., and Reiss, A. J., Jr. (1970). "Police control of juveniles," *American Sociological Review,* Vol. 35, pp. 63–77.

Botwinick, J. (1973). *Aging and Behavior.* New York: Springer-Verlag.

Bundy, M. L., and Whaley, R. G. (1977). *National Children's Directory: An Organizational Directory and Reference Guide for Changing Conditions for Children and Youth.* College Park, Md.: Urban Information Interpreters.

Carter, R. M., and Klein, M. (1976). *Back on the Street.* Englewood Cliffs, N.J.: Prentice Hall.

Colarusso, C. A., and Nemiroff, R. A. (1981). *Adult Development.* New York: Plenum Press.

Condit, T. W., et al. (1977). *Forgotten Victims: An Advocate's Anthology.* Sacramento, Calif.: California Office of Criminal Justice Planning.

DeSanto, J. A., and Moore, E. M. (1981). "Aggression and excessive force in the police portrait," *The Police Chief,* March, pp. 47–50.

Dreikurs, R. (1964). *Children: The Challenge.* New York: Hawthorne Books.

Ford, J. L. (1992). "Health care fraud: The silent bandit," *F.B.I. Law Enforcement Bulletin,* October, pp. 2–7.

Golan, N. (1981). *Passing Through Transitions: A Guide for Practitioners.* New York: Free Press.

Hahn, P. H. (1976). *Crimes Against the Elderly: A Study in Victimology.* Santa Cruz, Calif.: Davis Publications.

Havighurst, R. J. (1972). *Developmental Tasks and Education,* 3rd ed. New York: David McKay.

Hochstedler, E. (1981). *Crime Against the Elderly in 26 Cities.* NCJ-76706. Washington, D.C.: U.S. Department of Justice, Bureau of Justice Statistics.

Horn, J. L. (1975). "Psychometric studies of aging and intelligence," in S. Gershon and A. Raskin (Eds.), *Genesis and Treatment of Psychological Disorders in the Elderly.* New York: Raven Press.

In re Cault, 387 U.S. 1 87 S. Ct. 1428, 18 L.Ed. 1967.

In re Sampson, 317 N.Y.S. 2d 611.

Lent, C. J., and Harpold, J. A. (1988). "Violent crime against the elderly," *F.B.I. Law Enforcement Bulletin,* July, pp. 11–19.

Lund, R. E. (1978). *Development and Plasticity of the Brain.* New York: Oxford University Press.

Lundman, R. J., Sykes, R. E., and Clark, J. A. (1976). "Police control of juveniles: A replication," *Journal of Research in Crime and Delinquency,* Vol. 15, pp. 74–91.

Malinchak, A. A. (1980). *Crime and Gerontology.* Englewood Cliffs, N.J.: Prentice Hall.

Masters, W., and Johnson, V. (1966). *Human Sexual Response.* London: Churchill.

Mayhall, P. D., and Norgard, K. E. (1983). *Child Abuse and Neglect: Sharing Responsibility.* New York: Wiley.

Milton, C. (1977). *Little Sisters and the Law.* Washington, D.C.: Office of Juvenile Justice and Delinquency Prevention.

Morton, J. B., and Anderson, J. C. (1982). "Elderly offenders: The forgotten minority," *Corrections Today,* December, pp. 14–20.

National Association of Social Workers, (1983) March: 37.

National Institute of Law Enforcement and Criminal Justice (1981). *A Mutual Concern: Older Americans and the Criminal Justice System.* Washington, D.C.: U.S. Department of Justice.

Neugarten, B. (Ed.) (1968). *Middle Age and Aging.* Chicago: University of Chicago Press.

Parent, M. K. (1977). "The losses of middle age and related developmental tasks," in E. R. Prichard, et al. (Eds.), *Social Work with the Dying Patient and the Family.* New York: Columbia University Press, pp. 146–153.

Peck, R. C. (1968). "Psychological development in the second half of life," in B. Neugarten (Ed.), *Middle Age and Aging.* Chicago: University of Chicago Press.

Perlberg, M. (1978). "The distorted world of old age," *Human Behavior,* December.

Piaget, J. (1968). *On the Development of Memory and Identity.* Worcester, Mass.: Clark University Press.

Schafer, S. (1977). *Victimology: The Victim and His Criminal.* Reston, Va.: Reston Publishing.

Schmalleger, F. (1993). *Criminal Justice Today,* 2nd ed. Englewood Cliffs, N.J.: Prentice Hall.

Senna, J. J., and Siegel, L. J. (1993). *Introduction to Criminal Justice,* 6th ed. St. Paul, Minn.: West.

Spurlin, J., and Schwein, S. (1990). "G.R.A.M.P.A. Cops," *FBI Law Enforcement Bulletin,* May, pp. 2–4.

Vanagunas, S. (1979). "Police diversion of juvenile offenders: An ambiguous state of the art," *Federal Probation,* Vol. XXXXIII, September.

White House Conference on Aging (1981). *Final Report: The White House Conference On Aging, Vol. 2.* Washington, D.C.: Health and Human Services Department, 1981.

10

COMMUNITY RELATIONS IN THE CONTEXT OF CULTURE

I have a dream that one day my children will be judged by the strength of their character and not by the color of their skin. (Martin Luther King, Jr., 1963)

Racial classifications of any sort pose the risk of lasting harm to our society. They reinforce the belief, held for too much of our history, that individuals should be judged by the color of their skin. (Sandra Day O'Conner, 1993)

In Chapter 1 we discussed the exchange relationships among the various internal and external community groups with whom the police interact. In Chapter 2 cultural diversity within police organizations was discussed. In this chapter we examine the impact of culture in the United States, and how cultural considerations affect police–community relations.

"Culture is the total way of life shared by members of a society. It includes not only language, values, and symbolic meanings but also technology and material objects" (Brinkerhoff, White, and Ortega, 1993, p. 34). When applied to the United States, this definition would allow for individual and group differences according to region, ethnicity, religion, political orientation, class, and gender but would hold that despite these differences that Americans share a common culture based on our national heritage of personal freedom and democratic principles. While encouraging individuality, American citizens and resident aliens are expected to adhere to basic societal values and beliefs.

Other definitions of culture are not as inclusive. Rather than seeing a society in which there is great consensus despite regional, ethnic, religious, political, class, and gender diversity, these definitions stress the conflicts that occur within such a broad-based nation. They tend to see culture "as all that human beings learn to do, to use, to produce, to know, and to believe as they grow into maturity and live out their lives *in the social groups to which they belong*" (Tischler, 1993, p. 46). Such a definition would view America not as a cultural melting pot but as a complex mixture of diverse groups engaged in competitions which too frequently boil over into cultural conflicts.

Both of the definitions above are accurate and both are somewhat misleading. American culture may be distinguished from European, African, or Asian cultures. The American people, however (as is true of most large social groups, including European, Asian, and African), are not culturally homogeneous. In fact, the United States is culturally diverse. There are numerous ethnic groups, religious groups, and many age and sex attributes of communities across the United States which help to make them unique. Immigrants—newcomers who may have difficulty in understanding the common characteristics shared by American citizens (particularly our traditions and norms)—comprise still another culturally diverse group.

In this chapter we seek to understand how culture influences human behavior, on the part of both the police and the communities they serve. Our view will be that neither the common values and beliefs of American society as a whole nor the competing views produced by cultural diversity within American society can be ignored. Both the commonality of the former and the distinctions of the latter contribute to our strength as a nation.

Understanding and appreciating individuals within a cultural context—within the framework of the way their language and behavior express their feelings and beliefs as a part of a cultural group—will provide new opportunities for police and citizens to increase the effectiveness of their interpersonal communication; open avenues for increased mutual respect; and form a realistic base for clarifying common values and areas of mutual concern.

STUDYING THIS CHAPTER WILL ENABLE YOU TO:

1. Define *cultural context.*
2. Describe the cultural context of community relations.
3. Contrast characteristics of different cultural groups.
4. Analyze several cultural factors that may be misunderstood by police.
5. Describe several community relations strategies for improving community relations in the context of culture.

THE CULTURAL CONTEXT OF COMMUNITY RELATIONS

A *context* is a framework for understanding meaning. It is the environment, or the conditions in which something is said or done. Contexts are very important. Without them, what people mean by what they say and do would rarely be clearly understood. The media is often accused of quoting people "out of context," that is, of selecting some portion of a speech and using it in a way that infers a meaning that the speaker did not intend. Because people usually behave in culturally defined ways, culture is a part of the meaning of every interpersonal interaction.

Being Culturally Appropriate

It is possible to have excellent counseling skills and yet apply them in culturally inappropriate ways (see Weaver, 1992). It is possible to make decisions precisely by the letter of policy and procedure and to commit acts that are inappropriate and inhumane. Understanding the cultural context of our own beliefs and actions and the beliefs and actions of others can help to prevent such tragedy.

In order to understand how to deal with people of different cultures (or of divergent subcultures within a dominant culture), one must seek to examine the context of that particular culture. Weaver (1992) demonstrated that failure to understand the dynamics of another culture could cause police officers to misinterpret the intentions of others. The seeking of contextual understanding of different cultures is defined by sociologists as cultural relativism. *Cultural relativism* means that we seek to understand different cultures from their particular perspectives or on their own terms rather than imposing preconceived standards from our own cultural development (Tischler, 1993).

Achieving cultural relativism is not an easy task. We all have biases and preconceptions that we bring to every situation we encounter. Psychologists use the term *cognitive scripts* to refer to the application of past experiences to new situations or encounters (Bartol, 1991). How we approach these situations is thus colored by our personal development, which is largely influenced by our own cultural environment. How we respond to influences from our cultural environment shapes how we respond to other cultures. When we perceive cultures other than our own as flawed or inferior, we are being *ethnocentric*. People within a nation who see all other nations as inferior, individuals who see other races, religions, or regions as having lessor morality or intellect, are practicing ethnocentrism (Brinkerhoff, White, and Ortega, 1992; Eshleman, Cashion, and Basirico, 1993). Ethnocentrism is a form of *xenophobia* in that those things with which we are familiar and therefore perceive as preferable are influenced by cultural considerations. Catholics who have contempt for Baptists, African Americans who hate Hispanics, Northerners who perceive Southerners as inferiors, and upper-class elitists who consider those of other classes to be unworthy are all examples of ethnocentrism.

Cultural biases are not always to the detriment of those who are different from us. Frequently, people are so concerned about being fair to others that they discriminate against their own kind. *Xenophiles* are people who are ashamed of who or what they are. They feel that people who are different from them are either superior or warrant preferential consideration. When these feelings are applied to other cultures they are referred to as *xenocentrism* (Brinkerhoff, White, and Ortega, 1992; Eshleman, Cashion, and Basirico, 1993). If we have come to perceive our culture as flawed or inferior to others, we are being xenocentric. Such perceptions can be just as detrimental to cultural relations as those of ethnocentrists. Americans who are anti-American, Southerners who are anti-Southern, Native Americans who are ashamed of their ancestry, and individuals who are ashamed of their class level are examples of xenocentrism.

To deal fairly and objectively with other people within a culturally diverse society, one must be both accepting and understanding of his/her own culture as well as that of others. We must be sensitive to the norms and traditions of others but we must also understand that there are *cultural universals* which are dictated by the overall society in which we live (Popenoe, 1993). Determining and applying those behaviors or values that are appropriate universal standards (i.e., America ideals of individual freedoms, social equality, order under law, and democratic values) can be extremely difficult. The person must come to terms with his/her own moral and social perspectives as well as understand how compatible their views are within society as a whole. As we discuss in more detail in the following chapter, there is considerable disagreement on what behaviors are culturally appropriate. What is often perceived as being a societal standard is "often only a common strand found among the diverse elements of which it is composed" (Popenoe, 1993, p. 71).

In the following sections we discuss many of the cultural influences that the police must consider to properly enforce universal standards in a diverse American society.

Understanding Crime

In order to understand crime in minority communities we must take into account the ideas, feelings, and experiences of the people in the community (Livingston, 1992). Weis and Sederstrom (1981) state: "In essence an individual learns criminal behavior, particularly within social groups or social areas where there is a culture conflict or inconsistency surrounding the violation of the law." They argue for getting families, schools, peer groups, youth gangs, local officials, and social organizations involved in healthier social development opportunities for young people, and effectively organizing the community against crime. Accomplishing such a goal requires an understanding of cultural contexts.

Providing Services to the Community

New immigrant communities and other communities in transition need special police attention. Officers can help to ease the shock of entering a new culture by offering protection and informal education. But such work requires close personal contact, not remote observation through the windows of patrol cars (Cox and Fitzgerald, 1992). Services to any community must be matched to the citizen's perception of need and to the resources of the community. Distrust of established agencies, expectations of community members, different languages and different symbols, and many other factors must be considered in planning and providing for effective services (Pitter, 1992; Colvard, 1992). Many new immigrants (both legal and illegal) suffered abuses at the hands of government officials in their native lands. A product of those abuses is a strong distrust of government institutions in general and the police in particular (Pitter, 1992). These immigrants tend to perceive the police as oppressors rather than public servants (Colvard, 1992). Their fears are heightened by cultural conflicts and language barriers that block effective communication between the police and many ethnic communities.

These blocks to effective communication (discussed in detail in Chapter 6) are not only experienced in immigrant communities but are also observable within communities comprised of English-speaking ethnic minorities. In those areas the language may appear on the surface to be the same, but cultural variations in linguistic patterns and semantic meanings impair understanding and heighten tensions between officers and citizens. The results are police–citizen encounters in which individuals "talk at" one another rather than communicating.

Overcoming Stereotypes

Stereotyping of police by the community and of the community by the police interferes with effective community relations. Stereotyping is often based on prejudice. Prejudice creates and is created by hostility and mutual fear, and distrust is intensified in the process.

Officers and community members who can appreciate and respect cultural differences are less likely to be fearful and judgmental of people from cultures other than their own. They can be more open to assessing their own biases and in achieving mutual respect.

Understanding beliefs and behavior in a cultural context may help to debunk stereotypes about members of that culture, but even in the process of gaining understanding, a new danger exists. Because characteristics must be generalized to place them in a cultural context, we must take care not to replace the old stereotypes with new ones.

Discretionary Decision Making

Three major factors that influence decision making in the field are space, time, and appearance (Greenlee, 1980, p. 50). Perception and use of these are often culturally defined.

Space

The suspect's use of physical and personal space both during an alleged offense and during questioning influence decision making by the officer. Finally, the officer's decision is usually based on his or her own cultural definition of the proper use of space in such a situation, even though that definition may not be understood by the suspect.

Time

Time of day, elapsed time, and use of time on the part of the suspect are decision-making factors. "Proper" use of time usually is culturally defined. Time may be perceived specifically or globally, depending upon the cultural context of the perceiver.

Appearance

Males are more likely than females to commit some types of crimes (e.g., rape, voyeurism). Age, too, may be a factor in determining who to stop and question about a specific crime. The person who looks "out of place" in a neighborhood may be considered a primary suspect, as may a person who is stereotyped as a potential problem. Care must be taken not to mistake poverty and its impact on a group of people for culture.

As Greenlee states: ". . . a discretionary decision resulting in a just action depends on the officer's ability to assess cultural norms accurately and to be, in effect, the cultural and social engineer at that moment" (Greenlee, 1980, p. 51).

Characteristics of Culture

Culture is:

- *Organic and supraorganic.* It depends on people acting, thinking, and feeling to exist, but it outlives individual people and generations.
- *Overt and covert.* Overt parts of culture such as language and houses can be observed, but attitudes, philosophies, and spiritual elements are inferred.
- *Explicit and implicit.* Explicit culture can be described by the people who perform the behavior that is a part of it (e.g., playing football, brushing teeth). Implicit culture is more difficult to describe objectively (e.g., adults speak a common language but may not be able to explain objectively its grammar and syntax).
- *Ideal and manifest.* The ideal culture is what people believe their behavior should be; manifest culture is how people really behave.
- *Stable and changing.* System principles apply to cultures. Both change and a need for structure and predictability are constants.

No person adheres to all the values in a given culture; socialization is seldom complete. Within every culture there are distinctive subcultures (Popenoe, 1993). As a result, diversity within a culture is common. Hispanic includes Cuban, Puerto Rican, Mexican, Spanish, and other subcultural groups. Southeast Asian includes Laotian, Vietnamese, Cambodian, and so on. It is possible then to describe basic traditions and standards, or touchstones, of a culture because these are less subject to area variation. It is not possible, however, to define a culture precisely nor to find a person who perfectly represents a given culture.

CROSS-CULTURAL FACTORS

The following factors should be viewed only as examples of the variety of cross-cultural factors that lead to cultural understanding and misunderstanding.

African Americans

The term *African American* has supplanted *black* as the preferred terminology by which to refer to Americans who fall within the negroid categorization of racial groups. This terminology can be misleading, in that there are Americans of African descent who are not black and there are blacks residing in the United States who are neither American nor of direct African descent. Despite those distinctions, in this book the term *African American* is used to refer to U.S. residents who are negroid or identify themselves as being African American, Afro-American, Negro, or black.

African Americans are the majority minority within the United States. Their numbers, 29,986,070 (U.S. Bureau of the Census, 1990), comprise 12.1 percent of the U.S. population. The majority of African Americans reside within urbanized areas of the nation. They also represent 29.3 percent of all persons living below the poverty level (U.S. Bureau of the Census, 1992). These figures may be interpreted to mean that African Americans are overrepresented both within the lower class and within inner cities. The products of these findings are that large numbers of African Americans live under both economic and social hardships. The existence of such hardships places a direct burden on the relations between African Americans and the police who serve them.

Despite considerable progress in regard to race relations within American society, African Americans continue to be dramatically overrepresented within American correctional institutions (U.S. Bureau of the Census, 1990). This overrepresentation will continue until such time as economic and social conditions for African Americans improve. Although African Americans have for the most part become *culturally assimilated*—adopted behaviors, customs, language, dress, and values consistent with the norms of the overall society—large numbers are still striving to be *structurally assimilated*—integrated into the common institutional and social life of the country (Vander Zanden, 1983; Marger, 1991). This resistance to structural assimilation is a product of lingering ethnocentrism within both the white majority and African Americans.

African Americans have experienced more difficulty in becoming assimilated into American society than have many other ethnic minorities, for two primary reasons: (1) clearly notable racial characteristics, and (2) the legacy of slavery. The first difficulty has been reduced as American society has become less color conscious due to the civil rights movement, laws barring racial discrimination, and the continued development of human understanding. The second difficulty is actually more difficult. Even in a society committed to social equality which utilizes governmental programs to redistribute wealth and enhance the quality of life and opportunities for the lower class, change comes slowly. The change is hindered by political disagreements with regard to the appropriateness of change strategies utilized by governments and individuals.

Within both African-American communities and American society as a whole, there are constant disagreements over what should be done to enhance the quality of life for African Americans (Kitano, 1991). Should we follow the model of Martin Luther King, Jr., who sought an integrated, colorblind society in which all citizens were treated equally? Or, do we follow the Malcolm X model, which demands enhanced economic opportunities while maintaining separation of the races? Is racism only a white problem? Or is anyone who dislikes members of other races or seeks treatment distinctive from other races guilty of racism? Are affirmative action programs still beneficial? Or have they become more divisive than beneficial? These are but of a few of the complex and difficult questions with which we as a society continue to wrestle.

Within the ranks of African Americans, the perspectives are as varied as those found within American society as a whole. Many African Americans call for continued understanding and cooperation among the races (Washington, 1993). They stress mutual respect and opposition to racism and bigotry on the part of both blacks and whites (Holmes, 1993). Others, such as the National Coalition of Blacks for Reparations in America, argue that peaceful coexistence cannot be achieved until "white society" atones by apologizing for the enslavement of their ancestors and subsequent injustices which have continued to the present and then pays reparations to every African American. Still others hold more moderate positions as to what is best for both African Americans and other Americans.

The end result of the foregoing debates is that the police will continue to be seen by many African Americans as representatives of an unjust and oppressive society. Unfortunately, African Americans will continue to be a large part of the police clientele (both as victims and offenders). The police must therefore seek to understand the perspectives and problems of African Americans, and they must do so with true concern and sensitivity. This is best achieved through the enhanced selection, training, disciplinary, and accountability strategies discussed in previous chapters. It is also supported by continued emphasis on equitable minority representation at all levels within police agencies and increased community involvement in the police decision-making process. Hopefully, the successful implementation of these strategies will prevent racial riots such as those experienced in Los Angeles in 1992.

New Immigrants

The complexity of African-American relations within American society (and with the police in particular) is further compounded by the diversity of immigrants (both legal and illegal) who have recently begun arriving in the United States from Africa and the Caribbean. Most Africans have little in common with African Americans beyond racial similarities. The cultural norms, values, history, and traditions differ significantly. Tribal and family influences, language difficulties, religious differences, and divergent attitudes regarding democracy and legal order make assimilation into both American society as a whole and within African-American communities quite challenging for all but the better educated Africans.

The influx of recent Caribbean refugees who are negroid is creating a similar dilemma. Although many refugees speak English, most are poorly educated and can neither read nor write. Like African immigrants, they have distinctive cultural traditions and values that conflict with American society norms. This has led to heated debates as to what immigration policies should be regarding specific island nations. Haiti, where many of the poorly educated, French-speaking populace seek to escape abject poverty and political turmoil by entering the United States is a classic example.

Hispanic Americans

Hispanic Americans comprise the second-largest ethnic group behind African Americans. The 1990 Census found 22,354,059 residents of Hispanic descent, 9 percent of the total population (U.S. Bureau of the Census, 1990). It is thought that these numbers are grossly underrepresentative due to the fact that many Hispanics are undocumented aliens who avoided contact with census takers and many individuals did not identify themselves as Hispanic. It has been estimated that by 2015 the Hispanic population will exceed 40 million, making them the nation's largest minority group (Henslin, 1993, p. 330).

Hispanic Americans are unique among America's ethnic minorities in that they are categorized not by race but by ethnic heritage. Hispanics are a very diverse ethnic group whose racial membership includes individuals who could be racially classified as negroid, American mongoloid, or caucasoid, with most being varied mixtures of caucasoid and American mongoloid or caucasoid and negroid. According to the U.S. Census Bureau, Hispanics are those persons who identify themselves as Mexican American, Puerto Rican, Cuban, Central or South American, or of other Spanish culture or origin. Many do not choose to identify themselves under the umbrella of Hispanic, which they consider to be too broad, preferring designations more specific to their particular origins (Kitano, 1991). Others prefer to be referred to as Latinos. Still others prefer to be identified solely as Americans.

There are many differences among the ethnic subgroups of which Hispanic Americans are comprised. However, they share several common difficulties which set them apart from others in American society. The most notable distinction for many Hispanics who have recently immigrated to America or have lived their lives within segregated enclaves is that of the Spanish language. There are many Hispanic dialects, some so different from others that they may appear to be another language. However, except for some variations in the definition and use of specific terms, they are similar enough to be mutually understood. Unfortunately, to those who do not understand its subtle nuances and reliance on nonverbal gestures, the different use of surnames and last names to indicate heritage, the closer proximity of communications, the greater use of touching, and its heightened expressiveness, the Spanish language may appear to be both foreign and threatening. This can lead to serious misunderstanding between Spanish-speaking citizens and English-speaking police officers (Weaver, 1992; Colvard, 1992).

While language is a major distinction for Hispanics, there are other important cultural differences that deserve comment. Hispanic males tend to exhibit a strong sense of *machismo,* in which they place great emphasis on their personal honor and their position of power within traditionally male-dominated families (Henslin, 1993). Hispanics have very strong commitments to family and often live within large familial groups which include three or more generations. Religion (predominately Catholicism) plays an important role in their lives, and many have a fatalistic view of life (If it is God's will, it will occur) (Kitano, 1991). Like other ethnic minorities, they place a greater emphasis on the welfare of the group rather than on that of individuals. Hispanics have traditionally been less materialistic than other ethnic groups in America, which combined with discrimination contributes to their being overrepresented within the lower class. And like other ethnic minorities, their frustration with limited social and economic opportunities has frequently led to negative relations with the police.

There are over 5 million Hispanics from Central America, South America, or other Spanish cultures or origins. However, we confine our discussions to the three largest categories of Hispanic Americans: Mexican Americans, Puerto Ricans, and Cuban Americans.

Mexican Americans

Mexican Americans are by far the largest Hispanic group in the United States. There were 13,495,938 Mexican Americans identified by the 1990 Census, comprising 5.4 percent of the total population (U.S. Bureau of the Census, 1990). Like African Americans, Mexican Americans or Chicanos have a long history of oppression in American society. While we may tend to think of Mexican Americans as being recent immigrants (often illegal) from Mexico seeking better economic conditions, many have historical connections within the United States which are far older than those of all other ethnic groups except Native Americans (Marger, 1991). They became Americans because their homelands were forcibly annexed by American colonialism. As a Chicano living in New Mexico informed one of the authors: "My family never moved. The United States moved." This perspective is also held by many Mexican immigrants who feel that they have merely moved to lands that rightfully belong to their people (Vander Zanden, 1983).

Mexican Americans see themselves as quite distinct from other Hispanics both in racial composition and cultural history (Kitano, 1991). They are a racial amalgamation of European and Native American which while distinctly different to "Anglos" is the least divergent of all non-Caucasian groups (Kitano, 1991, p. 170). Their cultural development was shaped by early Spanish and Native American historical events that took place in Mexico and the American Southwest.

Mexican Americans have not created nationwide political organizations to promote their group interests as have African Americans and some other ethnic groups (Kitano, 1991). Nor have they been quick to use social unrest as a weapon against injustice. The 1977 drowning of a handcuffed Chicano by six white Houston police officers led to demonstrations by Mexican Americans and calls for reforms but did not lead to riots (Vander Zanden, 1983). Chicanos have seemed more content to use the established political process to address their grievances than have other ethnic groups. It has been argued that this is due to successful assimilation on the part of many Mexican Americans (Brookhiser, 1993).

Puerto Ricans

Puerto Ricans make up the second-largest grouping of Hispanics within the United States. In the 1990 Census 2,727,754 Puerto Ricans (1.1 percent of the total population) were identified (U.S. Bureau of the Census, 1990). This figure does not include people living in Puerto Rico, which is a U.S. possession. Like many Mexican Americans and all Native Americans, Puerto Ricans are Americans because their lands were incorporated into the United States (Marger, 1991). All Puerto Ricans are considered U.S. citizens who may freely move back and forth from the island to the continent, which many frequently do (Kitano, 1991). The privileges and responsibilities extended to Puerto Ricans (i.e., voting in presidential elections and paying federal income tax) varies depending on whether they reside in Puerto Rico or elsewhere in the United States.

Approximately one-third of all Puerto Ricans are black (U.S. Bureau of the Census, 1990), with the majority being varying mixtures of caucasoid, American mongoloid, and negroid (Kitano, 1991). The product of this ethnic and racial mixture is that while white Puerto Ricans may suffer from discrimination against Hispanics, black Puerto Ricans may suffer from racial discrimination as well. Due to discrimination and other cultural influences that make assimilation into society on the American mainland difficult, many Puerto Ricans move back to Puerto Rico.

Puerto Rico became an American possession in 1899 following the Spanish-American War. The attitudes of Puerto Ricans toward the United States varies considerably. Many Puerto Ricans view the United States as a colonial power which wrongly holds their island. They feel that Puerto Rico should be granted independence from the United States. Others feel that Puerto Rico is a distinct region within the United States and that as such it should be granted statehood. Still others feel that Puerto Rico is best served by being an American possession but having a degree of autonomy as currently provided by its status as a commonwealth. This debate has raged for several years, and at this writing it appears that the status quo will continue to exist in the foreseeable future.

Cuban Americans

Cuban Americans number 1,043,932 persons or 0.4 percent of the total population in the 1990 Census (U.S. Bureau of the Census, 1990). They are mostly concentrated within southeast Florida near their original homeland. While there was some migration to the United States during the 1800s and early 1900s due to the close proximity of Florida to Cuba, most did not immigrate until Fidel Castro took power in 1959. The initial Cuban immigrants were predominately well-educated members of the upper and middle class who were light skinned and either spoke English or learned readily to do so. These individuals maintained their Cuban identity but were easily absorbed into southeast Florida society. Later immigrants fleeing from Cuba's communist society were less affluent, more racially diverse, and few spoke English, but they were able to adapt due to American acceptance of refugees from communism and resources provided by previous immigrants. As the Cuban-American community grew in the Miami area, many immigrants were able to adapt without learning English or adopting "American" customs (Kitano, 1991; Marger, 1991).

In 1980 Castro agreed to allow over 100,000 Cubans to leave Cuba from the port of Mariel. In addition to political refugees, most of whom were poor, lacking in job skills, and unable to speak English, the Cuban government included several thousand people who had been imprisoned for committing nonpolitical crimes, being mentally ill, or being homosexual. The inclusion of this relatively small number of individuals resulted in a negative reaction toward the "Marielitos" which previous Cuban immigrants had not experienced. This negativism also heightened discriminatory attitudes by other ethnic groups toward Cuban Americans in general. Today, the Miami area is an ethnically and racially diverse area in which Cuban Americans comprise almost half of the populace (U.S. Bureau of the Census, 1990).

The political and social influence wielded by Cuban Americans in southeast Florida has provoked considerable resistance on the part of non-Cubans living there. Relations with lower- and middle-class whites, African Americans, and other Hispanics not of Cuban descent have frequently become strained. Twice during the 1980s, riots occurred as the result of police actions that led to the death of African

Americans. One was precipitated by the death of a motorcyclist at the hands of a predominately white group of officers. The second occurred after an African American was killed by a Cuban-American officer. In 1991 another riot occurred after a Hispanic officer of Colombian descent shot an African-American motorist. The fact that riots did not occur following the officer's acquittal on manslaughter charges in 1993 is testimony to enhanced efforts to mediate grievances within Miami's multicultural community.

Asian Americans

Asian Americans are a highly diverse group made up of persons of Chinese, Japanese, Filipino, Korean, Vietnamese, Cambodian, Hmong, Laotian, Thai, Asian Indian, Bangladeshi, Burmese, Indonesian, Malayan, Okinawan, Pakistani, Sri Lankan, and other nationalities. In 1990, Asians comprised 2.8 percent of the American populace or 6,908,638 persons (U.S. Bureau of the Census, 1990). As categorized by the U.S. Census Bureau, Asians include persons classified both by racial characteristics (i.e., individuals displaying mongoloid features) and geographic origin (areas in which the inhabitants reside are considered to be a part of Asia, but like Asian Indians, the residents do not display mongoloid features).

Like other immigrant groups, Asian Americans have suffered from discrimination due to differences in race, religion, culture, language, and social organization (Popenoe, 1993). During the 1800s, Asian immigrants were used when cheap labor was desirable but abused when they and their children were perceived as being in economic competition. In California, citizenship was denied to immigrants who were not white. As recently as 1952, the California constitution forbade the employment of Asian workers (Vander Zanden, 1983). This "fear" of Asians flooding the country led the U.S. government to impose restrictive immigration laws which severely limited the numbers of Asians that could enter the country (Kitano, 1991).

In addition to discrimination based on fear of economic competition by both whites and other ethnic groups, Asian Americans suffered from the view that they had unbreakable ties with their homelands which were stronger than any attachments they might have for the United States. This view was erroneous in that descendants of Asian immigrants had readily adopted mainstream American customs (including the use of English as a primary, if not a single, language) (Kitano, 1991). Their adherence to cultural traditions and heritage were in effect no stronger than what might be found among white ethnic groups. Another difficulty faced by Asian Americans is that members of other ethnic groups who have had little exposure to Orientals (other than Hollywood stereotypes) tend to look upon all Asians as being the same. This has often led to spillover bigotry from persons who dislike an Asian nation or another Asian-American group (Henslin, 1993). Such bigotry caused the 1982 beating death of a Vietnamese American by unemployed autoworkers who thought he was Japanese (Brinkerhoff, White, and Ortega, 1992).

The largest Asian groups in American society are Chinese Americans, Filipino Americans, Japanese Americans, Asian Indians, Korean Americans, and Vietnamese Americans. Other Americans of Asian descent make up only a small percentage of U.S. ethnic minorities. For brevity's sake, our discussion in this section will focus on the larger categories of Chinese Americans, Filipino Americans, Japanese Americans, and to a lesser degree, Asian Indians, Korean Americans, and Vietnamese Americans.

Chinese Americans

Chinese Americans were the earliest of the Asian groups to begin immigrating to the United States. They were first imported in the 1850s to work in mines, help build railroads, and to perform duties that were considered inappropriate for white males (Kitano, 1991). Today they remain one of the largest groupings of any new immigrants. There were approximately 1,645,472 Chinese Americans identified in 1990 (U.S. Bureau of the Census, 1990). Many of these citizens are descendants of immigrants who came to this country over 100 years ago. Others (both legal and illegal) are recent arrivals. The majority of Chinese Americans reside in California and Hawaii, but they may be found living throughout the United States.

Like other Asian Americans, Chinese Americans tend to have strong family ties, strict discipline, and a deep-seated respect for heritage and traditions. As mentioned earlier, Chinese Americans have historically experienced severe oppression within American society. They were denied both citizenship and work because of their race (Popenoe, 1993; Kitano, 1991). They were specifically excluded from immigration to the United States (Tishler, 1993; Eshleman, Cashion, and Basirico, 1993). They were barred from being able to testify against whites (Kitano, 1991). Despite these handicaps, Chinese Americans as a whole have persevered, in large part because of strong commitments to achieve both educational and economic success.

Despite the successes of many upper- and middle-class Chinese Americans, large numbers continue to live in poverty in racially segregated "Chinatowns." Racial discrimination and cultural conflict continues today. Although current stereotypes depict Chinese Americans as having economic affluence and political influence, large numbers (particularly recent immigrants) have not been assimilated into American society.

Filipino Americans

Filipino Americans numbered 1,406,770 in the 1990 Census, making them the second largest grouping of Asian Americans (U.S. Bureau of the Census, 1990). Like other Asian Americans, their numbers tend to be clustered in California and Hawaii. Unlike other Asian-American ethnic groups, Filipinos are more racially diverse. They are predominately of Malayan descent with varying mixtures of other races, due to varying periods in which the Philippines were controlled by other nations (i.e., Spain, the United States, and Japan). Indeed, Filipino Americans are frequently mistaken for Hispanic Americans due to their physical appearance and Spanish surnames (Kitano, 1991).

The Philippines were annexed by the United States following the Spanish-American War. Like Puerto Ricans, they had a unique status as both U.S. nationals and subjects. This ended when the Philippines were officially granted independence in 1934. Their ability to immigrate easily to the United States was halted following independence, but large numbers of Filipinos had already migrated in search of better economic conditions in Hawaii and California. Their lives as workers on Hawaiian plantations and West Coast farms were harsh, and they were paid meager wages (Popenoe, 1993). They were also segregated from other ethnic groups due to cultural differences and discrimination (Kitano, 1991).

Following World War II, restrictions on Filipino immigration were loosened and a second wave of immigrants came to America (Popenoe, 1993). Like other immigrants they experienced hardships both in adjusting to and being accepted into American society. Despite these obstacles, Filipino Americans have been able to achieve a median family income that is one of the highest among Asian-American groups (Popenoe, 1993).

Japanese Americans

Japanese Americans began arriving in the United States in fairly large numbers during the 1870s. Their experiences were very similar to those of Chinese Americans in regard to mistreatment and prejudice at the hands of the white majority and other ethnic groups (Popenoe, 1993). Although they were the subjects of bigotry and discrimination, Japanese Americans were more readily adaptable to American society than were many other immigrant groups. Like Chinese Americans, they were very industrious and sought to attain both educational and economic success. Unlike Chinese Americans and other Asian groups, the Japanese are less likely to segregate themselves within ethnic communities (Kitano, 1991) and they are more likely to intermarry outside their ethnic group (Henslin, 1993). As a result, they have been more easily assimilated than Chinese Americans.

One of the more shameful exhibitions of racism in American history was perpetrated upon Japanese Americans during World War II. Due to the war with Japan, over 110,000 Americans of Japanese descent were forcibly removed from their homes and placed in "relocation camps" (Eshleman, Cashion, and Basirico, 1993). Included were people whose families had lived in America for nearly a century. Any one of one-eighth or greater Japanese blood was considered a potential Japanese sympathizer (Henslin, 1993). It was not until 1988 that survivors of the Japanese relocation programs received an official apology and partial compensation from the U.S. government (Tischler, 1993).

Although they did not arrive in the United States in large numbers until after 1900, the Japanese-American population has grown steadily. Today they comprise the third largest group of Asian Americans, numbering 847,562 in the 1990 Census (U.S. Bureau of the Census, 1990). As a group, Japanese Americans have been very successful in both economic and educational achievements (Henslin, 1993). Yet they continue to suffer from discrimination and bigotry (Brinkerhoff, White, and Ortega, 1992). Much of this discrimination is based on racism, but a great deal may also be attributed to envy by other groups. Japanese Americans are resented not just because of their (exaggerated) success within American society but also because of Japan's success in the world economy.

Asian Indians

Asian Indians comprised the fourth-largest Asian group according to the 1990 Census, which found 815,447 residents of Indian ancestry. Like neighboring Pakistan,

Bangladesh, Burma, and Sri Lanka, India is populated by a very complex mixture of racial, ethnic, and religious groups who are in constant competition and frequently, open conflict with one another. These conflicts are exacerbated by the population density of India. In addition, widespread poverty may be found within the rigid class system that still exists within Indian society (Henslin, 1993). Due to these conditions, many Asian Indians have immigrated in search of a better life.

In that they have dark skins but Caucasian features, Asian Indians are an "in-between ethnic group" which differs from other racial classifications (Marger, 1991). This means that they are not readily assimilated into other groups which tend to have predominately caucasoid, mongoloid, or negroid features. In addition, their religious beliefs (Hinduism, Islam, Sikhism, Buddhism, and Jainism) and traditions are seen as threatening by many Americans. This has led to segregated communities and limited opportunities for Asian Indians of less affluence.

Korean Americans

Korean immigration has taken place in three waves. The first began in 1882 with the signing of the Shufeldt Treaty and ended in 1905 when Japan took control of Korea. The second took place during and after the Korean War when immigration policies were relaxed for war brides, war orphans, and students. The third wave began following the Immigration and Naturalization Act of 1965 and continues today (Kitano, 1991). The product of these successive waves is that there were 798,849 Korean Americans identified in the 1990 Census (U.S. Bureau of the Census, 1990).

Korean Americans have experienced difficulties similar to those of other Asian immigrants. Like Chinese Americans and Japanese Americans, Korean Americans have been relatively successful in adapting to American society (Tischler, 1993). A willingness to learn English and adopt Christianity has aided their success. Some may even argue that they have been too successful. These "hardworking, striving, studious people living in closely knit families" have begun to suffer from the same domestic problems (divorce, abuse, alcoholism, etc.) that plague the white majority (Henslin, 1993, p. 450). It should be further noted that the success of Korean Americans has led to strained relations with other minorities, as evidenced in the Los Angeles riot of 1992.

Vietnamese Americans

The fourth-largest Asian group in American society is that of Vietnamese Americans. In a manner similar to that of Korean Americans, the immigration of Vietnamese to the United States was largely the product of American involvement in an Asian conflict. Unlike Korea, war immigrants were not limited to American brides, orphans, and students. The fall of South Vietnam to Communist North Vietnam led to thousands of Vietnamese citizens seeking asylum in other countries (Popenoe, 1993). The initial wave of Vietnamese refugees immigrating to the United States consisted primarily of upper- and middle-class individuals, predominately Catholic, who left Vietnam to escape reprisals from the communists (Kitano, 1991). Assimilation for this group, while challenging, was not as difficult as for those who came later.

The second wave of Vietnamese refugees began arriving in the United States after 1975. As a whole they were less educated, poorer, younger, Buddhist, and less prepared for entry into American society (Kitano, 1991, p. 250). Many of these refugees were "Boat People" who had endured extreme hardships to escape Vietnam and eventually gain entry in the United States. The combined numbers of Vietnamese Americans that resulted from these immigration processes were 614,547 in the 1990 Census (U.S. Bureau of the Census, 1990).

Like previous Asian groups, those Vietnamese who spoke English, were better educated, and had economic assets and/or marketable skills experienced considerably less difficulty in gaining acceptance in the communities in which they settled. The poorer, less affluent refugees have experienced challenges more similar to those of earlier Asian immigrants. Prejudice and hostility toward Vietnamese immigrants has been extremely severe in areas in which Vietnamese customs and economic competition have brought them into direct conflict with working-class persons of other races.

The outcome of the Vietnam War did not result only in mass immigrations from Vietnam. Other Asian groups who had supported America involvement in Southeast Asia also fled their countries as political refugees. These groups were predominately Cambodians, Hmong (a separate ethnic group living in Laos), Laotians, and Thais. Their immigration added greatly to the numbers of Cambodians, Hmong, Laotians, and Thais living in the United States.

Native Americans

In the previous sections we discussed those persons who immigrated to the United States and the difficulties they have experienced in adjusting to and being accepted into American society. The racial and cultural distinctions among those ethnic minorities have significantly influenced how they interact with one another and with the white majority. Ironically, the challenges those groups have faced are overshadowed by those which the indigenous peoples of the lands that now comprise the United States have endured.

Pacific Islanders

Until 1980, Pacific Islanders were classified among Other Races within the U.S. Census. In the 1980 and 1990 censuses, Pacific Islanders were grouped with Asians. We have not classified them as such for two reasons. The first is that such a grouping was based more on geography than on race or culture. Pacific Islanders are predominately Polynesians, Micronesians, or Melanesians (Kitano, 1991, p. 254). These racial groups are distinctive from others discussed previously. The second reason is that the vast majority of Pacific Islanders residing within the United States are not immigrants from other nations but from lands that are part of the United States. In that these peoples are Americans due to American imperialism rather than to immigration, they are more correctly classified as Native Americans.

Hawaiian Americans

The majority of Pacific Islanders residing in the United States are Hawaiian Americans. Hawaii was a separate kingdom until 1893, when American businessmen, aided by the U.S. Navy, led a successful revolt against the monarchy. In 1900, Hawaii became a territory of the United States despite considerable opposition by native Hawaiians. Efforts to make Hawaii a state were resisted by Congress until 1959, primarily due to fears of its heavily Oriental population which had been imported during the late 1800s and early 1900s to work on the plantations (Lind, 1980). Today, Hawaii is a prosperous state noted for its natural beauty, its mild climate, its friendly treatment of visitors, and its cultural diversity. However, the negative impact of the American experience on Native Hawaiians tends to be overlooked.

Hawaiian Americans numbered 211,014 in the 1990 Census (U.S. Bureau of the Census, 1990). True Hawaiian Americans are of Polynesian descent. Today they are a minority population in the state of Hawaii. That few pure Hawaiians remain is the result of diseases transported to the islands by visitors, which nearly decimated the native populace during the 1800s, and Hawaiian intermarriage with Asian and white immigrants. The social product is a "melting pot" of diverse cultures and traditions (Kitano, 1991). Unfortunately, within this "multicultural society," Native Hawaiians have suffered discrimination and abuse at the hands of both white Americans and Asian Americans. Native Hawaiians (who were traditionally friendly and trusting) discovered that their lands had been taken over, their economic opportunities were limited, and their cultural heritage was being repressed by other ethnic groups. It has been the authors' observation that many Native Hawaiians residing in the "American Paradise" are currently experiencing economic and social adversities similar to those of other ethnic minorities.

Samoan Americans

The Samoan Islands were an independent kingdom in the South Pacific until 1899, when they were partitioned by the United States and Germany. The western islands, which had been seized by Germany, were administered by New Zealand following World War I. In 1962, Western Samoa became an independent nation. American Samoa, as the smaller group of eastern islands are known, has remained under the control of the United States since 1899 (Kitano, 1991).

The residents of American Samoa are of Polynesian descent and are predominately Catholics. They are not American citizens but as American nationals are free to travel to the United States. As the result of unrestricted immigration, mostly in search of better economic conditions, there were 62,964 Samoan Americans included in the 1990 census (U.S. Bureau of the Census, 1990). Many Samoans immigrate to Hawaii, where they are more readily assimilated than on the U.S. mainland (Kitano, 1991). The Samoan-American experience has been similar to that of other ethnic minorities.

Guamanian Americans

The United States obtained control of Guam at the conclusion of the Spanish-American War. Guam is located within the Marianas Islands and is now a part of the Commonwealth of the Northern Marianas. Most Guamians are "Chamoros," a mixture of Native Guamians, Filipinos, Mexicans, Anglos, and Japanese (Kitano, 1991). Increased economic competition caused Guamians to begin immigrating to the U.S. mainland in 1970 after the U.S. government opened immigration to Guam by other Asian groups. The 49,345 Guamian Americans identified in the 1990 Census (U.S.

Bureau of the Census, 1990) have encountered difficulties similar to those of other Pacific Islanders.

American Indians

Earlier we used the term *Native Americans* as an umbrella under which all the indigenous peoples of America were categorized. To distinguish them from Pacific Islanders, Eskimos, and Aleuts, we will use the term *American Indians* to refer to the 308 tribes of Native Americans residing within the continental United States (Burns et al., 1993). Some Native Americans object to the label *American Indian,* citing its derivation from the erroneous assumptions of early European explorers (Cummings and Wise, 1993). However, in that it is still in use by the U.S. Census Bureau, the Bureau of Indian Affairs, and the American Indian Movement, we shall utilize this terminology. The junior authors of this current edition are one-quarter Chickasaw and one-sixteenth Sioux, respectively, so we assure the reader that no disrespect is intended.

Thus far we have discussed American Indians as if they were a homogeneous group (a practice which the U.S. government too frequently followed). Nothing is further from the truth. Like Asian Americans and Hispanic Americans, these Native Americans are comprised of culturally diverse peoples who have little in common. The depiction of "blood-thirsty" half-naked warriors riding the plains made great Hollywood hype but bore little resemblance to reality. To discuss the diversity among the many tribes and their various cultures and traditions would require volumes. However, the reader should be aware that American Indians had (and continue to have) many different lifestyles which were greatly influenced by their tribal traditions and geographical area. Many were fishermen, farmers, shepherds, ranchers, and craftsmen who lived in permanent and well-governed communities (Kitano, 1991; Brinkerhoff, White, and Ortega, 1993). In fact, the model used by Benjamin Franklin in drafting the Articles of Confederation which originally governed the United States was based on the League of the Iroquois (Tishler, 1993).

American Indians are the most disadvantaged minority group in the United States (Brinkerhoff, White, and Ortega, 1993). They have suffered harsher and more prolonged discrimination than has any other minority group. Almost every ethnic group in America has been grievously exploited but none to the degree of American Indians. The enslavement of Indian tribes began in New England prior to the importation of African slaves and continued in the Southwest for several years after the freeing of African slaves (Barker, Hunter, and Rush, 1994). Entire Indian tribes were driven from their lands, confined to lives of poverty on dreary reservations, and/or massacred at the hands of white settlers and the U.S. government. The "Trail of Tears" in which members of the Eastern tribes were forcibly removed to lands west of the Mississippi River, the Sand Creek Massacre of peaceful Indians in Colorado, the Massacre at Wounded Knee in South Dakota, and the countless other acts of wanton aggression against Native American men, women, and children (Kitano, 1991; Henslin, 1993) exemplify one of the more shameful periods in the history of the United States.

Even in today's enlightened society, which seeks to promote ethnic harmony and which vigorously enforces laws prohibiting discrimination against ethnic minorities, approximately half of American Indians live on government reservations (Brinkerhoff,

White, and Ortega, 1993, p. 177). Conditions on those 278 reservations are predominately poor, with most residents living in poverty and lacking decent health care (Burns et al., 1993, p. 125). Of those who live off reservations, nearly one-fourth live in poverty (Cummings and Wise, 1993, p. 133).

American Indians are estimated to have numbered as high as 10 million at the time that Europeans began settling in North America. By 1850 their numbers had declined to approximately 250,000 as a result of starvation, disease, and deliberate massacre (Eshleman, Cashion, and Basirico, 1993, p. 243). It has only been within the latter portion of this century that the number of American Indians has experienced sizable growth. In the 1990 Census, American Indians numbered 1,878,285 or 0.8 percent of the U.S. population (U.S. Bureau of the Census, 1990). This increase has been attributed to high birth rates and somewhat better living conditions (Popenoe, 1993). It is also due in part to a greater willingness on the part of respondents to identify with their American Indian heritage (Tishler, 1993).

Due to increasing awareness of the continued plight of American Indians and the efforts of organizations such as the American Indian Movement and the National Indian Youth Council, it is hoped that the economic and social conditions of American Indians will be improved. But when one realizes that these first Americans were not granted U.S. citizenship until 1924, it appears that change will come slowly.

Eskimos and Aleuts

Like American Indians, Eskimos and Aleuts are considered Native Americans. These groups have distinct racial and cultural features similar to those of Siberian Asians, which distinguish them from American Indians (Cummings and Wise, 1993). In the 1990 Census, there were 57,152 Eskimos and 23,797 Aleuts residing in the United States (U.S. Bureau of the Census, 1990). Due to their segregation from most of American society in the Alaskan Arctic, Aleuts and Eskimos did not share the long history of oppression experienced by American Indians. However, with the coming of white settlers in the late 1800s and the development that has followed, they have experienced difficulties similar to those of other ethnic minorities.

White Americans

In previous sections we have detailed the difficulties ethnic minorities have experienced in gaining acceptance into American society. Based on those discussions, the reader might assume that all ethnocentric wrongs have been perpetuated on minorities by the "white majority." This view is incorrect for two reasons:

1. All peoples tend to be somewhat xenophobic. The products of this xenophobia are racism, bigotry, intolerance, and discrimination against other groups. Just as minorities have suffered from these social evils, so have they imposed them on one another as well as on whites. Historically, those within positions of power in the United States have been predominately white. This has led to the false impression that all whites have power and that all minorities are powerless. It

has also led white zenophiles and minority xenophobes to overlook, or too readily excuse, minority misconduct.

2. There is no cohesive "White America." White Americans are as culturally diverse as any other racial category. Indeed, white Americans are varying mixtures of many caucasoid ethnic groups. To classify all whites as Anglo Americans would be equivalent to labeling all Asians as Japanese, all Hispanics as Chicano, all Pacific Islanders as Samoan, or all American Indians as Cherokee. European American is a more accurate designation but still fails to note that many whites, while predominately of European descent, also have the blood of other races.

In the 1990 Census, whites numbered 199,686,070 or 80.3 percent of the U.S. population. Within this group 11,557,774 were also classified as Hispanic (U.S. Bureau of the Census, 1990). There has been an increasing interest in ethnic heritage among white Americans during the past decade, which ironically, gained impetus due to the televised presentation of Alex Haley's *Roots,* a history of an African-American family. Later films, such as Ron Howard's *Far and Away,* have aided in keeping white ethnic interests alive. Heightened awareness of cultural heritage among whites has also resulted from the current push for multicultural education by minorities and white liberals.

Due to the past success of "Americanization," which emphasized learning to speak English and abandoning national origin or cultural identity in favor of becoming an American (Tischler, 1993), many whites have only limited knowledge of their cultural heritage. Despite this loss, the majority of white Americans are still able to identify their national, if not specific area of origin. The largest nationality groupings indicated by white Americans are displayed in Table 10-1. The accuracy of these identifications is a matter of debate.

TABLE 10-1
LEADING EUROPEAN ANCESTRY GROUPS IN AMERICA

English	49,596,000
German	49,224,000
Irish	40,166,000
French	12,892,000
Italian	12,184,000
Scottish	10,049,000
Polish	8,228,000
Dutch	6,304,000
Swedish	4,345,000
Norwegian	3,454,000
Russian	2,781,000
Czech	1,892,000
Hungarian	1,777,000
Welsh	1,665,000
Danish	1,518,000
Portugese	1,024,000

Source: (U.S. Bureau of the Census, 1991).

European Americans

The original European immigrants to America were primarily from the colonial powers of England, France, Holland, and Spain. By 1700, the English culture was dominant along the East Coast (Brinkerhoff, White, and Ortega, 1992, p. 171). Later immigrants (both before and after the American Revolution) were expected to adopt the social standards of this earlier group of WASPS (White Anglo-Saxon Protestants). Affluent WASPS controlled the political and social environment of early America (many non-WASPS argue that they still do). As non-English immigrants from Western Europe arrived, they were indoctrinated as to how to conduct themselves. For Protestants from Scotland, Wales, Ireland, Sweden, Norway, Germany, France, and Switzerland, this was not a particularly difficult task (Eshleman, Cashion, and Basirico, 1993). For Catholics from those same nations, the adjustment was more difficult due to religious persecution. Irish Catholics, in particular, were the recipients of severe harassment and oppression at the hands of the WASP power structure.

As masses of non-Protestant immigrants began arriving in America from Southern and Eastern Europe, they also suffered from bigotry and discrimination. These "White Ethnics," as they are called (Eshleman, Cashion, and Basirico, 1993; Brinkerhoff, White, and Ortega, 1992), did not assimilate as readily as had previous white immigrants. Even in the 1990s, despite the constant pressures of Americanization, strong cultural identification can be found among their descendants. In addition to their cultural identification, one can also find a resentment among this group toward those who would declare that their "whiteness" has made for easy assimilation into American society. This resentment appears to be well founded if the reader considers that 66.5 percent of the nation's poor are white (U.S. Bureau of the Census, 1992, p. 12).

Jewish Americans

Approximately 6,500,000 Americans identify themselves as being Jewish (Eshleman, Cashion, and Basirico, 1993, p. 244). Unlike the other non-Protestant ethnic groups identified above, Jewish Americans did not identify with a common homeland (Marger, 1991). Nor can Jews be identified as a distinct racial group (despite the efforts of anti-Semites to do so). Their intermarriages with other ethnic cultures and the adoption of Judaism by members of diverse racial groups preclude such a racial identity. However, being Jewish transcends mere religious identification. Many people who do not practice Judaism still strongly identify with being Jewish. This strong cultural identification has been both beneficial and detrimental to Jews. Their adherence to a specific ethnic identity has enabled them to preserve their unique cultural heritage. Unfortunately, it has also led to their being targeted by others for being "different."

Jewish immigration to America began during the colonial period and continues today. The earliest Jewish immigrants came from Spain and Portugal. They were followed by immigrants from Germany and later from Eastern Europe. In recent years Jewish immigration has been primarily from Russia (Marger, 1991). As a group,

Jewish Americans have achieved economic success and considerable political power. Yet they have suffered from prejudice and discrimination throughout American history (Eshleman, Cashion, and Basirico, 1993). Anti-Semitism is no longer commonplace in the United States, but it continues.

Middle Easterners and Northern Africans

Another cultural grouping that may be found in the United States is that of Middle Easterners and Northern Africans. Members of this group either immigrated from or are descendants of immigrants from Northern Africa or the Middle East. Included in this grouping would be Arab Americans, Iranian Americans, and Turkish Americans. The exact numbers of Americans of Middle Eastern or Northern African descent are difficult to ascertain in that some members of this grouping are categorized as "Other Asian," others are classified within the general category of "White," and still others may be found within the category of "Other Race." However, utilizing data from the 1980 Census provided in the *1991 Statistical Abstract of the United States* (U.S. Bureau of the Census, 1991), it appears that their numbers would exceed 1 million. While many practice other religions, the majority are Muslim.

Immigration from Northern Africa and the Middle East has been a fairly recent phenomenon. Northern Africans and Middle Easterners did not begin arriving in the United States in large numbers until the relaxing of immigration restrictions by the Immigration and Naturalization Act of 1965. Although their numbers are relatively small in comparison to other ethnic groups, they have received considerable attention in recent years due to the hostile relations that the United States has had with Iran and Iraq, and due to terrorist activities by a variety of Arab and Middle Eastern groups. The product of this attention has been a dramatic increase in hostility, discrimination, and assaults on American citizens and resident aliens of Arab and Middle Eastern descent.

A Perspective on Diverse Cultures

The United States is comprised of numerous ethnic groups that are actively engaged in social and economic competition in our pluralistic society. Racism, ethnocentrism, and discrimination continue. We, too frequently, experience racial unrest in our urban areas. "Hate crimes" are perpetuated by frustrated individuals who act out against groups or persons who differ from them. A casual observer may wonder why outright cultural conflict such as that currently found in regions of Eastern Europe and Africa does not break out.

Although the authors cannot assure the reader that such incidents will never take place in the United States, we can offer hope that they will not. We will always have individuals who fear and hate peoples who are different than they are, and there will always be individuals and groups who will play on those fears and hatred for their own political and/or economic gain. Some will blatantly preach their bigotry, others will seek to conceal it within noble-sounding rhetoric. Despite the existence of those who harbor resentment and animosity toward other races or ethnic groups, the majority of Americans are actually quite tolerant of one another. The reason for this is quite simple: *we are more alike than we are different.*

IMPROVING COMMUNITY RELATIONS IN THE CONTEXT OF CULTURE

Generally, the following elements must exist in order for strategies designed to improve community relations in the context of culture to be successful, especially since we have such diverse cultural groups in most U.S. cities.

Appreciating the Culture(s)

Understanding and appreciating the cultural patterns and characteristics that exist in the community are prerequisite to making positive decisions in a cultural context. Developing a strategy in which the community can participate and retain a sense of community ownership and self-help must begin with this step.

Understanding the Language(s)

Lack of a common language creates the likelihood for misunderstanding, increased fear, and increased distance in interpersonal relations. It is not possible to be fluent in each of the many languages and ethnic dialects that exist in our larger, multicultural cities. It is possible, however, to learn key street-applicable phrases in the language, to have translators available in major language groups, and to appreciate some of the cultural values expressed in language. As members of the community teach new language skills to police officers, they may also learn from the officers some of the same elements of English.

Getting Involved in Meaningful Ways

Getting involved can reduce isolation and stereotyping and increase community morale and participation in policing. Those who live outside the community and spend little free time there are outsiders, even if they once were community residents. Face-to-face contact is important. A new immigrant may come to the United States with a view of the police based on an old-country value, which is one of fear and distrust. Police will need to understand that view and appreciate its cultural context if change is to be possible.

In another sense, the community will have to make the same commitment in reverse and seek to understand the police view and appreciate its cultural context. Rather than leading to stereotyping and distrust, such efforts could lead to helping both officers and the community achieve their goals. If it is true that the values of police officers are lower in context than the communities they serve, this understanding of context can be used by police and the community to build cooperation. Reward can be attached by the agency and the community to community relations projects, gaining social recognition for the officers. The challenge of confronting barriers and building a legacy of cooperation can be both exciting and lead to inner harmony. In this way, meeting community needs can also meet the needs of the officers.

Affecting Public Policy

Community members can be encouraged by police officers to get involved in the formation of public police policy that affects their lives. Police can help build a supportive network that involves the leadership of more than one cultural group.

Making a Firm, Full Commitment

The agency and its officers must make a firm, full commitment to improving relations in the context of culture if the effort is to be successful. It must be firm in the sense that what is promised is what is delivered; the commitment is not just rhetoric but real. It must be firm also in the sense that it will be supported over a long period of time and will not be abandoned at the first sign of problems. It must be full in the sense that energy, money, and time must be committed to the effort. This includes rewards for officers and enough flexibility within the program to meet new challenges as they arise.

Creatively Overcoming Barriers (New and Old)

Barriers to success will exist within the department, in the community, and probably from sources external to both. Much commitment will be required of individual officers so they will not be worn down by the obstacles that must be confronted. It may even be difficult to demonstrate that this approach is cost-effective. It lies within the ambiguous territory of crime prevention, community participation, and mutual respect.

Specific Targets

Recruitment

It is generally accepted that recruitment of officers must reflect the racial/cultural makeup of the community. The agency must seek the best candidates within these groups and then assist them to be culturally appropriate and to translate their understanding of their culture into positive action.

Training

Preservice and inservice training must build in an ongoing appreciation of culture. Training must be

> . . . designed to combat stereotypes about racial and ethnic minorities and to assure that police officers appreciate that people who are different from themselves also have worth as human beings . . . One of the most significant contributions a community organization could make would be to support a joint police–citizen coalition to review current funding resources for training, evaluate strengths and weaknesses with regard to intergroup relations, and determine what steps might be taken to increase training availability and upgrade programs. (Community Relations Service, U.S. Dept. of Justice, 1982, *Police Use of Deadly Force,* p. 18)

The Santa Ana Police Department was instrumental in setting up the Task Force on Police-Asian Relations (TOPAR) in Orange County, California. Several departments joined to produce a series of videotapes for both officers and immigrants. They held a series of seminars explaining Southeast Asian culture with the goal of increasing communication and understanding between refugees and police. Problems still exist, but most feel that progress has been made (Taft, 1982, pp. 17–21).

Language skills may be taught through the use of key words, role-play situations depicting cross-cultural incidents, case studies that demonstrated values, beliefs, and life-styles. Involvement of community members and practice is critical to the success of language training. Crash courses usually have little long-term use.

The Houston Police Department's academy and inservice program incorporates many of the key strategies discussed in this chapter in their effort to improve community relations with the Hispanic population. The program includes information about Hispanic culture and its variations; information and activities regarding stress—what causes it and how to recognize it. Part of the training also includes discussion about Hispanic culture and cultural differences at Ripley House, a community center in a Hispanic area. This encourages communication between police officers and members of the Hispanic community. Confronting stereotypes through asking and answering anonymous questions of officers, learning a basic system of communication in Spanish that is geared toward street use are also part of the overall program. Input from officers is an important part of the training. A fiesta attended by officers and community members concludes one part of the training. Attendance is supported by the department. Each officer is rewarded through points toward certification, an insignia, and opportunity to make changes in the program.

Tactics

Use of nonlethal weaponry, learning alternatives to violence, negotiation, conflict management, and crime prevention techniques will assist in reaching community relations goals. In each case, however, these tactics must reflect cultural relevancy.

Public Information Bulletins for Language Minorities

The U.S. Department of Justice has published a brochure containing ideas for developing materials for people who do not speak fluent English. The materials are geared toward involving these people in the nation's social, political, economic, and legal mainstream to avoid isolation and frustration.

Ongoing Community Participation

Involving the community in training programs and in volunteer and citizen review efforts helps to secure continuing input. Police can be personally involved in community activities, particularly in outreach activities with youth. Foot patrol and/or team policing in designated areas may also be helpful. Close personal connections with the community must be maintained both on duty and off. Los Angeles Police Department storefront center in Koreatown (Figure 10-1) is the joint effort of the department and the community.

In St. Paul, the police chief meets with leaders of the Hmong, a group of 10,000 Laotian hill people who have settled there. His goal is to stay up to date on community developments and provide meaningful inservice training in the police department on Hmong culture (Taft, 1982, p. 17).

FIGURE 10-1   The Los Angeles Police Department storefront center in Korea-town is the joint effort of the department and the community. (Courtesy of Travis L. Mayhall.)

The Community Relations Service (CRS)

CRS is an agency of the U.S. Department of Justice, created by the Civil Rights Act of 1964. The purpose of the agency is to assist in resolving community racial conflict and the method is through noncoercive, third-party intervention. The service has regional offices in Atlanta, Boston, Chicago, Dallas, Denver, Kansas City, New York, Philadelphia, San Francisco, and Seattle. CRS conducts formal negotiations and offers informal assistance to facilitate resolution of conflicts, frequently assisting communities in resolving disputes arising from alleged police use of excessive force.

Advocacy

"Action" committees can be formed that work with community social and legal services, civil rights, and other groups to promote police–citizen communication and citizen participation in formulating and monitoring police policies and practices that reflect the cultural needs of the community. For example, Hispanics are beginning to become increasingly involved in and committed to influencing public policy in justice areas.

CONCLUSIONS

People usually behave in culturally defined ways, and their behavior can often be understood in the context of culture. Positive police–community relations are easiest to achieve in a community that is relatively culturally integrated. They are most difficult to achieve in fragmented communities that are culturally diverse and where cultural rules are in transition and unclear.

We rarely have the ideal as an option, but even in the most fragmented community an aggressive ongoing program for improving community relations in the context of culture can be effective. The key elements of a successful program include appreciating the culture(s); understanding the language(s); getting involved in meaningful ways; making a firm, full commitment; and creatively overcoming barriers.

It is important to remember that we are one culture as well as many. We have some basic values and goals in common. We share common feelings of anger, sadness, happiness, and fear. We also wish to be valued and to belong. Ruth Benedict wrote this statement in 1934:

> What really binds men together is their culture—the ideas and the standards they have in common. If instead of selecting a symbol like common blood heredity and making a slogan of it, the nation turned its attention rather to the culture that unites its people, emphasizing its major merits and recognizing the different values which may develop in a different culture, it would substitute realistic thinking for a kind of symbolism which is dangerous because it is misleading." (p. 16)

STUDENT CHECKLIST

1. Define *cultural context.*
2. Describe the cultural context of community relations.
3. Contrast characteristics of different cultural groups.
4. Analyze several cultural factors that may be misunderstood by police.
5. Describe several community relations strategies for improving community relations in the context of culture.

TOPICS FOR DISCUSSION

1. List five values that you share with other members of your family. Are these values commonly held by all members of your community?

2. Discuss the cultural contexts that exist in your community. How has your community worked to resolve conflicts in values among these contexts?

3. What training is offered to police officers in your community that could improve community relations across cultures?

ONE STEP FORWARD

Coping with Cultural Diversity

In light of the many racial and ethnic groups in the United States, how do we as a nation deal properly with cultural diversity? In the 1990s, there are three distinct perspectives held by Americans in regard to cultural diversity. Each of these three perspectives offers a solution for coping with cultural diversity which is contradictory to the solutions offered by the others.

Leftist advocates of cultural pluralism claim that since the United States is a multicultural society, the political, economic, and educational systems must reflect that diversity. This "politically correct" group argues that straight, white, Anglo males have wrongly dominated American society (Gates, 1993). This wrong must be corrected by providing preferential treatment for females, ethnic minorities, and homosexuals until true equality of results has been achieved.

Political correctness calls for downplaying traditional studies of Western culture in favor of studies that emphasize the views of ethnic minorities, non-Christian religions, females, and gays (Eshleman, Cashion, and Basirico, 1993). "PC" advocates also support bilingual education by asserting that forcing immigrants to learn English is demeaning to minorities. Quotas designed to achieve equal results are considered both appropriate and necessary. They respond to allegations of reverse racism, sexism, and "straight bashing" by declaring that these actions are needed to pay back white males for their past oppressions of others. In short, not only must equality of results be accomplished, but atonement for past injustices must be made.

Conservative proponents of Americanization claim that political correctness is racist, sexist, anti-Christian, and heterophobic. These "fundamentalists" see the overemphasis of multiculturalism and discrimination against white males as harmful to all of society in that they promote separateness, bigotry, and intolerance. Actions that took place in the past cannot be undone in the present, particularly when those now targeted either had nothing to do with past injustices or were themselves victims of injustice. This group argues that English must be the official language of the United States in order to maintain the American culture (Eshleman, Cashion, and Basirico, 1993). They argue further that traditional American values must be upheld to protect our national identity, thwart moral decline, and prevent society from breaking down into cultural enclaves such as those currently found in Eastern Europe and Africa.

Americanization proponents partially agree with the concept of equal opportunity for individuals but oppose the use of quotas or other mechanisms to ensure equality of results. They state that ethnic minorities and females are being assimilated into the economic and political power structure, and that time will eventually remove any inequities. Stressing multiculturalism is seen as rewarding activists who are motivated by selfish desires for economic and political gain rather than contributing to society. They further argue that efforts to redistribute wealth and expand welfare programs stifle individual initiatives and lead to overreliance upon government (Brookhiser, 1993). Finally, these American fundamentalists view homosexuality as a deviant lifestyle which should be repressed rather than accepted by society. Critics of this extreme conservatism argue that it is close-minded, racist, sexist, classist, and homophobic.

A third view is held by moderates, joined by a mainstream coalition of both political liberals and conservatives. This group disagrees with the extremism of the two previous perspectives. Multiculturalism is seen as reasonable and healthy, but it is felt that societal norms and shared values must be preserved to protect all groups and maintain order within a pluralistic society. Affirmative action programs designed to provide equality of opportunity by ensuring a "level playing field" for women and minorities are felt to be appropriate. However, absolute guarantees of equal results are viewed with skepticism. Bilingual education is seen as beneficial in preserving ethnic identity as long as it does not ignore the competency in English needed to be competitive in American society (Tischler, 1993). And homosexuality is seen as a personal matter that should be used neither for nor against gays.

This moderate approach to multiculturalism is based on a desire to create an equitable, colorblind nation that is tolerant of differences among its diverse population. All groups, regardless of cultural heritage, gender, or sexual persuasion, are seen as contributing to American society. In this perspective, past injustices should be acknowledged in order to guard against similar unfairness in the future. However, efforts to exact vengeance for past evils (real or imagined) are seen as meaningless and divisive. Instead, cooperation based on education, tolerance, and a desire for a common good is seen as the appropriate means for coping with cultural diversity. Both left- and right-wing critics of moderation tend to see it as being allied with their ideological opponents at the other extreme.

Which of the foregoing perspectives is most compatible with your own views on culture? Why?

BIBLIOGRAPHY

Barker, T., Hunter, R. D., and Rush, J. P. (1994). *Police Systems and Practices: An Introduction.* Englewood Cliffs, N.J.: Prentice Hall.

Bartol, C. R. (1991). *Criminal Behavior: A Psychosocial Approach,* 3rd ed. Englewood Cliffs, N.J.: Prentice Hall.

Benedict, R. (1934). *Patterns of Culture.* Boston: Houghton Mifflin.

Brinkerhoff, D. B., White, L. K., and Ortega, S. T. (1992). *Essentials of Sociology,* 2nd ed. St. Paul, Minn.: West.

Brookhiser, R. (1993). "The melting pot is still simmering," *Time,* March 1, p. 72.

Burns, J. M., Peltason, J. W., Cronin, T. E., and Magleby, D. B. (1993). *Government by the People,* 15th ed. Englewood Cliffs, N.J.: Prentice Hall.

Colvard, A. L. (1992). "Foreign languages: A contemporary training requirement," *FBI Law Enforcement Bulletin,* Vol. 61, No. 9, pp. 20–23.

Cox, S. M., and Fitzgerald, J. D. (1992). *Police in Community Relations: Critical Issues,* 2nd ed. Dubuque, Iowa: Wm. C. Brown.

Cummings, M. C., and Wise, D. (1993). *Democracy Under Pressure: An Introduction to the American Political System,* 7th ed. Fort Worth, Texas: Harcourt Brace Jovanovich.

Eshleman, J. R., Cashion, B. G., and Basirico, L. A. (1993). *Sociology: An Introduction,* 4th ed. New York: HarperCollins.

Gates, D. (1993). "White male paranoia" *Newsweek,* March 29, pp. 48–53.

Greenlee, M. R. (1980). "Discretionary decision making in the field," *Police Chief,* February, pp. 50–51.

Henslin, J. M. (1993). *Sociology: A Down-to-Earth Approach.* Needham Heights, Mass.: Allyn and Bacon.

Holmes, G. (1993). Statement made on the Sally Jessie Raphael Show, June 9.

King, M. L., Jr. (1963). "I have a Dream" speech made on August 28, in Washington, D.C.

Kitano, H. H. L. (1991). *Race Relations,* 4th ed. Englewood Cliffs, N.J.: Prentice Hall.

Lind, A. W. (1980). *Hawaii's People,* 4th ed. Honolulu: University Press of Hawaii.

Livingston, J. (1992). *Crime and Criminology.* Englewood Cliffs, N.J.: Prentice Hall.

Marger, M. N. (1991). *Race and Ethnic Relations: American and Global Perspectives,* 2nd ed. Belmont, Calif.: Wadsworth.

O'Conner, S. D. (1993). Supreme Court majority opinion written by Justice O'Conner, June 28, in *Shaw* v. *Barr* 92–357.

Pitter, G. E. (1992). "Policing cultural celebrations," *FBI Law Enforcement Bulletin,* Vol. 61, No. 9, pp. 10–14.

Popenoe, D. (1993). *Sociology,* 9th ed. Englewood Cliffs, N.J.: Prentice Hall.

Taft, P. B., Jr. (1982). "Policing the new immigrant ghettos," *Police Magazine,* July, pp. 10–26.

Tischler, H. L. (1993). *Introduction to Sociology,* 4th ed. Fort Worth, Texas: Harcourt Brace Jovanovich.

U.S. Bureau of the Census (1990). *1990 Census of Population: General Population Characteristics of the United States: 1991.* Washington, D.C.: U.S. Government Printing Office.

U.S. Bureau of the Census (1991). *Statistical Abstract of the United States: 1991.* Washington, D.C.: U.S. Government Printing Office.

U.S. Bureau of the Census (1992). *Income, Poverty, and Wealth in the United States: A Chartbook.* Washington, D.C.: U.S. Government Printing Office.

Vander Zanden, J. W. (1983). *American Minority Relations,* 4th ed. New York: Alfred A. Knopf.

Washington, R. (1993). Statement made on the Sally Jessie Raphael Show, June 9.

Weaver, G. (1992). "Law enforcement in a culturally diverse society," *FBI Law Enforcement Bulletin,* Vol. 61, No. 9, pp. 1–7.

Weis, J. G., and Sederstrom, J. (1981). *The Prevention of Serious Delinquency: What to Do?* Reports of the National Juvenile Justice Assessment Centers. Washington, D.C.: U.S. Department of Justice.

11

THE DILEMMAS OF DISSENT AND POLITICAL RESPONSE

We hold these Truths to be self-evident, that all Men are created equal, that they are endowed by their Creator with certain unalienable Rights, that among these are Life, Liberty, and the Pursuit of Happiness—That to secure these Rights, Governments are instituted among Men, deriving their just Powers from the Consent of the Governed, that whenever any Form of Government becomes destructive of these Ends, it is the Right of the People to alter or abolish it, and to institute a new Government, laying its Foundation on such Principles, and organizing its Powers in such Form, as to them shall seem most likely to effect their Safety and Happiness.

(Declaration of Independence, 1776)

Change and resistance to change are part of every system. For change to occur, some amount of "deviance" takes place and the "normal way of things" is disturbed—or as perceived by some—threatened.

The rights guaranteed to individuals and groups by the First Amendment to the Constitution of the United States reflect a commitment to allowing dissent as a means of bringing about needed social, legal, and political change. In this country as elsewhere, however, powerful social and political forces have always been resistant to change, so that dissent has often led to intense and even violent confrontation.

Dissent may be active or passive, nonviolent or violent, individual or mass. In a democratic society, the major dilemma becomes how to avoid social disorder, while at the same time avoiding total social control.

To better understand the dilemmas of dissent and political response, we must first understand the concept of dissent. Toward that end in this chapter we will consider contrasting views of dissent and study current social conflicts as they relate to both the strategies of dissent and response and the consequences for all parties involved. We will address the processes of escalation, de-escalation, and resolution of social conflicts, and the involvement of police, courts, and corrections in them.

STUDYING THIS CHAPTER WILL ENABLE YOU TO:

1. Define the parameters of the right to dissent under the U.S. Constitution.
2. Present contrasting views of acceptable dissent.
3. Describe the interaction of the strategies of dissent and response.
4. Identify the significant aspects of escalation and de-escalation.
5. Analyze the ways in which police, courts, and corrections become instruments of power in relation to dissent.
6. Describe the necessary components for effectively neutralizing disorder without increasing violent dissent.

DISSENT: THE "CATALYST OF PROGRESS"

Change Versus Order

One of the problems in political history is the conflict between change and order. It is difficult to say that any specific historical time was in a "state of order" because the patterns of conflict and resolution that were current then have led to new conflicts. This process will continue to occur. Our present society is complex, technologically communicative, and composed of many groups of people who have different interests, life-styles, and values. Our political reality is that we are essentially a society of groups rather than of persons. These groups are pressing for change at an accelerating rate because more and more individuals feel they cannot bring about change unless they represent, or are represented by, a power base (Cummings and Wise, 1993).

Why Seek Change?

Why are so many groups seeking changes? The answer, perhaps, can be found by examining our culture. Our contemporary culture places great emphasis on achievement, but it also emphasizes dissatisfaction with one's present state. Thus, achievement and its companion value, individual self-determination, make the rights to protest and to have grievances addressed—indispensable elements of a "free society" (Burns et al., 1993).

The Right to Dissent

The First Amendment protects the freedom of speech, the press, the right of the people to assemble peacefully, and the right to petition the government for a redress of grievances (Figure 11-1). The amendment protects not only the *individual's* right to dissent but also the right of *groups* to dissent, assemble, petition, and demonstrate. The First Amendment is a principle—a symbolic commitment by our government to permit dissent and debate on public issues. Dissent, in the words of the National Commission on the Causes and Prevention of Violence, is the "catalyst of progress."

Congress shall make no law respecting an establishment of religion, or prohibiting the free exercise thereof; or abridging the freedom of speech, or of the press; or the right of the people peaceably to assemble, and to petition the Government for a redress of grievances.

FIGURE 11-1   First Amendment to the U.S. Constitution.

Keeping Dissent Peaceful

The survival of our democratic system is dependent on accommodating dissent, solving disagreements, peacefully containing social conflicts, righting wrongs, and modifying the structure of the system as conditions change. Although these changes are necessary to keep the government alive, the organization of government itself is fundamentally resistant to change. This resistance by the government to peaceful change leads to violence, a problem that the Violence Commission found has occurred throughout the history of the United States. The Commission's conclusions remain accurate.

1. America has always been a relatively violent nation. Considering the tumultuous historical forces that have shaped the United States, it would be astonishing were it otherwise.

2. Since rapid social change in America has produced different forms of violence with widely varying patterns of motivation, aggression, and victimization, violence in America has waxed and waned with the social tides. The decade just ending, for example, has been one of our most violent eras—although probably not the most violent.

3. Exclusive emphasis in a society on law enforcement rather than on a sensible balance of remedial action and enforcement tends to lead to a decaying cycle in which resistance grows and becomes ever more violent.

4. For remedial social change to be an effective moderator of violence, the changes must command a wide measure of support throughout the community. Official efforts to impose change that is resisted by a dominant majority frequently prompt counter-violence.

5. Finally, Americans have been, paradoxically, both a turbulent people but have enjoyed a relatively stable republic. Our liberal and pluralistic system has historically both generated and accommodated itself to a high level of unrest, and our turmoil has reflected far more demonstration and protest than conspiracy and revolution. (The National Commission on the Causes and Prevention of Violence, 1969, pp. 1-2).

Acceptable Dissent

Our current concern with militant and dissident groups involves the strategies they use to apply pressures in an attempt to bring about changes in society (see Figure 11-2). The men who wrote the Constitution did not define "acceptable dissent tactics" in the

First Amendment. Therefore, the meaning of what is considered acceptable strategies of dissent constantly changes. For example, the acceptability of such protest strategies as civil disobedience, direct action, violent confrontation, sit-ins, boycotts, parades, and draft-card burnings varies greatly, depending upon who is defining these actions. Such tactics may be acceptable to a protest leader or even a bystander, but not to a Supreme Court justice or a police officer. Even legal scholars concede that drawing constitutional lines on acceptable dissent procedures is a difficult task (Burns et al., 1993).

FIGURE 11-2   Birmingham, Alabama. American Nazi Party demonstration.

A Legalistic Position

A Model Definition

A model definition of acceptable dissent was developed by former Supreme Court Justice Abe Fortas, who wrote:

> The First Amendment protects dissent if it is belief and not acts, if it is speech and does not create a clear and present danger of injury to others, if it is against a specific law or enforcement thereof by silent and reproachful presence, in a place where the dissenter has every right to be. Violation of a valid law is not justified by either conscience or a good cause. (1968, pp. 106–111)

Supportive Legalistic Views

A similar position was taken by Archibald Cox, who said that the Constitution guarantees a wide variety of public actions to express sentiment, dramatize a cause, and to demonstrate aroused indignation, power, or solidarity. As Cox explained: "One may disregard with legal impunity, the commands of civil authorities if what the authorities forbid is in truth only the exercise of a privilege guaranteed by the Constitution" (1971, p. 386). Such action does not involve a violation of law in the ultimate sense because the orders given by the authorities are not law at all. However, the Constitution does not give us the right to disobey *valid* laws. Conducting a sit-in demonstration in someone's office, for example, would plainly violate valid and constitutional laws. The Constitution does not give anyone the privilege to violate a law even if the protest demonstration is designed to test the law's constitutionality. Citizens cannot pick and choose which laws they will obey without destroying the whole concept of law. The privilege of freedom and the right to peaceful change are eroded by such law-breaking, although some changes have occurred as a result of such tactics.

Most of the members of the Violence Commission took a similar position. They said that no matter how a person feels about the dissenters' cause, he must not violate valid laws. In their views, "respect for the judicial process is a small price to pay for the civilizing hand of law, which alone can give abiding meaning to constitutional freedom" (*Walker* v. *Birmingham*). The Violence Commission suggests that the best way to challenge the constitutionality of a law is by initiating legal action, and while the judicial test is in progress, all other dissenters should abide by the law (The National Commission on the Causes and Prevention of Violence, 1969, pp. 90–91). Every time a court order is disobeyed and each time an injunction is violated, the effectiveness of our judicial system is eroded. Defiance of the law is the surest road to tyranny. Disobeying valid laws does not contribute to the emergence of a more humane society, but leads instead to the emergence of a totalitarian state.

The Legalistic Position: A Summary

Under this view, protesters are justified in disobeying the commands of civil authorities who try to forbid actions that exercise privileges guaranteed by the Constitution.

Those who hold this view, however, insist that no one has the right to disobey valid laws. Three important corollaries of this position are:

- Protest actions that break valid laws weaken the legal system, thus creating a threat to the privilege of freedom and the right to peaceful change, and compel the state to resort to its power.
- A distinction must be made between laws violated through protest actions (e.g., trespass and traffic laws) and laws violated because they are the object of dissent.
- The law and legal institutions are the only viable mechanisms for change in a democracy. Consequently, the best way to challenge the constitutionality of a law is through legal action; while the judicial test is in progress, all other dissenters should abide by the law.

Contrasting Positions

In contrast to the legalistic positions taken by Fortas, Cox, and the Violence Commission, others feel that (1) the traditional methods of dissent are insufficient or have fallen on deaf ears; (2) dissent is often focused on organizational policies or administrative decisions and not laws; and (3) the dissent issue is often not negotiable to those in the power structure. Thus, one cannot legally protest those procedures or institutional practices which the legal system assumes to be "correct." For example, there are few legal options available to people who want to alter school curriculums or textbooks that devalue the role of minority groups in American history. Conversely, a person can protest discriminatory employment practices through the law but not through the economic system itself.

A Key Issue

Both the legalists and the advocates of dissent agree that creative disruptive tactics are legitimate, yet they also realize that many protest strategies pose that serious political problem: *how to avoid social disorder while at the same time avoiding total social control.*

A Classic Argument

Howard Zinn, a 1960s advocate of civil disobedience, argued that government has abdicated its duty to meet the needs of the people in order to serve the needs of those in power (1968). To right the balance, therefore, he urged strategies of dissent that go far beyond what is legally acceptable. He also argued that the Constitution should be interpreted boldly and broadly in order to augment what he called "the natural rights of the citizen."

> Why should not the equal protection clause of the Fourteenth Amendment be applied to economics, as well as race, to require the state to give equal economic rights to its citizens: food, shelter, education, medical care. Why should not the Thirteenth Amendment barring involuntary servitude be extended to military conscription? Why should not the cruel and unusual punishment clause of the Eighth Amendment be applied in such a way as to bar all imprisonment except in the most stringent of cases, where confinement is necessary to prevent a clear and immediate danger to others? Why should not the Ninth Amendment, which says citizens have unnamed rights beyond those enumerated in the Constitution, be applied to a host of areas: rights to carry on whatever family arrangements (marriage, divorce, etc.) are desired, whatever sexual relationships are voluntarily entered into, whatever private activities one wants to carry on, so long as others are not harmed (even if they are irritated)." (Zinn, 1968, pp. 115–116)

Zinn suggested some guidelines for deciding when to disobey the law through protest activity.

1. *Civil disobedience—the deliberate violation of the law for a vital social purpose*—is not only justifiable, but necessary whenever a fundamental human right is at stake and the right cannot be secured through existing legal channels.
2. Government and laws are *instruments* to life, liberty, and happiness, not ends in themselves. Consequently, obeying "the rule of law" has *no* social value—and has *negative* social value if laws are bad ones.

3. Civil disobedience can involve violating laws that are not in themselves wrong in order to protest an important issue (e.g., illegally occupying a building, although normally wrong, is justified as part of a protest against, say, racism).

4. If a specific act of civil disobedience is morally justifiable, then jailing those who performed the act is *immoral* and should be opposed.

5. The tactics used in civil disobedience should be *as nonviolent as possible,* and the distinction between harm to property and harm to people should be a paramount consideration. However, the appropriate degree of force or disorder must be determined in light of the significance of the issue at stake.

6. The degree of disorder in civil disobedience should be measured not against some misleading degree of "peace" or "order" associated with the status quo, but against the *real disorder* or *violence* produced by the abuse that led to protest.

7. The state and the citizen have *opposed* interests. The state seeks power, influence, and wealth as ends in themselves and is in a favored position to obtain them, even if this means depriving individuals of the health, peace, creative activity, and love they seek. Each citizen, therefore, must learn to think and act on his or her own or in concert with fellow citizens against the state. (Zinn, 1968, pp. 119–122)

ARENAS FOR DISSENT

The United States is a politically diverse nation. The numerous cultural influences discussed in Chapter 10, in conjunction with a wide variety of perspectives in regard to what the role of government and the extent of individual freedoms should be, frequently leads to bitter conflicts among competing political parties and interest groups. The major disagreements in the U.S. political system tend to occur between liberals and conservatives. *Liberals* seek to increase governmental (particularly federal) control over the modes of production and to promote social programs designed to help the poor. *Conservatives* argue for limited government and promotion of self-reliance by individuals. Both liberals and conservatives claim to cherish individual freedoms but tend to interpret them differently. Liberals argue that government must provide protections to ensure that the poor, minorities, and those living alternative lifestyles are treated fairly and equally. Conservatives argue that government intervention discriminates against the middle and upper classes, the white majority, and those who hold traditional American values (Burns et al., 1993, pp. 196–201).

The nature of the liberal–conservative debate is not as easily defined as the preceding paragraph might cause one to believe. There is not one type of conservative, nor is there one type of liberal. Instead, liberalism ranges from socialists on the far left, who make American social policies similar to those found in "democratic socialist" nations such as Sweden (Eshleman, Cashion, and Basirico, 1993), to "neoliberals," who are skeptical of welfare programs and governmental bureaucracies (Burns et al., 1993, p. 198). Conservatives range from "ultraconservatives" on the far right who favor religious fundamentalism and strict enforcement of morality in addition to strongly opposing a "welfare state" (Burns et al., 1993, p. 200), to "neoconservatives," who support limited government involvement in solving social problems but fear that "excessive liberalism" threatens individual liberties and threatens social stability.

A great many Americans occupy the middle of the political spectrum in that they consider themselves to be neither liberals nor conservatives. These citizens hold divergent views that cannot readily be classified by political scientists. Such a person might favor both capital punishment and abortion. He/she might vote for a Republican for one political office and a Democrat for another; and he/she would feel no obligation to abide by the wishes of a particular political party or interest group in making political decisions (Cummings and Wise, 1993).

Still other Americans may have political ideologies which are far more extreme than those found within the liberal–conservative spectrum. Communists (and many remain despite the decline of communism in the former Eastern Bloc nations) feel that even the welfare capitalism found in the United States is evil and must be eliminated. Anarchists (a limited few) argue that all government is evil. *Libertarians,* who are considerably more moderate, criticize both liberals and conservatives as abusing the power of the government and infringing on individual liberties. Like conservatives, libertarians would sharply limit the size and power of the federal government. Like liberals, libertarians are very concerned with protecting individual freedoms. Figure 11-3 depicts where libertarians see themselves within the political system.

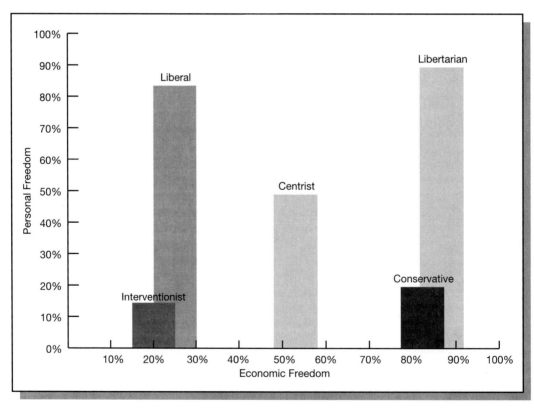

FIGURE 11-3   Libertarian political compass. [Adapted from Advocates for Self-Government, *Worlds Smallest Political Quiz*" (1988).]

Due to the nature of democracy in the United States, many compromises are made in order for the political system (and subsequently, the social and economic systems) to function. This compromise causes many (on the left, right, and in the middle) to feel that their views are being ignored by those in power. When this occurs, many Americans frequently utilize dissent in an effort to effect change. In our society, dissent can be said to occur in at least five major areas: political, social, economic, religious, and environmental. Although these are not mutually exclusive, they often serve individually as primary targets for dissent.

Political Dissent

Political dissent is concerned primarily with effecting change in political policy. Power is sought in political decision making. Examples of nonviolent political dissent include the historic protests that were waged during the 1960s in opposition to the Vietnam War and in support of civil rights protection for minorities. More recent demonstrations in the United States have resulted from the efforts of opponents seeking to eliminate lawful abortions within the United States and from gay rights advocates seeking to eliminate laws and regulations that are considered discriminatory against homosexuals.

When advocates of political change resort to violence, it is frequently the activities of a single person or a small group of extremists within a predominately peaceful organization. However, it may be calculated actions of an organization that is willing to use terrorism to bring attention to themselves or their cause (White, 1991). While most civilized peoples deplore terrorism, it is important to realize that a person classified as a terrorist by one group may be considered to be a hero or freedom fighter by others (Vetter and Perlstein, 1991). For example, to most Americans (including opponents of abortion), the bombing of abortion clinics and/or the murder of doctors who perform abortions are acts of terrorism. But to some, they are morally justified acts taken in defense of unborn children. However, those same persons would define terrorism quite differently if their churches were attacked by pro-abortion forces.

Social Dissent

Social dissent is concerned primarily with gaining social equality. Often, the conflict is over the counting and discounting of minority-group concerns in our society (Henslin, 1993). Social acceptance and rejection, changes in public opinion and social institutions, and having a "viable place" in the community are all social concerns. Social dissent in the United States was pioneered by Martin Luther King, Jr., who utilized nonviolent protests as a means of drawing attention to inequitable treatment of African Americans (Greenberg and Page, 1993).

During the 1990s the groups that most frequently utilize social dissent are gay rights advocates, feminists, and ethnic minorities. Many of these groups are also involved in political dissent, because changes in the law, a part of structuring social change, are a political perogative.

Economic Dissent

Economic dissent is concerned primarily with effecting change in the economy and meeting material needs. Economic dissent addresses issues of unemployment, underemployment, poverty, and food, clothing, and shelter issues in general. Strikes and protests regarding unfair labor practices, and demonstrations on behalf of the homeless, may be considered economic dissent. A recent example was the Los Angeles Riot of 1992. Although the initial spark was the acquittal of the police officers accused in the videotaped beating of black motorist Rodney King, the real issues dealt with living conditions, unemployment, lack of opportunity, and what residents saw as social and economic oppression.

Religious Dissent

Religious dissent is concerned primarily with effecting change in the definition of religious freedoms or specific religious practice that may violate existing law. In this instance conflict may be between opposing values or religious beliefs or between church and secular law. Much of the antiabortion dissent discussed earlier is couched in a religious context. Other examples include the ongoing debate over prayer in the schools, atheist–religious conflicts, Catholic–Protestant and Jewish–Gentile conflicts, and the refusal of religious groups such as the Amish and Mennonites to comply with compulsory school attendance laws. The attacks on doctors and abortion clinics by supporters of "Operation Rescue," the dramatic events that led to the 1993 deaths of approximately 90 people in the Branch Davidian compound near Waco, Texas, during an FBI assault, and the 1993 bombing of the World Trade Center by Muslim fundamentalists demonstrate the extremes to which religious dissent in the United States can reach.

Freedom to believe is absolutely protected by the First Amendment to the U.S. Constitution, but freedom to act is not totally free from interference (Cummings and Wise, 1993). This is particularly true if those actions obstruct the rights of others, are seen as detrimental to the health and well-being of group members (especially juveniles), if the group or individual is found to be only incidentally religious, or when fraud or deception is involved (Lucksted and Martell, 1982).

Environmental Dissent

Environmental dissent is concerned primarily with effecting change in the surroundings or settings in which we live. Issues might include zoning changes, health hazards, threats to wildlife, and so on. Recent environmental debates have ranged from preserving endangered species, environmental protection from inappropriate disposal of chemical waste, pollution of air and water, guarding against radioactive or toxic risk to populations, and the harvesting of public forests. This dissent can range from community resistance to building chemical incinerators, to assaults on hunters or people wearing furs by animal rights extremists, to acts of sabotage and terrorism against perceived environmental offenders.

STRATEGIES OF DISSENT AND RESPONSE

Legalists and advocates of dissent differ in many critical respects, but they all recognize the need for "justice," "order," and "change" and agree that dissent must be analyzed in relation to crises in American institutions. This factor was also recognized by the Violence Commission. In a staff report, the commission suggests that mass protest is an outgrowth of social, economic, and political conditions and the violence that occurs in these protests arises from an interaction between protesters and the authorities.

Commission observations include:

- Political processes establish what "violence" is. Whoever has the power to disseminate and enforce their definitions blames the other party for the violence.

- Both the authorities and the protesters often exaggerate the violence committed against them in order to discredit the other party, gain sympathy from third parties, and deflect attention from their own violence.

- The interplay of protest and violence must be seen in the light of the surrounding structure of power and authority and the conceptions held by the authorities of the nature of protest and the proper uses of official violence.

- Participants in mass protest today see their activity as political action aimed at the existing arrangements of power and authority that produced their grievances (See Popenoe, 1993; Tischler, 1993).

The Labeling Process

In most issues of social conflict, a variety of groups and individuals with differing demands and differing strategies of dissent wish to be heard. These dissenters, however, generally have much less power than the political authorities or other parties whose actions, beliefs, policies, or laws the dissenters are protesting. Because dissenters usually have the least amount of power in a social conflict, the views of the more powerful authorities or organizations generally become the accepted ones.

The authorities, or those who have power (the "establishment"), generally label dissenters as "militants." This label may be applied to whole groups of dissenters or to individual spokesmen for a particular group of dissenters. No clear-cut definitions exist for the word *militant*. This label has been used by the opponents of a movement to discredit everyone in the movement; it has also been used selectively by persons who partially agree with the objectives of the movement but who regard some of its demands as nonnegotiable. It is generally agreed that militants (1) approve of violence as a protest tactic, (2) are hostile toward their adversaries, and (3) do not accept the legitimacy of the structural system or its institutions.

Strategies of Dissent

Strategies of dissent differ with regard to three concerns: (1) the nature of the desired changes, (2) the means of achieving change (specifically, the degree of adherence to the rules of the system, and (3) attitudes toward the people who defend the system. Three strategies can be distinguished: *strategies of order, disorder,* and *violence.*

In the *strategy of order,* dissidents divide their attention between the changes to be accomplished and the accepted rules regarding legitimate ways of bringing about change; dissidents who use this strategy follow the rules.

In the *strategy of disorder,* dissidents have less interest in both the given rules and the powerful persons who stand in the way of change; they focus strongly on the changes needed.

In the *strategy of violence,* dissidents divide their attention between the changes needed and the powerful persons who stand in the way of change; dissidents who use this strategy attack their enemies.

Presumably, we can define any particular dissident group's strategy at any given time simply by analyzing its rhetoric and observing its deeds.

Strategies of Response

To understand the dynamics of dissent strategies, we must also understand the strategies of response utilized by political authorities or other parties who are the targets of dissident groups (Table 11-1). These can vary as widely as the strategies of protest groups and generally differ with respect to the same three concerns: the nature of desired

TABLE 11-1
STRATEGIES OF DISSENT AND RESPONSE

Dissent		Response	
Concerns:		*Concerns:*	
1. The nature of desired changes		1. The nature of desired changes	
2. The means of achieving change		2. The means of achieving change	
3. Attitudes toward people who defend system		3. Attitudes toward people who defend system	
Strategies:	Focus on:	*Strategies:*	Focus on:
1. Of order:	legitimate ways of bringing about change	1. Response of law:	no response or protective response
2. Of disorder:	changes needed; less concern with rules or powerful persons who stand in the way.	2. Response of order:	arresting and processing dissenters in legal and acceptable manner
3. Of violence:	attacking enemies; change needed and powerful persons who stand in the way of change.	3. Response of violence:	issue in conflict and people who are dissenting; attack enemies

Possible Interactional Outcomes
Changes in orientation and strategy
Violent action
Resolution of conflict

changes; the means of achieving change; and attitudes toward the people who defend the system. The strategies of response are the *response of law, of order,* and *of violence.*

In the *response of law,* authorities do not respond at all or only respond in a protective manner as long as dissenters adopt legal strategies of protest (i.e., strategies of order). If the dissenters adopt illegal means of protest, however, the *response of law* strategy involves arresting dissenters and processing them in a legally acceptable manner. In this response, authorities follow proper legal procedures.

In the *response of order,* authorities make no response or only a protective one to legal protest (strategies of order). Illegal dissent, however, is met by attempting nonviolent bargaining over the social issue. The authorities place less emphasis on the demanded change than on maintaining order or preventing violence.

In the *response of violence,* authorities are concerned with the issue in conflict and focus on the people who are dissenting (regardless of what strategy of dissent they use). In other words, they attack their enemies.

Interaction Between Strategies

When the strategies of dissent and response meet head-on, three outcomes are possible: changes in orientation and strategy, violent action, or resolution of the conflict.

Changes in Orientation and Strategy

Those who adopt a given strategy of dissent usually expect it to have a specific effect on third parties or to elicit a specific strategy of response from the authorities. Thus, the civil disobedience of Martin Luther King was a strategy of order designed to draw attention to a particular issue and to educate the public about it; to a large extent, it succeeded. Problems arise, however, when dissidents and those in power find that their efforts are not producing the results they want. Their strategy may change toward greater use of violence.

Violent Actions

Some dissident groups seem committed to violence from the outset, engaging in guerrilla warfare and terrorist activities. Moreover, many law enforcement officials favor violent response to dissent; if they disagree with the dissenters on the issues, they are likely to consider acts of civil disobedience as simply another type of crime, and they often try to divert attention from the issues by defining the dissidents as terrorists, "crazies," or common criminals.

Guerrilla warfare, as a strategy of violence, exists throughout the world. Underground armies and terrorist organizations are particularly prevalent in underdeveloped nations that are ruled by dictatorship.

Terrorism and guerrilla insurgency has appeared in this country in all segments of our major cities. The use of terrorism as a tactic of dissent usually is directed at persons who exercise power and at the symbols of that power. The goal of this form of dissent is often terror and anarchy.

Some observers predict that in the future, the police officer on the street will be required to deal with criminal violence arising from violent political dissent. The Task Force on Disorders and Terrorism (1976) and subsequent presidential commissions on terrorism have encouraged local police to increase their ability to deal with such activity.

A key element in violent dissent is that the dissenters seek to achieve their goals by whatever means are necessary. Some domestic terrorist groups that are active or have been active in the United States in recent years include the Aryan Nations; Black Liberation Army; Christian Patriots Defense League; The Covenant, the Sword, and the Arm of the Lord (CSA); Jewish Defense League; Ku Klux Klan; Macheteros; Move; Neo-Nazis; New World Liberation Front; Alpha 66; Omega 7; The Order; Posse Comitatus; Puerto Rican Armed Forces of the Revolution (FALN); United Freedom Front; Weather Underground; Fuqra; Armenian Secret Army for the Liberation of Armenia (ASLA); Justice Commandos for Armenian Genocide (JCAG); Croation National Liberation Forces; Animal Liberation Front; and arguably, Operation Rescue (Vetter and Perlstein, 1991; White, 1991). In addition to these politically motivated groups, many individuals and criminal gangs engage in activities that could also be classified as terrorism. As if there were not enough of a harm potential from these "home-grown terrorists," there is an increasing likelihood of international terrorists operating in America.

Resolution of the Conflict

This outcome, of course, would seem the most desirable, and it is often possible, although the struggle to reach it may be long. Those who adopt strategies or responses of violence, however, may not want any resolution other than the complete surrender or destruction of the other side.

The Role of Third Parties

Both dissidents and the authorities plan tactics, publicity, and media communication to win over third parties. This is especially important when power differences are great between the conflicting parties, and the weaker party can obtain a compromise or achieve its goals only if strong third parties become its allies. In the civil rights movement in the South, the goal the protesters sought was inclusion in the political system; thus, these groups aimed their messages not only at the persons directly affected but also at third-party persons sympathetic to these goals and at those who believed in the legal inclusion of blacks in the political system. As a result, media coverage and the violent response of political authorities to the civil rights movement had the consequences of affecting third-party intervention by the federal government, expanding the issues in conflict, and obtaining both participants in the movement as well as allies.

The Role of the Media

Because media coverage is so necessary for reaching third parties, both parties try to influence the way conflict and the parties to it are portrayed in newspaper and magazine articles and on radio and television. Dissenters create events for media that will draw attention to the conflict and hopefully build bargaining power for them. Political authorities, on the other hand, attempt to control what the media present by exercising power through regulatory agencies and political pressure. They attempt to control sources of information by making government documents secret, infiltrate dissident groups with agents of the government, cut off dissident groups from media visibility, and attack the media for their "underdog" bias. When political authorities are pressed by dissent, freedom of the press comes under increasing fire.

ESCALATION AND DE-ESCALATION OF CONFLICT

Once conflict has started, each party tends to undergo changes that make the conflict more intense. Conflict, however, cannot escalate indefinitely. Sooner or later, forces or events that de-escalate conflict will influence the behavior of the parties involved.

Escalation Factors

Increase in Loyalty and Commitment

Feelings of loyalty and commitment to one's position increase, especially if the other side responds with coercion, threats, or injuries. Increased commitment leads to and justifies further efforts toward the attainment of one's goals, creates anxiety, and heightens a sense that *now* is the time to act. For example, dissident or militant leaders state, "Seize the time!" "Freedom now!" "Peace now!," or other rhetoric emphasizing urgency:

> This is our last gasp as a sovereign people, and if we don't get these treaty rights recognized, then you might as well kill me because I have no reason for living. (Means, 1973)

He was not killed. And at this writing, 20 years later, Mr. Means has not given up on living.

> My hunger is for liberation of my people, my thirst is for the ending of oppression. I am a political prisoner, jailed for my beliefs that black people must be free. . . . Death can no longer alter our path to freedom. For our people death has been the only known exit from slavery and oppression. We must open others. Our will to live must no longer supersede our will to fight, for our fighting will determine if our race shall live. . . . Brothers and sisters, and all oppressed peoples, we must prepare ourselves both mentally and physically, for the major confrontation is yet to come. We must fight. (Brown, 1968)

Fortunately, the race war that Mr. Brown called for has not taken place. Despite frequent setbacks and the combined efforts of both white and black militants, race relations in the United States continue to progress.

Persistence in a Course of Action

Once conflict begins, it often escalates because leaders acting as representatives of an entire group usually persist on a course of action, even if no success is achieved. Mistakes are rarely admitted by either the dissenters or the responders. However, admission of mistakes does tend to occur when the group's constituency changes, when the futility of the strategy becomes apparent, or when escalation and reaction reaches the point where survival of the group is threatened. Thus, the Black Panther party retracted its focus on the police when party programs were seriously threatened by police actions. Party leaders recognized that other authorities are more important than the police, and began to concentrate more deeply on other issues.

Withdrawal of Moderate Membership

Another factor influencing the escalation of conflict is the withdrawal of members who are unwilling to participate in more intense conflict behavior, leaving the group to those who are more eager to engage in hostile actions. With the withdrawal of moderates, dissident groups which have previously been viewed as peaceful activists (e.g., Operation Rescue) may begin to emerge as terrorist threats.

An Upward Spiral of Violence

Hostility and aggression from one side will very likely be answered in kind from the other side, so that an upward spiral of violence is created. Once the spiral begins, a relatively weak response from one side is unlikely to stop it; the other side will react with even more violence in order to defeat a seemingly "weakened enemy." If the police see a group of dissidents as a threat or as a source of violence and respond with violence, the dissident group tends to increase its violent activities. Once intensely engaged, even efforts by police to de-escalate the conflict may be interpreted as retreat and evidence of weakness. Therefore, such efforts will require careful planning and execution in order to avoid increasing the level of violence.

De-escalation Factors

Conflict cannot escalate indefinitely. The processes of de-escalation are embedded in those of escalation. Although participation in conflict behavior produces greater commitment to the group and willingness to escalate conflict, it also becomes increasingly costly if the attainment of the group's demands are not in sight.

Superior Coercive Power

One side may use its superior coercive power to repress the opposition through harassment or by imprisoning its leaders. However, actions that are perceived as too extreme can lead to both heightened resistance on the part of the dissidents and increased sympathy from those who were neutral or somewhat opposed to dissent.

Divide and Conquer

One side may split the conflict by being conciliatory in a divisive way (e.g., by granting the demands of some members of the opposition and thus removing their reasons for continuing the conflict). Placating the more moderate factions within the opposition may seriously weaken those who hold more extreme positions. The product is a deeply divided opposition that may force extremists to either capitulate or be rejected by their previous allies.

Third Party Involvement

One side may introduce issues that involve third parties who then either act as negotiators or increase one side's power to the point where the other side can no longer bear the cost of intense conflict. For example, during the Vietnam War, raising the POW issue brought in new third parties to the peace movement. The intervention of third parties also can have a de-escalating impact by increasing the political costs to the authorities of continuing the practices which are being protested.

A Redefinition of "Reasonable"

The struggle may become so intense that leaders who formerly seemed militant now appear "reasonable"—an appearance that can only increase their bargaining power, if authorities have not repressed the entire movement.

Success Factors

In general, dissident groups are more likely to be successful if they have:

1. A specific goal or a broad goal (e.g., equality of job opportunity) that can realistically be achieved (e.g., by reserving a specific percentage of construction jobs for minority group applicants).
2. A specific, identifiable target (e.g., a particular political leader, landlord, or company).
3. Demands that realistically can be met. Some demands are defined as nonnegotiable by the conflict authority (e.g., state sovereignty, capitalism, or student control of school administration), and some demands are not grantable by the targets chosen (e.g., police, mayor).

OUTCOMES

Determinants of Outcomes

Differences in Power

Power differences seem to be the major determinant in the outcome of social conflict. Extreme power differences almost invite domination and repression if the conflict has escalated to highly coercive strategies. In general, the greater the power difference the more the outcome is likely to be withdrawal or domination of the dissidents.

Perceived Permanence of Conflict

The outcomes of different conflicts also vary according to the perceived permanence of the conflict. The Vietnam War has long since ended; mass rioting does not prevail over periods of weeks and months. Underlying social conflicts, however, such as the status of black, brown, and Native American citizens in our society seem to be continuing and painfully direct issues.

In a sense, the call for "black power" during the 1960s grew out of the perception that there would have to be many years of resistance and protest against white institutions and attitudes for African Americans to gain equality. In this view, to bargain from a position of strength, blacks first had to establish group solidarity. This same strategy is currently being utilized by advocates of gay rights, who are seeking to establish a group identity based on sexual preference.

Enhancing group solidarity to improve bargaining position is the objective of many other groups in our society with similar issues. Group solidarity is often defined in terms of self-defense, cultural autonomy, a sense of community, and community control.

The role of "militant" groups where conflict is perceived to be ongoing or permanent might include:

1. Correct the illusions of progress through critical, pessimistic attitudes.
2. Identify unresolved issues through confrontations.
3. Radicalize membership of the movement and increase polarization between the movement and its opposition.
4. Create an awareness of injustice among nonmovement third parties. Schools and the police are among the primary targets of such movements; other targets involve issues such as housing, welfare, and social services.

PERCEIVED INSTRUMENTS OF POWER

In the midst of conflict, police, courts, and corrections administration and personnel are often seen as political instruments of power rather than as instruments of law.

The Police

In the drama of dissent, police frequently find themselves acting as substitutes for necessary political and social reform. Labor history demonstrates that the police served as the main bulwark against the labor movement. Picket lines were violently dispersed; meetings were disrupted, and organizers and activists were shot, beaten, and jailed. Police harassment of unions, such as the United Farm Workers, was common. Denial of strikers' legal rights; physical and verbal abuse; detaining organizers for long periods of time; encouraging workers to cross picket lines; and arresting strikers for trespass, unlawful assembly, secondary boycott, and illegal picketing are current episodes of old alignments. The police have also sought at times to prevent the political organization of Native Americans, Chicanos, and blacks by harassing and intimidating organization members and arresting leaders.

Responses of Violence

In some of our larger cities, tenant groups, students, war protesters, gays, browns, and blacks have drawn similar responses from the police. For example, some of the most highly publicized *responses of violence* occurred at the 1968 Democratic Convention and in police confrontations with the Black Panther party. The shooting outbreaks between Panthers and police in San Francisco, Oakland, New Orleans,

Detroit, Toledo, Philadelphia, New York, Houston, and Chicago were touched off by harassment (the Panther view) or minor offenses (the police view). These incidents involved the selling of a Panther newspaper on a Detroit street corner, the assault upon two police infiltrators in New Orleans, and the stockpiling of weapons in the other cities. The Black Panthers argued that police respond violently because:

- Many of them are "racists."
- Few minority persons serve on police forces.
- The police are isolated from the people they serve.
- They are ill-trained for sensitive peacekeeping jobs.
- Police have a special view of dissent and dissenters.

This same theme was echoed in the Los Angeles Riot of 1992.

Police View of Dissent

Many police officers (and administrators) view protest as unequivocally illegitimate. They tend to regard organized protest as the conspiratorial product of authoritarian agitators, communists, rabble-rousers, spoiled kids, outsiders, or anarchists. This view does not distinguish dissent from subversion, and lumps all dissent strategies into one category (Skolnick, 1969, p. 199). As a result, police may tend to be hostile to most strategies of dissent and make the reduction of dissent their goal. The dangers of such a position are many. The police may underestimate both the number of people involved and the emotionality of dissent. They may arrest leaders or speakers at mass rallies, thereby heightening the cycle of escalating violence. They may equate the law with their own situational use of power. As the police have become more comfortable with their role as protectors of individual rights rather than as strictly law enforcers, this view of protest has become less prevalent (Barker, Hunter and Rush, 1994).

Dissenters as Deliberate Provokers of Violence

Violent dissent and violent response are generally an interactional product of short-term situational escalation or a product of a history of unsuccessful dissent and/or response strategy. Some dissenters, however, purposely provoke hostility and violence in order to gain attention, increase membership, enlist third-party support, or simply to show how "violent" the system is. Thus, the greater the resistance which groups encounter, the greater their motivation to continue their "just" struggle. Threats of punishment have little deterrent value on dissenters of this type, because they can use such threats to increase sympathy for their cause (White, 1991; Vetter and Perlstein, 1991).

Power and the Response of Order

The response of order is more likely to occur if the power of the dissenting group approaches that of the powerful group. When large numbers of people become involved in dissent and when their goals become specific and clear, police response of order is more frequent. If negotiation is on side issues that are not seen as critical by a majority of the dissenters, the strength of the dissent becomes diffused.

The Police and "Dirty Work"

The police frequently provide the most visible direct response to dissent. It is a response that the powerful and/or larger segments in society wish to see made, even though they themselves do not wish to be personally involved in the response. In such instances, the police find themselves doing the "dirty work" of larger political and social forces. As the police have become more representative of the communities they serve, many are beginning to resent that position (Barker, Hunter, and Rush, 1994).

Sometimes police seem to have been forced unwillingly into violent confrontations by the actions of legislative and judicial bodies over which they had no control. For example, city officials may decide to take steps to block what might have been a peaceful demonstration. The dissenters, with increased commitment, decide to demonstrate anyway. The police are caught in the middle.

Political Surveillance

The FBI, CIA, IRS, Army, Secret Service, Civil Service Commission, Department of Justice, and other government agencies sometimes, like the police, equate dissent with subversion. As a result, they maintain surveillance of the activities of dissidents. One major purpose of this surveillance is political control of dissent. Fortunately, the misuse of surveillance has led to congressional inquiries and the imposition of restrictions on those agencies with surveillance capabilities (Cummings and Wise, 1993).

Agents Provocateurs. To keep tabs on dissident groups, law enforcement agencies often try to infiltrate them with undercover agents, who may well commit provocative acts—or encourage others to commit them—to gain the dissenters' confidence and to obtain concrete evidence of illegal activity. The need for undercover agents is quite clear. Without them, terrorist acts would be extremely difficult to prevent. As this chapter was being written, two separate terrorist incidents were prevented due to information provided by undercover operatives. One was a planned assault upon an African-American church and assassinations of several African-American leaders in Los Angeles by a neo-Nazi group. Another was a plan on the part of Muslim extremists to assassinate a number of political leaders and blow up several tunnels in New York City. However, despite the benefits of undercover operatives as information sources, they must not be allowed to entrap or entice others into committing criminal acts.

National Security

When the national security is believed to be at stake, political intelligence sweeps up dissenters of all styles. To protect the national security, all groups and individuals committed to social or political change, however peaceful, nonviolent, or legal, must be scrutinized because they may be "subversive." These intelligence activities are designed to demoralize, intimidate, and frighten citizens into not dissenting.

The harassment, invasion of privacy, prosecution on drug charges, vandalism of offices and homes, blacklisting, or illegal searches, are chilling. When a covert force plays an important role in political decisions, the selection of candidates, the publication of false opinion polls, and the conducting of "smear" campaigns, then this nation's stated democratic political processes cease to exist. The First Amendment becomes meaningless when dissenting individuals are not allowed to exercise their rights. If there are great personal costs involved in the process of dissent, then there is no freedom. Driving political activity underground tends to escalate strategies to the more organized forms of violence, paramilitarism, terror, sabotage, assassination, guerrilla warfare, espionage, counter-intelligence, and extreme political repression (Henslin, 1993).

New Limits on Political Surveillance

To the concern of those who believe intelligence efforts are important, the trend in the recent past has been for legislatures, courts, and administrators to establish a tighter rein on police intelligence units. Some of the most restrictive guidelines have been placed on the FBI. After the guidelines went into effect in 1976, domestic security investigations by that agency fell dramatically. Most state guidelines are not as restrictive as those of the FBI. For those who believe that every "scrap of information" should be kept, such guidelines are a great handicap to police. For those who believe that intelligence gathering should be a highly selective activity and should exclude much political information, the new rules are a means of streamlining and professionalizing the intelligence process.

The Courts

The passage of laws that attempt to stifle dissent, such as riot conspiracy laws, mob action laws, and administrative laws, all make the court an arena for the politics of protest. Intelligence gathering, selective prosecution, and the response of violence tend to underwrite the perception that the courts are also political instruments of power.

The court process assumes that the activities defined as crimes are disapproved of by the community as a whole. In contemporary dissent situations, however, these conditions may not be met. As dissent increases and as a strategy of dissent gains acceptability, a majority of the citizens may not define the activity as criminal. Moreover, they may not accept the court's authority to decide the dispute. This presents a crisis for the courts and the legal system. The court becomes a political arena in which actors attempt to win third parties to their side (Skolnick, 1969, p. 243).

The Issue of Impartiality

It is difficult for the court to function as an impartial arbiter of conflict when the government itself is a party to the conflict. In the United States, lower courts have often set aside their independence and become instruments of political need, without regard for legality. In the civil turmoil of the 1960s and early 1970s courts often took the view that:

1. Civil disorders were emergency situations that required extraordinary measures of control and resistance.
2. The courts must support the police and other public agencies acting to restore order.
3. Because of the emergency, defendants must be presumed guilty (until proven innocent).
4. High bail was required to prevent rioters from returning to the riot.
5. The niceties of due process cannot and should not be observed while an emergency lasts.
6. Due process should be restored as soon as the emergency passes (Skolnick, 1969, p. 237).

No recent period in history has provided such powerful examples of the courts as political arenas than the decade in which the government moved against well-known dissidents such as Dr. Benjamin Spock, the Chicago Seven, the Panther Twenty-one, Angela Davis, and others in several dramatic trials. The government sought conviction; the defendants sought acquittal. Both parties also had other, perhaps greater, concerns. The dissenters were willing to accept the legal penalties for their acts to raise the moral justice of their cause. The government's main purpose, particularly in the Spock trial, was probably to deter draft resistance and adult support of this resistance. But the event was also used to discredit these dissenters symbolically, to blame dissent on Spock for his permissive child-rearing philosophy, and to rally patriotic third parties to the government's side of the conflict. Actually, the Spock trial may have produced the opposite effect. It became a rallying point for the entire movement. Through the trial, citizens were informed about the issues of war.

Attacks on the Courts

During their trials, dissidents of that period frequently tried not only to publicize their grievances, but also to attack the courts themselves, the criminal justice system and, ultimately, the entire socioeconomic and political system of the nation.

Corrections: The Prison

The Realities of Prison Life

Citizens want "deviants" disposed of safely, quickly, and invisibly. This invisibility creates a need for prisoners to escalate the strategy of dissent if they wish to obtain attention. Most prison dissent—hunger strikes, building takeovers, hostage-taking—is directed toward making third parties aware that "just" ideals are perverted both inside prison and out. Prisons are the breeding grounds of the strategy of violence and the marketplace of the response of total control.

Dissenters often claim that prisons, like the courts, are instruments of political oppression. Whether or not the claim is justified, punitive confinement is the essence of American penal institutions.

Reactions to Prison Life

Reaction to prison life may be docility, cooperativeness, and uncomplaining conformity, or it may be rebellion in the name of liberty. Often prisoners feel that to be subject to the arbitrary exercise of power is to be a slave (Zimbardo, 1972, p. 8). Prison authorities may feel that prison dissent is caused by a small band of militants, the circulation of militant revolutionary literature, the influence of militant lawyers, and the strategies of dissent occurring outside the institution. They respond to threat by transferring inmates, placing them in solitary confinement, censoring mail and reading materials, and limiting contacts.

Systems for Solution

The National Task Force on Disorders and Terrorism, whose report was released in late 1977, addressed setting standards and goals for the criminal justice system and for the nonofficial community in prevention, evaluation of threats, and management strategies of riots, urban disorders, prison disorders, and terrorism (National Advisory Committee, 1977).

Currently, much emphasis is being placed on the use of negotiation, which stresses human dynamics, rather than "power" tactics, as an effective means of neutralizing disorder. However, as exemplified by the 1993 FBI assault on the Branch Davidian compound near Waco, Texas, when negotiations fail, authorities tend to revert to the use of force. Whether the FBI response was correct will remain a matter of debate for many years.

Awareness

The best solution is prevention. If the police maintain close, ongoing contact with community members and help to keep channels for communication open, mutual trust will help to open legitimate peaceful options for dissent and deter the escalation of dissent to violent action. Close positive contact will also allow the police and community members to be aware of increasing tensions in a community, the factors involved in that tension, and ways to diffuse it.

Police officers also need to be self-aware. Their own assumptions and reactive behavior may increase the intensity of problems. Their level of hopefulness that what they do can make a difference influences the behavior of dissenters.

Agency administrators affect the officer's level of hopefulness and his or her ability to deal with fear and anxiety. They affect the officer's emotional and physical preparedness for situations of dissent. Support for the officers in the form of guidelines, education and training, planning and coordination of function is a key element of success.

Education

Officers who understand human dynamics and mass behavior (e.g., that riots have a classic lull between 3 and 9 A.M.), who understand the interaction of strategies of dissent and political response, who understand the element of surprise, who have learned to deal with their own fear and anxiety, and who have learned how to gain consistently reliable information, are better prepared to respond to dissent in ways that prevent violence. In addition to gaining information as a resource, officers need to gain response skills. This may be accomplished through role play and needs to be provided over a period of time so that skills can be acquired, tested, and sharpened.

Planning and Preparation

Planned, practiced tactical response can be successful. If police agencies are prepared, they can effectively use the wide range of options that they have and seize the initiative in a situation. Perhaps many different responses will be needed. If planning has been effective, the roles of each cooperating agency and jurisdiction are defined, and coordination of resources exists, disorder can be neutralized without extinguishing dissent or imposing excessive social control.

Cooperation and coordination among units in a single police agency (e.g., those trained in the various tactics of countersniper, assault, negotiation, and intelligence) is critical. Just as critical is cooperation of police with other agencies. A system response must be an organized one. Usually such response is from the "bottom up." The local agency is the key decision maker, and other agencies provide support. If this division of responsibility is not followed, procedures may be imposed from the "top down" (e.g., federal agencies making decisions for the local police).

Jealousies, conflicting philosophies, and poor planning can lead to immobility and disaster. Many of these problems can be avoided if police–community relations are conducted effectively with members of the justice community and clear guidelines for cooperation are developed. This includes not only other police agencies, but also courts and corrections.

Human Dynamics Versus Power Tactics

Political response to dissent may shape the intensity of the dissent. Restraint on the part of the police will help to prevent violent confrontation. In contrast, heavy-handed harassment increases anger and invites violence.

Establishing dialogues with dissenting groups and applying an understanding of human dynamics is much more effective than power tactics in maintaining long-term peace, even if it is somewhat uneasy. Further discussion of human dynamics as a part of conflict management is found in the next chapter.

CONCLUSIONS

Change and resistance to change are part of every system. For change to occur, some amount of "deviance" takes place and the "normal way of things" is disturbed. Dissent—acts designed to bring about needed social, legal, and political change—grows out of people's desire to shape their own destiny and to be more active in the processes and structures that shape their lives.

Political authority can, if it chooses, adapt and be responsive to change by encouraging solutions that will alleviate the conditions that have led to dissent. Political authority can also respond to dissent by trying to control it, either through persuasion, reward or compromise, or through force. The latter alternative will induce some people to be docile, but may drive others to violent resistance.

If authority recognizes the issues raised by dissent, our institutions may be transformed; if authority defines these issues as nonnegotiable and tries to control or stifle dissent, our democratic political institutions will turn into prisons that are run without the consent of the governed.

STUDENT CHECKLIST

1. Define the parameters of the right to dissent under the U.S. Constitution.
2. Present contrasting views of acceptable dissent.
3. Describe the interaction of the strategies of dissent and response.
4. Identify the significant aspects of escalation and de-escalation.
5. Analyze the ways in which police, courts, and corrections become instruments of power in relation to dissent.
6. Describe the necessary components for effectively neutralizing disorder without increasing violent dissent.

TOPICS FOR DISCUSSION

1. Discuss the conflict between the right to dissent and the need to maintain order.
2. Discuss several positive ways of resolving social conflict.
3. In what ways is power a central issue in dissent and political response?

ONE STEP FORWARD

Greetings

You are the Chief of Police in a major Southern city. A group of 300 unemployed workers have taken over City Hall. They are unarmed. They have food and water supplies to last for a week. They are breaking out windows and destroying furniture but they have no hostages. They are demanding that they be provided jobs or they will not leave city hall.

How will you solve the problem without escalating violence?

BIBLIOGRAPHY

Advocates For Self-Government (1988) "Worlds Smallest Political Quiz."

Barker, T., Hunter, R. D., and Rush, J. P. (1994). *Police Systems and Practices: An Introduction.* Englewood Cliffs, N.J.: Prentice Hall.

Brown, R. (1968). March speech on "The Black Panther."

Burns, J. M., Peltason, J. W., Cronin, T. E., and Magleby, D. B. (1993). *Government by the People,* 15th ed. Englewood Cliffs, N.J.: Prentice Hall.

Cox, A. "Direct action, Civil Disobedience and the Constitution," in Grossman, J. B., and Grossman, M. H., Law and *Change in Modern America.* Pacific Palisades, Calif.: Goodyear, 1971.

Cummings, M. C., and Wise, D. (1993). *Democracy Under Pressure: An Introduction to the American Political System,* 7th ed. Fort Worth, Texas: Harcourt Brace Jovanovich.

Eschleman, J. R., Cashron, B. G., and Basirico, L. A. (1993). *Sociology: An Introduction,* 4th ed. New York: HarperCollins.

Fortas, A. (1968). *Concerning Dissent and Civil Disobedience.* New York: New American Library.

Greenberg, E. S., and Page, B. I. (1993). *The Struggle for Democracy.* New York: Harper-Collins.

Henslin, J. M. (1993). *Sociology: A Down-to-Earth Approach.* Needham Heights, Mass.: Allyn and Bacon.

Lucksted, O. D., and Martell, D. F. (1982). "Cults: A conflict between religious liberty and involuntary servitude? Part I," *FBI Law Enforcement Bulletin,* April, pp. 16–20.

Means, R. (1973). "American Indian movement" *Chicago Express,* p. 1.

National Advisory Commission on Criminal Justice Standards and Goals (1976). *Disorders and Terrorism: Report of the Task Force on Disorders and Terrorism.* Washington, D.C.: U.S. Government Printing Office.

The National Commission on the Causes and Prevention of Violence (1969). *To Establish Justice, To Insure Domestic Tranquility.* Washington, D.C.: U.S. Government Printing Office.

Popenoe, D. (1993). *Sociology, 9th ed. Englewood Cliffs, N.J.: Prentice Hall.*

Skolnick, J. (1969). *The Politics of Protest: Violent Aspects of Protest and Confrontation,* a staff report to the National Commission on the Causes and Prevention of Violence. Washington, D.C.: U.S. Government Printing Office.

Tischler, H. L. (1993). *Introduction to Sociology,* 4th ed. Fort Worth, Texas: Harcourt Brace Jovanovich.

Vetter, H. J., and Perlstein, G. R. (1991). *Perspectives on Terrorism.* Pacific Grove, Calif.: Brooks/Cole.

White, J. R. (1991). *Terrorism: An Introduction.* Pacific Grove, Calif.: Brooks/Cole.

Zimbardo, P. G. (1972). "Pathology of imprisonment," *Society,* April, p. 8.

Zinn, H. (1968). "The need for increased civil disobedience," in *Democracy; Nine Fallacies on Law and Order.* New York: Random House.

12

CONFLICT MANAGEMENT

*. . . we must not be locked into one view of response or fear constructive change. It is
especially important that we carefully define the problem of tactical crisis
management and vigorously pursue innovation in that area.* (Olin, 1980)

The concept of conflict management emphasizes alternatives to arrest. This is an
important but sometimes neglected aspect of police–community relations. Society is
continually groping for an understanding of the proper position of arrest in the fulfill-
ment of its needs. No one believes that arrest can be completely discarded, but in
many situations the usefulness of arrest is questionable.

The power to arrest is a necessary and useful tool in police work, but many
times arrest, particularly mass arrest and arrest relating to civil disobedience, is likely
to be inconsistent with the responsive, effective, considerate police operations so
essential to police–community relations. Mass arrest has always been associated with
the suspension of individual rights. In the area of mass dissent and civil disobedience,
the line that separates the positive and negative impact of arrest is unclear, especially
because the ranks of dissenters have been joined by college professors, members of
Congress, religious leaders, and other community leaders. Many arrests may aggravate rather than resolve impending problems.

Conflict management focuses on working with the community to identify areas
of conflict, defusing problems when (or before) they arise, minimizing or preventing
property damage and violence through communication, education, and/or advocacy of
community interests. This approach emphasizes policies, procedures, and attitudes
that are different from the punitive policies and procedures traditionally associated
with police work. Community relations is an important part of and a beneficiary of
conflict-management approaches.

STUDYING THIS CHAPTER WILL ENABLE YOU TO:

1. Contrast conflict management approaches with traditional police policy.
2. Identify several alternatives to arrest.

3. Describe the defusement process.

4. Apply the concept management approach and its application to the variety of disputes that the police encounter.

5. Understand why civil disturbances were avoided after the first Rodney King verdict in some cities.

MAINTAINING AN ORDERLY COMMUNITY

Since the late 1950s, police agencies in the United States have been especially attuned to the difficult and critical problem of maintaining an orderly community. But how do we maintain an orderly community? Unfortunately, there is no pre-scribed formula to tell us how to accomplish this task. Each situation is unique and must be resolved through intricate knowledge of the community—its concerns and its priorities.

Self-Critical Analysis

Before a police agency can develop an effective order-maintenance program, it must first initiate a program of self-critical analysis; the goal of this program is to sci-entifically and rationally place the police role into proper perspective as it relates to community needs, tolerances, and expectations. Such an analysis must include the realization that police–community relations means responsive, effective, considerate police operations.

Community Concerns and Changing Priorities

The primary consideration of police operations should be the concerns and changing priorities of the community's citizens. The police department must make an effort to provide the community with staff assistance directed toward identifying and resolving the causes of crime and violence, whether those causes are legal or social.

A Partnership

Police officers are involved in a balancing act between rigid enforcement and community tolerances, which is complicated by their own personal beliefs. Before any alternatives, contingencies, or strategies are developed, the department must first acquire an in-depth knowledge of the community and its problems, which can only be accomplished by police operating as a part *of,* and not apart *from,* the community. In addition, the community must be convinced that its police department is operating objectively and is serving the community's legitimate interests to the best of its abil-ity. A partnership must exist between the police and the community. This partnership is one step in laying the groundwork for an accommodation within the department and the community organization, information, and education efforts initiated by the police.

Exemplary Projects

Many departments are now becoming more committed to developing conflict-management policies and procedures, usually targeting certain types of problems, such as family crisis, hostage situations, mass dissent, and civil disobedience. The Family Crisis Intervention efforts of the New York City Police Department have proven to be very successful not only in defusing the conflict, but also in protecting the lives of the officers who respond to such crises. Hostage negotiation, rather than force, has produced impressive records of preserving lives in Cincinnati, San Francisco, Chicago, New York, and Los Angeles, and in less populated communities such as Virginia Beach, Virginia, St. Petersburg, Florida, and Concord, California. Since 1976 the Los Angeles County Sheriff's Department alone has handled over 250 hostage or barricade situations. Only one death, a suicide, occurred once negotiators were on the scene (Gettinger, 1983, p. 12).

HOSTAGE NEGOTIATION

Hostage situations are crisis situations with some special characteristics. Hostage negotiation differs in some ways from crisis intervention; length of time involved is a factor. Hostage negotiations may occur over an extended number of hours (24 to 48 are not unusual). The level of imminent danger may be greater, also, and the necessity for cooperation among agencies and among units within an agency may be critical because of the need to secure the area, and prepare for alternative solutions in case of failure of the negotiation.

Qualities of a Good Negotiator

Qualities of hostage negotiators and crisis counselors are similar. Gettinger (1983) states that the qualities of a good negotiator are "patience, an ability to keep the conversation going, and an ability to suspend value judgment (p. 17). According to Lowenberg and Forgach (1982), a crisis counselor shows respect, warmth, and empathy through words, tone, and actions. Personal qualities include maturity, honesty, and genuineness, because people with these qualities are more likely to be able to handle crisis situations with objectivity and confidence (Lowenberg and Forgach, 1982). All of these sources agree that the best person for the job is one who can make genuine connections with others. Most references suggest that the best hostage negotiator is a police officer with these qualities and "street knowledge," and one who has been trained in hostage negotiation techniques.

Key Elements of Negotiation Training

Central to most emergency situations is a need for planning and preparation; achieving contact; clarifying needs and hopes; exploring possible mutually acceptable solutions; and contracting for a solution and feedback. Gaining skills in these areas is part of negotiation training.

Nielson and Shea suggest that effective negotiators need to be self-confident; recognize that negotiating is more than bargaining; focus on needs rather than on solutions; work toward agreements that can be mutually acceptable; and seek creative alternatives to impasse. Extensive training using role play and situations that are designed to challenge the officer's creativity in seeking alternatives is critical as is continued practice after training in order to maintain skills (Nielson and Shea, 1982).

A BROADER CONCEPT

Conflict management is not limited to hostage negotiations and family crisis situations. Police departments of every size are recognizing the importance of applying conflict management strategies to disputes that may involve a few people, disputes between hundreds of people, and conflicts that occur over the use of public space (Goldstein, 1990, pp. 111–112).

In some agencies, conflict management is still a very narrow concept that is packaged for delivery by one unit to a specific category of problems (such as hostage negotiation). This unit, because it is "different" may be an agency stepchild and may not receive general officer and administrative support. There may be little coordination between this unit and other police units within the department, and even less coordination between this unit and other members of the justice community. Lacking the supportive resources that can be gained through this sort of coordination, the success of the unit may be limited even though its officers have excellent personal rapport with community members.

Disputes Between a Few People

The disputes between a few people that police officers deal with could involve people who live with one another, tenants and landlords, customers and merchants, and neighbors. The typical reaction to any incident that disturbs the public peace or involves a dispute between two or more persons is to "call the cops." As Egon Bittner pointed out:

> In place of the freedom of self-help we have devised an exceedingly cumbersome and time-consuming method of dealing with transgressions and omissions, known as the administration of justice. For most purposes this method works, if not well, at least well enough. Thus, if I desire to prevent my neighbor's dog from tearing up my flower bushes, I can go to court to obtain some satisfaction for past damages and an injunction against future trespasses. But if the neighbor sics his dog on me and threatens to do it again, then I can scarcely be expected to wait for the wheels of justice to turn. Instead, I will do what every American would, namely, "Call the cops!" (Bittner, 1972, p. 95).

Domestic Disputes

Nowhere is this more evident than in the handling of domestic disturbances. According to Sherman (1992), domestic assault is the single most frequent form of violence that police officers encounter. At least 8 million times each year police officers will confront a victim who has been beaten by a spouse or lover. One police trainer has said that "living in a home racked by domestic violence is like living in a POW camp (Winn, 1993). Another trainer has said that "American women are safer in the streets than in their homes" (Pyle, 1993). The public and the police have long recognized the need for skilled crisis intervention in these police calls. However, police alternatives for dealing with these incidents is now subject to debate.

In the mid-1980s, mandatory arrests of suspects in misdemeanor domestic violence arrests became widely accepted. Numerous states passed laws that allowed police officers to make misdemeanor arrests in domestic disturbance when they did not view the assault or did not have a warrant. Up to this time the police hardly ever made an arrest unless there was serious visible injury or they had a warrant. This was an expansion of police powers and seen as a breakthrough in the handling of domestic disputes.

Several factors combined to make mandatory arrest the most feasible alternative. A research study conducted by Sherman and Berk in Minneapolis during the years 1981–1982 on the effects of mandatory arrests showed that it was successful in reducing the violence and repetition of domestic disturbances. The Sherman and Berk report recommended that police in all 50 states be allowed (not mandatory) to make warrantless arrests in misdemeanor domestic violence cases (Sherman, 1992). In 1984, the U.S. Attorney General's Task Force on Family Violence urged police departments to adopt arrest as the preferred response to domestic violence. Also, at this same time the Torrington, Connecticut, police department lost a $2.6 million lawsuit to Tracy Thurman, whose husband had continued to assault her while police officers hesitated to act. These events combined to make mandatory arrest the preferred police alternative (Benson, 1993, p. 37).

Recent research has convinced Sherman (1992) and others that mandatory arrests may have been doing more harm than good. Replications of the Minneapolis research has shown that arrest deters domestic violence in some cities and not others based on a combination of factors, such as race, socioeconomic status, and the history of violence among the participants (Sherman, 1992). He suggests that instead of requiring mandatory arrest, that state statutes require mandatory actions from a list of options. The options would be determined by the needs and makeup of the community and could include such things as transporting the victim to a shelter, transporting either victim or suspect to a detox center, letting the victim decide whether or not the suspect is to be arrested, or providing short-term protection. In any event, this recent research has shown that there is no one answer to conflict management in domestic settings and that the police must combine training with policy and use the law along with other social service agencies to reduce the violence and manage the conflict.

The Milwaukee, Wisconsin Police Department uses a combination of mandatory arrests and social services in their handling of domestic violence. The department has had a policy of mandatory arrest since 1986, three years before the state made it a law. In addition, the department also works closely with two battered women's shelters. Police officers are instructed to call the shelters from the scene and social workers assess the victim's condition and need for counseling, emergency shelter, or a protection order. The Sojourner Truth House, the city's largest battered women's shelter, also participates in police training and Batterers Anonymous, a 20-week program to which offenders may be diverted (Benson, 1993, p. 39).

Disputes Between Neighbors

Tasker Street in Philadelphia, Pennsylvania, is similar to a number of streets in large urban cities throughout the United States. It runs through a 1-mile-square area of the city known as Gray's Ferry. This section of the city is mostly a lower-income black community surrounded by pockets of middle-income white neighborhoods and it has a predominantly black housing project situated in the area. In 1989, when black police Captain Arthur Berry assumed command of the 17th District, which included the Grey's Ferry area, it was a racial battle field where "neighbors really hated each other" (Berry, in Parker, 1992).

Soon after Captain Berry took command there was a racial incident which resulted in the tragic death of a 16-year-old white youth. To resolve this incident and lessen the conflict in the area, Berry approached the leaders of the main community groups: the Grey's Ferry Community Council, which represented the white neighborhoods; the Stinger Square Council, which represented blacks in surrounding communities; and two Tasker Home Associations, one representing blacks in surrounding communities and the other representing blacks in the housing project (Parker, 1992, p. 26). It was his intention to have these groups meet and come to a cooperative solution to the conflict between neighbors.

The first attempts to meet were less than successful but Berry continued to meet with the leaders of the groups individually. Before long, the leaders began to meet on a regular basis and discuss community conflicts. The program has been a success and violence has been curtailed and black and white neighbors are beginning to get along together (Parker, 1992, p. 27).

Disputes Between Youths and Merchants

A particularly disturbing source of neighborhood conflict is the presence of large groups of youths, particularly teenagers "hanging out" on business property during business hours and when they are closed. The majority of the teenagers who hang out cause no serious problems. However, some drink and fight with one another and carelessly litter on private property. The police can rely on a strict law enforcement approach or they can try to resolve the conflict in a manner that is agreeable to both the youths and the property owners. In 1992, officers from the Joliet, Illinois Police Department took this approach (Parker, 1992).

Officers developed a trespassing agreement to be signed by owners and managers that would allow them to arrest trespassers without having the owners and managers verbally warning trespassers to get off their property. The officers also had school liaison officers explain the trespass agreement in school and solicit anonymous comments from the teenagers. The officers also located areas for the youths to hang out. This combined effort resulted in less conflict between youth and merchants and increased interaction between the police and the youths.

Tenant–Landlord Disputes Program of the Dayton, Ohio Police Department

Traditionally, there has always been friction between tenants and landlords. Tenants often take advantage of landlords who do not carefully supervise and maintain rental property, and landlords often take advantage of tenants who do not understand the legal technicalities of rental contracts or landlord obligations. Disputes are common occurrences. The police have traditionally regarded such disputes as strictly civil matters that do not call for police involvement, and often one of the participants falls victim to the other. The tenants may suffer unfair landlord practices, ranging from illegal rent increases to eviction. Or the landlords may have their rental property completely destroyed by the tenants. When landlord–tenant disputes continue over a period of time, criminal acts often occur. These may be property destruction, assaults that may result in serious injury or death, and other types of violence. Disputes in many cities reach proportions where angry groups of tenants or a civil rights organization enter into large-scale demonstrations against the landlord; as a result, there is a breakdown in order. This means that in many tenant–landlord disputes police become involved at one point or another, with a considerable expenditure of man-hours in the conducting of investigations or quelling disorder.

The Dayton police department's conflict-management unit established a program to intervene in tenant–landlord disagreements at the initial stage. The program is an ongoing crime and violence prevention project, a definite police responsibility.

This program requires part of one conflict management officer's time. Upon being notified of a dispute (either by a beat officer who identifies a dispute during his course of duty or by a call from one of the parties involved), the officer meets with the tenant and landlord to find out what the problem is. Then, employing the training in this area, the officer informs both participants of their mutual obligations and of what they legally can and cannot do. The officer keeps in contact with the cases to see that both sides reach reasonable and satisfactory agreements. Often the officer is able to handle a dispute quickly by referring the tenants and landlords to the proper service agencies or by informing the agency that a dispute exists.

This program deals with police responsibilities (crime and violence prevention) at a level traditionally ignored by police. The program saved the Dayton Police Department countless manhours that would otherwise have been expended.

Disputes Between Hundreds of People

The police are often called upon to handle disputes between hundreds of people whenever there are political disputes or disputes over such current social issues as abortion, gay rights, environmental issues, and any number of highly charged topics (Figure 12-1). They are also present at civil rights demonstrations, labor–management disputes, rallies of extremists groups, and urban riots. All of these events require the police to take on a conflict-management approach emphasizing mediation and negotiating skills.

The issues that bring about these disputes and their locations has changed in the last 30 to 40 years. Civil rights protests were predominant in the 1950s and 1960s and Vietnam was the issue behind most protests in the late 1960s and 1970s. In the 1990s it appears that the majority of the protests and demonstrations occur as a result of environmental issues and over such social issues as abortion and the right to life. The demonstrations of the 1990s are not as likely to occur in urban areas as was the case in the 1960s, 1970s, and 1980s. The demonstrations of today are increasingly occurring

FIGURE 12-1   Crowd control New York City.

in rural and small-town America (Fanton, 1990). Unfortunately, many of the departments in rural and small-town America are ill equipped and not trained in handling
disputes between hundreds of peoples (Figure 12-2).

Civil Disturbances Following the First Rodney King Verdict

The April 29, 1992 acquittal of the four Los Angeles police officers charged
with the beating of Rodney King unleased a riot of burning, looting, killing, and general mayhem in Los Angeles and led to disturbances in many other U.S. cities. This
incident created an image of urban unrest that this nation had not seen since the 1960s.
However, several large urban cities, particularly Boston, Chicago, Miami, and San
Diego, were able to avoid these disturbances through strategic planning and deployment of police forces, the willingness of police and city officials to maintain close
communication with their constituents, the debunking of rumors and good old-
fashioned luck (Clark, 1992).

The police in each of these four cities had contingency plans ready in the event
that they were needed to maintain calm and quell disorder. The police administrators in
these cities recognized that an acquittal verdict would produce disturbances. In each of
these cities, police and city officials made public pronouncements voicing their dismay
about the verdicts and asking for calm. Chicago Police Superintendent Matt Rodriguez
released a public statement conveying his "amazement and concern" over the verdict

The first environmental demonstration in Allegheny County, New York occurred May 31, 1989, caught everyone by surprise and took place on the front steps of the county court house. Several hundred demonstrators assembled in front of the courthouse and 48 of them surrounded a car carrying two members of a state commission who had come to inspect the site of a nuclear dump site. The protestors blocked the wheels and refused to let the commission members out of their car.

"It presented a big problem," Allegheny County Sheriff Larry Scholes said later. His department consisted of 21 full-time staff whose primary duties were maintaining the county jail. Scholes recalls, "I walked out there with one uniformed deputy. As soon as that vehicle pulled in and was surrounded by 48 people, I asked my office to get additional staff."

Two civil deputies were called in and then the New York State Police were summoned when it became clear that the objective of the people surrounding the car was to be arrested. Eventually, the demonstrators were arrested and the two shaken commissioners were allowed to leave. Sheriff Scholes stated, "I feel like Andy of Mayberry on a bad day."

Following the initial demonstration of May 31, Sheriff Scholes met with representatives of the protest groups to advise them of his concerns about violence and the need for communications. "We set up a rapport right from the very first meeting," the sheriff reported. "They feel comfortable calling and asking me something, knowing that if I can't give the information, I'll tell them so and if I do give them the information it's going to be accurate. They, in turn, have done the same thing for me." Sheriff Scholes' approach did not stop the demonstrations, that was not his intent. However, his handling of the demonstrations did lessen the potential for violence and reduced the likelihood of surprise for both parties.

Source: Adapted from B. Fanton, "Rural demonstrations," *Law and Order,* November 1990, pp. 92–97.

FIGURE 12-2   Anatomy of a rural demonstration.

(Clark, 1992, p. 1). Other police executives met with community leaders and spoke at the spontaneous demonstrations that sprang up in their cities. The San Diego police department let residents know that they could protest the verdicts peacefully, but they would not allow opportunists to engage in violence, looting, or burning.

Each of the cities set up networks to control the spread of rumors and keep community leaders informed of police activities. Community leaders were praised in each of the cities for their part in keeping the cities calm. In fact, the relationships created between police and community leaders during this crisis have led to positive developments in conflict management. The San Diego Coalition for Equality-Year 2000 was formed by residents and the police department after the immediate crisis was over. There have been meetings in Chicago between community leaders and the police to explore solutions to other possible sources of conflict.

Disputes over the Use of Public Space

The police are often involved in conflict situations when there are disputes over the use of public space. Sometimes these disputes involve the illegal use of public space such as when prostitutes or drug pushers use the public streets to engage in their illegal enterprises. However, peddlers, alcoholics, the mentally ill, or the homeless may compete with merchants, shoppers, pedestrians, and others for public space which they both feel they are entitled to use. In the latter instances, the police would prefer to resolve the conflict without resorting to arrest whenever possible.

Homeless

Research on homelessness has revealed that although these unfortunate people have a high arrest rate, they are not involved in crimes that involve violence or threats of violence against others (Snow, Baker, and Anderson, 1989). Their crimes mainly involve acts that indicate personal dysfunction, such as public intoxication, theft/shoplifting, and violation of city ordinances. Nevertheless, a recent survey by the Police Executive Research Forum (PERF) indicates that the responding police executives view the homeless as a source for concern because they increase the fear of crime among citizens and the conditions in which they live poses a public health hazard (Carter and Sapp, 1993).

Although respondents to the PERF survey were aware that the police are often the only resource available to provide aid to the homeless, they recognized that a law enforcement response was not the answer.

> [This] is not strictly a police problem and requires, like domestic abuse, a multidisciplinary approach. Police are strictly a stopgap measure dealing with immediate problems and are not equipped to deal with root causes. (Carter and Sapp, 1993, p. 7)

Over 80 percent of the police executives reported that their departments provided transportation when they came in contact with homeless requiring shelter. The majority of the contacts the police had with homeless involved "public nuisances" such as panhandling, public intoxication, or problematic behavior indicating mental illness.

CONFLICT INTERVENTION AT THE COMMUNITY LEVEL

Although the conflict management unit of the Dayton, Ohio police department mentioned earlier no longer exists, it has been incorporated into their community policing strategy (Ritchey, 1992); the conflict intervention team of this unit still provides a useful model.

Conflict Intervention Team

The conflict intervention team of the Dayton conflict management unit was responsible for seeking out, identifying, and intervening in areas of potential conflict before they became serious disruptions. Police departments may not be able to recognize conflict before it reaches major proportions unless the department develops close communication and contact with the community. The primary responsibility of the Dayton conflict intervention team was to develop and nurture this kind of close contact. Team members spent most of their time in the community in an effort to create the open exchanges of opinion that are necessary for a working police–community interaction. The team members met with ministers, presidents, and leaders of neighborhood organizations and service clubs, directors and staff members of service agencies, business and industrial leaders, school administrators and faculty, leaders and members of paramilitary and youth groups, gang members, and others who had no formal connections to anyone or any group but who could still exert influence over large numbers of people.

The Defusement Process

The relationships mentioned above gave team members a chance to learn about the conflicts and community problems that might lead to violence and confrontation situations. These relationships played a major role in the so-called *defusement process*—a conflict management technique employed to smooth over potentially abrasive police–community interaction when a large group forms, either spontaneously or as a planned demonstration.

The Major Aspects of Conflict Intervention

The first aspect of conflict intervention, then, is to identify conflict and potential conflict situations in the community and to respond to potentially explosive situations as they arise in the community.

The second aspect is actual intervention in the conflict and working out a solution to the conflict situation so that the necessity for forceful police response is eliminated. This includes keeping command officers informed as conflicts develop and preparing a number of alternatives that the department can adopt in handling each situation. During this stage, the conflict intervention team acts as a resource and research arm for the department, attempting to find a means of responding that will maintain a maximum of order, yet not result in an open confrontation.

At other times, intervention may mean going immediately into the problem area and bringing initial relief to the community through defusement before developing the longer-term solution. This permits the department to control a situation through conflict management techniques using as few as six officers (number on Dayton's conflict intervention team), and to alleviate problems that might otherwise call for a more extensive use of force. The ability of the team to defuse potentially dangerous situations illustrates the value of a conflict management approach toward law enforcement at the community level. The conflict intervention unit cannot only be a specialized task force that acts as a planning source for the department; it can also be a practical, on-the-street operation that intervenes in crises as they arise. Its approaches are those of mediation, communication, and advocacy. When a conflict and its participants have been identified, a meeting or series of meetings is arranged between the team and those community members who are parties to the conflict.

The Dayton Conflict Intervention Team intervened in such varied disputes as two quarreling neighbors, two youth groups, labor and management during a strike situation, and a group of college students hostile to the school administration.

In many cases, a conflict could result from a lack of proper services from some other public agency. Advocacy by the conflict intervention team could be used to ensure that the proper service is rendered. This concept could also be employed during intensive conflict situations when an in-depth study is necessary to discover the causes of the conflict and develop recommendations for action.

CONCLUSIONS

Conflict management will become an increasingly vital area of police work in the 1990s as our population expands and changes. Disputes between persons, hundreds of persons, and others over the use of public space will increase. The public and the police will seek alternatives to arrest whenever it is possible. Police departments, rural and urban, will be forced to examine the inventory of tools and resources they have at their disposal to deal with conflict. Departments will consider their coercive powers, their discretionary powers (the ability to sanction or do nothing when faced with conflict), and the power to arrest and to issue warrants or warnings when dealing with conflict.

Police departments will also call on other community resources, such as the news media, churches and civic organizations, regulatory agencies, neighborhood organizations, and social service agencies, to assist them in the management of conflict. These departments will have to provide training and specialized personnel in conflict management.

It is imperative that arrest be viewed from a reasonable and proper perspective. There are too many persons in the police service and within our communities who view arrest as the final problem solver. This simplistic point of view has served as an inhibiting factor in allowing police to increase their options for response. The coercive powers of the police are certainly necessary for the performance of their duties; however, those same coercive powers (arrest) sometimes contribute to the chaotic conditions in today's communities. Police, as the community's resource in the control of deviant behavior, must look beyond traditional ways so that their contribution to society may be even more effective.

STUDENT CHECKLIST

1. Contrast conflict-management approaches with traditional police policy.
2. Identify several alternatives to arrest.
3. Describe the defusement process.
4. Describe several strategies for developing close communication between the police and the community.

5. Apply conflict-management strategies to typical situations needing police intervention.

TOPICS FOR DISCUSSION

1. Set up a conflict-management program in your class. "Respond" to the situations described in the One Step Forward section.
2. Discuss the advantages to police of having such a program.

ONE STEP FORWARD

Try Your Hand at Conflict Management

Problem 1

Situation. Several paramilitary and loosely organized youth groups are responsible for considerable apprehension in the city's neighborhoods and for assaults and destruction to property.

Potential. Because of the quick, "hit-and-run" nature of gang activities, only rarely are witnesses and victims able to identify assailants or provide enough information to effect arrests. It is virtually impossible for the department to legally halt such activities.

However, all gangs do not engage in antisocial behavior, nor are all members of a gang that engages in antisocial behavior destructive or violence-oriented. Indeed, some of these groups have assisted the department in keeping tense situations from exploding. Therefore, an attempt by the department to "get the gangs off the streets" by gathering intelligence information and making arrests will be both unfair and of little value in reaching the real sources of trouble. Additionally, such police action has proven to be disastrous; it serves as a recruiting mechanism for the gangs and, as experience across the country has shown, further alienates young people, drawing police into an imaginary "war" with the youths. Neither does such action offer more than stopgap measures. It only commits the department to respond to gang activities again and again.

What Would You Do? Actual Conflict-Management Unit Response. The conflict-management unit recognized its double predicament. The gangs were becoming more influential in Dayton, and a confrontation with them would heavily drain the department and the city of vital resources. Therefore, the conflict-management unit sought to develop a longer lasting solution to this problem area.

Operating under the premise that "if you can't lick 'em, join 'em," two conflict intervention team officers practically became gang members. But this was not an intelligence or undercover operation. The two officers wore their police uniforms and rode marked police motorcycles in their interaction with the gangs. This gave the team a chance to meet the gangs "on their own grounds," developing an honest relationship with them which allowed the officers to become familiar with gang leaders, their habits, and other related matters. The officers cautioned the gang members if they were causing trouble and explained the consequences of their behavior.

Evaluation. This relationship between the officers and the gangs proved to be valuable. The department was able to reduce the late night noise created by gangs, the general vandalism and littering, and the roughhousing that often leads to assaults on innocent people. It prevented a potential gang–police confrontation and reduced the need to investigate complaints due to gang activities. In addition, the conflict-management operation provided the community with a visible police presence, assuring residents that the department is monitoring gang activity.

Problem 2

Situation. Growing urban schools, beginning to integrate, and the complex problems of young people experiencing the first challenges of responsibility have been a source of difficulty. This is complicated by racial antagonisms, often reflected in the homes and carried into schools by the students, apprehension on the part of city residents who live in school neighborhoods, and the fear of "new" people (integration).

Potential. There is a real strain on intergroup relations among students in the public school system, and even unintentional acts can produce confrontations between black and white youngsters. Traditional responses—sending in troops to separate and disperse youngsters—have resulted in making the police the object of the confrontation and creating just as serious a problem. In many cases, this type of response only aggravates the situation and makes it necessary for the department to return to the school on a continual basis which places an exhausting strain on departmental resources. It also irritates students, who resent massive police presence at the schools and are drawn more and more into the situation.

What Would You Do? Actual Conflict-Management Unit Response. Recognizing that the Dayton Police Department could not afford to respond day after day to such situations, yet realizing that the department had an obligation to assure that the schools remain peaceful learning centers, the conflict-management unit sought to develop longer lasting solutions.

Conflict intervention team members met with students in seminars, assemblies, conferences, workshops, classrooms, and street parties to explore and dissect myths, rumors, false and malicious statements, and ignorant beliefs. This brought about an understanding on the part of both black and white students that the fast-moving pace of our times calls for interdependence. These discussions were expanded to include parents and residents of the school neighborhoods. In addition, the team members promoted the establishment of student-faculty-administration councils, which brought normally separated people into a more positive alliance.

The team also developed a special course that was taught to high school students in civic classes. This course was led by a conflict-management officer who discussed such topics as the laws of search and seizure, the American system of justice and constitutional rights, police responsibilities and limitations, and basic police operations.

Evaluation. The Dayton Police Department was able to maintain a healthy, learning atmosphere in the schools, reducing the negative attitudes that students often have toward police. Racial tensions and hostilities among students and in school neighborhoods were reduced, and the department no longer has to contend with continuous, abrasive contacts between students and neighborhood residents.

BIBLIOGRAPHY

Benson, K. (1993). "Domestic violence: The house divided," *Police,* March, pp. 32–36.

Bittner, E. (1972). *The Functions of the Police in Modern Society.* Washington, D.C.: National Institute of Mental Health.

Carter, D. L., and Sapp, A. (1993). "Police response to street people: A survey of perspectives and practices," *FBI Law Enforcement Bulletin,* March, pp. 5–9.

Clark, J. R. (1992). "Keeping a lid on things," *Law Enforcement News,* May 31, p. 6 ff.

Fanton, B. (1990). "Rural demonstrations," *Law and Order,* November, pp. 92–97.

Gettinger, S. (1983). "Hostage negotiations bring them out alive," *Police Magazine,* Vol. 6, pp. 10–28.

Goldstein, H. (1990). *Problem-Oriented Policing.* New York: McGraw-Hill.

Lowenberg, D. A., and Forgach, P. (1982). *Counseling Crime Victims in Crisis.* Washington, D.C.: Aurora Associates.

Nielson, R. C., and Shea, G. F. (1982). "Training officers to negotiate creatively," *The Police Chief,* Vol. XLIX, August, pp. 65–67.

Olin, W. R. (1980). "Tactical crisis management: The challenge of the 80s." *FBI Law Enforcement Bulletin*, November, pp. 20–25.

Parker, P. (1992). "Starting with the kids," *Police,* August, pp. 26–27.

Pyle, V. (1993). Pima County Arizona Victim-Witness Program, quoted in Benson.

Ritchey, D., Officer Dayton, Ohio Police Department (1992). Personal telephone conversation, September 9.

Sherman, L. W. (1992). *Policing Domestic Violence: Experiments and Dilemmas.* New York: Free Press.

Snow, D. A.; Baker, S. G. and Anderson, L., "Criminality and Homeless Men: An Empirical Assessment." *Social Problems* 36:5, 1989: 532–549.

Winn, M., Sergeant, Nashville, Tenn., Police Department. (1993). Quoted in Benson.

13

COMMUNITY POLICING

*The first thing to understand is that public peace . . . of cities is not kept primarily by
the police. . . . It is kept primarily by an intricate, almost unconscious network of
voluntary controls and standards among the people . . . and enforced by the people.*
(Jacobs, 1966, pp. 31–32)

*Where [community involvement] has been properly obtained, the people are
much more secure. Where they are secure, they are closer to the ideal created
by the founders of this Republic. And, where they are secure, the torch of freedom
is burning brightly.* (Davis, 1977, p. 8)

Throughout this book we have stressed the need for the police to develop relationships with the public that are based on mutual respect and trust in order to provide
proper police services to that public. Such a relationship is not created merely by
soliciting support from the public but by establishing lines of communication that
enable the police to become an integral part of the community being served. As we
noted in Chapters 1 and 2, this is a difficult undertaking. The police are drawn in
many directions by the complex and frequently competing groups that comprise each
"community." These relationships are further complicated by the organization of the
police system in the United States and the restrictions that are placed on it.

In this chapter we discuss how American police organizations have evolved in
their efforts to maintain law and order within a democratic society. Community policing is seen as the product of this evolutionary process. The focus of our discussion
will be to present the development, philosophy, and application of community policing in the United States.

STUDYING THIS CHAPTER WILL ENABLE YOU TO:

1. Understand the evolution of police service delivery models within the United
   States.
2. Describe the difference between police–community relations and community-
   oriented policing.

3. Describe the development of community policing models.

4. Discuss the philosophy and role of community policing.

5. Describe the strengths and weaknesses of community policing.

6. Assess the future of community-oriented models in American policing.

THE POLICE IN THE UNITED STATES

The focal concern within the criminal justice systems of democratic nations is determining how to balance crime control against freedom and justice. Too little control results in the loss of freedoms due to crime and the fear of crime. Too much control results in the loss of freedoms due to governmental interference and fear of persecution. This concern is directly reflected in the models of policing utilized by democratic nations.

Unlike totalitarian states, the police in democracies must elicit the support of the populace to carry out their duties. In deciding what the role and structure of the police will be in a given nation, the government must determine how much freedom its citizens are willing to give up to feel safe from crime. The flip side of this issue is: How much crime is the populace willing to tolerate to feel safe from the police? As U.S. police organizations have evolved, they have sought to deal with the foregoing dilemma by increasing both their effectiveness and their responsiveness to the public. As we shall see, this has not been an easy task.

The United States is a nation of small police agencies. The majority of the approximately 17,000 police departments (FBI, 1993) employ fewer than 30 officers (Cole, 1992; Walker, 1992). Despite the existence of huge agencies such as the New York City Police Department, the provision of police services is predominately a small agency responsibility. As a result of the large number of agencies and the regional diversity found within the United States, no two police agencies are exactly alike. Therefore, the provision of police services varies considerably within the nation.

Political, cultural, and economic factors influence the organizational structure, financial support, management styles, and enforcement policies of police agencies (Wilson, 1968). While a small city police may focus on order maintenance, its larger neighbor may have a strong service orientation. They may share their jurisdiction with a sheriff's department that is strictly legalistic. All three approaches may be viewed as appropriate by the communities they serve.

THE EVOLUTION OF POLICE SERVICE MODELS

The current state of policing within the United States is the product of a series of developments that have taken place over the past two centuries. While considerable progress has occurred, the reader may observe that in many ways, policing has not moved far from its roots.

The Watch and Ward

As English society evolved during the later Middle Ages, the decline of feudalism brought significant changes in law enforcement. The migration of serfs from the manors to towns and cities and the rise of a merchant class created a need for a more formal police system. In the ninth century, Alfred the Great established the "frankpledge" system (Beckman, 1980; Cole, 1992). Under this Saxon system, the head of each family was responsible for the conduct of all family members over the age of 12. Ten landless families grouped together into a "tithing" were responsible for one another. The "Tithingman" was responsible for raising a "hue and cry" if a criminal act occurred. Tithing members were then required to join in the apprehension of the offender(s). Ten tithings constituted a "hundred," which was headed by a "reeve" appointed by a local magistrate. Several hundreds made up a shire, which was overseen by a "shire reeve" (Beckman, 1980; Senna and Siegal, 1993).

The Statute of Winchester, enacted in 1285, replaced the frankpledge with the "watch and ward." This military system established parish "constables" (successors to the old Saxon reeves) to assist the sheriffs by maintaining order in the cities and towns. Every male between 15 and 60 was required to assist the constable by (1) keeping an assize of arms, (2) maintaining the peace, (3) participating in the apprehension of criminals, and (4) serving as a member of a night watch (Critchley, 1985).

The system described above remained in effect in England for the next 600 years. As England conquered the remainder of the British Isles, its system of law enforcement was imposed on the inhabitants of Wales, Scotland, and Ireland. When the United Kingdom began expanding its empire to North America, it was this system, augmented by martial law, which was implemented. In the towns and cities that sprang up, the constable and watch were used to enforce the laws of the community, the colony, and of England. A sheriff would be elected by the populace or appointed by government officials to provide law enforcement for those areas outside the cities. In remote areas, the citizens in small settlements relied on the militia for protection. Those families and individuals living alone in isolated parts of the frontier had to rely on themselves and any neighbors who might be close enough to render assistance (Johnson, 1981; Bopp and Schultz, 1977).

The Peelian Model

The system of law enforcement that had existed in Great Britain performed reasonably well within the small towns and rural areas for several centuries. However, by the eighteenth century, the collapse of feudalism and the onset of the Industrial Revolution had led to congestion and social disorder within the large cities. The old system of law enforcement could not contend with the resulting chaos. London was a particularly troubled city in which there was almost a total breakdown of law and order (Cole, 1992).

Robert Peel was an ambitious young politician who was elected to Parliament in 1809 at the age of 21. By the age of 24 he was Chief Secretary to Ireland (then a British possession), where he established the Royal Irish Constabulary to bolster English rule in Ireland (Miller, 1977). This military force, commonly called "Peelers," had only limited success, due to fierce opposition from the populace. When Peel left

Ireland in 1818, it was with an understanding that the police must work to achieve and maintain legitimacy from the public (Miller, 1977). This lesson would serve him in good stead when as Home Secretary to England he guided an "Act for Improving the Police in and Near the Metropolis" (Cole, 1992) through Parliament. Peel saw the creation of a "New Police" as necessary to contend with the increasing crime, class conflict, and social disorder that threatened England in general and metropolitan London in particular (Reppetto, 1978).

Due to Peel's efforts, the Metropolitan Police Act passed in June 1829 (Critchley, 1977). The act established a force, initially of 1000 men and soon expanded to 3400, to police the London metropolis with the exception of the 1 square mile area within the old City of London. The mission of the Metropolitan Police was crime prevention (Walker, 1992) (Figure 13-1). They sought to accomplish this task by providing continuous "preventive patrols" throughout the metropolis. To stress that the police were there to serve rather than repress the public, it was agreed that constables would not carry firearms. While the organization itself was structured after the military, Peel went to great lengths to ensure that it was perceived as a civilian force. With the exception of the rank of sergeant, no military titles were used in the police organizational structure (Reppetto, 1978). Strict discipline was enacted to ensure that no actions (i.e., excessive force or unnecessary interventions) were taken that might alienate the public (Cole, 1992).

The Metropolitan Police gained acceptance so rapidly and served so effectively that Parliament passed the "County and Borough Police Act of 1856" (Stead, 1985). This act required that every borough and county in England form its own police force. In time, the Metropolitan Police came to be the model not only for British forces but for police forces in democracies throughout the world.

FIGURE 13-1

PEELIAN PRINCIPLES

1. To prevent crime and disorder, as an alternative to their repression by military force and severity of legal punishment.

2. To recognize always that the power of the police to fulfil their functions and duties is dependent on public approval of their existence, actions and behavior,a nd on their ability to secure and maintain public respect.

3. To recognize always that to secure and maintain the respect and approval of the public means also the securing of the willing cooperation of the public in the task of securing observance of law.

4. To recognize always that the extent to which the cooperation of the public can be secured diminishes, proportionately, the necessity of the use of physical force and compulsion for achieving police objectives.

5. To seek and preserve public favor, not by pandering to public opinion, but by constantly demonstrating absolutely impartial service to law, in complete independence of policy, and without regard to the justice or injustice

of the substance of individual laws, by ready offering of individual service and friendship to all members of the public without regard to the justice or injustice of the substance of individual laws, by ready offering of
individual service and friendship to all members of the public without
regard to their wealth or social standing; by ready exercise of courtesy and
good humor; and by ready offering of individual sacrifice in protecting
and preserving life.

6. To use physical force only when the exercise of persuasion, advice and
   warning is found to be insufficient to obtain public cooperation to an
   extent necessary to secure observance of law or to restore order; and to
   use only the minimum degree of physical force which is necessary on any
   particular occasion for achieving a police objective.

7. To maintain at all times a relationship with the public that gives reality to
   the historic tradition that the police are the public and that the public are
   the police; the police being only members of the public who are paid to
   give full-time attention to duties which are incumbent on every citizen in
   the interests of community welfare and existence.

8. To recognize always the need for strict adherence to police–executive
   functions, and to refrain from even seeming to usurp the powers of the
   judiciary of avenging individuals or the State, and of authoritatively judging guilt and punishing the guilty.

9. To recognize always that the rest of police efficiency is the absence of
   crime and disorder and not the visible evidence of police action in dealing
   with them.

Source: C. Reith, *The Blind Eye of History.* London: Faber and Faber, Ltd., 1952, p. 154. See
also M. W. L. Lee, *A History of Police in England,* London: Methuen & Co., 1901.

FIGURE 13-1 (continued)

The Traditional Model

In the nineteenth century in the United States, the larger cities of the North were
experiencing chaos similar to that which Britain had gone through. As in Britain, the
old system of policing could not cope with the wave of riots and disorders that swept
through the large cities. The combined effects of industrialization, urbanization, and
immigration transformed the Northern cities into hotbeds of economic, ethnic, racial,
and cultural strife (Walker, 1992). Crime was rampant on the streets and mob violence
was a frequent occurrence.

To the leaders of America's large cities it was all too apparent that the police
system had to be changed if control was to be regained. The same difficulties that had
slowed the creation of the Metropolitan Police arose in such cities as New York,
Boston, and Philadelphia. There was uncertainty about creating a "police state," political groups feared that rival factions would use the police to repress them, and there
was reluctance to bear the financial costs (Walker, 1992). Despite these concerns,

political leaders began to explore the various options available to them. The Metropolitan Police model was the alternative of choice (Johnson, 1988; Reppetto, 1978; Walker, 1992).

The creation of police forces within the large Northern cities helped regulate social disorders but did not alleviate the underlying problems of congestion and class conflict. Within a relatively short period, the police had become a tool with which politicians rewarded their friends and punished their enemies. In New York, Boston, Philadelphia, and Chicago, politics and corruption dominated the police (Reppetto, 1978). Recent immigrants, particularly the Irish and Germans, gained considerable influence in the political machines that dominated the large cities throughout the nineteenth century. Subsequently, the police departments in cities such as Boston, New York, Philadelphia, Chicago, St. Louis, Cincinnati, and Milwaukee became the domains of the dominant ethnic groups. The amount of law enforcement received, if any, was dependent on one's political connections (Walker, 1977). Crime and social tumult plagued the metropolitan areas. Once again, it was obvious that the police systems of the large cities needed overhauling.

The second half of the century saw a number of efforts at police reform. In New York and a number of other cities, the state legislatures seized control of their police forces (Reppetto, 1978). The majority of these efforts were designed to wrest control of the police from the ethnic groups and return to the "higher morality" of the upper-class Anglo-Saxon Protestants (Berman, 1987). The reforms actually accomplished very little in improving police performance. In effect, they only replaced control by one political faction with that of another (Walker, 1992).

The Professional Model

In the early years of the twentieth century, the need for police reforms continued. There was still a call to "get politics out of the police and get the police out of politics" (Walker, 1992). This continued to be based on political competition to control city governments, but now the focus was on hiring professional administrators in order to limit political influence.

In addition to hiring professional administrators, advocates for reform, such as Richard Sylvester, police chief of Washington, D.C. and founder of the International Association of Chiefs of Police, called for personnel standards for police officers. One person, August Vollmer, police chief of Berkeley, California and future founder of the American Society of Criminology, would spread the message across the nation that police officers needed to have higher education, extensive training, professional integrity, and a clearly defined organizational structure to regulate their activities (Carte and Carte, 1975; MacNamara, 1977).

Orlando Winfield Wilson attended college at the University of California and became a protegé of Vollmer. He became a Berkeley police officer and through Vollmer's influence, later obtained positions as police chief in Fullerton, California and Wichita, Kansas. His success in Wichita served as yet another model for police reform. He would later become dean of the School of Criminology at the University of California, where he wrote *Police Administration,* the text that would become the bible for American police chiefs. Wilson would later be called upon to reform the

Chicago Police Department, an effort that resulted in only modest success but laid the groundwork for future improvements (Carte and Carte, 1977).

Political turbulence dominated America in the 1960s. War protests, the civil rights movement, street crime, union actions, and unrest on college campuses created problems for city police. These problems were accentuated by the abuses of the Chicago police while "maintaining order" at the 1968 Democratic convention, the tactics that the Los Angeles police used in quelling racial unrest in that city, and by the discovery of "rampant corruption" in the New York City Police Department (Johnson, 1988). Once again the call for reform was heard.

THE DEVELOPMENT OF COMMUNITY POLICE MODELS

A new group of reformers, led by New York City Police Commissioner Patrick Murphy, began to emerge during the 1960s and 1970s. New techniques that emphasized community relations and enhanced service delivery became popular (Walker, 1992). New procedures regulating the discretion and conduct of the police began to take effect. These changes, in conjunction with rulings of the U.S. Supreme Court which dramatically expanded the rights of those accused of criminal behavior, significantly affected the role and performance of law enforcement officers in general and of big city police in particular.

American police forces became more representative of the community, and more disciplined than ever before. Administrators were constantly experimenting with ways in which to enhance the delivery of police services. The public and the media became more aware of what the police are supposed to be doing and, more important, what they are not supposed to do.

Today the mission of police is recognized as going beyond "crime fighting"—catching bad guys—and "order maintenance"—keeping potential threats to the peace in line (Walker, 1992; Senna and Siegal, 1993). Service to the public through community awareness and crime prevention programs is now in vogue. The police and the public are once again learning that law enforcement requires a cooperative effort, not alienation from one another. To achieve this cooperative goal, American police agencies have experimented with a number of community-oriented models.

Team Policing

The professional model of policing had sought to move away from the favoritism, corruption, and inefficiency of the contextual law enforcement provided by the traditional model. Effectiveness in reducing crime rates and in apprehending criminals was stressed. Later, efficiency and accountability in providing police services became a focal concern. Although these efforts resulted in "better law enforcement," they did so at the expense of community relations. "Professional officers" were better disciplined, less biased, less corrupt, and more efficient. They were also more effective in fighting crime. However, their fixation with crime fighting and the strictly legalistic provision of services viewed as necessary for professional accountability caused them to become isolated from the communities they served (Barker,

Hunter, and Rush, 1994). Team policing was an attempt to restore those needed ties to the community while maintaining the standards of the professional model.

Team policing sought to enhance police–community relations by increasing police–citizen interaction within designated communities. Patrol officers, with some assistance from specialists, were assigned to specific geographic areas. These areas were to become "their community." Service delivery would become more personal and would gain community support as a result of this interaction. Team policing concepts varied from conventional patrol delivery in the following aspects:

1. Geographic stability of the patrol team.
2. A combination of patrol and investigative functions.
3. Lower-level flexibility in policymaking.
4. Maximum interaction among team members.
5. Maximum communication among team members and the community (Roberg and Kuykendall, 1990, pp. 169–170).

Although the intentions of team policing were commendable, the attempts to turn large city policing into small town policing failed. Community relations were somewhat improved, but lack of support from middle managers who perceived the decentralized geographic areas and team concept as threatening to their control, lack of dispatching technology that resulted in patrol movement within geographic communities, a lack of clarity as to the role of team officers, and resentment from other officers who perceived the teams as being elitist doomed the early efforts of team policing (Roberg and Kuykendall, 1990; Sherman, Milton and Kelly, 1973).

Integrated Criminal Apprehension Program

In 1975, the Law Enforcement Assistance Administration began funding of the Integrated Criminal Apprehension Program (ICAP) that would eventually be implemented, in varying degrees in more than 500 cities. Originally developed as the Patrol Emphasis Program, ICAP was intended to direct patrol resources toward crime problems that were identified through intensive crime analysis. It was envisioned as an operations support concept that would enhance patrol operations, thus providing more efficient service delivery and more effectively addressing community needs (Carter, 1994; Hunter, 1991).

ICAP was both a program and a process for enhanced service delivery. It was a program in that it sought to establish key components that would structure service delivery efforts. These components were crime analysis, operations analysis, secondary receiving, directed patrol activities, managing criminal investigations, career criminal monitoring, and tactical crime prevention. ICAP was a process in that it sought to enhance the provision of services based on data collection, analysis planning, service delivery, and feedback (Grassie and Crowe, 1978).

The success of ICAP was limited due to the complexity of the concept, the requirement for sophisticated planning and analysis, and resistance to change on the part of police officials (Carter, 1994). While many of the components of ICAP were implemented by the participating agencies, most tended to utilize only those portions that fit within their particular service delivery scheme rather than adopting the overall process. As a result, benefits to the communities being served were limited (Hunter, 1990). However, the emphasis on problem identification and response through crime analysis would influence the development of later service enhancement strategies, most notably that of problem-oriented policing.

Neighborhood Foot Patrol

Neighborhood foot patrol emerged during the 1970s as an effort to correct the deficiencies of team policing. Like team policing, this police service delivery style utilized teams assigned within a geographical area. Unlike team policing, it was not an attempt to change overall service delivery strategies within that area. Nor did it require organizational changes to implement its tactics. Instead, the teams emphasized foot patrols within designated neighborhoods. The efforts of these patrol generalists was to interact within the small community that they served. The regular patrol and investigations service delivery within the larger geographical area surrounding the designated neighborhoods was not affected (Carter, 1994).

Two of the early foot patrol programs were experimental programs in Newark, New Jersey and Flint, Michigan. The primary efforts of these programs were to deter crime by maintaining a police presence and to involve citizens in crime prevention efforts. The successes of those programs led to the development of similar programs in Madison, Wisconsin, Baltimore County, Maryland, and Houston, Texas. It also led to the establishment of the National Neighborhood Foot Center at Michigan State University (Trojanowicz and Bucqueroux, 1990).

The reports of enhanced community involvement and reduced crime rates from the early neighborhood foot patrol programs have resulted in expansion of the program to many other cities as well as expansion of the community involvement concept. Foot patrol is not a necessary part of community-oriented policing. Nor does a police agency have to adopt community-oriented policing to utilize foot patrols. However, the neighborhood foot patrol concepts of police and citizens working together, developing trust and sharing power, became the basis for community-oriented policing (Trojanowicz and Bucqueroux, 1990).

Community-Oriented Policing

The successful implementation of neighborhood foot patrol led to the development of more comprehensive strategies designed to enlist community support within designated geographical areas. These strategies have become identified as community-oriented policing.

Community Policing is a new philosophy of policing, based on the concept that police officers and private citizens working together in creative ways can help solve contemporary problems related to crime, the fear of crime, social and physical disorder, and neighborhood decay. The philosophy is predicated on the belief that achieving these goals requires that police departments develop a new relationship with the law-abiding people in the community, allowing them a greater voice in setting local police priorities and involving them in efforts to improve the overall quality of life in their neighborhoods. It shifts the focus of police work from handling random calls to solving community problems.

The Community Policing philosophy is expressed in a new organizational strategy that allows police departments to put theory into practice. This requires freeing some patrol officers from the isolation of the patrol car and the insistent demands of the police radio, so that these officers can maintain direct, face-to-face contact with people in the same defined geographic (beat) area every day. This new Community Policing Officer (CPO) serves as a generalist, an officer whose mission includes developing imaginative, new ways to address the broad spectrum of community concerns embraced by the Community Policing philosophy. The goal is to allow CPO's to own their beat areas, so that they can develop the rapport and trust that is vital in encouraging people to become involved in efforts to address the problems in their neighborhoods. The CPO acts as the department's outreach to the community, serving as the people's link to other public and private agencies that can help. The CPO not only enforces the law, but supports and supervises community-based efforts aimed at local concerns. The CPO allows people direct input in setting day-to-day, local police priorities, in exchange for their cooperation and participation in efforts to police themselves.

Community Policing requires both a philosophical shift in the way that police departments think about their mission, as well as a commitment to the structural changes this new form of policing demands. Community Policing provides a new way for the police to provide decentralized and personalized police service that offers every law-abiding citizen an opportunity to become active in the police process. (Trojanowicz and Bucqueroux, 1990, pp. 5–6)

The definition above is perhaps the most extreme vision of community-oriented policing as a philosophy and would doubtless be the most difficult to implement. Others have attempted to address the topic using more simplistic terminology. Holden (1992, p. 133) defined community-oriented policing as an "approach based on the assumption that policing a city's neighborhoods is best done at the individual neighborhood level rather than by centralized command" in which police "focus on value statements rather than mission statements as a means to direct and control officer behavior." Skolnick and Bayley (1986) emphasized that community-oriented policing consisted of the four innovations of reciprocity, a real decentralization of command, reorientation of patrol, and civilianization. Walker (1992, p. 176) refers to community-oriented policing as "a new strategy for delivering basic police services. It includes a shift away from responding to calls for service and an emphasis on police officer involvement in long-term strategies to improve the quality of life in neighborhoods."

Community-oriented policing is seen by its advocates as the solution to the reactive practices of traditional service delivery models. The community-oriented model utilizes a flexible philosophy of community involvement that transcends community relations but is not strategy specific. This flexibility is community-oriented policing's greatest asset. Unfortunately, it is also community-oriented policing's greatest weakness. Police practitioners, as well as police scholars, often do not understand how to apply this concept successfully. The results are attempts to classify all community relations efforts as being true community-oriented policing.

Problem-Oriented Policing

Another innovation operational style that has been utilized by police in recent years is problem-oriented policing. While community-oriented policing is a broad effort to develop new relationships within all or designated parts of a community, problem-oriented policing is a narrower effort to deal with a specific problem (Goldstein, 1990). In problem-oriented policing there are no demands for the total restructuring of police organizations, nor is there insistence that decision making be shared with the community (Trojanowicz and Bucqueroux, 1990). Community involvement is encouraged, but it is noted that those areas of cities which require the greatest police attention often have little sense of community (Goldstein, 1990).

Problem-oriented policing attempts to engage productively with the community by "(1) assigning officers to areas for longer periods of time to enable them to identify the problems of concern to the community; (2) developing the capacity of both officers and the department to analyze community problems; (3) learning when greater community involvement has the potential for significantly reducing a problem; and (4) working with those specific segments of the community that are in a position to assist in reducing or eliminating the problem" (Goldstein, 1990, pp. 26–27).

Problem-oriented policing is considered to be superior to traditionally reactive service delivery in that like the previously discussed Integrated Criminal Apprehension Program, proactive planning and analysis governs resource allocation decisions. In this model, "problem solving is a central element, not a peripheral activity as in traditional policing. Everyone in the department contributes to its mission, not just a few innovative officers or a special unit. And, this problem solving approach places special emphasis on careful analysis of problems before developing solutions and seeks to avoid instant answers that are unsupported by good information" (Eck and Spelman, 1989, p. 96).

According to its proponents, problem-oriented policing is also superior to community-oriented policing in that it does not require departments to decentralize decision making or abandon crime control and service functions (Eck and Spelman, 1989; Goldstein, 1990). Unfortunately, problem-oriented policing has been wrongly associated with community-oriented policing to the point that both police practitioners and police scholars are hesitant to embrace it.

Like community-oriented policing, the application of problem-oriented policing suffers when police administrators adopt the terminology without understanding the concept or its applications. To be successful, problem-solving efforts, which address the needs of the public, not the police administration, should become the standard method of policing rather than an occasional tactic. And police administrators should attempt to get all departmental members involved in solving problems based upon thorough analysis. The creation of special "POP squads" or encouraging specific officers to utilize problem-solving techniques is not enough (Eck and Spelman, 1990).

COMMUNITY POLICING TODAY

The emphasis in policing today is on community-oriented operational styles which will bring the community and the police together in a concerted effort to prevent disorder. Unfortunately, the success of such a service model is hampered by the lack of community consensus within a diverse and increasingly fragmented nation. There is no single geographical community with whom the police must relate but as we have said earlier, a complex system of overlapping and frequently competing internal and external communities in constant interaction.

The community-oriented approaches are further hampered by the lack of clarity provided by their proponents in regard to application. Police agencies have great difficulty implementing these models because no one really seems to know whether they are programs or philosophies. In addition, community policing terminologies have been usurped by many police administrators who desire to appear progressive and wish to enhance community relations but who have neither the desire nor the intent to abandon the contemporary reactive model of delivering police services. To do so would require enhanced fiscal resources, a consensus of public support, a widespread acceptance by rank-and-file police employees, and solid commitment by top administrators.

THE FUTURE OF COMMUNITY POLICING

Community policing, as currently practiced, has limited application to those diverse police organizations (local, state, federal, and special district) which perform a myriad of duties outside of patrolling inner-city neighborhoods. The new community orientation, where applicable, may give the citizens a warm feeling toward the police but does not actually appear to enhance protection for the public. This approach projects a great deal of style but too frequently reveals little substance. Yet the need to obtain citizen involvement in the delivery of police services is so crucial that community-oriented models are expected to dominate American policing in the near future (Trojanowicz and Bucqueroux, 1994). However, until the previously discussed problems are resolved through the development of an operational model that is easily understood and readily implemented, the benefits of community policing will be limited.

Traditional Disguised as Community Policing

Due to the lack of clarity as to the role and philosophy of community-oriented policing and its confusion with the proactive strategies of problem-oriented policing, many of today's police administrators seek to appear progressive by labeling their traditional service delivery techniques with community-oriented or problem-oriented titles. Despite valiant efforts by community-oriented proponents to foster understanding, management strategies, while disguised by buzzwords (Hunter and Barker, 1993), continue to be reactive in nature. Despite "catchy" labels assigned to specific units or functions, the basis for service delivery continues to be response to citizen-generated calls for service and pressures brought by civic and political leaders (Walker, 1992; Hunter, 1991).

Professional with Concessions to Community Policing

Professionalization was an attempt to build on the previous police innovations of legalization and militarization. The goals of professionalization were higher-caliber personnel, enhanced technical service, increases in the use of research, and greater autonomy from politics (Walker, 1992). The desired products of these professional innovations were enhanced efficiency and strict accountability.

Professionalization, for the most part, focused on developing professional police administrators who would use rigorous selection criteria, intensified training, and strict discipline to ensure that police personnel performed their duties in a proper manner. Police services to the public benefited from this model and its emphasis on efficiency. Unfortunately, professionalism relied on and (continues to rely on) a reactive philosophy of service delivery that tends to overemphasize crime fighting. We would argue that today, most police agencies continue to operate under the professional model despite arguments for more proactive efforts.

Professional Services Policing: A New Community Policing Model

A new proactive police service model is sorely needed, but it should not (and cannot) discard all previous service strategies in order to do so. The professional model, while reactive and arguably lacking in community interaction, is well known and understood by police administrators and line personnel. Officers are taught in their basic training that they are to act in a professional manner, and this emphasis is continually reinforced within police agencies by both line and staff personnel. That the police are not a true profession is a moot point.

The advantage of building on the professional model is that professionalism is not a complex academic philosophy nor an administrative buzzword (like community-oriented policing) but a term that police at all levels are already familiar with and which is frequently used in police training. By adding the proactive policing strategies of problem-oriented policing to the professional model and stressing that *professional services include all police activities, not just crime control,* the needs of today's communities can be met.

What is needed is a model that utilizes the strategies of problem-oriented policing, is easily understood by police officers and administrators, addresses all types of police service delivery, is appealing to the communities served, and which actually enhances both crime control and community relations. Such a model is available and can be implemented in any police agency regardless of mission. We refer to this model as *professional services policing.* It is, to a large extent, a return to the Peelian concept of policing (Hunter and Barker, 1994).

Professional services policing would readily incorporate problem-oriented policing's service enhancement strategies. It would move beyond previous service models by including *all* police functions, not just patrol. In addition, it has the potential to cover all types of agencies, not just municipal police departments. By presenting professional services as total services, those agencies that have historically viewed themselves as crime fighters could not emphasize protection of rights and proactive crime prevention. The product would maintain the professional model's emphasis on integrity, discipline, education, and training, while adding proactive services which focus on community involvement and coordination of efforts.

Many police agencies are not at the stage of development where they can benefit from a community policing style. They are still struggling with basic issues such as the development of policies and procedures and how to organize themselves. A combined model is needed to give them the guidance they require. Fortunately, this is being done in part through the standards developed for law enforcement accreditation. Unfortunately, those agencies that most need assistance are among the last to enter the accreditation process. The professional services model, which is compatible with accreditation, would fill this void by emphasizing efficiency, effectiveness, and civic accountability within contemporary police organizational structures.

CONCLUSIONS

The provision of police services in the United States has seen considerable change during the past two centuries. Initially, citizens were responsible for policing themselves, due to the lack of adequate police organizations capable of providing police services. As police organizations have evolved, they have utilized a variety of service delivery styles. Unfortunately, efforts to enhance discipline, effectiveness, and efficiency have too frequently resulted in isolation from the communities being served. Today's community policing strategies seek to restore the ties to those communities.

Like its predecessors, community policing as a model of police service delivery is in a constant state of evolution. Problems of conceptual complexity and difficulty of implementation have yielded mixed results among the strategies utilized thus far. Police scholars and practitioners are currently seeking to develop a community policing model that addresses these issues. Despite these challenges, community involvement in the delivery of police services is the police style of the future.

STUDENT CHECKLIST

1. Describe the evolution of police service delivery styles in the United States.
2. Discuss the differences between police–community relations and community policing.
3. Discuss the differences between the traditional model of policing, the professional model of policing, and community policing.
4. Contrast the differences between community-oriented policing and problem-oriented policing.
5. What are the strengths and weaknesses of community policing?
6. What must be done to make community policing work in the United States?

TOPICS FOR DISCUSSION

1. What degree of community involvement in policing do you believe is appropriate in your community?

2. If you were a police chief in a large city, would you attempt to implement community policing? Why or why not?

3. Assume that you are a police chief in a large city and you have been ordered by the city council to initiate some form of community policing. What strategies would you choose, and how would you seek to implement them?

ONE STEP FORWARD

Comparison of Community Policing to Police–Community Relations[1]

Community Policing	*Police–Community Relations*
Goal: Solve problems—improved relations with citizens is a welcome by-product.	**Goal:** Change attitudes and project a positive image—improved relations with citizens is a main focus.
Line Function: Regular contact between officers and citizens	**Staff Function:** Irregular contact between officers and citizens.
A department-wide philosophy and department-wide acceptance.	Isolated acceptance often localized in the PCR unit.
Internal and external influence and respect for officers.	Limited influence and respect for officers.
Well defined role—does both proactive and reactive policing—a full-service officer.	Loose role definition; focus on dealing with problems of strained relations between police and citizens; crime prevention encouraged.
Direct service—same officer takes complaints and gives crime prevention tips.	Indirect service—advice on crime prevention from PCR officer but "regular" officers respond to complaints.
Citizens identify problems and cooperate in setting up the police agenda.	"Blue Ribbon" committees identify the problems and "preach" to police.
Police accountability is ensured by the citizens receiving the service in addition to administrative mechanisms.	Police accountability is ensured by civilian review boards and formal police supervision.
Officer is the leader and catalyst for change in the neighborhood to reduce fear, disorder, decay and crime.	Officer provides consultation on crime issues without having identified beat boundaries or "field responsibilities."
Chief of police is an advocate and sets the tone for the delivery of both law enforcement and social services in the jurisdictions.	Chief of police reacts to only the law enforcement concerns of special interest groups.
Officers educate public about issues (like response time or preventive patrol) and the need to prioritize services.	Officers focus on racial and ethnic tension issues and encourage increased services.
Increased trust between the police officer and citizens because of long-term,	Cordial relationship between police officer and citizens but often superfi-

[1]From R. Trojanowicz and B. Bucqueroux (1994) *Community Policing: How To Get Started.* Cincinnati, OH: Anderson.

regular contact results in an enhanced flow of information to the police.

Officer is continually accessible in person, by telephone, or in a decentralized office.

Regular visibility in the neighborhood.

Officer is viewed as having a "stake in the community."

Officer is a role model because of regular contact with citizens (especially youth role model).

Influence is from "the bottom up"—citizens receiving service help set priorities and influence police policy.

Meaningful organizational change and departmental restructuring—ranging from officer selection to training, evaluation, and promotion.

When intervention is necessary, informal social control is the first choice.

Officer encourages citizens to solve many of their own problems and volunteer to assist neighbors.

Officer encourages other service providers like animal control, firefighters, and mail carriers to become involved in community problem solving.

Officer mobilizes all community resources, including citizens, private and public agencies, and private business.

Success is determined by the reduction in citizen fear, neighborhood disorder, and crime.

All officers are sworn personnel.

cial trust with minimum information flow to prevent and solve crime.

Intermittent contact with the public because of city-wide responsibility; contact is made through central headquarters.

Officer seldom seen "on the streets."

Officer is viewed as an "outsider."

Citizens do not get to know officer on an intense basis.

Influence is from "the top down"—those who "know best" have input and make decisions.

Traditional organization stays intact with "new" programs periodicaly added; no fundamental organizational change."

When intervention is necessary, formal means of control is typically the first choice.

Citizens are encouraged to volunteer but are told to request and expect more government (including law enforcement) services.

Service providers stay in traditional roles.

Officers do not have mobilization responsibility because there is no specific beat area for which they are responsible.

Success is determined by traditional measures—i.e., crime rates and citizen satisfaction with the police.

Most staff members are sworn personnel but some are non-sworn.

BIBLIOGRAPHY

Barker, T., Hunter, R. D., and Rush, J. P. (1994). *Police Systems and Practices: An Introduction.* Englewood Cliffs, N.J.: Prentice Hall.

Beckman, E. (1980). *Law Enforcement in a Democratic Society.* Chicago: Nelson-Hall.

Berman, J. S. (1987). *Police Administration and Progressive Reform: Theodore Roosevelt as Police Commissioner of New York.* New York: Greenwood Press.

Bopp, W. J., and Schultz, D. O. (1977). *A Short History of American Law Enforcement.* Springfield, Ill.: Charles C Thomas.

Carte, G. E., and Carte, E. H. (1975). *Police Reform in the United States: The Era of August Vollmer, 1905–1932.* Berkeley, Calif.: University of California Press.

Carte, G. E., and Carte, E. H. (1977). "O. W. Wilson: police theory in action," in P. J. Stead (Ed.), *Pioneers in Policing.* Montclair, N.J.: Patterson Smith.

Carter, D. L. (1994). "Community policing," Chapter 13 in T. Barker, R. D. Hunter, and J. P. Rush (Eds.), *Police Systems and Practices: An Introduction.* Englewood Cliffs, N.J.: Prentice Hall.

Cole, G. F. (1992). *The American System of Criminal Justice,* 6th ed. Pacific Grove, Calif.: Brooks/Cole.

Critchley, T. A. (1977). "Peel, Rowan, and Mayne: The British model of urban police," in P. J. Stead (Ed.), *Pioneers in Policing.* Montclair, N.J.: Patterson Smith.

Critchley, T. A. (1985). "Constables and justices of the peace," in W. C. Terry III (Ed.), *Policing Society: An Occupational View.* New York: Wiley.

Davis, E. M. (1977). "Developing police involvement" *The Police Chief,* April.

Eck, J. E., and Spelman, W. (1989). "A problem-oriented approach to police service delivery," in D. J. Kenney (Ed.), *Police and Policing: Contemporary Issues.* New York: Praeger.

Eck, J. E., and Spelman, W. (1990). "Problem-solving: problem-oriented policing in Newport News," in R. G. Dunham and G. P. Alpert (Eds.), *Critical Issues in Policing: Contemporary Readings.* Prospect Heights, Ill.: Waveland Press.

Federal Bureau of Investigation (1993). *Crime in the United States.* Washington, D.C.: U.S. Department of Justice.

Goldstein, H. (1990). *Problem-Oriented Policing.* New York: McGraw-Hill.

Grassie, R. G., and Crowe, T. D. (1978). *Integrated Criminal Apprehension Program: Program Implementation Guide.* Washington, D.C.: U.S. Department of Justice.

Holden, R. (1992). *Law Enforcement: An Introduction.* Englewood Cliffs, N.J.: Prentice Hall, Inc.

Hunter, R. D. (1990). "Three models of policing," *Police Studies,* Vol. 13, No. 3; pp. 118–124.

Hunter, R. D. (1991). "The failure of ICAP at the Tallahassee Police Department," paper presented at the Southern Criminal Justice Association Annual Meeting, Montgomery, Ala.

Hunter, R. D., and Barker, T. (1993). "BS and buzzwords: The new police operational style," *American Journal of Police,* (X11)(3): 157–168.

Jacobs, J. (1966). *Prelude to Riot.* New York: Vantage Books.

Johnson, D. R. (1981). *American Law Enforcement: A History.* St. Louis, Mo.: Forum Press.

Johnson, H. A. (1988). *History of Criminal Justice.* Cincinnati, Ohio: Pilgrimage Press.

MacNamara, D. E. J. (1977). "August Vollmer: The vision of police professionalism," in Phillip John Stead (Ed.), *Pioneers in Policing.* Montclair, N.J.: Patterson Smith.

Miller, W. R. (1977). *Cops and Bobbies: Police Authority in New York and London, 1830–1870.* Chicago: University of Chicago Press.

Reppetto, T. A. (1978). *The Blue Parade.* New York: Free Press.

Roberg, R. R., and Kuykendall, J. (1990). *Police Organization and Management: Behavior, Theory and Process.* Pacific Grove, Calif.: Brooks/Cole.

Senna, J. J., and Siegal, L. J. (1993). *Introduction to Criminal Justice,* 6th ed. New York: West.

Sherman, L., Milton, C., and Kelly, T. (1973). *Team Policing: Seven Case Studies.* Washington, D.C.: Police Foundation.

Skolnick, J., and Bayley, B. H. (1986). *The New Blue Line: Police Innovation in Six American Cities.* New York: Free Press.

Stead, P. J. (1985). *The Police of Britain.* New York: Macmillan.

Trojanowicz, R., and Bucqueroux, B. (1990). *Community Policing: A Contemporary Perspective.* Cincinnati, Ohio: Anderson.

Trojanowicz, R. C., and Bucqueroux, B. (1994). *Community Policing: How to Get Started.* Cincinnati, Ohio: Anderson.

Walker, S. (1977). *A Critical History of Police Reform.* Lexington, Mass.: Lexington Books.

Walker, S. (1992). *The Police in America: An Introduction,* 2nd ed. New York: McGraw-Hill.

Wilson, J. Q. (1968). *Varieties of Police Behavior.* Cambridge, Mass.: Harvard University Press.

14

COMMUNITY CONTROL:
A CONTINUUM
OF PARTICIPATION

Perhaps, the most significant aspect of police–community relations remains as the context in which the police and the community work together in an effort to reduce criminal activity and insure the safety of citizens. (Miller and Braswell, 1993)

Throughout this book, the word *community* has included all the many environments where police work. Community as a term means common unity, common goals meeting common needs, but such a definition seems out of place in most urban settings. Small towns, too, may be separated into many communities with sometimes conflicting needs. Group interests and values are varied and complicated and have a direct impact on the working environment of the police officer.

There is little argument today with the statement that citizen participation in the justice process is crucial to its effectiveness. Never before in this country has each individual citizen been so aware of crime and its personal cost. Citizens are also more aware that they must participate in their own protection and be responsible for their own actions. We have come to appreciate Greenberg's urging that "there is something magical about the power of self-help" (1977, p. 60). But at what level should this participation exist? Do we need modern-day vigilantes? Should we spend huge sums of money on security devices and security personnel? Should we have civilian review boards to control police misconduct? What should volunteers be allowed to do within justice agencies?

In this chapter we address the concept of community control. It is not our purpose to advocate any particular model of community control, nor even to convince the reader of the value of such a concept. Rather, it is our purpose to provide the reader with an objective description and analysis of some of the methods of community participation currently being considered or implemented in criminal justice.

STUDYING THIS CHAPTER WILL ENABLE YOU TO:

1. Define the concept of community control.
2. Describe the factors that influenced the development of community control efforts.
3. Describe the factors that create resistance to community control.
4. Contrast several methods of community participation in the provision of police services.
5. Compare the effectiveness of different styles of community control.

THE CONCEPT OF COMMUNITY CONTROL

Little agreement exists on a definition of community control. The term is generally defined to suit the purposes of a specific analysis, and depends to a large extent on what subject is being investigated. Definitions range from meaning the community's absolute control over an organization (of which there are few examples) to the ability of a community to exercise some degree of input into the organization (of which there are many examples) (Figure 14-1).

What Is a Community?

To understand the concept of community control, we must first review the major characteristics of community:

1. Group interaction that may be deliberate or unintentional, positive or negative, ranging from conflict to cooperation.
2. Shared boundaries that may be largely geographical (simply a common physical location), common interests (professional, social, economic, or political), or common history, values, goals, needs, or some combination of these.

Not Enough Community Participation	Appropriate Community Participation	Too Much Community Participation

Not enough community participation results in isolation of the police from the communities they are supposed to serve. This may lead to inappropriate behavior on the part of the police which is detrimental to democratic principles and the welfare of citizens.

Appropriate levels of community participation results in crime prevention strategies and involvement in police decision making which serve the best interests of both the police and citizens.

Too much community participation results in power struggles among competing interest groups which may lead to discriminatory practices, corruption, and ineffectiveness on the part of the police.

FIGURE 14-1   Community control continuum: the need for balance.

In the first chapter we stated the fact that realistically, the environment where police work is fragmented, segmentalized, and sometimes many "communities" with competing goals making up a larger community of people living together within a common geographical area and sharing some common needs. The justice community is described as systems within systems interacting with one another within legal boundaries. One of the key problems of community relations is that all of these communities are part of the relationship and their uncommon needs, as well as their common ones, must be defined and addressed.

What Is Control?

The use of the word *control* is equally difficult to pinpoint. Some writers have used control in an absolute context to mean "the ability to impose one's views upon others by the threat or use of power." Control can also mean the "opportunity to check, regulate, or keep within certain limits the actions of others," or "the legitimate authority and power to govern." Defined in this manner, control is used in the context of providing an equilibrium and a measure of accountability. Finally, control can be used more indirectly to include the ability to communicate with, to influence, to vote for, to participate, or to exercise impact with important decision makers. Used in this manner, control emphasizes the ability to interact with people. Each of these definitions of control can be found to some extent in the criminal justice system. Prisoners' riots can be reviewed as an attempt to exercise control by threat or use of force. Civilian review boards, developed to handle citizen complaints against the police, are examples of the community's attempt to control by way of regulation and accountability. Recent citizen voting initiatives to reinstate the death penalty, citizen support of community-based correctional and diversionary programs, and citizen participation on criminal justice advisory councils are examples of community control by interaction.

What Is Community Control?

Community control is a continuum of citizen participation. It is multifaceted, ever-changing, and encompasses a wide range of citizen involvement. Degree of participation varies with community characteristics and community goals. If the intent is to destroy the political system, threat or use of violence might be considered an effective use of control. If improving the relationship between police and citizens is the goal, efforts might be centered around assessing mutual needs and fears and opening new avenues of communication. The continuum of citizen participation includes a wide range of activities pursued at various levels of the criminal justice system.

Several key questions may be helpful in analyzing the nature of existing citizen participation (Altshuler, 1970, pp. viii–ix). From what community is the demand for increased involvement coming? How likely is it to persist or mushroom? What type of increased participation does the community desire? How does the demand for increased participation fit into the general framework of American culture and politics? What are the types of interest affected by increased community control? How is the community being defined? What mode of representation or accountability does it seek?

DEVELOPMENT OF COMMUNITY CONTROL

New Demands

Today, more and more citizens are demanding a greater voice in the decisions that affect them. They feel that government has become too far removed from their needs and from public accountability.

The criminal justice system has not remained isolated from these accusations. The police, who are the most visible arm of the government at the community level, are often accused of representing the force of the dominant white class and of employing differential treatment and unnecessary brutality. The courts, too, have been criticized. These criticisms range from accusations of uneven justice to a questioning of judicial standards and accountability. The bail system, plea bargaining, and sentencing criteria are viewed as arbitrary decisions that are no longer responsive to the changing mores of the communities being served. Attacks aimed at the correctional system center around its perceived inability to rehabilitate the criminal so that he/she is no longer a threat to society.

The demand for increased participation by various communities comes from an apparent realization on the part of the citizens that they have a stake in making the components of the criminal justice system operate at a level responsive to their needs. This realization of citizen responsibility is being translated into citizen action. No longer is the aroused citizen content to permit the professionals to solve alone the problems of the police, courts, and corrections. Instead, the emphasis has seemingly switched from "*They* should do more" to "*We* can do more." Examples of this are numerous. Groups of citizens have organized to monitor the performance levels of the police, courts, and corrections.

When the community is dissatisfied, pressure to improve the performance is generated from the community to the relevant administrator or elected official. The pressure is sometimes direct in the form of filing numerous complaints against a specific agency; at other times, it is more indirect and takes the form of citizen ballot initiatives or community support of alternative candidates. Judging from recent municipal, state, and national elections, "law and order" has become a visible issue that few office-seekers can afford to ignore.

A Clear Necessity

As the National Advisory Commission on Criminal Justice Standards and Goals pointed out:

> Government programs for the control of crime are unlikely to succeed all alone. Informed private citizens, playing a variety of roles, can make a decisive difference in the prevention, detection, and prosecution of crime, the fair administration of justice, and the restoration of offenders to the community. (National Advisory Commission, 1973, p. CC-7)

Citizen and community involvement in the justice system is not viewed as merely desirable: It is a necessity.

An Old Concept

Community control of the justice system is not a new or a radical concept. It dates back to the time when peace was kept by the entire community (e.g., when citizens spotted crimes, they were supposed to notify their neighbors so that they all could apprehend the criminal). As time passed and society became more complex, communities delegated these responsibilities to criminal justice specialists, but they did not abdicate them. Thus many feel that responsibility and accountability for planning, decision, and action regarding criminal justice should be returned, insofar as is practicable, to the community.

Systems and Community Values

The police occupy a strategic position in any society, because they are charged with the responsibility of enforcing the norms of society. In order to perform this role, they must interact with the members of society. The importance of this interaction and cooperation varies with the nature of the total society. In a strictly regulated society, conflict in values becomes less important because individual values tend to be less important. In societies where the individual member is considered to be important, value conflicts become vital to the system's maintenance of the community, and the police value system must accommodate community values to a greater degree.

Problems of Community Control

Community Resistance to Community Control

The recognition of the usefulness of citizen involvement or community control is not universally accepted by either the average citizen or by the professionals employed in the criminal justice system. By its very nature, community control is reactive. It is only when conditions become unacceptable that citizens are aroused from apathy and are motivated to devote time, imagination, and energy to a particular cause. The civil rights movement of the 1960s, the college student demonstrations over the invasion of Cambodia in 1970, and demonstrations by women's rights organizations, Gay Liberation, Gray Panthers and Women Against Rape, Antinuclear groups, and others that continue to represent strong issues in the 1990s, are examples of an aroused citizenry.

Even most of the organized Neighborhood Crime Prevention efforts occur after several people in a neighborhood have been victimized rather than as true primary prevention. Communities react when the services provided are no longer acceptable to them. Even then, it is not the entire community that responds, but rather only the energetic and sufficiently aroused citizen. It is a difficult task to enlist the support of the unaffected citizen. The National Advisory Commission on Criminal Justice Standards and Goals emphasized this point and its implications.

> There appears to be a widespread assumption that it is the business of the criminal justice system to respond to this demand and to marshall all available resources to choke off crime at its roots. This viewpoint neglects the certainty that unless a worried citizenry

can translate its indignation into active participation in the search for and implementation of an effective solution, the criminal justice system must inevitably fall even farther behind in its crime control and rehabilitation efforts. Awakening the conscience of America is a necessity because if the multiplicity of factors that produce crime and delinquency are not recognized and remedied, more crime will occur, more of it will go undetected, and the inadequateness of the system will thus become even stronger incentive to further illegal activity. (National Advisory Commission, 1973, p. CC-2)

Professional Resistance to Community Control

Beyond marshaling citizen support and involvement in the criminal justice system, advocates for increased citizen participation point out the need to instill a willingness on the part of the police, courts, and corrections to use available citizen input effectively. Many studies indicate that the three components of the justice system are reluctant to involve citizens in their operations. Many employees view such participation as an attempt to minimize their professional expertise (Trojanowicz and Bucqueroux, 1994).

In addition, there is a natural suspicion of outsiders on the part of any organization. As was pointed out earlier in this chapter, scientific management is, of itself, sometimes a barrier to citizen participation. It is established public administration theory that much organizational energy is spent in self-sustaining activities. Proposed reforms tend to be evaluated in terms of their efficiency in protecting the organization's welfare and their ability to minimize the required expenditure of energy (Roberg and Kuykendall, 1990). The organization's employees reinforce this tendency by developing patterns of behavior that further insulate the organization from the community. Their members often prefer to maintain the status quo despite public demands for change. They may be more resistant to community input than members of other organizations, because of the fragmentation of their services into separate local units, their method of recruitment and promotion, and their degree of isolation from the general public as well as from one another.

TWO TYPES OF COMMUNITY CONTROL

According to the role assigned to citizens, community control can take two general forms: pure and participative. In pure community control, members of the community regulate operations of components of the criminal justice system. In participative community control, the community supplements and complements operations of the system. The following discussion describes examples of pure and participative community control.

Pure Community Control

A unique characteristic of pure community control is that it has been directed primarily at the police, policing agencies are the most visible form of government at the community level, and police officers the primary initiators of action in the entire justice system. When police officers make the decision to arrest, they are making a formal determination of whether or not the potential arrestee should be processed into the criminal justice system. What happens at the police level determines to a greater degree what the rest of the criminal justice system is capable of doing. The initial and most expansive sorting out of "criminals" from "average citizens" is done by the police officer: Only those arrested by the police can be adjudicated by the courts and rehabilitated by corrections. For these reasons, much public attention and concern centers around the operations of law enforcement agencies.

This section reviews briefly five major developments in the area of pure community control of the police. These developments are (1) the attempt to establish civilian complaint review boards, (2) the attempt to create an ombudsman to review citizen complaints against the police, (3) the attempt to decentralize the police politically and administratively, (4) the attempt to ride patrol on the police in the community, and (5) the attempt to affect the establishment of enforcement priorities.

Civilian Review Boards

Origins. Most law enforcement agencies have some internal machinery for reviewing allegations of misconduct against their agents. Dissatisfaction with this machinery, particularly among members of minority groups, has led to the establishment of civilian review boards in several American cities, usually in the face of severe police opposition.

The Nature of Civilian Review Boards. The typical civilian review board consists of seven to nine members, including some members of the police, but with a civilian majority. Usually, the civilians were appointed by the mayor and the police members were named by the police commissioner. The size of the administrative and investigative staffs varies from board to board.

The Controversy over the Boards. Wherever they have been proposed or implemented, civilian review boards have provoked controversy, and some have been reorganized or disbanded (e.g., the New York City board was voted out of existence after a heated campaign). Below are some of the leading arguments pro and con.

1. *Pro.* Advocates of the boards claim that they:
   a. Create a climate in which citizens can freely state their complaints about police misconduct.
   b. Educate the public about their legal rights.
   c. Provide for public exoneration of police officers by an impartial agency.
   d. Are primarily concerned with getting at the truth (not with protecting the police department).
2. *Con.* Opponents of the boards argue that they:
   a. Destroy police administrators' authority to investigate and discipline their officers.
   b. Demoralize police officers and make them hesitant to act on complaints.

c. Are probably biased against the police and, in any case, are staffed by civilians unqualified to judge the performance of police officers.

The Office of Professional Standards (OPS)

The Office of Professional Standards was established in 1974 in Chicago in an attempt to combine the best qualities of civilian and internal review. It operates as a part of the personal staff of the police superintendent. OPS investigators are civilians, and the office is closer to the police department than a civilian review board. It is administered separately but reports to the superintendent, works out of police headquarters, and is part of the police budget. The superintendent retains the final decision-making power on disciplinary action. No objective measure of the success of OPS is available, but it appears to have a wide support base (Rodriguez, 1992).

The Ombudsman

Some cities and states have explored the idea of establishing an ombudsman as an alternative to the civilian review board concept. The ombudsman concept in government is fairly new to Americans, but it has been in existence in Sweden since 1809.

The ombudsman concept is similar to the civilian review board in that it is external to the police department and has the power to act upon any complaints received from aggrieved citizens. It differs from the civilian review board in the sense that it handles complaints lodged against all governmental agencies, including the city manager's office, fire department, and department of public works. The department or agency named in the complaint is obligated to assist the ombudsman in the investigation of the complaint. If the complaint is found to be justified, the ombudsman notifies the concerned agency and advises the proper administrator of the action required to relieve the situation. The administrator reports back to the ombudsman when the corrective steps have been taken. At this point, the ombudsman notifies the complainant of the disposition of his complaint.

The ombudsman approach appears to have several advantages in terms of the community. Again, like the civilian review board, it provides the opportunity for citizen complaints to be aired in an environment of seeming impartiality. A measure of government accountability is inherent in the process.

The opposition to the concept has been primarily from law enforcement. The police argue that their work is unique, especially when compared with that of firefighters, public works employees, the city manager's office, or even city council members. Many law enforcement administrators question whether someone unfamiliar with police practices can adequately appraise what would constitute correct police procedure in a given situation.

Community Policing

In response to various communities' demands for greater participation in the functioning of law enforcement agencies, many police administrators have initiated changes designed to bring officers into closer contact with the communities being served. These changes have taken a number of forms, many of which fall under the name "community policing." The basic goals of community policing are to return greater responsibility to those doing the actual policing at the community level and to provide for increased citizen involvement in crime prevention and police service delivery. Community policing was discussed in detail in Chapter 13.

Citizen and Community Alert Programs

In August 1966, a civic group was organized in San Francisco called "Citizens Alert." This program was developed as an alternative to police review boards, and was composed of people interested in police work. Its purpose was to facilitate communication between the police and the community and to collect, analyze, and report police misconduct. One method used was to have someone on call day and night who could respond to complaints of alleged police misconduct. Legal and medical services were also available. The organization investigated the complaint independently and registered its findings with the relevant police agency.

The proponents of the group emphasize the importance of its independent status and its grass roots appeal. The opponents stress its ineffectiveness in handling complaints; because the group is not present at the incidents, their investigations are based solely on the testimony of the complainants.

The "Community Alert Patrol" is similar in some ways to the "Citizens Alert." The former has augmented its approach by using community residents to follow police cars in the neighborhood to observe and document police activity. The participants use "community alert" cars and carry flash cameras, tape recorders, and two-way radios. This approach was developed in the Watts community of Los Angeles and has been implemented with varying degrees of success in several other communities.

Participative Community Control

Participative community control has been defined as the community's willingness to function in the capacity of supplementing and complementing the operations of the criminal justice system. Four key roles may be identified as being central to participative community control. They are: the volunteers—those who work directly with the person being assisted; the social persuaders—persons of influence or elite status in the dominant social system who are willing to persuade others to support criminal justice programs; the gatekeepers of opportunities—those who control the access to important social systems; and intimates—persons who possess a common background or understanding of the problems confronting the person to be assisted (O'Leary, 1969, p. 99). The effective balancing of these roles by a program coordinator can be of valuable assistance in generating a successful program in the community.

Unlike *pure* community control, *participative* community control is directed toward augmenting and providing supportive services to the justice system. The most obvious examples of participative control are found in the support and development of diversionary and community-based treatment facilities.

Volunteers in Criminal Justice Agencies

Volunteer work in justice agencies has increased tremendously in recent years. Some programs for police volunteers are limited to specific areas of service (e.g., search and rescue), whereas others are much more broadly based. Some police agencies now use volunteers in records, patrol, traffic control, community liaison, and crime prevention functions. Police reserve officer programs are now found in most major American cities. Although the training and duties of these volunteer officers vary from agency to agency, they are generally extensively trained and function in most of the ways paid officers function. Many agencies draw their officers from this volunteer pool. Most citizens in reserve programs, however, are not seeking full-time police service. They come from many professions, usually with above average incomes. They volunteer to provide a public service and to enjoy the challenge of the job (Sklarewitz, 1979, pp. 86–88)

Volunteers now have a place in most justice agencies. Many juvenile courts have well-organized volunteer programs. Corrections agencies, prosecutors' offices, and adult criminal courts are, as a group, less consistent in their use of volunteers than police and juvenile agencies. Even here, however, acceptance of volunteers has increased, and their services are now being utilized in a wide range of functions.

Self-protection Outside the System

Vigilante Patrols.   Volunteer patrols have been formed in some neighborhoods to patrol the area on a regular schedule. Their function is said to be preventive, and if they observe suspicious behavior, they are to report it to the police. Although many patrol members follow such guidelines very well, others take the responsibility for apprehension and/or meeting out justice into their own hands. It is this latter action that concerns the police.

Private Security.   According to a *New York Times* estimate, $12 billion is spent annually on private security in the United States. Many police officers are allowed by their agencies to provide individual guard service (but usually not private investigation). Many sources estimate that the private security officers in the United States now outnumber public police officers by more than 2 to 1. Many large companies now hire and train their own security forces. Hospital security has been among the fastest growing areas in the recent past.

Environmental or target-hardening crime prevention efforts have led individual citizens to invest large sums of money for security devices, attack dogs, firearms, and so on, for personal property protection.

Guardian Angels.   This well-organized group of youths originated in New York City and now functions in 40 other major metropolitan areas. They receive no public funding and perform a security function in high crime areas. Their efforts have received public support and police criticism. They are credited with reducing criminal activity in target areas. They are generally well trained and disciplined, and they intervene to protect citizens (physically, if necessary). They make a citizen's arrest and hold the suspect for the police (Barker, Hunter, and Rush, 1994).

Police Attitudes Toward These Groups

Generally police are critical of these groups, usually citing such problems as the lack of professionalism in private security and the danger of overzealousness in the vigilante patrols. They argue that the Guardian Angels are a potential problem because they are not held accountable for their actions in the ways that police are. They also are unable to screen prospective members adequately and could therefore allow someone with excessive power needs into the group.

Family Crisis Intervention Projects.   The New York City Police Department established a unit to intervene in conflict-ridden family situations and mediate or resolve them before they escalated into violence that would require arrests. The project achieved its designated objectives and also helped to improve police–community relations. Consequently, it has been emulated in other urban areas (see Figure 14-2).

Community Responsibility Programs.   Frequently located in low-income, ethnic, and racial communities, these projects provide an alternative to the official juvenile justice system. Thus, instead of going to court, a juvenile offender in these communities may appear before a panel of residents, adults and youths, who determine his or her responsibility. If found guilty, the juvenile offender may be asked to do some supervised work for the good of the community and perhaps also participate in a counseling program.

Victim-Witness Advocate Programs.   Victims and witnesses are often the "forgotten men and women" of the criminal justice system. In 1976, Pima County, Arizona, set up a program to provide them with short-term counseling, social service referral, and court information. Later the program added a juvenile unit, a mobile unit to deal with family crisis situations, and other programs. Similar models now exist in many areas.

FIGURE 14-2   Officers trained to intervene in family disturbance calls often can mediate or resolve the conflict on the scene. They also may refer the family to various community agencies for counseling. (Courtesy of Tom Mulligan.)

CONCLUSIONS

As long as the criminal justice systems fails to do what citizens expect it to do, demands for community control will exist. Because the police, or indeed the justice system as a whole, cannot function properly in a free society without the help and support of the people it serves, community participation is essential for success.

At every point in the system concerned citizens can become involved in the justice process. The stage, manner, and level of involvement are determined both by the sources available and by the individual's area of interest and level of motivation.

Many models of community control exist. Choosing the "best" model in a specific situation is a matter of understanding the unique characteristics of the community, its citizens, and its criminal justice clientele.

STUDENT CHECKLIST

1. Define *community control.*
2. Why are some communities more desirous of control than other communities?
3. Contrast several different methods of community participation in the criminal justice system.
4. How is police organization a factor in police resistance to community control?
5. Compare the effectiveness of different styles of community control.
6. Investigate the various types of programs available in your community.

TOPICS FOR DISCUSSION

1. What degree of community control do you believe is appropriate in your community?
2. How would you know that a method of community control was effective?
3. Based on your answer to topic 2, what methods of community control mentioned in this chapter are most effective?

ONE STEP FORWARD

The Vera Institute Style of Participation

Merely involving the community is not sufficient. When a community is contemplating making a change in the system, it must recognize the importance of selecting an appropriate method for exerting influence and control. The Vera Institute of Justice in New York City provides a positive example of a private group of citizens working together to improve the criminal justice system. A brief review of their approach to improving the criminal justice system may serve as a model to others who are considering similar actions.

Vera's control strategy was to identify specific problem areas and to experiment with changes that could benefit both the defendant and relevant criminal justice agencies (police, prosecution, courts, and corrections). The efforts of the Vera Institute have resulted in several successful projects in the New York City Police Department. Their latest collaborative effort resulted in the establishment of the Community Patrol Officer Program (CPOP) in the 72nd Precinct in Brooklyn. This program is currently being expanded to include other precincts in New York City (McElroy, Cosgrove, and Sadd, 1993).

The style of participation selected by the Vera Institute is an important facet of their success. Basically, their approach has five steps:

1. The Vera staff identifies the problem, considers the alternatives, and proposes a solution to the affected criminal justice agencies.

2. The institute then provides the personnel to operate the project on a trial basis, thus minimizing the concerned agencies' expenditure of valuable resources.

3. The institute assumes responsibility for the trial phase and continues to remain in close contact with the involved agencies.

4. When the trial phase has been evaluated and is considered to be a success, the institute assumes an advisory role and permits the involved agency to take control of the project.

5. Although no longer formally involved with the project, the institute remains in close association with the agency, available to discuss problems as they arise.

The Vera example illustrates that bureaucratic inaction or citizen apathy need not hamper the development of effective community involvement in the criminal justice system.

BIBLIOGRAPHY

Altshuler, A. A. (1970). *Community Control: The Black Demand for Participation in Large American Cities.* Indianapolis, Ind.: Pegasus.

Barker, T., Hunter, R. D., and Rush, J. P. (1994). *Police Systems and Practices: An Introduction.* Englewood Cliffs, N.J.: Prentice Hall.

Greenberg, M. A. (1977). "Volunteer crime prevention program: A proposal for survival in the third century," *The Police Chief,* April, Vol. XLIV, pp. 60–61.

McElroy, J. E., Cosgrove, C. A., and Sadd, S. (1993). *Community Policing: The CPOP in New York.* Newbury Park, Calif.: Sage Publications.

Miller, L., and Braswell, M. (1993). *Human Relations and Police Work.* Prospect Heights, Ill.: Waveland Press.

National Advisory Commission on Criminal Justice Standards and Goals (1973). *Working*

Papers for the National Conference on Criminal Justice. Washington, D.C.: Law Enforcement Assistance Administration.

O'Leary, V. (1969). "Some directions for citizen involvement in corrections," *The Annals,* Vol. 381, January.

Roberg, R. R., and Kuykendall, J. (1990). *Police Organization and Management: Behavior, Theory and Process.* Pacific Grove, Calif.: Brooks/Cole.

Rodriguez, M. L. (1992). Materials on the Chicago Police Department provided to the authors by Superintendent Rodriguez.

Sklarewitz, N. (1979). "Citizen cop," *American Way,* March.

Trojanowicz, R. C., and Bucqueroux, B. (1994). *Community Policing: How to Get Started.* Cincinnati, Ohio: Anderson.

EPILOGUE:

POLICE–COMMUNITY RELATIONS: A PERSPECTIVE

Police–community relations is very much like a marriage. At its best, a marriage is an ongoing, person-to-person relationship that

- Involves mutual respect and acceptance.
- Involves self-awareness and other-awareness.
- Involves interdependence rather than dependence, so that participants retain their individuality and their separate roles.
- Involves commitment and continuing work on the relationship.
- Involves effective communication and a mutual willingness to listen.
- Involves crises, mutual problem solving, and fun.

These are also the elements of positive, effective police–community relations. Community relations also has the same pitfalls that a marriage has

- We bog it down in details and red tape.
- Sometimes we take it for granted and it suffers from neglect.
- Sometimes our commitment is halfhearted, and then so is the relationship.
- Sometimes we make the assumption that the announced joining of the two parties involved is a reward for effort expended, when in reality, it is the beginning of an agreement to work together.
- Sometimes we pay lip service to the concept but are afraid to risk involving ourselves in the reality of it.

There is at least one major difference. In police–community relations, neither party can file for divorce. For better or worse, they will have a relationship. Wouldn't this be reason enough, even if there were no other reason, for both parties to make the relationship a positive one?

APPENDIX:

CASE STUDIES

1. AS A POLICE OFFICER, WHAT WOULD YOU DO?

Officer Harris was dispatched to 7676 N. Nebraska Avenue in reference to a family fight involving a father and his teenage son. Although, according to police records, fights are frequent occurrences at the Keyes's residence, Officer Harris has never previously been the officer called to the scene.

Upon arrival at the residence, the officer heard yelling and female screaming coming from inside the residence. Officer Harris went to the front of the residence; he noticed that the front door was wide open. Officer Harris went inside and observed that Mr. Robert Keyes had a bloody nose and Dick Keyes, age 17 years, appeared to have a cut mouth and a cut under his left eye.

Officer Harris separated the two combatants. Mr. Robert Keyes began yelling at the officer, "I want my no good son out of this house. Take him to juvie and lock him up!"

Dick Keyes was very upset. He told the officer that he was tired of his father coming home drunk every day and starting a fight with his mother.

Mrs. Mary Keyes was sitting on the living room sofa crying and sobbing.

A backup officer, Officer Daniels, arrived on the scene and also entered the residence. Officer Daniels had been at the residence approximately six hours earlier and told the Keyes that if he came back again, someone was "going to jail."

Officer Daniels told Officer Harris that he had been there earlier and that the situation was somewhat calmer when he left the scene the first time.

Mr. Robert Keyes stated that he wanted his son out of the house and that his wife could leave also. Officer Daniels told Mr. Keyes to keep quiet and he would settle the problem once and for all. Mrs. Keyes stated she wanted her husband arrested for hitting her son and disturbing the peace. Officer Harris asked Mrs. Keyes if she would go to court and prosecute Mr. Robert Keyes. She replied that she would.

Officer Daniels went over to Mr. Keyes and arrested him, handcuffing him with no resistance. As the officers were leading Mr. Keyes outside, Mr. Keyes's son, Dick, came after the officers yelling that they couldn't take his father to jail. Dick Keyes struck and kicked Officer Harris and also struck Officer Daniels. Officer Daniels placed Mr. Robert Keyes in the patrol car and went to assist in physically subduing Dick Keyes. Dick Keyes was arrested for obstruction of justice.

Mrs. Mary Keyes stood in the front doorway of the residence crying uncontrollably as she watched her husband and son being placed in the patrol cars and taken to the city jail and juvenile detention center.

2. WHAT DO YOU THINK OF MR. NEVINS' STORY?

While on patrol, Officer Pope observed a white male hitchhiking on the roadway at approximately 3:00 A.M. at the corner of Frontier and Casas Road. The intersection is poorly lighted, and Casas Road is not heavily traveled.

As the officer stopped his patrol car, he asked the subject for identification. The subject was very nervous and kept trying to bend as if tying his shoes. Officer Pope noticed that the subject was wearing boots.

The subject advised the officer that he had just been robbed. The thief had taken his vehicle also. Officer Pope asked the subject if he wished to file a theft report. The subject stated that he would.

The officer then asked the subject, later identified as Mr. Robert Nevins, to please place his hands on the hood of the patrol car. Mr. Nevins did so. While searching Mr. Nevins, Officer Pope felt a bulge on the outside of the right leg under Mr. Nevins' trousers by the top of the boot. Officer Pope lifted the pant leg and found a six and one-half inch blade of a scuba-type knife. Mr. Nevins stated that it was a weapon for protection.

Mr. Nevins was arrested for carrying a concealed weapon. Officer Pope did not make a theft report on the vehicle.

What do you think of Mr. Nevins' story?

A vehicle belonging to Mr. Nevins was found, stripped, in the county, just outside the city limits two weeks later. Mr. Nevins' personal property was found inside the vehicle.

3. HOW WOULD YOU HAVE HANDLED THIS SITUATION?

Deputy Johnson was dispatched to 41 E. Applegrove to meet the security guard of the Applegrove apartment complex in reference to an 11-year-old boy who was the alleged victim of an aggravated assault. Deputy Johnson and a second officer, Deputy Miller, arrived at the security guard shack. There the officers observed that the victim, Jimmy Jones, had blood coming out of his nose and blood and a cut on his upper and lower lips.

The young boy stated that Mr. Alex Steinberg, his mother's boyfriend, had punched Jimmy with his closed fist. Jimmy's mother and Mr. Steinberg had been fighting, and he went in to check on his mother. This, according to Jimmy, was when, and why, he was struck.

Deputy Johnson and Deputy Miller went to the Jones's apartment with the victim. Upon arrival, the officers observed that the door was partially open. Both deputies identified themselves and asked if they could come in. A male voice stated that they could come in. Deputy Johnson went inside, and Deputy Miller stayed outside with the victim.

Deputy Johnson was then confronted with the victim's mother, Mrs. Jones. She stated that everything was fine. She was not going to press charges against Mr. Steinberg for hitting her son. Deputy Johnson requested that Mrs. Jones go outside with her son.

Mr. Steinberg stated loudly that he was in the kitchen. Deputy Johnson joined him there. Mr. Steinberg said he had been fighting with Mrs. Jones but that everything was okay now. Mr. Steinberg apologized for causing trouble.

At that moment, Sergeant Glenn arrived at the scene and was briefed by the two officers regarding the situation. Deputy Johnson advised Mr. Steinberg of his Miranda rights which he read from the Miranda card. Mr. Steinberg stated that he understood his rights.

When asked how the victim, Jimmy Jones, got his bloody nose and cut lip, Mr. Steinberg stated that he had just pushed the little boy. At this, Sergeant Glenn advised the officers to arrest Mr. Steinberg for aggravated assault and for child abuse. Sergeant Glenn told Mr. Steinberg that if he wanted to fight, he should choose someone his size.

Deputy Johnson and Deputy Miller then arrested Mr. Steinberg, who physically resisted and was subdued. Mrs. Jones came inside, yelling that they were hurting her boyfriend. Mrs. Jones stated that she would not press charges.

Mr. Steinberg was taken to the county jail and booked.

Mrs. Jones was referred to child protective services, and Jimmy was taken to the child protective services shelter care facility for his safety.

4. IF YOU WERE THE JUDGE . . .

Deputies Martin and Miller were dispatched to 881 W. Timber Street in reference to a larceny that had occurred at that address. Upon arrival, the officers were met by Mrs. Jan Harris, the victim, and Mr. Brass, the victim's employer. The victim stated she is employed by the Dixie Escort Service.

The victim stated she had been sent to 881 W. Timber Street to meet a client at approximately 2:00 A.M. The victim went on to say that when she arrived at the residence, she told the client that the fee was $100. He paid her with five $20 bills. The victim placed these inside her purse and placed the purse on the kitchen table. At approximately 5:00 A.M., the victim was getting ready to leave and, upon checking her purse, discovered that her money was missing. The victim confronted the suspect about the missing money. The suspect told the victim that he did not know anything about it. The victim advised him that she would call the police unless he returned the money.

According to the victim, at this point the suspect became enraged. He told her not to leave or call the "cops" because he had "a bunch of guns and a loaded shotgun in the closet." As the victim moved toward the front door, the suspect moved toward the closet.

The victim ran out of the residence and hurried to an all night grocery store. From there she called her boss. He, in turn, called the police. Mrs. Harris stated that the suspect's name is Dan Winner.

The officers knocked on the door at the suspect's residence. There was no answer. Deputy Martin found a brown purse lying outside the residence, near the front porch. Mrs. Harris identified the purse as belonging to her. Deputy Miller had the communication center call the suspect on the phone and advise him to meet the officers at his front door. The suspect finally came to the door. He stated that the woman was only a "whore" and "you shouldn't worry about anything."

Mr. Winner stood in the doorway. The door was partially opened. Mr. Winner's right arm and hand were concealed from the officers.

Deputy Martin asked him to step outside and talk to the officers about the incident. Suspect Winner just smiled.

At this time, another officer arrived at the scene to ascertain the welfare of the officers at this location. Deputy Simms, the squad leader, approached to where the officers were talking to the suspect. Mr. Winner was still standing in the doorway. Deputy Simms asked Mr. Winner to step outside. There was no response.

Deputy Martin was standing in front of the suspect; Deputy Miller and Deputy Simms were standing on each side of the doorway. Deputy Martin then took a step toward Mr. Winner. As he did so, Mr. Winner came out of the residence and tried to strike Deputy Martin. The suspect was restrained and was told to calm down.

The suspect then stated that maybe he took the purse from the girl . . . "but you can't prove it!"

As Deputy Martin started to read Mr. Winner his Miranda rights, the suspect pushed Deputy Martin. The officers physically subdued and arrested Mr. Winner. Mr. Winner was taken into custody.

Mr. Brass stated that Mrs. Harris was going to file charges and, if necessary, go to court to testify against Mr. Winner.

Will he be convicted?

5. DO YOU AGREE?

Officer Jones was dispatched to Mrs. Paul's residence to take a report on a stolen vehicle and some stolen jewelry. Officer Jones had been to Mrs. Paul's home many times. He was aware that she was a heavy drinker. She often complained about crimes that allegedly had been committed against her. In Officer Jones's experience, the complaints had always been unfounded. As he started toward Mrs. Paul's home, a fellow officer said to him, "Oh, you get that nutty Mrs. Paul again. She belongs in a mental ward."

Upon arrival at the residence, Officer Jones was met by Mrs. Paul. She was very intoxicated and spoke incoherently. She told Officer Jones that someone (a suspect named Steve), had been to her house to do yard work and to clean out her swimming pool. Steve had borrowed Mr. Paul's car to go to the store to buy some cigars. Steve had not returned. Also, Mrs. Paul was missing about $2000 worth of jewelry which she believed that Steve had taken.

During the questioning, Mrs. Paul gave a very sketchy description of the suspect. She was not sure exactly when the incident occurred.

Officer Jones duly made his report, but he and the other officers in his squad felt sure that no incident had occurred. No follow-up was necessary. Do you agree with Officer Jones and squad?

Approximately one week later the vehicle was found in a town about 200 miles away. Indeed a crime was committed. What were the prejudgments that were made in this situation?

6. HOW COULD THIS SITUATION BE HANDLED DIFFERENTLY?

Two off-duty officers had gone to a swap meet to buy some items. While there, they separated, wandering up one aisle and down another. Officer Smith saw a jewelry box that he liked. The marked price was $10. Officer Smith asked the attendant if he would take $5. The attendant, Bill Wells, age 15, stated that he had to check it out with his partner, Don Stacey, age 17. In a moment, Bill returned and sold Officer Smith the box for $5.

Officer Smith rejoined his friend, Officer Ray, at a hardware stand where Ray was purchasing a pick ax. Bill Wells approached the two men, took the jewelry box, and gave Smith his money back, saying, "You were just trying to cheat me because I was a kid." He then went back to his display.

A short time later, Officer Smith went back to where Bill Wells was working. Officer Ray was with him, still carrying his newly purchased pick ax. Bill Wells, obviously frightened, pulled out a knife and told the two to leave. He shouted for Don Stacey to join him. The youth could be seen approaching from the next aisle. The officers continued to stand in front of Bill. As Don Stacey arrived and picked up an ice pick from the display, Bill Wells said, "If you try to hurt us, we'll get one of you first."

At this point, the two officers identified themselves and took the boys into custody. They were physically referred to the county juvenile detention facility.

AMENDMENTS TO THE CONSTITUTION OF THE UNITED STATES

Articles in addition to, and amendment of, the Constitution of the United States of America, proposed by Congress, and ratified by the several states, pursuant to the fifth article of the original Constitution. (Ratification of the first ten Amendments was completed December 15, 1791.)

Amendment I

Congress shall make no law respecting an establishment of religion, or prohibiting the free exercise thereof; or abridging the freedom of speech, or of the press; or the right of the people peaceably to assemble, and to petition the Government for a redress of grievances.

Amendment II

A well regulated Militia, being necessary to the security of a free State, the right of the people to keep and bear Arms, shall not be infringed.

Amendment III

No Soldier shall, in time of peace be quartered in any house, without the consent of the Owner, nor in time of war, but in a manner to be prescribed by law.

Amendment IV

The right of the people to be secure in their persons, houses, papers, and effects, against unreasonable searches and seizures, shall not be violated, and no Warrants shall issue, but upon probable cause, supported by Oath or affirmation, and particularly describing the place to be searched, and the persons or things to be seized.

Amendment V

No person shall be held to answer for a capital, or other infamous crime, unless on a presentment or indictment of a Grand Jury, except in cases arising in the land or naval forces, or in the Militia, when in actual service in time of War or public danger; nor shall any person be subject for the same offence to be twice put in jeopardy of life or limb; nor shall be compelled in any criminal case to be a witness against himself, nor be deprived of life, liberty, or property, without due process of law; nor shall private property be taken for public use, without just compensation.

Amendment VI

In all criminal prosecutions, the accused shall enjoy the right to a speedy and public trial, by an impartial jury of the State and district wherein the crime shall have been committed, which district shall have been previously ascertained by law, and to be informed of the nature and cause of the accusation; to be confronted with the witnesses against him; to have compulsory process for obtaining witnesses in his favor, and to have the Assistance of Counsel for his defence.

Amendment VII

In Suits at common law, where the value in controversy shall exceed twenty dollars, the right of trial by jury shall be preserved, and no fact tried by a jury, shall be otherwise reexamined in any Court of the United States, than according to the rules of the common law.

Amendment VIII

Excessive bail shall not be required, nor excessive fines imposed, nor cruel and unusual punishments inflicted.

Amendment IX

The enumeration in the Constitution, of certain rights, shall not be construed to deny or disparage others retained by the people.

Amendment X

The powers not delegated to the United States by the Constitution, nor prohibited by it to the States, are reserved to the States respectively, or to the people.

Amendment XI (January 8, 1798)

The Judicial power of the United States shall not be construed to extend to any suit in law or equity, commenced or prosecuted against one of the United States by Citizens of another State, or by Citizens or Subjects of any Foreign State.

Amendment XII (September 25, 1804)

The Electors shall meet in their respective states and vote by ballot for President and Vice President, one of whom, at least, shall not be an inhabitant of the same state with themselves; they shall name in their ballots the person voted for as President, and in distinct ballots the person voted for as Vice President, and they shall make distinct lists of all persons voted for as President and of all persons voted for as Vice President, and of the number of votes for each, which lists they shall sign and certify, and transmit sealed to the seat of the government of the United States, directed to the President of the Senate;—The President of the Senate shall, in the presence of Senate and

House of Representatives, open all the certificates and the votes shall then be counted;—The person having the greatest number of votes for President, shall be the President, if such number be a majority of the whole number of Electors appointed; and if no person have such majority, then from the persons having the highest numbers not exceeding three on the list of those voted for as President, the House of Representatives shall choose immediately, by ballot, the President. But in choosing the President, the votes shall be taken by states, the representation from each state having one vote; a quorum for this purpose shall consist of a member or members from two-thirds of the states, and a majority of all the states shall be necessary to a choice. And if the House of Representatives shall not choose a President whenever the right of choice shall devolve upon them, *before the fourth day of March next following,*[1] then the Vice President shall act as President, as in the case of the death or other constitutional disability of the President.—The person having the greatest number of votes as Vice President shall be the Vice President, if such number be a majority of the whole number of Electors appointed, and if no person have a majority, then from the two highest numbers on the list, the Senate shall choose the Vice President; a quorum for the purpose shall consist of two-thirds of the whole number of Senators, and a majority of the whole number shall be necessary to a choice. But no person constitutionally ineligible to the office of President shall be eligible to that of Vice President of the United States.

Amendment XIII (December 18, 1865)

Section 1. Neither slavery nor involuntary servitude, except as a punishment for crime whereof the party shall have been duly convicted, shall exist within the United States, or any place subject to their jurisdiction.

Section 2. Congress shall have the power to enforce this article by appropriate legislation.

Amendment XIV (July 28, 1869)

Section 1. All persons born or naturalized in the United States, and subject to the jurisdiction thereof, are citizens of the United States and of the State wherein they reside. No State shall make or enforce any law which shall abridge the privileges or immunities of citizens of the United States, nor shall any State deprive any person of life, liberty, or property, without due process of law; nor deny to any person within its jurisdiction the equal protection of the laws.

Section 2. Representatives shall be apportioned among the several States according to their respective numbers, counting the whole number of persons in each State, excluding Indians not taxed. But when the right to vote at any election for the choice of electors for President and Vice President of the United States, Representatives in Congress, the Executive and Judicial officers of a State, or the members of the Legislature thereof, is denied to any of the male inhabitants of such State, being twenty-one years of age, and citizens of the United States, or in any way abridged, except for participation in rebellion, or other crime, the basis of representation therein shall be reduced in the proportion which the number of such male citizens shall bear to the whole number of male citizens twenty-one years of age in such State.

[1]Revised by the Twentieth Amendment.

Section 3. No person shall be a Senator or Representative in Congress, or elector of President and Vice President, or hold any office, civil or military, under the United States, or under any State, who, having previously taken an oath, as a member of Congress, or as an officer of the United States, or as a member of any State legislature, or as an executive or judicial officer of any State, to support the Constitution of the United States, shall have engaged in insurrection or rebellion against the same, or given aid or comfort to the enemies thereof. But Congress may by a vote of two thirds of each House, remove such disability.

Section 4. The validity of the public debt of the United States, authorized by law, including debts incurred for payment of pensions and bounties for services in suppressing insurrection or rebellion, shall not be questioned. But neither the United States nor any State shall assume or pay any debt or obligation incurred in aid of insurrection or rebellion against the United States, or any claim for the loss or emancipation of any slave; but all such debts, obligations, and claims shall be held illegal and void.

Section 5. The Congress shall have power to enforce by appropriate legislation, the provisions of this article.

Amendment XV (March 30, 1870)

Section 1. The right of citizens of the United States to vote shall not be denied or abridged by the United States or by any State on account of race, color, or previous conditions of servitude.

Section 2. The Congress shall have power to enforce this article by appropriate legislation.

Amendment XVI (February 25, 1913)

The Congress shall have power to lay and collect taxes on incomes, from whatever source derived, without apportionment among the several States, and without regard to any census or enumeration.

Amendment XVII (May 31, 1913)

The Senate of the United States shall be composed of two Senators from each State, elected by the people thereof, for six years; and each Senator shall have one vote. The electors in each State shall have the qualifications requisite for electors of the most numerous branch of the State legislatures.

When vacancies happen in the representation of any State in the Senate, the executive authority of such State shall issue writs of election to fill such vacancies: *Provided,* That the legislature of any State may empower the executive thereof to make temporary appointments until the people fill the vacancies by election as the legislature may direct.

This amendment shall not be so construed as to affect the election or term of any Senator chosen before it becomes valid as part of the Constitution.

Amendment XVIII (January 29, 1919)

Section 1. After one year from the ratification of this article the manufacture, sale, or transportation of intoxicating liquors within, the importation thereof into, or the exportation thereof from the United States and all territory subject to the jurisdiction thereof for beverage purposes is hereby prohibited.

Section 2. The Congress and the several States shall have concurrent power to enforce this article by appropriate legislation.

Section 3. This article shall be inoperative unless it shall have been ratified as an amendment to the Constitution by the legislatures of the several States, as provided in the Constitution within seven years from the date of the submission hereof to the States by the Congress.[2]

Amendment XIX (August 26, 1920)

The right of citizens of the United States to vote shall not be denied or abridged by the United States or by any State on account of sex.

Congress shall have power to enforce this article by appropriate legislation.

Amendment XX (February 6, 1933)

Section 1. The terms of the President and Vice President shall end at noon on the 20th day of January, and the terms of Senators and Representatives at noon on the 3rd day of January, of the years in which such terms would have ended if this article had not been ratified; and the terms of their successors shall then begin.

Section 2. The Congress shall assemble at least once in every year, and such meeting shall begin at noon on the 3rd day of January, unless they shall by law appoint a different day.

Section 3. If, at the time fixed for the beginning of the term of the President, the President elect shall have died, the Vice President elect shall become President. If a President shall not have been chosen before the time fixed for the beginning of his term, or if the President elect shall have failed to qualify, then the Vice President elect shall act as President until a President shall have qualified; and the Congress may by law provide for the case wherein neither a President elect nor a Vice President elect shall have qualified, declaring who shall then act as President, or the manner in which one who is to act shall be selected, and such person shall act accordingly until a President or Vice President shall have qualified.

Section 4. The Congress may by law provide for the case of the death of any of the persons from whom the House of Representatives may choose a President whenever the right of choice shall have devolved upon them, and for the case of the death of any of the persons from whom the Senate may choose a Vice President whenever the right of choice shall have devolved upon them.

Section 5. Sections 1 and 2 shall take effect on the 15th day of October following the ratification of this article.

Section 6. This article shall be inoperative unless it shall have been ratified as an amendment to the Constitution by the legislatures of three-fourths of the several States within seven years from the date of its submission.

---

[2]Repealed by the Twenty-first Amendment.

Amendment XXI (December 5, 1933)

Section 1. The eighteenth article of amendment to the Constitution of the United States is hereby repealed.

Section 2. The transportation or importation into any State, Territory, or possession of the United States for delivery or use therein of intoxicating liquors, in violation of the laws thereof, is hereby prohibited.

Section 3. This article shall be inoperative unless it shall have been ratified as an amendment to the Constitution by conventions in the several States, as provided in the Constitution, within seven years from the date of submission hereof to the States by the Congress.

Amendment XXII (February 26, 1951)

Section 1. No person shall be elected to the office of the President more than twice, and no person who has held the office of President, or acted as President, for more than two years of a term to which some other person was elected President shall be elected to the office of President more than once. But this Article shall not apply to any person holding the office of President when this Article was proposed by the Congress, and shall not prevent any person who may be holding the office of President, or acting as President, during the term within which this Article becomes operative from holding the office of President or acting as President during the remainder of such term.

Section 2. This article shall be inoperative unless it shall have been ratified as an amendment to the Constitution by the legislatures of three-fourths of the several States within seven years from the date of its submission to the States by the Congress.

Amendment XXIII (March 29, 1961)

Section 1. The District constituting the seat of Government of the United States shall appoint in such manner as the Congress may direct:

A number of electors of President and Vice President equal to the whole number of Senators and Representatives in Congress to which the District would be entitled if it were a State, but in no event more than the least populous State; they shall be in addition to those appointed by the States, but they shall be considered, for the purposes of the election of President and Vice President, to be electors appointed by a State; and they shall meet in the District and perform such duties as provided by the twelfth article of amendment.

Section 2. The Congress shall have the power to enforce this article by appropriate legislation.

Amendment XXIV (January 23, 1964)

Section 1. The right of citizens of the United States to vote in any primary or other election for President or Vice President, for electors for President or Vice President, or for Senator or Representative in Congress, shall not be denied or abridged by the President or any State by reason of failure to pay any poll tax or other tax.

Section 2. The Congress shall have the power to enforce this article by appropriate legislation.

Amendment XXV (February 10, 1967)

Section 1. In the case of the removal of the President from office or of his death or resignation, the Vice President shall become President.

Section 2. Whenever there is a vacancy in the office of the Vice President, the President shall nominate a Vice President who shall take office upon confirmation by a majority vote of both Houses of Congress.

Section 3. Whenever the President transmits to the President pro tempore of the Senate and the Speaker of the House of Representatives his written declaration that he is unable to discharge the powers and duties of his office, and until he transmits to them a written declaration to the contrary, such powers and duties shall be discharged by the Vice President as Acting President.

Section 4. Whenever the Vice President and a majority of either the principal officers of the executive departments or of such other body as Congress may by law provide, transmit to the President pro tempore of the Senate and the Speaker of the House of Representatives their written declaration that the President is unable to discharge the powers and duties of his office, the Vice President shall immediately assume the powers and duties of the office as Acting President.

Thereafter, when the President transmits to the President pro tempore of the Senate and the Speaker of the House of Representatives his written declaration that no inability exists, he shall resume the powers and duties of his office unless the Vice President and a majority of either the principal officers of the executive departments or of such other body as Congress may by law provide, transmit within four days to the President pro tempore of the Senate and the Speaker of the House of Representatives their written declaration that the President is unable to discharge the powers and duties of his office. Thereupon Congress shall decide the issue, assembling within forty-eight hours for that purpose if not in session. If the Congress, within twenty-one days after receipt of the latter written declaration or, if Congress is not in session, within twenty-one days after Congress is required to assemble, determines by two-thirds vote of both Houses that the President is unable to discharge the powers and duties of his office, the Vice President shall continue to discharge the same as Acting President; otherwise, the President shall resume the powers and duties of his office.

Amendment XXVI (June 30, 1971)

Section 1. The right of citizens of the United States, who are eighteen years of age or older, to vote shall not be denied or abridged by the United States or any State on account of age.

Section 2. The Congress shall have the power to enforce this article by appropriate legislation.

INDEX